CM0082S984

RATNA
English-Nepali
POCKET DICTIONARY

RATNA
English-Nepali
POCKET DICTIONARY
(With Devanagari and Roman Transcriptions)

Compiled by
Shyam P. Wagley

Revised, enlarged and updated by
R.B. Maharjan, M. Sharma, S.P. Shrestha

Ratna Pustak Bhandar
Kathmandu, Nepal

Shyam P. Wagley

RATNA ENGLISH -NEPALI POCKET DICTIONARY

3rd Edition 2009, revised

Published by **Ratna Pustak Bhandar,** Kathmandu, Nepal

1st Edition 2005

© **Publisher**

Typesetting & printed in Nepal at Dongol Printers

ISBN: 99933-0-360-7

Publisher's Note

This dictionary is based on **English-Nepali Pocket Dictionary*** which is in Romanized Nepali. Here the Nepali meanings to the English words have been given in Devanagari. This, we hope, would not only help the users to learn how to speak but also facilate them to read and write Nepali. Native speakers of Nepali should also find this dictionary a handy one.

We are very grateful to **Shyam P. Wagley** who compiled the above mentioned dictionary and like to thank many people who have helped in bringing out *this* edition. We regret any errors that might have cropped up in this dictionary and would welcome all valuable suggestions and comments.

---

* Shyam P. Wagley, *English Nepali Pocket Dictionary*, Ratna Pustak Bhandar, 1992

Nepali Language and Notes on Pronunciation, Devanagari Script, Roman Nepali Equivalents

Nepali language belongs to the Indo-Aryan family and has a deep root in Sanskrit. It has words borrowed form Sanskrit, Hindi, Urdu and in the recent times, English (particularly the technical terms like radio, television, computer, etc.).

From a regional spoken language of the western hills of Nepal (then known as Khas Bhasa), it spread and developed as a literary language during the past few centuries and became the national language of Nepal in the 1960's. It has been adopted by people who have their own spoken (and in some cases, written) languages like Newari, Tamang, Rai, Limbu, Magar, Sherpa, Maithil, Bhojpuri, etc. It is the lingua franca among the various peoples inhabiting the country. It is also used in Darjeeling, Sikkim and north-eastern parts of India, Bhutan and some parts of Tibet.

Nepali is written in Devanagari script, which is phonetic in nature. The system comprises of three kinds of characters: vowels, consonants and conjuncts. There are, however, no capital letters.

The Nepali words in this book are given both in Devanagari and Romanized versions, with the latter serving as the pronunciation guide. But there are some discrepancies between written and spoken Nepali. The short and long vowels इ and ई, उ and ऊ (and the corresponding signs, 'ि' and 'ी', 'ु' and 'ू') are distinguished in written Nepali but not in pronunciation.

Moreover, there is a strong tendency to pronounce **sh** as **s** and vice versa. ब **(b)** and व **(w, v)** are also interchangeable.

In some parts of Nepal, ष is often pronounced as ख. Similarly, य is pronounced as ज. आँप is pronounced both as /Aँp/ and /Amp/. संभाल्नु is written also as सम्भाल्नु. Such variations are shown in both parts of dictionary including British and American spellings and words. Especially, in Nepali-English part, sub-entries are placed in parantheses in bold and italics and marked as **_phr._** wherever possible. Other such words are mentioned as major entries and marked as due part of speech. It also contains common spelling like संक्षेप, unlike in English-Nepali part. The given word has many variations – सङ्क्षेप, सङ्क्षेप but all are pronounced as सन्क्षेप.

Part I

Vowels

अ a	as **'a'** in 'ago', 'around'	
आ A	as **'a'** in 'are', 'father'	
इ i	as **'i'** in 'it', 'dig'	
ई I	as **'ee'** in 'feet', 'read'	
उ u	as **'u'** in 'put', 'rule'	
ऊ U	as **'oo'** in 'food', 'pool'	
ऋ ri*	as **'ri'** in 'drink', 'trip'	
ए e	as **'e'** in 'pen', 'men'	
ऐ ai	as **'ai'** in 'paisa', 'mynah'	
ओ o	as **'o'** in 'old', 'total'	
औ au	as **'ou'** in 'plough', 'bowl'	
अँ/अं ṅ/ṃ, n̂	nasalize the preceding alphabet of the word	
अः ah**	as in 'दुःख, अतः'	

Consonants – velar

क ka	as **'k'** in 'kill', 'call'	
ख kha (aspirated)	as **'kh'** in 'khukuri', 'khaki'	
ग ga	as **'g'** in 'God', 'give'	
घ gha (aspirated)	as **'gh'** in 'ghee', 'ghaut'	
ङ ṅa (nasal)	as **'n'** in 'bang', 'sing'	

---

* This vowel is a loan sound from Sanskrit. In this book, there is no distinction between Romanized Nepali र and ऋ.

** While first is pronounced also without 'h' sound and spelt without (:) letter ('dukha' - 'दुख'), the latter is not.

Consonants – palatal

च cha   as **'ch'** in '**ch**eese', '**ch**eck'

छ chha (aspirated)   as **'chh'** in 'Tsering'. '**chh**urpi'

ज ja   as **'j'** in '**j**ug', '**j**elly'

झ jha (aspirated)   as **'jh'** in '**jh**ola', '**jh**iti'

ञ ña (nasal)   as **'n'** in 'be**n**ch', 'wre**n**ch'

Consonants – retroflex

ट Ta   as **'t'** in '**t**ap', 's**t**op'

ठ Tha (aspirated)   as **'th'** in 'Ka**th**mandu', '**Th**amel'

ड Da   as **'d'** in '**d**o', '**d**ig'

ढ Dha (aspirated)   as **'dh'** in '**dh**unga', '**dh**indo'

ण Na (nasal)   as **'n'** in 'Ramaya**n**a', 'wa**n**'

Consonants – dental

त ta   as **'t'** in 'Tantra', '**t**abala'

थ tha (aspirated)   as **'th'** in 'Thimi', '**th**una'

द da   as **'d'** in '**th**en', '**d**ip'

ध dha (aspirated)   as **'dh'** in '**dh**oti', '**dh**obi'

न na   as **'n'** in '**n**il', '**n**ame'

Consonants – bilabial

प pa   as **'p'** in '**p**en', '**p**eace'

फ pha (aspirated)   as **'ph'** in '**ph**one', '**ph**ysics'

ब ba   as **'b'** in '**b**ook', '**b**ird'

भ bha (aspirated)   as **'bh'** is '**Bh**aktapur', '**Bh**utan'

म ma   as **'m'** in '**m**an', '**m**edal'

Semi-vowels

य	ya	as '**y**' in 'yes', 'yak'
र	ra	as '**r**' in 'rain', 'race'
ल	la	as '**l**' in 'land', 'love'
व	wa	as '**w**' in 'water', 'well'

Sibilant consonants

श	sha	as '**sh**' in 'shy', 'shop'
ष	sha/ṣ[1]	as '**sh**' in 'shatkona', 'shadayantra'
स	sa	as '**s**' in 'sun', 'soul'

Aspirate consonant

ह	ha	as '**h**' in 'hat', 'head'

Conjuncts

क्ष	ksha	a consonant cluster, made of क + ष as '**ksh**' in 'Kuru**ksh**etra', '**Ksh**atriya'; placed under क
त्र	tra	a consonant cluster, made of त + र as '**tr**' in '**tr**ishul', 'kshatriya'; placed under त
ज्ञ	gȳa/jna[2]	a consonant cluster, made of ग + य as '**gy**' in '**gy**an', '**Gy**awali'; placed under ज

Half letter (*halant* ⟋ /)

क्, व्,   as in दिक्क्, दिक्क etc.

---

1 The dictionary uses **sha**
2 The dictionary uses **gȳa**

Part II

a	अ	as 'a' in 'ago', 'around'
A	आ	as 'a' in 'father', 'car'
ai	ऐ	as 'ai' in 'paisa', 'mynah'
au	औ	as 'au' in 'plough', 'bowl'
aṅ	अं	as 'un' in 'song', 'bunk'
aṅ	अं	same as above
ah	अः	as 'h' in 'wah', 'duhkh'
b	ब	as 'b' in 'boy', 'cab'
bh	भ	as 'v' in 'very', 'believe'
ch	च	as 'ch' in 'church', 'hatch'
chh	छ	as 'chh' in 'chhimeki', 'Tseten'
d	द	as 'd' in 'rather', 'that'
dh	ध	as 'dh' in 'dhoti', 'Dhulikhel'
D	ड	as 'd' in 'dad', 'card'
Dh	ढ	as 'dh' in 'dhunga', 'dhindo'
e	ए	as 'e' in 'air', 'play'
f	फ़[1]	as 'f' in 'fat', 'fish'
g	ग	as 'g' in 'God', 'give'
gh	घ	as 'gh' in 'ghaut', 'ghee'
h	ह	as 'h' in 'hotel', 'head'
i	इ	as 'i' in 'tip', 'in'
I	ई	as 'ee' in 'each', 'tree'
j	ज	as 'j' in 'jug', 'John'
jh	झ	as 'jh' in 'jhagada', 'rujhnu'
k	क	as 'k' in 'cat', 'kite'
kh	ख	as 'kh' in 'khukuri', 'khaki'
l	ल	as 'l' in 'lady', 'land'

m	म	as '**m**' in '**m**an', '**m**oon'
n	न	as '**n**' in 'pe**n**', '**n**ame'
N	ण	as '**n**' in 'Ramaya**n**a', 'Rawa**n**'
ñ	ङ	as '**n**' in 'ba**n**g', 'si**n**g'
ñ	ञ	as '**n**' in 'be**n**ch', 'wre**n**ch'
o	ओ	as '**o**' in '**o**ld', 'expl**o**re'
p	प	as '**p**' in '**p**oor', '**p**eace'
ph	फ[1]	as '**ph**' in '**ph**one', '**ph**ysics'
q	क	as '**k**' in 'bou**q**uet', 'cli**q**ue'
r	र	as '**r**' in '**r**ight', 'dea**r**'
s	स	as '**s**' in '**s**it', '**s**un'
sh	श	as '**sh**' in '**sh**y', 'ra**sh**'
ṣ	ष[2]	as '**sh**' in '**sh**adyantra', '**sh**atakon'
t	त	as '**t**' in '**T**aruni', 'ben**t**'
th	थ	as '**th**' in '**Th**ailand', 'ba**th**'
T	ट	as '**t**' in '**t**rekking', '**t**ent'
Th	ठ	as '**th**' in '**th**ug', '**Th**amel'
u	उ	as '**u**' in 'p**u**t', 'g**u**ru'
U	ऊ	as '**oo**' in 'm**oo**n', 's**oo**n'
v	भ/व[3]	as '**v**' in 'e**v**ery', '**v**alue'
w	व[3]	as '**w**' in '**w**ord', '**w**ater'
x	क्स	as '**ks**' in 'fo**x**', 'Me**x**ico'
y	य	as '**y**' in '**y**eti', '**y**es'
z	ज	as '**z**' in '**z**oo', '**z**ebra'

---

1 The dictionary uses **ph**
2 The dictionary uses **sh**
3 The dictionary uses **w**

Symbols and Punctuations

,   to separate main entry, list things, and before *etc*

.   to abbriviate, except in acronyms like HMG

~   to refer to the main entry

-   to hyphenate a compound word; to show variant spellings

( )   to give additional information; to include British and American spellings, phrases under the main entry, and Devanagari transcription

/ /   to transcribe the Devanagari word entries and sub-entries

/   to avoid unnecessary repetition and provide options

Abbreviations

abbr.   abbreviation संक्षिप्त रूप

adj.   adjective नामविशेषण

adv.   adverb क्रियाविशेषण

Am.   American English अमेरिकामा प्रयोग हुने अंग्रेजी भाषा

approx.   approximately सालाखाला

arch.   archaic पुरानो प्रयोग

arith.   arithmetic अंकगणित

aux.   auxiliary verb सहायक क्रिया

bot.   botany वनस्पतिशास्त्र

Br.   British English ब्रिटेनमा प्रयोग हुने अंग्रेजी भाषा

bus.   business व्यापार

colloq.   colloquial आम बोलीचाली

com.   common आम

comm.   communication संचार

comp.   computer कम्प्युटर

conj.	conjunction संयोजक
def. art.	definite article निश्चयबोधक उपपद
derog.	derogatory अपमानजनक
dial.	dialect बोलचाल, भर्रो भाषा
dimin.	diminutive छोटो वा लघु रूप
eco.	economics अर्थशास्त्र
eg.	for example जस्तै, उदाहरणका लागि
elec.	electricity विद्युत्
emph.	emphatic जोड वा बल दिने
esp.	especially विशेषगरी
exam.	examination(s) परीक्षा, जाँच
fem.	feminine स्त्रीलिङ्गी
fig.	figurative आलंकारिक
for.	formal औपचारिक
gen.	general आम
geo.	geography भूगोल
govt.	government सरकारी
gram.	grammar व्याकरण
his.	history इतिहास
HMG	His Majesty's Government श्री ५ को सरकार
hon.	honorific आदरार्थी
hum.	humorous हास्यास्पद
imp.	imperative आज्ञार्थी
ind. art.	indefinite article अनिश्चयबोधक उपपद
inf.	informal अनौपचारिक
int.	interrogative प्रश्नवाचक
inter.	interjection विष्मयादिबोधक
lg.	language भाषा
ling.	linguistics भाषाविज्ञान

lit.	literary	साहित्यक
mas.	masculine	पुलिङ्ग
math.	mathematics	गणित
mech.	mechanical of	यान्त्रिक, मेशीनसम्बन्धी
med.	medicine	चिकित्साशास्त्र
mil.	military	सैनिक
mod.	modal (auxiliary)	मोडल सहायक क्रिया
mt./Mt.	mountain, Mount	पर्वत, हिमाल, पहाड
mus.	music	संगीत
myth.	mythology	मिथक
n.	noun	संज्ञा, नाम
neg.	negative	नकारात्मक
num.	number, numerical	संख्या, सांख्यिकी
oft.	often	प्रायः
opp.	opposite	विपरीतार्थी
orgn.	organization	संगठन
part.	particle	निपात
pass.	passive	कर्मवाच्य
per.	person	पुरुष
phil.	philosophy	दर्शनशास्त्र
pl.	plural	बहुवचन
pol.	politics, political science	राजनीति, राजनैतिक शास्त्र
poss.	possessive	स्वामित्व भाव बुझाउने
pref.	prefix	प्रत्यय
prep.	preposition	सम्बन्धवाचक
pres.	present	वर्तमान
pron.	pronoun	सर्वनाम
psy.	psychology	मनोविज्ञान
pt.	past tense	भूतकाल

rel.	relative सम्बन्धवाचक
sb.	somebody कोही
sl.	slang अश्लील
so.	someone कोही
sth.	something केही
suff.	suffix उपसर्ग
univ.	university विश्वविद्यालय
usu.	usually साधारणतया
v.	verb क्रिया

A

a, *ind. art.* ek (एक),
euTA (एउटा)

abandon, *v.* chhoDnu
(छोड्नु), tyAgnu (त्याग्नु)

ABC, *n.* prArambhik kurA
(प्रारम्भिक कुरा)

ability, *n.* yogyaTA (योग्यता),
sAmarthya (सामर्थ्य)

able, *adj.* yogya (योग्य),
lAyak (लायक)

abnormal, *adj.* asAmAnya
(असामान्य), anauTho (अनौठो)

abominable snowman, *n.*
yatI (यती)

abort, *v.* garbh tuhAunu
(गर्भ तुहाउनु)

abortion, *n.* tuhAi (तुहाइ),
garbh pAt (गर्भपात)

abound, *v.* dherai/prashasta
hunu (धेरै/प्रशस्त हुनु)

about, *prep. (around)* wara
para (वरपर),
(approx.) lag bhag
(लगभग), karib (करिब),
(concerning) bAre (बारे),
(time) tira (तिर)

above, *adv./prep.* mAthi
(माथि)

abroad, *adv.* pardesh (परदेश)

abrupt, *adj.* akasmAt
(अकस्मात्), ekkAsi (एक्कासि)

abscess, *n.* phoDA (फोडा),
khaTirA (खटिरा)

absence, *n.* anupasthiti
(अनुपस्थिति), gayal (गयल)

absent, *adj.* anupasthit
(अनुपस्थित), gayal (गयल)

absorb, *v.* sosnu (सोस्नु),
samAwesh garnu
(समावेश गर्नु)

absurd, *adv./adj.* wAhiyat
(वाहियात), nirarthak (निरर्थक)

abundant, *adj.* prashasta
(प्रशस्त), managge (मनग्गे)

abuse, *n.* gAlI (गाली),
nindA (निन्दा)
v. gAlI garnu (गाली गर्नु),
nindA garnu (निन्दा गर्नु)

accept, *v.* swIkAr/manjur
garnu (स्वीकार/मन्जुर गर्नु)

access, *n.* pahuňch (पहुँच)

accessible, *adj.* pugna sakine
(पुग्न सकिने), sugam (सुगम)

accident, *n.* durghaTanA
(दुर्घटना),
choT paTak (चोटपटक)

acclimatize, *v.* hAwA pAnI
mA milnu (हावापानीमा मिल्नु)

accommodate, *v.* milAunu
(मिलाउनु), rAkhnu (राख्नु)

accommodation, *n.* DerA
(डेरा), bAs basne ThAuň
(बास बस्ने ठाउँ)

accompany, *v.* sAth dinu /
lAgnu (साथ दिनु/लाग्नु)

according to, *adv.* anusAr
(अनुसार), bamojim (बमोजिम)

account, *n. (in figures)* hisAb-
kitAb (हिसाब-किताब),
lekhA (लेखा),
(book) khAtA (खाता),
(description) bayAn (बयान)
v. hisAb garnu (हिसाब गर्नु)

accountant, *n.* lekhA pAl
(लेखापाल)

accurate, *adj.* ThIk (ठीक),
achUk (अचूक)

accurately, *adv.* ThIk saňga
(ठीकसँग)

accusation, *v.* dosh (दोष),
Arop (आरोप)

accuse, *v.* dosh lagAunu
(दोष लगाउनु),
bAt lAunu (बात लाउनु)

ace, *n. (cards)* ekkA (एक्का),
nipuN wyakti
(निपुण व्यक्ति)

ache, *n.* pIDA (पीडा)
v. dukhnu (दुख्नु)

achieve, *v.* prApt garnu
(प्राप्त गर्नु), kAm phatte
garnu (काम फत्ते गर्नु)

achievement, *n.* uplabdhi
(उपलब्धि)

acid, *n.* tejAb (तेजाब),
amla (अम्ल)

acidity, *n.* amal pitta
(अमलपित्त)

acknowledge, *v.* AbhAr
mAnnu (आभार मान्नु),
pahuňch dinu (पहुँच दिनु)

acknowledgement, *n.* swIkriti
(स्वीकृति), Abhar (आभार),
pahuňch (पहुँच)

acquaint, *v.* chinAunu
(चिनाउनु), parichaya garAunu
(परिचय गराउनु)

acquaintance, *n.* chinjAn
(चिनजान), chinhArI (चिन्हारी)

acquit, *v.* chhuTkArA /
chhoDI dinu
(छुट्कारा/छोडी दिनु)

across, *prep.* wArpAr
(वारपार), pAri (पारि)

act, *n.* kAm (काम)
v. kAm / abhinaya garnu
(काम/अभिनय गर्नु)

Act, *n. (legislation)* ain (ऐन)

action, *n.* kAm (काम),
kArbAI (कारबाई)

active, *adj.* jAňgarilo
(जाँगरिलो), sakriya (सक्रिय)

actor, *n.* abhinetA (अभिनेता)

actress, *n.* abhinetrI (अभिनेत्री)

actual, *adj.* wAstawik (वास्तविक), sAṅcho (साँचो)

ad, *n.* *(advertisement)* wigyÃpan (विज्ञापन)

add, *v.* joDnu (जोड्नु), thapnu (थप्नु), *(math.)* jammA garnu (जम्मा गर्नु)

addict, *v.* lat lAgnu (लत लाग्नु) *n.* ammalI (अम्मली), durwyasanI (दुर्व्यसनी)

addiction, *n.* lat (लत), ammal (अम्मल)

additional, *adj.* thap (थप), atirikta (अतिरिक्त)

address, *n.* ThegAnA (ठेगाना), pattA (पत्ता), *(talk)* prawachan (प्रवचन) *v.* sambhodhan garnu (सम्बोधन गर्नु)

adept, *adj.* sipAlu (सिपालु), nipuN (निपुण)

adequate, *adj.* pugdo (पुग्दो), paryApt (पर्याप्त)

adhere, *v.* TAṅsinu (टाँसिनु), lesinu (लेसिनु)

adjust, *v.* ThIk pArnu (ठीक पार्नु), milAunu (मिलाउनु)

administer, *v.* prashAsan chalAunu (प्रशासन चलाउनु)

administration, *n.* prashAsan (प्रशासन), shAsan (शासन)

administrator, *n.* prashAsak (प्रशासक), shAsak (शासक)

admirable, *adj.* prashamsanIya (प्रशंसनीय)

admire, *v.* tAriph / prashamsA garnu (तारिफ/प्रशंसा गर्नु)

admission, *n.* prawesh (प्रवेश), bhartI (भर्ती), bharnA (भर्ना)

admit, *v.* bharnA garnu (भर्ना गर्नु), mAnnu (मान्नु)

adorable, *adj.* AdarNIya (आदरणीय), pUjnIya (पूजनीय)

adore, *v.* premI ko Adar / pUjA garnu (प्रेमीको आदर/ पूजा गर्नु)

adorn, *v.* siṅgArnu (सिंगार्नु), sajAunu (सजाउनु)

adult, *n.* umer pugeko (उमेर पुगेको), wayaska (वयस्क)

advance, *n.* *(money)* peskI (पेस्की), bainA (बैना) *v.* aghi baDhnu (अघि बढ्नु), unnati garnu (उन्नति गर्नु)

advantage, *n.* phAidA (फाइदा), guN (गुण)

adventure, *n.* sAhasik kAm (साहसिक काम)

adventurous, *adj.* sAhasilo (साहसिलो), AṅTilo (आँटिलो)

advertise, *v.* wigyÃpan / sUchanA garnu (विज्ञापन/ सूचना गर्नु)

advertisement, n. wigỹApan (विज्ञापन), sUchanA (सूचना)

advice, n. sallAh (सल्लाह), artI (अर्ती)

advise, v. sallAh dinu (सल्लाह दिनु), samjhAunu (सम्झाउनु)

advisor, n. sallAh kAr (सल्लाहकार)

aeroplane, n. hawAI jahAj (हवाईजहाज), wimAn (विमान)

affair, n. kurA (कुरा), wishaya (विषय)

affect, v. prabhAw pArnu (प्रभाव पार्नु), lahsinu (लहसिनु)

affectation, n. jhUTo prem (झूटो प्रेम), swAṅg (स्वाँग)

affection, n. mAyA (माया), prem (प्रेम), sneha (स्नेह)

affectionate, adj. mAyAlu (मायालु), mAyA garne (माया गर्ने)

affirm, v. nishchaya saṅga bhannu (निश्चयसँग भन्नु)

affluent, adj. dhanI (धनी), sampanna (सम्पन्न)

afford, v. dina/kharch garna saknu (दिन/खर्च गर्न सक्नु)

afloat, adj. pAnI mA utreko (पानीमा उत्रेको)

afoot, adv. paidal (पैदल)

afraid, adj. DarAeko (डराएको)

after, prep. pachhi (पछि)

afternoon, n. aprAnha (अपरान्ह)

afterwards, adv. pachhi (पछि)

again, adv. pheri (फेरि)

against, prep. wiruddha (mA) (विरुद्ध)(मा)

age, n. umer (उमेर)

age-old, adj. bUDho (बूढो), purAno (पुरानो)

agent, n. ejeNT (एजेण्ट), gumAstA (गुमास्ता), wAris (वारिस)

agile, adj. phurtilo (फुर्तिलो)

agility, n. phurtI (फुर्ती)

ago, adv. aghi (अघि)

agree, v. swIkAr garnu (स्वीकार गर्नु), rAjI hunu (राजी हुनु)

agreeable, adj. mAnya hune (मान्य हुने), man sukhI tulyAune (मन सुखी तुल्याउने)

agreement, n. swIkriti (स्वीकृति), manjurI (मन्जुरी), (deed) samjhautA (सम्झौता)

agriculture, n. krishi (कृषि), khetI (खेती)

aid, n. sahAyatA / maddat (सहायता/मद्दत) v. sahAyatA / maddat garnu (सहायता/मद्दत गर्नु)

AIDS, n. eDs rog (एड्स रोग)

aim, n. irAdA (इरादा), laksha (लक्ष) v. tAknu (ताक्नु), chitAunu (चिताउनु)

air, n. hAwA (हावा)

airhostess, *n.* wimAn parichArikA (विमान परिचारिका)

airline, *n.* wimAn sewA (विमानसेवा)

airport, *n.* wimAn sthal (विमानस्थल)

alarm, *n.* khatarA ko sañket (खतराको संकेत)
v. sAwadhAn garAunu (सावधान गराउनु), tarsAunu (तर्साउनु)

alas, *inter.* hAy (हाय), aphsos (अफसोस)

album, *n.* taswIr rAkhne kitAb (तस्वीर राख्ने किताब)

alcohol, *n.* raksI (रक्सी)

alert, *adj.* satarka (सतर्क), chanAkho (चनाखो)
v. sAwdhAn / satarka garnu (सावधान/सतर्क गर्नु)

alien, *n.* pardeshI (परदेशी)

alike, *adj.* samAn (समान), ekai nAs ko (एकैनासको)

alimony, *n.* chhuTTiekI mahilA lAI diine mAnA pAthI (छुट्टिएकी महिलालाई दिइने मानापाथी)

alive, *adj.* jiuñdo (जिउँदो), bAñcheko (बाँचेको)

all, *adj.* sabai (सबै), jammai (जम्मै)

allow, *v.* anumati dinu (अनुमति दिनु)

allowance, *n.* bhattA (भत्ता)

Almighty, *n.* Ishwar (ईश्वर), sarwa shakti mAn (सर्वशक्तिमान्)

almond, *n.* badAm (बदाम)

almost, *adv.* prAyah (प्रायः), jhaNDai (झण्डै)

alms, *n.* bhikshA (भिक्षा)

alone, *adj.* eklo (एक्लो)
adv. eklai (एक्ले)

along, *prep.* sAth mA (साथमा)

aloof, *adj.* TADhA (टाढा), chuTTai (छुट्टै), udAsIn (उदासीन)

aloud, *adv.* ThUlo swarmA (ठूलो स्वरमा), joD le (जोडले)

alphabet, *n.* warN mAlA (वर्णमाला)

already, *adv.* aghi nai (अघि नै), pahile nai (पहिले नै)

also, *adv.* pani (पनि)

alter, *v.* badalnu (बदल्नु), phernu (फेर्नु)

alteration, *n.* adal badal (अदलबदल), pher phAr (फेरफार)

alternate, *adj.* ek ek birAera (एक एक बिराएर), pAlai pAlo (पालैपालो)
v. pAlai pAlo garnu (पालैपालो गर्नु)

alternately, *adv.* pAlai pAlo sañga (पालैपालोसँग)

```

**alternative,** *adj.* waikalpik (वैकल्पिक) *n.* wikalpa (विकल्प)

**although,** *conj.* huna ta (हुन त), yadyapi (यद्यपि)

**altitude,** *n.* uchAi (उचाइ), aglAi (अग्लाइ)

**altogether,** *adv.* jammai (जम्मै), pUrNa rUp le (पूर्णरूपले)

**always,** *adv.* sadhaiñ (सधैँ), sadaiwa (सदैव)

**amateur,** *n.* sikArU (सिकारू) *adj.* sokhin (सोखिन)

**amazing,** *adj.* achamma ko (अचम्मको), adbhut (अद्भुत)

**ambassador,** *n.* rAj dUt (राजदूत)

**ambition,** *n.* abhilAshA (अभिलाषा), AkAñkshA (आकांक्षा)

**ambulance,** *n.* embulens (एम्बुलेन्स)

**amenity,** *n.* suwidhA (सुविधा)

**among,** *prep.* bIch (बीच), mAjh (माझ)

**amount,** *n.* rakam (रकम), dhan (धन)

**amulet,** *n.* jantar (जन्तर), bUTI (बूटी)

**amuse,** *v.* ramAunu (रमाउनु), bahalAunu (बहलाउनु)

**amusement,** *n.* manorañjan (मनोरञ्जन), khelbAD (खेलबाड)

**anarchy,** *n.* arAjaktA (अराजकता)

**ancestor,** *n.* purkhA (पुर्खा), purkhyaulI (पुर्ख्यौली)

**ancient,** *adj.* purAno (पुरानो), prAchIn (प्राचीन)

**and,** *conj.* ra (र), tathA (तथा)

**angel,** *n.* dew dUt (देवदूत)

**angle,** *n.* kunA (कुना), koN (कोण)

**angry,** *adj.* risAeko (रिसाएको), kruddha (क्रुद्ध)

**animal,** *n.* jantu (जन्तु), janAwar (जनावर), pashu (पशु)

**ankle,** *n.* golI gAñTho (गोलीगाँठो)

**anklet,** *n.* pAujeb (पाउजेब), nUpur (नूपुर), kallI (कल्ली)

**anniversary,** *n.* wArshikI (वार्षिकी), janma diwas (जन्मदिवस)

**announce,** *v.* prakaT / ghoshaNA garnu (प्रकट/घोषणा गर्नु)

**announcement,** *n.* ghoshaNA (घोषणा)

**annoy,** *v.* dikka lAunu (दिक्क लाउनु), jhok chalAunu (झोक चलाउनु)

**annual,** *adj.* wArshik (वार्षिक), sAlAnA (सालाना)

**annuity,** *n.* sAlAnA bhattA (सालाना भत्ता)
```

another, *adj.* arko (अर्को)

answer, *n.* jawAph (जवाफ),
uttar (उत्तर)
v. jawAph dinu (जवाफ दिनु),
uttar dinu (उत्तर दिनु)

ant, *n.* kamilA (कमिला)

antelope, *n.* hariN (हरिण),
mrig (मृग)

anthem, *n.* dhun (धुन),
stuti gAn (स्तुतिगान)

antique, *adj.* purAno
(पुरानो), prAchIn (प्राचीन)

antiseptic, *n.* ghAu khaTira
pAkna nadine aushadhi
(घाउ खटिरा पाक्न नदिने
औषधि)

antonym, *n.* ulTo artha ko
shabda (उल्टो अर्थको शब्द)

anxiety, *n.* surtA (सुर्ता),
chintA (चिन्ता), pIr (पीर)

anxious, *adj.* chintit (चिन्तित),
wyAkul (व्याकुल)

any, *adj./pron.* kunai (कुनै),
kohI (कोही)

anyhow, *adv.* jasarI pani
(जसरी पनि)

anyone, *pron.* kunai wyakti
(कुनै व्यक्ति)

anyway, *adv.* je hos (जे होस्),
khair (खैर)

anywhere, *adv.* kahIň pani
(कहीँ पनि),
jahAň pani (जहाँ पनि)

apart, *adv.* alag (अलग),
chhuTTai (छुट्टै)

aparthied, *n.* rañg bhed
(रङ्गभेद)

apartment, *n.* DerA (डेरा),
koThA (कोठा)

apology, *n.* kshamA yAchnA
(क्षमायाचना)

apparel, *n.* poshAk (पोशाक),
lugA (लुगा)

apparent, *adj.* spashTa (स्पष्ट)

appeal, *n.* apIl (अपील)
v. ujur/bintI garnu (उजुर/
बिन्ती गर्नु)

appear, *v.* dekhA parnu
(देखा पर्नु)

appearance, *n.* anuhAr (अनुहार),
sakal (सकल), rUp (रूप)

appetite, *n.* bhok (भोक)

applaud, *v.* tAriph /prashamsA
garnu (तारिफ/प्रशंसा गर्नु)

apple, *n.* syAu (स्याउ)

application, *n.* darkhAsta
(दरखास्त), bintI patra
(बिन्तीपत्र), Awedan (आवेदन)

apply, *v.* prayog mA lyAunu
(प्रयोगमा ल्याउनु),
darkhAst dinu (दरखास्त दिनु)

appoint, *v.* niyukta garnu
(नियुक्त गर्नु),
khaTAunu (खटाउनु)

appointment, *n.* niyukti
(नियुक्ति)

appropriate, *adj.* suhAuṅdo (सुहाउँदो), uchit (उचित)

approval, *n.* manjurI (मन्जुरी), swIkriti (स्वीकृति)

approve, *v.* manjurI/swIkriti dinu (मन्जुरी/स्वीकृति दिनु)

approximately, *adv.* andAjI (अन्दाजी), lag bhag (लगभग)

apricot, *n.* khurpAnI (खुर्पानी)

aptitude, *n.* kaushal (कौशल), sIp (सीप)

arc, *n.* chAp (चाप), britta khanD (वृत्तखण्ड)

arcade, *n.* duwai tira pasal harU bhaeko DhAkieko bATo (दुवैतिर पसलहरू भएको ढाकिएको बाटो)

arch, *n.* dhanushAkAr samrachna (धनुषाकार संरचना), *adj.* mukhya (मुख्य), ugra (उग्र)

architect, *n.* wAstukAr (वास्तुकार)

architecture, *n.* bhawan nirmAN kalA (भवन निर्माण कला), wAstu kalA (वास्तुकला)

are, *v. (first per.)* chhauṅ (छौं), *(second per.)* chhau (छौ), *(third per.)* chhan (छन्)

area, *n.* kshetra phal (क्षेत्रफल), kshetra (क्षेत्र), ilAkA (इलाका)

argue, *v.* wiwAd/bahas garnu (विवाद/बहस गर्नु)

argument, *n.* wiwAd (विवाद), tark (तर्क)

arid, *adj.* sukkhA (सुक्खा)

arise, *v.* uThnu (उठ्नु)

arithmetic, *n.* aṅk gaNit (अंकगणित)

arm, *n.* pAkhurA (पाखुरा)

armpit, *n.* kokhA (कोखा), kAkhI (काखी)

arms, *n.* hAt hatiyAr (हातहतियार)

army, *n.* senA (सेना), phauj (फौज)

around, *adv.* chArai tira (चारैतिर), lag bhag (लगभग)

arouse, *v.* jagAunu (जगाउनु), uttejit garAunu (उत्तेजित गराउनु)

arrange, *v.* bandobast garnu (बन्दोबस्त गर्नु)

arrangement, *n.* bandobast (बन्दोबस्त), intjAm (इन्तजाम)

arrest, *v.* giraphtAr garnu (गिरफ्तार गर्नु), pakranu (पक्रनु) *n.* giraphtArI (गिरफ्तारी)

arrival, *n.* Agaman (आगमन)

arrive, *v.* Aipugnu (आइपुग्नु)

arrow, *n.* bAN (बाण), tIr (तीर)

arson, *n.* AgjanI (आगजनी)

art, *n.* kalA (कला), *(skill)* sIp (सीप)

artist, *n.* kalA kAr (कलाकार)

article, *n.* chIjbIj (चीजबीज),
(*write-up*) lekh (लेख),
(*clause*) dhArA (धारा)

artifact, *n.* mAnis le banAeko
bastu (मानिसले बनाएको वस्तु)

artificial, *adj.* nakkalI (नक्कली),
banAwaTI (बनावटी)

as, *adv.* jasto (जस्तो),
jhaiñ (झैं), (*since*)
kina bhane (किनभने)

ascend, *v.* uklanu (उक्लनु)

ascent, *n.* ukAlo (उकालो),
chaDhAi (चढाइ)

ashamed, *adj.* lAj lAgeko
(लाज लागेको), lajjit bhaeko
(लज्जित भएको)

ashes, *n.* kharAnI (खरानी),
bhasma (भस्म)

aside, *adv.* ekA paTTi
(एकापट्टि), alaggai (अलग्गै)

ask, *v.* sodhnu (सोध्नु)

ask for, *v.* mAgnu (माग्नु)

asleep, *v.* nidAeko (निदाएको),
suteko (सुतेको)

asparagus, *n.* kurilo (कुरिलो)

aspect, *n.* rUp (रूप),
paksha (पक्ष)

asphalt, *n.* alkatrA (अलकत्रा),
pich (पिच)

ass, *n.* gadhA (गधा)

assassin, *n.* hatyArA (हत्यारा),
jyAn mArA (ज्यानमारा)

assassination, *n.* hatyA (हत्या)

assault, *n.* kuT piT (कुटपिट),
AkramaN (आक्रमण),
v. hAt hAlnu (हातहाल्नु),
jAi lAgnu (जाइलाग्नु)

assemble, *v.* jammA hunu
(जम्मा हुनु), milnu (मिल्नु),
jaDAn garnu (जडान गर्नु)

assembly, *n.* sabhA (सभा)

assess, *v.* mUlyAñkan garnu
(मूल्याइकन गर्नु),
dar toknu (दर तोक्नु)

assessment, *n.* mUlyAñkan
(मूल्याइकन)

assign, *v.* nirdishTa garnu
(निर्दिष्ट गर्नु),
khaTAunu (खटाउनु)

assignment, *n.* khaTan (खटन)
sumpieko kAm
(सुम्पिएको काम)

assist, *v.* saghAunu (सघाउनु),
sahAyatA garnu (सहायता गर्नु)

assistant, *n.* sahAyak (सहायक)

associate, *v.* milnu (मिल्नु),
sAth dinu (साथ दिनु),
n. sahayogI (सहयोगी)

association, *n.* samsthA (संस्था)
sañgaThan (संगठन)

assure, *v.* AshwAsan dinu
(आश्वासन दिनु)

assurance, *n.* AshwAsan
(आश्वासन), bharosA (भरोसा)

asthma, *n.* dam (दम),
dam ko rog (दमको रोग)

astonishment, *n.* achamma
(अचम्म), Ashcharya (आश्चर्य)

astrologer, *n.* jyotishI (ज्योतिषी)

astrology, *n.* jyotish shAstra
(ज्योतिष शास्त्र)

astronaut, *n.* antariksha yAtrI
(अन्तरिक्ष यात्री)

at, *prep.* mA (मा), mAthi (माथि)

atheist, *n.* nAstik (नास्तिक)

athlete, *n.* khelADI (खेलाडी)

atmosphere, *n.* wAyu
maNDal (वायुमण्डल),
wAtAwaraN (वातावरण)

attach, *v.* natthI garnu
(नत्थी गर्नु), gA~snu (गाँस्नु)

attache, *n.* sahachArI (सहचारी)

attachment, *n.* lagAw (लगाव),
sneha (स्नेह)

attack, *v.* AkramaN/hamlA
garnu (आक्रमण/हमला गर्नु)
n. AkramaN (आक्रमण),
hamlA (हमला)

attempt, *v.* prayatna garnu
(प्रयत्न गर्नु), A~Tnu (आँट्नु)
n. prayatna (प्रयत्न),
kosis (कोसिस)

attend, *v.* dhyAn dinu (ध्यान
दिनु), *(meeting)* hAjir hunu
(हाजिर हुनु)

attendance, *n.* hAjirI
(हाजिरी), sAmel (सामेल)

attention, *n.* dhyAn (ध्यान)

attire, *v.* pahirAunu
(पहिराउनु), lagAunu (लगाउनु)
n. poshAk (पोशाक)

attitude, *n.* man ko bhAw
(मनको भाव), DhA~chA (ढाँचा)

attract, *v.* Akarshit garnu
(आकर्षित गर्नु),
khichnu (खिच्नु)

attraction, *n.* AkarshaN
(आकर्षण)

auction, *n.* lilAm (लिलाम)
v. lilAm garnu (लिलाम गर्नु)

audible, *adj.* sunna sakine
(सुन्न सकिने)

audience, *n.* darshak wrind
(दर्शकवृन्द), shrotA wrind
(श्रोतावृन्द), *(formal meeting)*
darshan (दर्शन)

audit, *v.* lekhA jA~chnu
(लेखा जाँच्नु)

auditor, *n.* lekhA parIkshak
(लेखा परीक्षक)

auditorium, *n.* sabhA kaksha
(सभाकक्ष)

aunt, *n. (paternal uncle's wife)*
kAkI (काकी), *(mother's
sister)* sAnImA (सानीमा),
ThulImA (ठूलीमा), *(maternal
uncle's wife)* mAijU (माइजू),
(father's sister) phupU (फुपू)

auspices, *n.* tattwAwdhAn
(तत्त्वावधान), mAt hat (मातहत)

auspicious, *adj.* shubha (शुभ),
mangalmaya (मङ्गलमय)

authentic, *adj.* wishwasnIya (विश्वसनीय), sAñcho (साँचो)

author, *n.* lekhak (लेखक)

authority, *n.* akhtiyAr (अख्तियार), adhikAr (अधिकार)

automatic, *adj.* Aphai chalne (आफै चल्ने), swachAlit (स्वचालित)

automobile, *n.* moTar gADI (मोटरगाडी)

autumn, *n.* sharad ritu (शरद् ऋतु)

available, *adj.* pAine (पाइने), uplabdha (उपलब्ध)

avenue, *n.* mArg (मार्ग)

average, *n.* ausat (औसत),

sAlA khAlA (सालाखाला)

avoid, *v.* TArnu (टार्नु), chhalnu (छल्नु)

awake, *adj.* biuñjheko (बिउँझेको)

v. biuñjhAunu (बिउँझाउनु), biuñtAunu (बिउँताउनु)

award, *n.* puraskAr (पुरस्कार), inAm (इनाम)

awful, *adj.* bhayAnak (भयानक), Dar lAgdo (डरलाग्दो)

awhile, *adv.* ek chhin (एक छिन), kehI ber (केही बेर)

awkward, *adj.* chhanda na banda ko (छन्द न बन्दको), bhaddA (भद्दा)

axe, *n.* bancharo (बन्चरो)

B

baby, *n.* bachchA (बच्चा), nAnI (नानी)

bachelor, *n.* wiwAh na bhaeko mAnis (विवाह नभएको मानिस), kumAr (कुमार)

back, *n.* Añg (अङ्ग), pITh (पीठ), piThyUñ (पिठ्यूँ)

adv. (rear) pachhil tira (पछिल्तिर)

v. samarthan/maddat garnu (समर्थन/मद्दत गर्नु)

backbone, *n.* DhAD (ढाड), DañDAlno (डँडाल्नो)

backdrop, *n.* prishTha bhUmi (पृष्ठभूमि)

background, *n.* prishTha bhUmi (पृष्ठभूमि)

backwards, *adv.* pachhil tira (पछिल्तिर)

bad, *adj.* kharAb (खराब), na rAmro (नराम्रो)

badge, *n.* billA (बिल्ला),

byAj (ब्याज)

bag, *n.* jholA (झोला),
thailo (थैलो), byAg (ब्याग)
v. thailA mA rAkhnu
(थैलामा राख्नु),
hAt pArnu (हात पार्नु)

baggage, *n.* mAl mattA
(मालमत्ता), jhiTI (झिटी),
gunTA (गुन्टा)

bail, *n.* jamAnI (जमानी),
dhan jamAnI (धन जमानी)
v. jamAnI linu/dinu (जमानी
लिनु/दिनु)

bait, *n.* balchhI (बल्छी),
chArA (चारा)
v. lobhyAunu (लोभ्याउनु),
balchhI mA chArA hAlnu
(बल्छीमा चारा हाल्नु)

bake, *v.* pakAunu (पकाउनु),
seknu (सेक्नु)

bakery, *n.* roTI/pAuroTI
banAune pasal/ThAuñ
(रोटी/पाउरोटी बनाउने
पसल/ठाउँ)

balance, *n.* *(scales)* tarAju
(तराजु), *(account)* bAñkI (बाँकी),
(equal) santulan (सन्तुलन)
v. taulanu (तौलनु),
barAbar garnu (बराबर गर्नु)

balcony, *n.* bArdalI (बार्दली),
balkonI (बालकोनी)

bald, *adj.* tAlu khuile (तालु-
खुइले), chiNDe (चिण्डे)

ball, *n.* bhakuNDo (भकुण्डो),
bal (बल),
(dance) bal nAch (बल नाच)

balloon, *n.* belun (बेलुन),
gubbArA (गुब्बारा)
v. phulnu (फुल्नु),
uksinu (उक्सिनु)

ballot, *n.* mat (मत),
mat patra (मतपत्र)
v. mat dinu (मत दिनु)

balm, *n.* malam (मलम),
sugandhit lep (सुगन्धित लेप)

bamboo, *n.* bAñs (बाँस)

ban, *n.* rok (रोक),
nishedh (निषेध)
v. roknu (रोक्नु),
nishedh garnu (निषेध गर्नु)

banana, *n.* kerA (केरा)

band, *n.* gherA (घेरा),
paTTI (पट्टी), *(tape)* phittA
(फित्ता), *(group)* dal (दल),
samUha (समूह)
v. dal/TolI banAunu
(दल/टोली बनाउनु)

bandage, *n.* paTTI (पट्टी),
byAñDej (ब्यान्डेज)

bandit, *n.* DAñku (डाँकु)

bangle, *n.* churA (चुरा)

bank, *n.* baiñk (बैंक),
(river) kinArA (किनारा)

bankrupt, *adj.* diwAliyA
(दिवालिया),
TAT palTeko (टाट पल्टेको)

banner, *n.* toraN (तोरण),
    dhwajA patAkA
    (ध्वजापताका), tUl (तूल)

banquet, *n.* bhoj (भोज)

banyan, *n.* bar ko rUkh
    (बरको रूख)

bar, *n.* DaNDA (डण्डा),
    (door) Aglo (आग्लो),
    (pub) piune ThAuṅ
    (पिउने ठाउँ)
    v. roknu (रोक्नु),
    chheknu (छेक्नु)

barber, *n.* hajAm (हजाम),
    nAu (नाउ)

bare, *adj.* nAṅgo (नाङ्गो),
    khulA (खुला)

barely, *adv.* muskil le
    (मुस्किलले)

bargain, *n.* mol tol (मोलतोल),
    mol molAi (मोलमोलाइ)
    v. molAi garnu (मोलाई गर्नु)

bark, *n.* rUkh ko bokrA
    (रूखको बोक्रा),
    (dog) bhukAi (भुकाइ)
    v. bhuknu (भुक्नु)

barley, *n.* jau (जौ)

barrel, *n. (oil)* byArel
    (ब्यारेल), pIpA (पीपा),
    (gun) nAl (नाल), nalI (नली)

barrier, *n.* chhek bAr
    (छेकबार), tagAro (तगारो)

barter, *n.* sAT pher (साटफेर)
    v. sATnu (साट्नु),

sAT pher garnu (साटफेर गर्नु)

base, *n.* pIṅdh (पींध),
    AdhAr (आधार)
    adj. nIch (नीच),
    adham (अधम)
    v. AdhAr banAunu (आधार
    बनाउनु)

basic, *adj.* AdhAr bhUt
    (आधारभूत)

basin, *n.* bhAṅDA (भाँडा),
    (pond) talAu (तलाउ)

basis, *n.* AdhAr (आधार),
    jag (जग), mUl kurA (मूल कुरा)

basket, *n.* DAlo (डालो),
    TokarI (टोकरी), Doko (डोको)

bat, *n. (animal)* chamero
    (चमेरो), *(cricket)* DaNDa
    (डण्डा), byAT (ब्याट)

batch, *n.* bathAn (बथान),
    TolI (टोली)

bath, *n.* snAn (स्नान),
    nuhAune koThA
    (नुहाउने कोठा)

bathe, *v.* nuhAunu (नुहाउनु)

battery, *n.* byATrI (ब्याट्री)

battle, *n.* laDAiṅ (लडाई),
    yuddha (युद्ध)
    v. laDAiṅ garnu (लडाई गर्नु)

bazaar/bazar, *n.* bajAr (बजार)

be, *v./aux.* hunu (हुनु),
    rahanu (रहनु)

beach, *n.* kinArA (किनारा),
    bagar (बगर)

bead, *n.* dAnA (दाना),
  pote ko geDA (पोतेको गेडा)
  v. dAnA unnu (दाना उन्नु)

beak, *n.* chuchcho (चुच्चो)

beam, *n. (ray)* kiraN (किरण),
  (wood) sattarI (सत्तरी)
  v. ujyAlo mukh lAunu
  (उज्यालो मुख लाउनु)

bean, *n.* simI (सिमी), boDI (बोडी)

bear, *n.* bhAlu (भालु)
  v. sahanu (सहनु),
  khapnu (खप्नु)

beard, *n.* dARhI (दाढी)

beast, *n.* pashu (पशु),
  janAwar (जनावर)

beat, *n.* dhukdhukI (ढुकढुकी)
  v. piTnu (पिट्नु)

beautiful, *adj.* sundar (सुन्दर),
  rAmro (राम्रो)

beauty, *n.* saundarya (सौन्दर्य),
  sundartA (सुन्दरता)

because, *conj.* kinaki (किनकि),
  kina bhane (किनभने)

become, *v.* hunu (हुनु),
  bannu (बन्नु)

becoming, *adj.* suhAuňdo
  (सुहाउँदो)

bed, *n.* bichhyaunA
  (बिछ्यौना), khAT (खाट),
  (river) bagar (बगर),
  (field) DyAňg (ड्याङ्ग)

bedbug, *n.* uDus (उडुस)

bedridden, *adj.* thala pareko

(थला परेको)

bee, *n.* maurI (मौरी),
  mAhurI (माहुरी)

beehive, *n.* mAhurI ko chAkA
  (माहुरीको चाका)

beef, *n.* gAI ko mAsu
  (गाईको मासु)

beer, *n.* biyar (बियर),
  (home-made) jAňD (जाँड)

beet, *n.* chukandar (चुकन्दर)

beetle, *n.* gobre kIrA (गोब्रे
  कीरा), bhaňwarA (भँवरा)

before, *prep. (place)* agADi
  (अगाडि), sAmunne (सामुन्ने),
  (time) aghi (अघि),
  pahile (पहिले)

beforehand, *adv.* pahile nai
  (पहिले नै)

beg, *v.* mAgnu (माग्नु),
  bintI garnu (बिन्ती गर्नु)

beggar, *n.* mAgne (माग्ने),
  bhikhArI (भिखारी)

begin, *v.* thAlnu (थाल्नु),
  shuru garnu (शुरु गर्नु)

beginning, *n.* shuruwAt
  (शुरुवात), thAlanI (थालनी)

behave, *v.* wyawahAr garnu
  (व्यवहार गर्नु)

behavio(u)r, *n.* wyawahAr
  (व्यवहार), AcharaN (आचरण)

behind, *adv.* pachhADi
  (पछाडि),
  pachhil tira (पछिल्तिर)

belch, *v.* DakArnu (डकार्नु)
  n. DakAr (डकार)

belief, *n.* wishwAs (विश्वास),
  wichAr (विचार)

believe, *v.* wishwAs garnu
  (विश्वास गर्नु),
  patyAunu (पत्याउनु)

bell, *n.* ghaNTA (घण्टा),
  ghaNTI (घण्टी)

belly, *n.* peT (पेट),
  bhuṅDI (भुँडी)

belong, *v.* **(to)** kasai ko hunu
  (कसैको हुनु)

belongings, *n.* mAl (माल),
  jethA (जेथा)

below, *adv.* tala (तल),
  muntira (मुन्तिर)

belt, *n.* kamar peTI (कमरपेटी),
  paTukA (पटुका)

bench, *n.* bench (बेन्च),
  phalaiṅchA (फलैंचा)

bend, *n.* moD (मोड),
  ghumtI (घुम्ती)
  v. jhuknu (भुक्नु),
  nihuranu (निहुरनु)

beneath, *adv.* tala (तल),
  muni (मुनि)

beneficial, *adj.* lAbh dAyak
  (लाभदायक), guNI (गुणी)

benefit, *n.* hit (हित),
  phAidA (फाइदा), guN (गुण)

benevolent, *adj.* dayAlu
  (दयालु), upkArI (उपकारी)

bereavement, *n.* wiyog
  (वियोग), bichhoD (बिछोड)

berry, *n.* geDA phal (गेडा फल),
  aiṅselu (ऐंसेलु),
  kAphal (काफल), chutro (चुत्रो),
  jAmun (जामुन)

berth, *n.* basne ra sutne ThAuṅ
  (बस्ने र सुत्ने ठाउँ)

besides, *prep.* bAhek (बाहेक),
  siwAya (सिवाय)

best, *adj.* sab bhandA asal
  (सबभन्दा असल),
  sarwottam (सर्वोत्तम)

bet, *n.* bAjI (बाजी)
  v. bAjI thApnu (बाजी थाप्नु)

betel, *n.* pAn (पान)

betel nut, *n.* supArI (सुपारी)

betray, *v.* dhokhA dinu
  (धोखा दिनु)

better, *adj.* bhandA rAmro
  (भन्दा राम्रो)

between, *adv./prep.* mAjh
  (माभ), bIch (बीच)

beverage, *n.* piune wastu
  (पिउने वस्तु)

beware, *v.* sAwdhAn hunu
  (सावधान हुनु)

bewilder, *v.* haDbaDAunu
  (हडबडाउनु),
  jilla pArnu (जिल्ल पार्नु)

beyond, *adv.* para (पर),
  TADhA (टाढा),
  bhandA bAhira (भन्दा बाहिर)

bias, *n.* paksha pAt (पक्षपात)

bicycle, *n.* sAikal (साइकल)

big, *adj.* ThUlo (ठूलो), baDemAn (बडेमान)

bike, *n.* sAikal (साइकल)

bile, *n.* pitta (पित्त)

bilingual, *n.* dobhAse (दोभाषे)

bill, *n.* bil (बिल), noT (नोट)

billion, *n.* *(Brit.)* dash kharab (दश खरब), *(Am.)* ek arab (एक अरब)

bin, *n.* bhakArI (भकारी)

bind, *v.* bAňdhnu (बाँध्नु), kasnu (कस्नु)

binoculars, *n.* durbin (दुर्बिन)

biped, *n.* dui khuTTe (दुईखुट्टे)

bird, *n.* charA (चरा), pakshI (पक्षी)

birth, *n.* janma (जन्म)

birthday, *n.* janma din (जन्मदिन), janmotsaw (जन्मोत्सव)

biscuit, *n.* biskuT (बिस्कुट)

bit, *n.* TukrA (टुक्रा), khaND (खण्ड)

bitch, *n.* kukurnI (कुकुर्नी)

bite, *n.* TokAi (टोकाइ) *v.* Toknu (टोक्नु), chilnu (चिल्नु)

black, *adj.* kAlo (कालो)

blacksmith, *n.* kAmI (कामी), kau (कौ)

bladder, *n.* mUtrAshaya (मूत्राशय), hAwA bhareko byAg (हावा भरेको ब्याग)

blade, *n.* dhAr (धार), chhurA (छुरा), *(grass)* tyAndro (त्यान्द्रो)

blame, *n.* dosh (दोष) *v.* dosh dinu (दोष दिनु)

blank, *n.* shUnyatA (शून्यता), riktatA (रिक्तता) *adj.* khAlI (खाली), ritto (रित्तो)

blanket, *n.* kambal (कम्बल), rADI (राडी), pAkhI (पाखी)

blaze, *v.* bAlnu (बाल्नु), salkanu (सल्कनु) *n.* jwAlA (ज्वाला), prakAsh (प्रकाश)

bleed, *v.* ragat bagnu/bagAunu (रगत बग्नु/बगाउनु)

bleeding, *n.* rakta srAw (रक्तस्राव)

bless, *v.* AshIrwAd/Asik dinu (आशीर्वाद/आसिक दिनु)

blessing, *n.* AshIrwAd (आशीर्वाद), Asik (आसिक)

blind, *adj.* andho (अन्धो), andhA (अन्धा)

blindly, *adv.* AňkhA chimlera (आँखा चिम्लेर)

blink, *v.* AňkhA jhimjhim garnu (आँखा झिमझिम गर्नु)

bliss, *n.* Anand (आनन्द), sukh (सुख)

blister, *n.* pAnI phokA
(पानी फोका)

block, *n.* kATh ko muDho
(काठको मुढो), gaṅTho (गाँठो)
v. roknu (रोक्नु),
band garnu (बन्द गर्नु)

blood, *n.* ragat (रगत)

blood pressure, *n.* rakta chАp
(रक्तचाप)

bloodshed, *n.* rakta pАt
(रक्तपात)

bloom, *v.* phulnu (फुल्नु),
n. kopilA (कोपिला),
phUl (फूल)

blossom, *n.* phUl (फूल),
kopilA (कोपिला)
v. phakranu (फक्रनु),
phulnu (फुल्नु)

blouse, *n.* blAuj (ब्लाउज),
cholo (चोलो)

blow, *n.* prahАr (प्रहार),
Thakkar (ठक्कर),
muDkI (मुड्की),
(disaster) wipatti (विपत्ति)
v. phuknu (फुक्नु),
bajAunu (बजाउनु)

blue, *adj.* nIlo (नीलो)

blunder, *n.* bhUl (भूल)
v. ThUlo bhUl garnu
(ठूलो भूल गर्नु)

blunt, *adj.* dhAr na bhaeko
(धार नभएको), bhutte (भुत्ते)
v. dhAr mArnu (धार मार्नु)

blush, *n.* sharam (शरम),
lajjA (लज्जा)
v. lАj mАnnu (लाज मान्नु),
sharmAunu (शर्माउनु)

boar, *n.* baṅdel (बँदेल),
banel (बनेल)

board, *n.* pАTI (पाटी),
phalyАk (फल्याक),
samiti (समिति)

boast, *v.* dhАk/phuiṅ lAunu
(धाक/फुइँ लाउनु)
n. dhАk (धाक),
dhakku (धक्कु)

boat, *n.* DuṅgA (डुङ्गा),
nAu (नाउ)

body, *n.* sharIr (शरीर),
jIu (जीउ), aṅg (अङ्ग)

bog, *n.* dal dal (दलदल),
dhАp (धाप)

bogus, *adj.* nakkalI
(नक्कली), jhUTho (झूठो)

boil, *n.* phokA (फोका),
khaTirA (खटिरा)
v. umAlnu (उमाल्नु), umlanu
(उम्लनु), usinnu (उसिन्नु)

bold, *adj.* shUro (शूरो),
AṅTilo (आँटिलो)

bolt, *n.* chheskinI (छेस्किनी),
Aglo (आग्लो), chukul (चुकुल)
v. chukul lAunu (चुकुल लाउनु)

bomb, *n.* bam golA (बम गोला)

bombard, *v.* bambArI garnu
(बमबारी गर्नु)

bonanza, *n.* dhan ko khAnI
(धनको खानी)

bond, *n.* bandhan (बन्धन),
tamasuk (तमसुक)

bone, *n.* hAD (हाड),
haDDI (हड्डी)

bonus, *n.* bhattA (भत्ता),
anudAn (अनुदान)

book, *n.* kitAb (किताब),
pustak (पुस्तक)
v. TikaT kinnu (टिकट
किन्नु), dartA garnu (दर्ता गर्नु)

booklet *n.* pustikA (पुस्तिका)

boon, *n.* wardAn (वरदान)

boot, *n.* juttA (जुत्ता), buT (बूट)

booty, *n.* lUT ko mAl
(लूटको माल)

booth, *n.* koThA (कोठा),
(election) matdAn sthal
(मतदान स्थल)

border, *n.* simAnA (सिमाना),
kinArA (किनारा)
v. kinArA hAlnu
(किनारा हाल्नु)

bore, *n. (gun)* nAl (नाल)
v. uchchAT lagnu
(उच्चाट लाग्नु)

born, *adj.* janmeko (जन्मेको)

borrow, *v.* sApaT linu
(सापट लिनु),
udhAro linu (उधारो लिनु)

boss, *n.* hAkim (हाकिम),
mAlik (मालिक)

both, *adj.* duwai (दुवै)

bother, *v.* kashT dinu
(कष्ट दिनु)
n. jhyAulo (भ्याउलो),
TanTA (टन्टा)

bottle, *n.* sisI (सिसी),
botal (बोतल)
v. sisI mA hAlnu
(सिसीमा हाल्नु)

bottom, *n.* pIndh (पींध),
phed (फेद)

bounce, *v.* uphranu (उफ्रनु),
uchhiTTinu (उछिट्टिनु)
n. uphRAi (उफ्राइ),
phUrti (फूर्ति)

bound, *v.* uphranu (उफ्रनु),
kudnu (कुद्नु)
n. sImA (सीमा), kinArA (किनारा)
adj. jAna lAgeko
(जान लागेको)

boundary, *n.* simAnA (सिमाना)

bountiful, *adj.* dAn shIl
(दानशील), kripAlu (कृपालु)

bouquet, *n.* phUl ko
guchchha (फूलको गुच्छा),
jhuppA (भुप्पा)

bourgeois, *n.* madhyam warg
(मध्यम वर्ग)
adj. bhautik wAdI
(भौतिकवादी)

bow, *n.* dhanush (धनुष)
v. jhuknu (भुक्नु),
nihurinu (निहुरिनु)

bowl, *n.* kachaurA (कचौरा),
DabkA (डबका)
v. phyAṅknu (फ्याँक्नु)

bowler, *n.* phyAṅkne mAnis
(फ्याँक्ने मानिस),
bolar (बोलर)

box, *n.* bAkas (बाकस),
kantur (कन्तुर),
sanduk (सन्दुक)
v. ghussA/mukkA hAnnu
(घुस्सा/मुक्का हान्नु)

boxer, *n.* mukke bAj
(मुक्केबाज)

boy, *n.* keTA (केटा),
ThiTA (ठिटा), laDkA (लड्का)

boycott, *v.* bahishkAr garnu
(बहिष्कार गर्नु)
n. bahishkAr (बहिष्कार)

bra, *n.* DhAkne cholI (ढाक्ने
चोली), brA (ब्रा)

bracelet, *n.* bAlA (बाला),
bAju (बाजु), churA (चुरा)

brain, *n.* dimAg (दिमाग),
buddhi (बुद्धि)

brake, *n.* brek (ब्रेक),
gati rodhak (गतिरोधक)
v. thAmnu (थाम्नु),
roknu (रोक्नु)

branch, *n.* hAṅgo (हाँगो),
hAṅgA (हाँगा),
shAkhA (शाखा)
v. hAṅgA hAlnu (हाँगा हाल्नु)

brand, *n.* DAmeko chinha
(डामेको चिन्ह), DAm (डाम),
kisim (किसिम)
v. DAmnu (डाम्नु)

brass, *n.* pittal (पित्तल),
pital (पितल)

brave, *adj.* bahAdur (बहादुर),
wIr (वीर), sUro (सूरो)

bread, *n.* roTI (रोटी),
pAu roTI (पाउरोटी)

breadth, *n.* chauDAi (चौडाइ),
moTAi (मोटाइ)

break, *v.* TuTAunu
(टुटाउनु),
phuTAunu (फुटाउनु),
(string) chuṅDnu (चुँड्नु),
chuṅDAlnu (चुँडाल्नु)
n. awrodh (अवरोध),
toD (तोड)

breakfast, *n.* nAstA (नास्ता),
jal pan (जलपान),
khAjA (खाजा)

breast, *n.* chhAtI (छाती),
(woman) dUdh (दूध),
stan (स्तन)

breath, *n.* sAs (सास),
dam (दम), prAN (प्राण)

breathe, *v.* sAs phernu/linu
(सास फेर्नु/लिनु)

bribe, *n.* ghUs (घूस)
v. ghUs khwAunu/dinu
(घूस ख्वाउनु/दिनु)

brick, *n.* IṅT (ईंट), IṅTA (ईंटा)
v. IṅT lAunu (ईंट लाउनु)

bride, *n.* dulahI (दुलही),
  behulI (बेहुली),
  byAulI (ब्याउली)

bridegroom, *n.* dulahA (दुलहा),
  behulo (बेहुलो),
  byAulo (ब्याउलो)

bridge, *n.* pul (पुल),
  sAṅgu (साँगु), *(suspension)*
  jhuluṅge pul (झुलुङ्गे पुल)
  v. jornu (जोर्नु),
  pul bAṅdhnu (पुल बाँध्नु)

bridle, *n.* lagAm (लगाम),
  rokAwaT (रोकावट)
  v. lagAm lagAunu
  (लगाम लगाउनु)

brief, *adj.* chhoTo (छोटो),
  chhoTkarI (छोटकरी),
  saṅkshipta (संक्षिप्त)

bright, *adj.* chahakilo
  (चहकिलो), chamkilo
  (चम्किलो), ujyAlo (उज्यालो),
  (person) tej (तेज),
  jehendAr (जेहेन्दार)

brilliant, *adj.* chaDko (चड्को),
  chahakilo (चहकिलो),

bring, *v.* lyAunu (ल्याउनु)

bring down, *v.* jhArnu (झार्नु),

bring out, *v.* nikAlnu (निकाल्नु)

bring up, *v.* hurkAunu (हुर्काउनु)

brisk, *adj.* TATho (टाठो),
  phurtilo (फुर्तिलो),
  (bus.) chaltI ko (चल्तीको)

brittle, *adj.* nAjuk (नाजुक),

broad, *adj.* chauDA (चौडा),
  chAklo (चाक्लो)

broke, *adj. (person)* TAT
  palTeko (टाट पल्टेको),
  kaṅgAl (कङ्गाल)
  v. bhAṅchyo (भाँच्यो),
  bhAṅchiyo (भाँचियो)

broker, *n.* dalAl (दलाल)

bronze, *n.* kAṅs (काँस),
  DhaloT (ढलोट)

brook, *n.* kholA (खोला)
  v. sahanu (सहनु),
  besAunu (बेसाउनु)

broom, *n.* kucho (कुचो),
  jhADu (झाडु)

brothel, *n.* ranDI ghar
  (रन्डीघर), weshyAlaya
  (वेश्यालय), koThI (कोठी)

brother, *n. (older)* dAju (दाजु),
  dAi (दाइ),
  (younger) bhAi (भाइ)

brother-in-law, *n. (husband's
  elder brother)* jeThAju
  (जेठाजु), *(husband's younger
  brother)* dewar (देवर),
  (wife's elder brother) jeThAn
  (जेठान), *(wife's younger
  brother)* sAlA (साला),
  (younger sister's husband)
  jwAiṅ (ज्वाईं), *(elder sister's
  husband)* bhinAju (भिनाजु)

brow, *n*. AṅkhI bhauṅ (आँखीभौं)

brown, *adj*. khairo (खैरो),
kailo (कैलो), geruwA (गेरुवा)

brunette, *n*. sAṅwalI (साँवली),
kAlo kapAl bhaekI AimAI
(कालो कपाल भएकी आइमाई)

brush, *n*. burus (बुरुस),
kucho (कुचो)
v. (teeth) dAṅt mAjhnu
(दाँत माझ्नु),
burus lAunu (बुरुस लाउनु),
kucho lAunu (कुचो लाउनु)

brutal, *adj*. nirdayI (निर्दयी),
krUr (क्रूर)

bubble, *n*. pAnI phokA
(पानी फोका)
v. phokA uThnu (फोका
उठ्नु), umlanu (उम्लनु)

buck, *n*. bhAle hariN
(भाले हरिण)
v. uphranu (उफ्रनु)

bucket, *n*. bAlTI (बाल्टी),
bAlTin (बाल्टिन), Dol (डोल)

buckle, *n*. khIp (खीप)
v. khIp lAunu (खीप लाउनु)

buckwheat, *n*. phApar (फापर)

bud, *n*. kopilA (कोपिला)
v. kopilA niskanu
(कोपिला निस्कनु)

budge, *v.* sarnu (सर्नु),
haTnu (हट्नु),
Deg chalnu (डेग चल्नु)

budget, *n*. bajeT (बजेट),

Aya-wyayak (आय-व्ययक)

buff, *n*. rAṅga ko mAsu
(राँगाको मासु)
adj. (colour) chhAlA ko raṅg
(छालाको रङ्ग),
(bare) nAṅgo (नाङ्गो)

buffalo, *n*. *(female)* bhaiṅsI
(भैंसी), *(male)* rAṅgo (राँगो),
(wild) arnA (अर्ना)

buffer, *n*. dhakkA thAmne
wastu (धक्का थाम्ने वस्तु)

buffet, *n*. baphe (बफे), tebul
ma rAkhekA khAne kurA
Aphai jhikI khAne bhoj
(टेबुलमा राखेका खानेकुरा आफै
झिकी खाने भोज)

bug, *n*. uDus (उडुस), kIrA (कीरा)

bugle, *n*. bigul (बिगुल)

build, *n*. jIu DAI (जीउडाल),
gaThan (गठन)
v. banAunu (बनाउनु)

builder, *n*. DakarmI (डकर्मी),
banAune (बनाउने)

building, *n*. ghar (घर),
bhawan (भवन)

bulb, *n*. *(plant)* gAnu (गानु),
(electric) chim (चिम)

bulge, *n*. sUj (सूज), poko (पोको)
v. uksanu (उक्सनु)

bulk, *n*. mAtrA (मात्रा),
thok (थोक)

bulky, *adj*. bhArI (भारी),
thasallo (थसल्लो)

bull, *n.* sAñDhe (साँढे),
  (young) bahar (बहर)
bullet, *n.* golI (गोली)
bulletin, *n.* samAchAr /
  sUchanA patra
  (समाचार/सूचनापत्र)
bullock, *n.* goru (गोरु)
bump, *n.* gAñTho (गाँठो),
  Thakkar (ठक्कर)
  v. thachchinu (थच्चिनु),
  thachArnu (थचार्नु)
bun, *n.* ban roTI (बनरोटी)
bunch, *n. (flower)* jhuppA
  (झुप्पा), guchchhA (गुच्छा),
  (group) jamAt (जमात)
bundle, *n.* poko (पोको),
  muThA (मुठा), kallI (कल्ली)
  v. poko/muThA pArnu
  (पोको/मुठा पार्नु)
burden, *n.* bhAr (भार),
  bhArI (भारी)
  v. bokAunu (बोकाउनु)
bureau, *n.* gharrA bhaeko
  tebul (घर्रा भएको टेबुल,
  (department) wibhAg (विभाग)
bureaucracy, *n.* nokar shAhI
  (नोकरशाही), karm chArI
  tantra (कर्मचारी तन्त्र),
  adhikArI prathA
  (अधिकारी प्रथा)
burglar, *n.* chor (चोर)
burial, *n.* chihAn mA gADne
  kAm (चिहानमा गाडिने काम)

burn, *n.* poleko/DAmeko
  ghAu (पोलेको/डामेको घाउ)
  v. polnu (पोल्नु),
  bAlnu (बाल्नु), DaDhnu (डढ्नु)
burst, *n.* jhokkA (झोक्का)
  v. phuTnu (फुट्नु),
  paDkanu (पड्कनु)
bury, *v.* gAdnu (गाडिनु)
bus, *n.* bas (बस)
bush, *n.* jhADI (झाडी),
  buTo (बुटो)
business, *n.* kAm (काम),
  wyApAr (व्यापार),
  kArobAr (कारोबार)
businesslike, *adj.* wyAwhArik
  (व्यावहारिक),
  wyawasthit (व्यवस्थित)
businessman, *n.* wyApArI
  (व्यापारी), bepArI (बेपारी)
bust, *n.* chhAtI (छाती), sharIr
  ko mAthillo AdhA bhAg
  (शरीरको माथिल्लो आधा भाग)
busy, *adj.* kAm mA lAgeko
  (काममा लागेको),
  wyasta (व्यस्त)
but, *conj.* tara (तर),
  kintu (किन्तु)
butcher, *n.* bagare (बगरे)
butter, *n.* makkhan (मक्खन),
  naunI (नौनी)
  v. naunI lagAunu (नौनी
  लगाउनु), chAplusI garnu
  (चापलुसी गर्नु)

butterfly, *n.* putalI (पुतली)
buttocks, *n.* puTThA (पुट्ठा), chAk (चाक)
button, *n.* Taṅk (टाँक), baTan (बटन)

buy, *n.* kharid (खरिद)
v. kinnu (किन्नु)
by, *prep.* saṅga (सँग), dwArA (द्वारा), le (ले)
bye, *n.* bidAi (बिदाइ)

C

cab, *n.* TyAksI (ट्याक्सी)
cabbage, *n.* bandA (बन्दा), bandA kobhI (बन्दाकोभी)
cabin, *n.* koThA (कोठा)
cabinet, *n.* darAj (दराज), *(pol.)* mantri maNDal (मन्त्रिमण्डल)
cable, *n.* DorI (डोरी), tAr (तार), TeligrAm (टेलिग्राम) *v.* tAr paThaunu (तार पठाउनु)
cactus, *n.* siuṅDI (सिउँडी), kyAchuk (क्याचुक)
cafeteria, *n.* chamenA ghar (चमेनाघर)
cage, *n.* piñjaDA (पिंजडा), khor (खोर)
cake, *n.* kek (केक)
calamity, *n.* Apatti (आपत्ति), wipatti (विपत्ति)
calculate, *v.* hisAb garnu (हिसाब गर्नु)
calculation, *n.* hisAb (हिसाब), gaNanA (गणना)
calendar, *n.* pAtro (पात्रो)

calf, *n. (cow)* bAchchho (बाछ्छो), bAchchhI (बाछ्छी), *(buffalo)* pADo (पाडो), pADI (पाडी), *(leg)* piṅDaulA (पिंडौला)
call, *n.* bolAwaT (बोलावट) *v.* bolAunu (बोलाउनु), DAknu (डाक्नु)
call girl, *n.* weshyA (वेश्या)
calm, *n.* shAnti (शान्ति) *adj.* shAnt (शान्त), sunsAn (सुनसान)
camel, *n.* UṅT (ऊँट)
camera, *n.* kyAmerA (क्यामेरा)
camouflage, *n. (war)* bhesh badalne kAm (भेष बदल्ने काम) *v.* bhesh badalnu (भेष बदल्नु)
camp, *n.* kyAmp (क्याम्प), shiwir (शिविर) *v.* bAs basnu (बास बस्नु)
campaign, *n. (mil.)* kaTak (कटक), abhiyAn (अभियान)

v. abhiyAn chalAunu
(अभियान चलाउने)

camphor, *n.* kapUr (कपूर)

campus, *n.* kyAmpas
(क्याम्पस), pITh (पीठ),
(area) prAṅgaN (प्राङ्गण)

can, *n.* Tin ko baTTA
(टिनको बट्टा),DhwAṅg (ढ्वाङ्ग)
mod. saknu (सक्नु)

canal, *n.* nahar (नहर), kulo (कुलो)

cancel, *v.* radda/badar garnu
(रद्द/बदर गर्नु)

cancer, *n. (zodiac)* karkaT
(कर्कट),
(med.) arbud rog (अर्बुद रोग)

candid, *adj.* khulA (खुला),
khulast (खुलस्त)

candidate, *n.* ummed wAr
(उम्मेदवार)

candle, *n.* main battI (मैनबत्ती)

candy, *n.* misrI (मिस्री),
miThAI (मिठाई)

cane, *n.* bet (बेत),chhaDI (छडी)

canister, *n.* DhwAṅg (ढ्वाङ्ग),
DibbA (डिब्बा)

canopy, *n.* chaṅduwA (चँदुवा),
jhallar (झल्लर)

canteen, *n.* chamenA ghar
(चमेनाघर)

canvas, *n.* TAT (टाट),
moTo kapaDA (मोटो कपडा)

cap, *n. (headgear)* TopI (टोपी),
(lid) birko (बिर्को)

v. DhAknu (ढाक्नु)

capable, *adj.* yogya (योग्य),
samarth (समर्थ)

capacity, *n.* haisiyat (हैसियत),
kshamatA (क्षमता)

capital, *n. (city)* rAj dhAnI
(राजधानी), sadar (सदर),
(money) pUñjI (पूँजी),
dhan (धन), *(letter)* ThUlo
akshar (ठूलो अक्षर)

capitalism, *n.* pUñjI wAd
(पूँजीवाद)

capricorn, *n.* makar (मकर)

capsule, *n.* kosh (कोष),
(med.) chakkI (चक्की)

captain, *n.* kaptAn (कप्तान),
saha senAnI (सहसेनानी),
netA (नेता)

captivate, *v.* mohit pArnu
(मोहित पार्नु),
wash garnu (वश गर्नु)

capture, *n.* pakrAu (पक्राउ),
giraphtArI (गिरफ्तारी)
v. pakranu (पक्रनु),
samAtnu (समात्नु)

car, *n.* kAr (कार),
moTar gADI (मोटर गाडी)

caravan, *n.* yAtrI samUh
(यात्री समूह)

card, *n.* moTo/bAklo kAgaj
(मोटो/बाक्लो कागज,
kArD (कार्ड),
(game) tAs (तास)

cardamom, *n.* *(big)* alaiñchI
(अलैंची),
(small) sukumel (सुकुमेल)

care, *n.* her chAh (हेरचाह),
surtA (सुर्ता),
(charge) jimmA (जिम्मा)
v. wAstA/her wichAr garnu
(वास्ता/हेरविचार गर्नु),
dhyAn dinu (ध्यान दिनु)

career, *n.* jIwan charyA
(जीवनचर्या)

careful, *adj.* hoshiyAr
(होशियार),
sAwdhAn (सावधान)

careless, *adj.* beparwAh
(बेपरवाह), behoshI (बेहोशी)

caress, *v.* sum sumyAunu
(सुमसुम्याउनु),
mAyA garnu (माया गर्नु)

cargo, *n.* jahAj/gADI mA
lagine mal mattA (जहाज/
गाडीमा लगिने मलमत्ता)

caricature, *n.* wyaṅgya chitra
(व्यङ्ग्य चित्र)

carnivorous, *adj.* mAsu
khAne (मासुखाने),
mAṃsAhArI
(मांसाहारी)

carpenter, *n.* sikarmI (सिकर्मी)

carpet, *n.* galaiñchA (गलैंचा),
satranjA (सतरन्जा)

carriage, *n.* gADI (गाडी),
rath (रथ)

carrier, *n.* bokne mAnis
(बोक्ने मानिस), kullI (कुल्ली),
(mech.) samwAhak (संवाहक),
kyAriyar (क्यारियर)

carrot, *n.* gAjar (गाजर)

carry, *v.* laijAnu (लैजानु),
boknu (बोक्नु)

cart, *n.* gADA (गाडा),
bail gADI (बैलगाडी)

cartoon, *n.* wyaṅgya chitra
(व्यङ्ग्य चित्र)

carve, *v.* kuňdnu (कुँद्नु),
kATnu (काट्नु)

cascade, *n.* chhAṅgo (छाँगो),
chhaharA (छहरा)

case, *n.* muddA (मुद्दा),
mAmilA (मामिला),
(container) baTTA (बट्टा),
khol (खोल)

cash, *n.* nagad (नगद),
rokaD (रोकड)
v. bhajAunu (भजाउनु),
paisA sATnu (पैसा साट्नु)

cashew nut, *n.* kAju (काजु)

cashier, *n.* khajAnchI (खजान्ची)

casino, *n.* jUwA ghar
(जूवा घर)

cassette, *n.* kyAseT (क्यासेट),
Tep (टेप)

cast, *n.* sAñcho (साँचो),
Akriti (आकृति)
v. phyAñknu (फ्याँक्नु),
hAlnu (हाल्नु)

caste, *n.* jAt (जात)

casual, *adj.* bhaiparI Aune (भैपरी आउने), *(dress, remarks)* anaupchArik (अनौपचारिक)

casualty, *n.* noksAn (नोक्सान), hatAhat (हताहत)

cat, *n.* birAlo (बिरालो)

catalog(ue), *n.* sUchI patra (सूचीपत्र)

catastrophe, *n.* utpAt (उत्पात), Apat (आपत्)

catch, *n.* pakaD (पकड) *v.* samAtnu (समात्नु), pakranu (पक्रनु)

category, *n.* shreNI (श्रेणी), samUha (समूह)

caterpillar, *n.* jhusil kIrA (भुसिलकीरा)

cattle, *n.* gAI-goru (गाई-गोरु), gAI wastu (गाईवस्तु)

cauliflower, *n.* kAulI (काउली), phUl kobhI (फूलकोभी)

cause, *n.* kAraN (कारण) *v.* garnu (गर्नु), garAunu (गराउनु)

cautious, *adj.* hoshiyAr (होशियार), sachet (सचेत)

cave, *n.* guphA (गुफा), oDAr (ओडार)

cease, *v.* band garnu (बन्द गर्नु), thAmnu (थाम्नु)

ceaseless, *adj.* lagAtAr (लगातार), nirantar (निरन्तर)

ceiling, *n.* siliñ (सिलिङ), chhAnA (छाना), dalin (दलिन)

celebrate, *v.* utsaw manAunu (उत्सव मनाउनु)

celebration, *n.* utsaw (उत्सव), samAroha (समारोह), khusIyAlI (खुसीयाली)

celestial, *adj.* AkAshIya (आकाशीय), diwya (दिव्य)

celibacy, *n.* awiwAhit jIwan (अविवाहित जीवन), brahma charya (ब्रह्मचर्य)

cell, *n.* jIw kosTh (जीवकोष्ठ), kosh (कोष)

cement, *n.* simaNTI (सिमण्टी) *v.* jornu (जोर्नु), baliyo pArnu (बलियो पार्नु)

cemetery, *n.* chihAn (चिहान), kabristAn (कब्रिस्तान)

censor, *n.* jAñch (जाँच), nirIkshak (निरीक्षक) *v.* jAñch garnu (जाँच गर्नु)

census, *n.* jan gaNanA (जनगणना)

centenary, *n.* shat wArshikI (शतवार्षिकी)

central, *adj.* mAjh ko (माझको), kendrIya (केन्द्रीय)

centre (ter), *n.* kendra (केन्द्र), madhya (मध्य) *v.* kendrit/jammA garnu (केन्द्रित/जम्मा गर्नु)

century, *n.* shatAbdI (शताब्दी), shatak (शतक)

ceremony, *n.* samAroh (समारोह), utsaw (उत्सव)

certain, *adj. (any)* kunai (कुनै), *(convinced)* pakkA (पक्का), nishchit (निश्चित)

certificate, *n.* pramAN patra (प्रमाणपत्र)

certify, *v.* pramANit garnu (प्रमाणित गर्नु)

chain, *n.* janjIr (जन्जीर), sikrI (सिक्री), *(series)* silsilA (सिलसिला) *v.* bAñdhnu (बाँध्नु)

chair, *n.* mech (मेच), kursI (कुर्सी), Asan (आसन) *v.* adhyakshatA garnu (अध्यक्षता गर्नु)

chairman, *n.* adhyaksha (अध्यक्ष), sabhA pati (सभापति)

chalk, *n.* kharI (खरी), chak (चक)

challenge, *n.* hAñk (हाँक), chunautI (चुनौती) *v.* hAñk dinu (हाँक दिनु), jorI khojnu (जोरी खोज्नु)

chamber, *n.* koThA (कोठा), *(orgn.)* sañgh (सङ्घ)

champion, *n.* wijetA (विजेता), laDAkA (लडाका)

chance, *n.* maukA (मौका), sanjog (सन्जोग)

chancellor, *n.* kul pati (कुलपति)

chancery, *n.* rAj dUtAwAs ko kAryAlaya (राजदूतावासको कार्यालय)

chandelier, *n.* jhAD phAnas (झाडफानस)

change, *n.* adal badal (अदलबदल), pariwartan (परिवर्तन), her pher (हेरफेर), *(money)* khudrA paisA (खुद्रा पैसा), *(clothes)* arko lugA (अर्को लुगा) *v. (clothes, etc.)* phernu (फेर्नु), badalnu (बदल्नु), *(money)* sATnu (साट्नु)

chant, *n.* bhajan (भजन), gIt (गीत) *v.* bhajan/pATh garnu (भजन/पाठ गर्नु)

chaos, *n.* ast wyasta (अस्त-व्यस्त), ganjAgol (गन्जागोल), lathAliñga (लथालिङ्ग)

chapter, *n.* adhyAya (अध्याय), khaND (खण्ड)

character, *n. (nature)* charitra (चरित्र), swabhAw (स्वभाव), *(letter)* akshar (अक्षर)

characteristic, *n.* lakshaN (लक्षण), wishishT guN (विशिष्ट गुण)

charcoal, *n.* gol (गोल)

charge, *n.* jimmA (जिम्मा),

(attack) hamlA (हमला),
(blame) Arop (आरोप),
(fee) dastur (दस्तुर)
v. (blame) Arop lAunu
(आरोप लाउनु), *(attack)*
hamlA garnu (हमला गर्नु),
(fee) dastur linu (दस्तुर लिनु),
(task) jimmA linu/dinu
(जिम्मा लिनु/दिनु)

chariot, *n.* rath (रथ)

charisma, *n.* IshwarIya dAn
(ईश्वरीय दान), sAmarthya
(सामर्थ्य), AkarshaN (आकर्षण)

charity, *n.* dAn (दान),
dAtawya (दातव्य)

charm, *n. (amulet)* jantar
(जन्तर), *(attraction)*
AkarshaN (आकर्षण),
moh (मोह)
v. mohit/Akarshit garnu
(मोहित/आकर्षित गर्नु)

charming, *adj.* mohak (मोहक),
sundar (सुन्दर),

chart, *n.* naksA (नक्सा),
chitra (चित्र), paT (पट)
v. (plan) yojanA banAunu
(योजना बनाउनु)

chase, *n.* lakheTai (लखेटाइ),
khedo (खेदो)
v. lagArnu (लगार्नु),
khednu (खेद्नु)

chauffeur, *n.* DAibar (डाइबर),
moTar chAlak (मोटरचालक)

chat, *v.* gaph garnu (गफ गर्नु),
bAt mArnu (बात मार्नु)

cheap, *adj.* sasto (सस्तो),
sulabh (सुलभ)

cheat, *n.* Thag (ठग),
luchcho (लुच्चो)
v. Thagnu (ठग्नु), chhalnu (छल्नु)

check, *n.* rok (रोक), bAdhA
(बाधा), *(exam.)* jAñch (जाँच)
v. roknu (रोक्नु), thAmnu
(थाम्नु), jAñchnu (जाँच्नु)

cheek, *n.* gAlA (गाला)

cheer, *n.* Anand (आनन्द),
prasannatA (प्रसन्नता)
v. hausalA dinu (हौसला दिनु),
prasanna tulyAunu
(प्रसन्न तुल्याउनु)

cheerful, *adj.* prasanna
(प्रसन्न), khusI (खुसी)

cheese, *n.* chIj (चीज)

chemical, *adj.* rAsAyanik
(रासायनिक)

cheque/check, *n.* chek (चेक)

chess, *n.* buddhi chAl
(बुद्धिचाल)

chest, *n. (body)* chhAtI
(छाती), *(box)* sanduk (सन्दुक),
sandus (सन्दुस)

chestnut, *n.* kaTus (कटुस)

chew, *v.* chapAunu (चपाउनु)

chicken, *n.* kukhurA (कुखुरा),
kukhurA ko challA/mAsu
(कुखुराको चल्ला/मासु)

chicken pox, *n.* TheulA
(ठेउला), Theulo (ठेउलो)

chide, *v.* hapkAunu (हप्काउनु)

chief, *n.* pradhAn (प्रधान),
mukhya mAnis
(मुख्य मानिस),
(village) mukhiyA (मुखिया),
thakAlI (थकाली)

child, *n.* bachchA (बच्चा),
bAlak (बालक), nAnI (नानी)

children, *n.* bachchA harU
(बच्चाहरू),
keTA keTI (केटाकेटी)

chill, *n.* shIt (शीत),
ThaNDI (ठण्डी)

chilli/chili, *n.* khorsAnI
(खोर्सानी), khursAnI (खुर्सानी)

chilly, *adj.* ThaNDA (ठण्डा),
jADo (जाडो), chiso (चिसो)

chimney, *n.* chimnI (चिम्नी),
dhuwAñ kas (धुवाँकस)

chin, *n.* chiuñDo (चिउँडो)

china, *n.* chiniyAñ mATo kA
bhAñDA (चिनियाँ माटोका भाँडा)

chip, *n.* TukrA (टुक्रा),
choiTA (चोइटा), roDA (रोडा)

chit, *n.* purjA (पुर्जा),
TippaNI (टिप्पणी)

chocolate, *n.* chakleT (चकलेट),
(colour) gADhA khairo rañg
(गाढा खैरो रङ्ग)

choice, *n.* chhanoT (छनोट),
chayan (चयन),

wikalp (विकल्प)

cholera, *n.* haijA (हैजा),
jhADA bAntA (झाडाबान्ता)

choose, *v.* chhAnnu (छान्नु),
chunnu (चुन्नु), rojnu (रोज्नु)

chop, *n.* chap (चप)
v. TukrA pArnu (टुक्रा पार्नु),
kATnu (काट्नु)

Christian, *n.* isAI (इसाई),
kristAn (क्रिस्तान)

Christmas, *n.* krismas chAD
(क्रिस्मस चाड)

chrysanthemum, *n.* godAwarI
phUl (गोदावरी फूल)

church, *n.* girjA ghar (गिर्जाघर)

churn, *n.* madAnI (मदानी)
v. mathnu (मथ्नु),
huñDalnu (हुँडल्नु)

CID, *n.* gupt char (गुप्तचर),
khuphiyA (खुफिया)

cigarette, *n.* churoT (चुरोट),
sigareT (सिगरेट)

cinema, *n. (movie)* chal chitra
(चलचित्र), filim (फिलिम)

cinnamon, *n.* dAl chinI
(दालचिनी)

circle, *n.* gherA (घेरा),
writta (वृत्त)
v. ghernu (घेर्नु),
ghumnu (घुम्नु)

circular, *adj.* bATulo (बाटुलो),
golo (गोलो)
n. (notice) sUchanA (सूचना)

circulation, *n.* prachAr (प्रचार), prasAr (प्रसार), *(blood)* rakta sañchAr (रक्तसञ्चार)

circumference, *n.* paridhi (परिधि), gherA (घेरा), girdA (गिर्दा)

circumstance, *n.* sthiti (स्थिति), awasthA (अवस्था), paribAnd (परिबन्द)

circus, *n.* sarkas (सर्कस), chaTak (चटक)

citizen, *n.* nAgrik (नागरिक)

citron, *n.* bimiro (बिमिरो)

city, *n.* shahar (शहर), nagar (नगर)

civil, *adj.* nijAmatI (निजामती), *(manner)* sushIl (सुशील)

civilization, *n.* sabhyatA (सभ्यता)

civilized, *adj.* sabhya (सभ्य), somatilo (सोमतिलो)

claim, *n.* dAbI (दाबी), dAbA (दाबा) *v.* dAbI/dAbA garnu (दाबी/दाबा गर्नु)

clamo(u)r, *n.* hallA (हल्ला), khalyAñg balyAñg (खल्याङ्गबल्याङ्ग) *v.* hallA garnu (हल्ला गर्नु), sor machchAunu (सोर मच्चाउनु)

clamp, *n.* chyApne purjA (च्याप्ने पुर्जा)

v. chyApnu (च्याप्नु), kasnu (कस्नु)

clap, *n.* thapaDI (थपडी), tAlI (ताली) *v.* tAlI/thapaDI bajAunu (ताली/थपडी बजाउनु)

clarify, *v.* spashT garnu (स्पष्ट गर्नु), khulAunu (खुलाउनु)

clash, *n.* bhiDanta (भिडन्त), ladAiñ (लडाईं) *v.* bhiDnu (भिड्नु), laDnu (लड्नु)

class, *n.* darjA (दर्जा), shreNI (श्रेणी), warg (वर्ग), kakshA (कक्षा)

classify, *v.* shreNI baddha / wargIkaraN garnu (श्रेणीबद्ध/वर्गीकरण गर्नु)

clay, *n.* chiplo mATo (चिप्लो माटो)

clean, *adj.* saphA (सफा), sugghar (सुग्घर) *v.* saphA garnu (सफा गर्नु)

clear, *adj.* saphA (सफा), spashT (स्पष्ट), chharlañg (छर्लङ्ग) *v.* saphA garnu (सफा गर्नु), khulAunu (खुलाउनु), ughranu (उघ्रनु)

clearly, *adv.* saphA/khulast sañga (सफा/खुलस्तसँग)

cleft, *n.* dhAñjA (धाँजा), kApo (कापो)

clerk, *n.* kArindA (कारिन्दा), klark (क्लर्क)

clever, *adj.* sipAlu (सिपालु), bATho (बाठो), chalAkh (चलाख)

cliff, *n.* bhIr (भीर)

climate, *n.* hAwA pAnI (हावापानी), jal wAyu (जलवायु)

climb, *v.* chaDhnu (चढ्नु), uklanu (उक्लनु)

cling, *v.* TAṅsinu (टाँसिनु), lAgi rahanu (लागिरहनु)

clinic, *n.* swAsthya/upchAr griha (स्वास्थ्य/उपचार गृह)

clip, *n.* kilip (किलिप) *v.* chyApnu (च्याप्नु), kATnu (काट्नु)

cloak, *n.* bAhirI khukulo lugA (बाहिरी खुकुलो लुगा) *v.* lukAunu (लुकाउनु)

clock, *n.* ghaDI (घडी)

close, *n.* ant (अन्त) *adj.* najik (नजिक), band (बन्द) *v.* band garnu (बन्द गर्नु), thunnu (थुन्नु)

closet, *n.* sAnu koThA (सानु कोठा), *(cabinet)* darAj (दराज)

cloth, *n.* kapaDA (कपडा), wastra (वस्त्र)

clothes, *n.* lugA phATo (लुगाफाटो),

poshAk (पोशाक)

clothing, *n.* lugA (लुगा)

cloud, *n.* bAdal (बादल)

cloudy, *adj.* badalI lAgeko (बदली लागेको), dhummieko (धुम्मिएको)

clove, *n.* lwAṅ (ल्वाङ)

clown, *n.* pAkhe (पाखे), mUrkh (मूर्ख), *(circus)* jokar (जोकर)

club, *n. (stick)* DaNDA (डण्डा), lauro (लौरो), *(orgn.)* saṅgh (संघ)

clubs, *n. (cards)* chiD (चिड), chiDiyA (चिडिया)

clue, *n.* suiṅko (सुइँको), patto (पत्तो), surAkh (सुराख)

clumsy, *adj.* beDhaṅg ko (बेढङ्गको), bhaddA (भद्दा)

coach, *n. (sport)* prashikshak (प्रशिक्षक), *(carriage)* gADI (गाडी), DibbA (डिब्बा) *v.* talIm dinu (तालीम दिनु), sikAunu (सिकाउनु)

coal, *n.* koilA (कोइला)

coarse, *adj.* khasro (खस्रो), bhaddA (भद्दा)

coast, *n.* kinArA (किनारा), taT (तट)

coat, *n. (dress)* koT (कोट), *(painting)* taha (तह), molammA (मोलम्मा)

cobbler, *n.* sArkI (सार्की)

cobra, *n.* goman (गोमन),
gahuman (गहुमन)

cobweb, *n.* mAkurA ko jAlo
(माकुराको जालो)

cock, *n.* bhAle kukhurA
(भाले कुखुरा)

cockroach, *n.* sAnglo (साँग्लो)

coconut, *n.* nariwal (नरिवल)

code, *n. (law)* ain (ऐन),
samhitA (संहिता),
(sign) sanket (सङ्केत)

co-education, *n.* saha shikshA
(सहशिक्षा)

co-existence, *n.* saha astitwa
(सहअस्तित्त्व)

coffee, *n.* kaphI (कफी)

coffin, *n.* lAsh rAkhne bAkas
(लाश राख्ने बाकस)

coil, *n.* guñDulko (गुँडुल्को),
guchchhA (गुच्छा)
v. guñDulkinu (गुँडुल्किनु),
Dallo parnu (डल्लो पर्नु)

coin, *n.* paisA (पैसा), sikkA (सिक्का)

coincide, *v.* sanjog parnu
(सन्जोग पर्नु)

coincidence, *n.* sanjog (सन्जोग),
kAktAlI (काकताली)

coke, *n.* kok (कोक)

cold, *adj.* jADo (जाडो), chiso
(चिसो), ThanDA (ठन्डा)

colic, *n.* sUl (सूल), solA (सोला)

collapse, *v.* laDnu (लड्नु),
Dhalnu (ढल्नु),

behos hunu (बेहोस हुनु)

collar, *n.* kaThAlo (कठालो)
v. pakDanu (पक्डनु), ghAñTI
samAunu (घाँटी समाउनु)

colleague, *n.* mitra (मित्र),
sAthI (साथी), sahyogI (सहयोगी)

collect, *v.* jammA garnu (जम्मा
गर्नु), baTulnu (बटुल्नु)

collection, *n.* sangAlo (सँगालो),
sañkalan (सङ्कलन)

college, *n.* kalej (कलेज),
kyAmpas (क्याम्पस)

collide, *v.* Thakkar khAnu
(ठक्कर खानु), judhnu (जुध्नु),
dhakkA lAgnu (धक्का लाग्नु)

collision, *n.* dhakkA (धक्का),
Thakkar (ठक्कर)

colloquial, *adj.* bol chAl ko
(बोलचालको)

collyrium, *n.* gAjal (गाजल)

colonialism, *n.* upniwesh wAd
(उपनिवेशवाद)

colony, *n.* bastI (बस्ती),
upniwesh (उपनिवेश)

colo(u)r, *n.* rang (रङ्ग)
v. rangAunu (रङ्गाउनु)

colo(u)rs, *n.* jhaNDA (झण्डा),
dhwajA (ध्वजा)

colt, *n.* ghoDA ko bachchA
(घोडाको बच्चा)

column, *n. (pillar)* khambA
(खम्बा),
(newspaper) stambh (स्तम्भ)

coma, *n.* mUrchhA (मूर्छा),
behos (बेहोस)

comb, *n.* kAṅgiyo (काँगियो)
v. kapAl kornu (कपाल कोर्नु)

combine, *v.* milAunu
(मिलाउनु), jornu (जोर्नु)

come, *v.* Aunu (आउनु),
(come out) niskanu
(निस्कनु), *(come upon)*
phelA pArnu (फेला पार्नु),
(come together) milnu
(मिल्नु), *(come what may)* je
hos (जे होस्)

comedy, *n.* prahasan (प्रहसन),
samyogAnt nATak
(संयोगान्त नाटक)

comely, *adj.* sundar (सुन्दर),
rAmro (राम्रो)

comet, *n.* puchchhre tArA
(पुच्छ्रेतारा), dhUmketu (धूमकेतु)

comfort, *n.* sukha (सुख),
ArAm (आराम)
v. phulyAunu (फुल्याउनु)

comfortable, *adj.* ArAm dAyI
(आरामदायी), sukhI (सुखी)

comma, *n.* ardh wirAm
(अर्धविराम)

command, *n.* AgȳA (आज्ञा),
Adesh (आदेश),
hukum (हुकुम)
v. AgȳA dinu (आज्ञा दिनु),
aDar garnu (अडर गर्नु),
arhAunu (अर्हाउनु)

commemorate, *v.* samjhanA
ma samAroh manAunu
(सम्झनामा समारोह मनाउनु)

commence, *v.* thAlnu (थाल्नु),
suru garnu (सुरु गर्नु)

commend, *v.* tAriph garnu
(तारिफ गर्नु)

comment, *n.* TikA-TippaNI
(टिका-टिप्पणी)
v. TippaNI/charchA garnu
(टिप्पणी/चर्चा गर्नु)

commerce, *n.* wANijya
(वाणिज्य), wyApAr
(व्यापार), bepAr (बेपार)

commercial, *adj.* wyApArik
(व्यापारिक)

commission, *n.* *(authority)*
Ayog (आयोग),
(bus.) kamisan (कमिसन),
chUT (छूट)
v. adhikAr dinu (अधिकार
दिनु), arAunu (अराउनु)

commit, *v.* saṃlagna /wachan
baddh hunu
(संलग्न/वचनबद्ध हुनु)

committee, *n.* samiti (समिति)

commodity, *n.* bepArI
sAmagrI (बेपारी सामग्री)

common, *adj.* sAjhA (साझा),
samAn (समान),
mAmulI (मामुली)

common sense, *n.* sAmAnya
gȳAn (सामान्य ज्ञान)

communicate, *v.* sandesh dinu (सन्देश दिनु), lekhA paDhI garnu (लेखापढी गर्नु)

communication, *n.* samwAd (संवाद), sañchAr (सञ्चार)

communism, *n.* sAmya wAd (साम्यवाद)

communist, *n.* kamyunishT (कम्युनिष्ट), sAmya wAdI (साम्यवादी)

community, *n.* samudAya (समुदाय), samAj (समाज)

companion, *n.* sAthI (साथी)

company, *n.* (bus.) samsthA (संस्था), (person) sañgat (संगत)

compare, *v.* dAñjnu (दाँज्नु), tulanA garnu (तुलना गर्नु)

comparison, *n.* dañjAi (दँजाइ), tulanA (तुलना)

compass, *n.* kampAs (कम्पास), parkAl (पर्काल) *v.* ghernu (घेर्नु)

compassion, *n.* dayA (दया), kripA (कृपा)

compassionate, *adj.* dayAlu (दयालु), kripAlu (कृपालु)

compel, *v.* kar lAunu (कर लाउनु), karepnu (करेप्नु)

compensation, *n.* bharnA (भर्ना), kshati pUrti (क्षतिपूर्ति)

compete, *v.* pratiyogitA garnu (प्रतियोगिता गर्नु)

competent, *adj.* sipAlu (सिपालु), lAyak (लायक)

competition, *n.* pratispardhA (प्रतिस्पर्धा), pratiyogitA (प्रतियोगिता)

complaint, *n.* gunAso (गुनासो), ujurI (उजुरी)

complain, *v.* ujur/sikAyat garnu (उजुर/सिकायत गर्नु)

complete, *adj.* pUrA (पूरा), siñgo (सिङ्गो) *v.* pUrA garnu (पूरा गर्नु), sidhyAunu (सिध्याउनु)

completely, *adv.* pUrai (पूरै)

completion, *n.* samApti (समाप्ति), sampanna (सम्पन्न)

complex, *n.* shriñkhalA (श्रृड्खला) *adj.* kaThin (कठिन), jaTil (जटिल)

complexion, *n.* anuhAr (अनुहार), cheharA (चेहरा), (colour) warN (वर्ण)

complication, *n.* aljho (अल्झो), jatiltA (जटिलता)

compliment, *n.* tAriph (तारिफ), prashamsA (प्रशंसा) *v.* tAriph garnu (तारिफ गर्नु)

compose, *v.* rachnu (रच्नु), rachnA garnu (रचना गर्नु)

composer, *n.* rachayitA (रचयिता), rachnA kAr (रचनाकार)

composition, *n.* rachnA
(रचना), banoT (बनोट)

compound, *n.* mishraN
(मिश्रण), yaugik (यौगिक)
v. milAunu (मिलाउनु),
joDnu (जोड्नु)

comprehend, *v.* bujhnu (बुझ्नु)

compromise, *n.* samjhautA
(सम्झौता), milA patra (मिलापत्र)
v. samjhautA garnu
(सम्झौता गर्नु)

compulsion, *n.* kar (कर),
kar kAp (करकाप)

compulsory, *adj.* garnai parne
(गर्नै पर्ने),
aniwArya (अनिवार्य)

computer, *n.* kampyuTar
(कम्प्युटर)

comrade, *n.* sAthI (साथी)

conceal, *v.* lukAunu (लुकाउनु)

concentration, *n.* ekAgratA
(एकाग्रता),
tallIntA (तल्लीनता)

concern, *n.* chAso (चासो),
phikrI (फिक्री), chintA (चिन्ता)

concerning, *prep.* bAre mA
(बारेमा)

concert, *n.* saṅgIt kAryakram
(संगीत कार्यक्रम)

concession, *n.* chhUT (छूट),
suwidhA (सुविधा)

conch shell, *n.* saṅkh (सङ्ख)

conciliation, *n.* mel milAp
(मेल मिलाप)

concise, *adj.* chhoTkarI
(छोटकरी), saṅkshep (संक्षेप)

conclude, *v.* nishkarsh
nikAlnu (निष्कर्ष निकाल्नु)

conclusion, *n.* nichoD
(निचोड), samApti (समाप्ति)

concrete, *adj.* roDA (रोडा),
(solid) Thos (ठोस)

concur, *v.* swIkAr garnu
(स्वीकार गर्नु), mAnnu (मान्नु)

condemn, *v.* nindA garnu
(निन्दा गर्नु),
doshI ThaharyAunu
(दोषी ठह-याउनु)

condition, *n.* gati (गति), hAlat
(हालत), awasthA (अवस्था)

condolence, *n.* shraddhAñjalI
(श्रद्धाञ्जली),
sahAnubhUti (सहानुभूति)

conduct, *n.* charitra (चरित्र),
chAl chalan (चालचलन)
v. sañchAlan garnu
(सञ्चालन गर्नु)

confectionery, *n.* miThAI
(मिठाई)

confer, *v.* pradAn/parAmarsh
garnu (प्रदान/परामर्श गर्नु)

conference, *n.* sabhA (सभा),
sammelan (सम्मेलन)

confess, *v.* swIkAr garnu
(स्वीकार गर्नु),
kAyal hunu (कायल हुनु)

confession, *n.* kAyal nAmA (कायलनामा), sAbitI (साबिती)

confidence, *n.* bharosA (भरोसा), wishwAs (विश्वास)

confident, *adj.* wishwAsI (विश्वासी)

confirm, *v.* pushTi garnu (पुष्टि गर्नु)

confiscate, *v.* japhat/sarwaswa haraN garnu (जफत/सर्वस्व हरण गर्नु)

conflict, *n.* wirodh (विरोध), bhiDant (भिडन्त)

confluence, *n. (river)* dobhAn (दोभान), saṅgam (संगम)

confront, *v.* sammukh parnu (सम्मुख पर्नु), bhiDant garnu (भिडन्त गर्नु)

confuse, *v.* almalla parnu /pArnu (अलमल्ल पर्नु/पार्नु)

confused, *adj.* bhramit (भ्रमित), bhram mA pareko/pAreko (भ्रममा परेको/पारेको)

confusion, *n.* golmAl (गोलमाल), gaDbaD (गडबड)

congratulate, *v.* badhAI dinu (बधाई दिनु)

congratulation, *n.* badhAI (बधाई), shubh kAmnA (शुभकामना)

congress, *n.* sabhA (सभा), *(party)* kAṅgres (काँग्रेस)

connect, *v.* joDnu (जोड्नु),

milAunu (मिलाउनु)

connecting, *adj.* milAune (मिलाउने), samyojak (संयोजक)

connection, *n. (join)* joD (जोड), *(link)* sambandh (सम्बन्ध), silsilA (सिलसिला), milAp (मिलाप)

conquer, *v.* jitnu (जित्नु), wijaya garnu (विजय गर्नु)

conquest, *n.* wijaya (विजय), jIt (जीत)

conscious, *adj.* hos mA bhaeko (होसमा भएको), sachet (सचेत)

consciousness, *n.* hos (होस), sur (सुर), chetnA (चेतना)

consent, *v.* mAnnu (मान्नु), swIkAr garnu (स्वीकार गर्नु) *n.* swIkriti (स्वीकृति)

consequence, *n.* phal (फल), pariNAm (परिणाम)

conservation, *n.* samrakshaN (संरक्षण), rakshA (रक्षा)

consider, *v.* wichAr garnu (विचार गर्नु), ThAnnu (ठान्नु)

consideration, *n.* wichAr (विचार), wiwek (विवेक)

consistent, *adj.* anurUp (अनुरूप), bamojim (बमोजिम)

consolation, *n.* tasallI (तसल्ली), sAntwanA (सान्त्वना)

consonant, *n. (alphabet)* wyañjan (व्यञ्जन)

conspiracy, *n.* shaDyantra (षड्यन्त्र), kapaT (कपट)

constant, *adj.* sthir (स्थिर), achal (अचल)

constantly, *adv.* nitya (नित्य), baRabar (बराबर)

constellation, *n.* tArA gaN (तारागण), nakshatra gaN (नक्षत्रगण)

constipation, *n.* kabjiyat (कब्जियत)

constitution, *n.* samwidhAn (संविधान), widhAn (विधान)

construct, *v.* banAunu (बनाउनु), nirmAN garnu (निर्माण गर्नु)

construction, *n.* nirmAN (निर्माण), banoT (बनोट)

consul, *n.* mahA wANijya dUt (महावाणिज्यदूत)

consult, *v.* sallAh linu (सल्लाह लिनु), paRAmarsh garnu (परामर्श गर्नु)

consume, *v.* khapat/upbhog garnu (खपत/उपभोग गर्नु), mAsnu (मास्नु)

consumption, *n.* khapat (खपत), *(med.)* kshaya rog (क्षयरोग), TB (टीबी)

contact, *n.* sampark (सम्पर्क), chhutchhAt (छुतछात)

v. sampark/samsarg garnu (सम्पर्क/संसर्ग गर्नु)

contagious, *adj.* sarne (सर्ने), saRuwA (सरुवा)

contain, *v.* mA hunu (मा हुनु), Rahanu (रहनु), *(stop)* Roknu (रोक्नु)

contained, *adj.* Raheko (रहेको), aTAeko (अटाएको)

container, *n.* bhAñDo (भाँडो)

contaminate, *v.* phohor/dUshit pArnu (फोहोर/दूषित पार्नु)

contamination, *n.* dUshaN (दूषण), bigAr (बिगार)

contempt, *n.* ghriNA (घृणा), anAdar (अनादर), upekshA (उपेक्षा)

contend, *v.* wiwAd garnu (विवाद गर्नु), judhnu (जुध्नु) *n.* wishaya sUchi (विषयसूची)

contest, *n.* wiwAd (विवाद), dwandwa (द्वन्द्व), pratispardhA (प्रतिस्पर्धा) *v.* laDnu (लड्नु), jhagaDnu (झगड्नु)

continent, *n.* mahA dwIp (महाद्वीप), mahA desh (महादेश)

continuation, *n.* kram (क्रम), sthAyitwa (स्थायित्व), silsilA (सिलसिला)

continue, *v.* lAgi rahanu (लागिरहनु), chAlu rAkhnu (चालु राख्नु)

continuously, *adv.* lagAtAr (लगातार), nirantar (निरन्तर)

contraband, *n.* awaidh mAl (अवैध माल)

contract, *n.* ThekkA (ठेक्का) *v.* seprinu (सेप्रिनु), khumchinu (खुम्चिनु)

contractor, *n.* ThekedAr (ठेकेदार)

contradict, *v.* khaNDan garnu (खण्डन गर्नु)

contrary, *adj.* wiparIt (विपरीत), ulTo (उल्टो)

contrast, *n.* bhed (भेद), antar (अन्तर), pharak (फरक)

contribute, *v.* madat/paisA dinu (मदत/पैसा दिनु), yogdAn garnu (योगदान गर्नु)

contribution, *n.* yogdAn (योगदान), madat (मदत)

control, *n.* niyantraN (नियन्त्रण), wash (वश) *v.* niyantraN/wash garnu (नियन्त्रण/वश गर्नु)

controversy, *n.* wiwAdAspad (विवादास्पद)

convenient, *adj.* pAyak (पायक), suwidhA janak (सुविधाजनक)

conversation, *n.* kurA kAnI (कुराकानी), bAtchit (बातचित)

convert, *n.* dharm badalne wyakti (धर्म बदल्ने व्यक्ति) *v.* badalnu (बदल्नु)

convey, *v.* sandesh puryAunu/sunAidinu (सन्देश पुर्‍याउनु/सुनाइदिनु)

convict, *n.* abhiyukta (अभियुक्त), kaidI (कैदी) *v.* aprAdhI Thahar garnu (अपराधी ठहर गर्नु)

convince, *v.* wiswAs garAunu (विश्वास गराउनु)

convoy, *n.* sañgai jAne jahAjI beDA (सँगै जाने जहाजी बेडा), gADI ko lahar (गाडीको लहर), surakshA (सुरक्षा)

cook, *n.* bhAnchhe (भान्छे), pakAune mAnis (पकाउने मानिस) *v.* pakAunu (पकाउनु)

cool, *adj.* chiso (चिसो), shItal (शीतल)

cooperate, *v.* sahyog garnu (सहयोग गर्नु)

cooperation, *n.* sahyog (सहयोग), saghAu (सघाउ)

coordinate, *v.* samanwaya garnu (समन्वय गर्नु)

copper, *n.* tAñbA (ताँबा), tAmA (तामा)

copulate, *v.* sambhog/maithun garnu (सम्भोग/मैथुन गर्नु)

copy, *n.* *(document)* pratilipi (प्रतिलिपि), *(book)* kApI (कापी) *v.* nakkal garnu (नक्कल गर्नु)

coral, *n.* mUgA (मूगा)

cord, *n.* DorI (डोरी)

cordial, *adj.* hArdik (हार्दिक)

coriander, *n.* dhaniyA (धनिया)

corn, *n.* *(grain)* anAj (अनाज),
anna (अन्न),
(maize) makai (मकै)

corner, *n.* kunA (कुना)

coronation, *n.* rAjyAbhishek
(राज्याभिषेक)

corporation, *n.* nigam (निगम)

corpse, *n.* murdA (मुर्दा),
lAs (लास), shawa (शव)

correct, *adj.* ThIk (ठीक),
shuddha (शुद्ध)
v. sachyAunu (सच्याउनु)

correspondence, *n.* lekhA
paDhI (लेखापढी),
patrAchAr (पत्राचार)

corridor, *n.* maTAn (मटान),
baraNDA (बरण्डा)

corruption, *n.* bhrashtAchAr
(भ्रष्टाचार)

cosmetics, *n.* shriṅgAr kA
sAmAn (श्रृंगारका सामान)

cosmos, *n.* sampUrN
brahmAND (सम्पूर्ण ब्रह्माण्ड)

cost, *n.* mUlya (मूल्य),
kimmat (किम्मत)
v. mol parnu (मोल पर्नु)

costly, *adj.* mahaṅgo (महँगो)

costume, *n.* poshAk (पोशाक),
pahiran (पहिरन)

cottage, *n.* kuTI (कुटी),
jhopaDI (झोपडी)

cottage industry, *n.* gharelu
udyog (घरेलु उद्योग)

cotton, *n.* kapAs (कपास),
ruwA (रुवा)

couch, *n.* kawach (कवच)

cough, *n.* khokI (खोकी)
v. khoknu (खोक्नु)

council, *n.* parishad (परिषद्),
sabhA (सभा)

counsellor, *n.* *(orgn.)*
sallAhkAr (सल्लाहकार),
(law) wakIl (वकील)

count, *n.* gantI (गन्ती)
v. gannu (गन्नु)

country, *n.* desh (देश),
muluk (मुलुक)

countryside, *n.* gAuṅ ghar
(गाउँघर)

coup d'etat, *n.* widroh (विद्रोह)

couple, *n.* joDA (जोडा),
joDI (जोडी), dampatI (दम्पती)
v. jornu (जोर्नु),
gAṅsnu (गाँस्नु)

coupon, *n.* kupan (कुपन)

courage, *n.* sAhas (साहस),
AṅT (आँट)

courageous, *adj.* sAhasI
(साहसी), AṅTilo (आँटिलो)

course, *n.* pAThya kram
(पाठ्यक्रम), gati (गति),
(way) mArg (मार्ग)

court, *n.* *(law)* adAlat (अदालत), *(palace)* darbAr (दरबार) *v.* prem garnu (प्रेम गर्नु), phakAunu (फकाउनु)

courteous, *adj.* sushIl (सुशील), shishTa (शिष्ट)

courtyard, *n.* chok (चोक), Aṅgan (आँगन)

courtesy, *n.* Adar (आदर), shishTAchAr (शिष्टाचार)

cousin, *n.* kAkA, mAmA, sAnimA ra ThulI AmA kA santAn (काका, मामा, सानिमा र ठूली आमाका सन्तान)

cover, *n.* birko (बिर्को), khol (खोल), *v.* chhopnu (छोप्नु), DhAknu (ढाक्नु)

cow, *n.* gAI (गाई)

coward, *adj.* kAthar (कातर)

cowshed, *n.* gAI goTh (गाईगोठ)

crab, *n.* gaṅgaTo (गँगटो), gaṅTo (गङ्टो)

crack, *n.* chirA (चिरा), charkeko dharkA (चर्केको धर्का), *v.* charkanu (चर्कनु), *(sound)* paDkanu (पड्कनु)

craft, *n.* sIp (सीप), kalA (कला)

cramp, *n.* bAuṅDine rog (बाउँडिने रोग)

v. bAuṅDinu (बाउँडिनु), akaDinu (अकडिनु)

crane, *n.* *(bird)* sAras (सारस), *(mech.)* kren (क्रेन)

crash, *n.* dhaDAkA (धडाका), Thakkar (ठक्कर) *v.* TakarAunu (टकराउनु), *(plane)* khasnu (खस्नु)

crawl, *v.* ghasranu (घस्रनु), ghisranu (घिस्रनु)

crazy, *adj.* baulAhA (बौलाहा), sankAhA (सन्काहा), pAgal (पागल)

cream, *n.* malam (मलम), krim (क्रिम)

crease, *n.* dobryAeko Doro/rekhA (दोब्य्राएको डोरो/रेखा), krij (क्रिज), mujA (मुजा)

create, *v.* srijanA/rachnA garnu (सृजना/रचना गर्नु)

creator, *n.* srishTi kartA (सृष्टिकर्ता), Ishwar (ईश्वर)

creature, *n.* prANI (प्राणी), jIw (जीव)

credible, *adj.* patyArilo (पत्यारिलो), wishwAs yogya (विश्वासयोग्य)

credit, *n.* *(reputation)* ijjat (इज्जत), *(merit)* mAn (मान), *(bus.)* udhAro (उधारो)

cremation, *n.* dAh saṃskAr (दाहसंस्कार)

crest, *n. (bird)* juro (जुरो),
   (hill) TAkuro (टाकुरो)

cricket, *n. (game)* krikeT
   (क्रिकेट), *(insect)*
   phaTyAṅgro (फट्याङ्ग्रो)

crime, *n.* aprAdh (अपराध)

criminal, *n.* aprAdhI (अपराधी)

cripple, *n.* laṅgaDo (लङ्गडो),
   khoraNDo (खोरण्डो)

crisis, *n.* saṅkaT (संकट)

critical, *adj.* nAjuk (नाजुक)

criticize, *v.* AlochanA garnu
   (आलोचना गर्नु)

crocodile, *n.* gohI (गोही),
   magar (मगर), makar (मकर)

crop, *n.* bAlI (बाली),
   phasal (फसल)

cross, *n.* sUlI (सूली),
   v. pAr garnu (पार गर्नु),
   pAkhA lAgnu (पाखा लाग्नु),
   nAghnu (नाघ्नु)

cross-examination, *n.* band
   sawAl (बन्द सवाल),
   kerkAr (केरकार)

crossroads, *n.* chaubATo
   (चौबाटो)

crossword, *n.* shabd pahelI
   (शब्द पहेली)

crow, *n.* kAg (काग),
   kauwA (कौवा)

crowd, *n.* bhID (भीड), hUl (हूल)

crowded, *adj.* bhIDbhAD
   pUrN (भीडभाडपूर्ण),
   khachAkhach (खचाखच)

crown, *n.* shrI pech (श्रीपेच),
   mukuT (मुकुट)

cruel, *adj.* nirdayI (निर्दयी),
   niThurI (निठुरी)

crutch, *n.* baisAkhI (बैसाखी)

cry, *v.* runu (रुनु),
   karAunu (कराउनु)

crystal, *n.* kAṅch (काँच),
   phaTik (फटिक)

cub, *n.* chhAuro (छाउरो),
   Damaru (डमरु), pATho (पाठो)

cuckoo, *n.* koyalI (कोयली),
   koyal (कोयल)

cucumber, *n.* kAṅkro (काँक्रो)

cultivate, *v.* khetI garnu
   (खेती गर्नु)

cultivation, *n.* khetI (खेती),
   khetI pAtI (खेतीपाती)

cultural, *adj.* sAmskritik
   (सांस्कृतिक)

culture, *n.* saṃskriti (संस्कृति)

cunning, *n.* dhUrt (धूर्त),
   chalAkh (चलाख)

cup, *n.* kachaurA (कचौरा),
   baTukA (बटुका), kap (कप)

cupboard, *n.* darAj (दराज),
   AlmArI (आल्मारी)

curable, *adj.* niko huna sakne
   (निको हुनसक्ने)

curb, *n.* pratibandh (प्रतिबन्ध),
   Dil (डिल),
   v. roknu (रोक्नु)

curd, *n.* dahI (दही)

curfew, *n.* karphyu (कर्फ्यु), rokkA (रोक्का)

cure, *v.* niko tulyAunu (निको तुल्याउनु)

curious, *adj.* utsuk (उत्सुक), anauTho (अनौठो)

currency, *n.* mudrA (मुद्रा)

current, *n. (elec.)* kareNT (करेण्ट)
adj. (time) hAl sAl ko (हालसालको)

curry, *n.* tarkArI (तरकारी)
v. khusI pArne kosis garnu (खुसी पार्ने कोसिस गर्नु)

curse, *n.* sarAp (सराप)
v. sarAp dinu (सराप दिनु),
gAlI garnu (गाली गर्नु)

curtain, *n.* pardA (पर्दा)

cushion, *n.* gaddA (गद्दा)

custard apple, *n.* sariphA (सरिफा)

custody, *n.* hirAsat (हिरासत)

custom, *n.* rIti thiti (रीतिथिति), chalan (चलन)

customer, *n.* gAhak (गाहक)

Customs, *n.* bhansAr aDDA (भन्सार अड्डा)

cut, *n.* kaTAn (कटान), kaTautI (कटौती)
v. kATnu (काट्नु)

cycle, *n.* chakra (चक्र), maNDal (मण्डल)

cymbals, *n.* jhyAlI (भ्याली)

D

dacoit, *n.* DAňku (डाँकु), DAňkA (डाँका)

daddy, *n.* bAbu (बाबु), bA (बा)

dagger, *n.* chhurA (छुरा), kaTArI (कटारी)

dahlia, *n.* lAhure phUl (लाहुरे फूल)

daily, *adv.* din dinai (दिनदिनै), dinahuň (दिनहुँ), rojindA (रोजिन्दा)
adj./n. dainik (दैनिक)

dairy, *n.* dUdh pAine ThAuň (दूध पाइने ठाउँ), DerI (डेरी)

dale, *n.* upatyakA (उपत्यका), ghATI (घाटी)

dam, *n.* bAňdh (बाँध)
v. bAňdh bAňdhnu (बाँध बाँध्नु)

damage, *n.* hAni (हानि), noksAnI (नोक्सानी)
v. bigArnu (बिगार्नु), nashT garnu (नष्ट गर्नु)

damp, *adj.* osilo (ओसिलो),
chiso (चिसो), bhijeko (भिजेको)

dance, *n.* nAch (नाच),
nritya (नृत्य)
v. nAchnu (नाच्नु),
nritya garnu (नृत्य गर्नु)

dandruff, *n.* chAyA (चाया)

danger, *n.* khatarA (खतरा),
jokhim (जोखिम),
saṅkaT (संकट)

dangerous, *adj.* khatar nAk
(खतरनाक),
Dar lAgdo (डरलाग्दो)

dangle, *v.* laTkinu (लटकिनु),
jhunDinu (भुन्डिनु)

dare, *v.* sAhas/himmat garnu
(साहस/हिम्मत गर्नु)

daring, *adj.* sUro (सूरो), niDar
(निडर), sAhasI (साहसी)

dark, *adj.* aňdhyAro (अँध्यारो),
(colour) gADhA (गाढा),
(complexion) kAlo (कालो)

darling, *n./adj.* priye (प्रिये),
priya (प्रिय), pyAro (प्यारो)

darn, *v.* raphphu bharnu
(रफ्फु भर्नु)

dash, *v.* huttinu (हुत्तिनु),
Thakkar lAgnu (ठक्कर लाग्नु),
jottinu (जोत्तिनु)
n. chhiTo (छिटो), danak (दनक),
(line) dharko (धर्को)

dashing, *adj.* phurtilo (फुर्तिलो),
josilo (जोसिलो)

date, *n.* miti (मिति),
tArikh (तारिख), *(fruit)* khajUr
(खजूर), chhoharA (छोहरा),
(meeting) bheT (भेट)
v. miti lekhnu (मिति लेख्नु),
(meeting) bheTne samaya
milAunu (भेट्ने समय
मिलाउनु)

dating, *n. (lovers)*
milne/bheTne kAm
(मिल्ने/भेट्ने काम)

daughter, *n.* chhorI (छोरी),
putrI (पुत्री)

daughter-in-law, *n.* buhArI
(बुहारी)

dawn, *n.* bihAna saberai
(बिहान सबेरै), mirmir
(मिरमिर) jhismis (फिसमिस)

day, *n.* din (दिन), *(week)* bAr
(बार), *(date)* gate (गते)

day after tomorrow, *n.* parsi
(पर्सि)

day before yesterday, *n.* asti
(अस्ति)

daybreak, *n.* jhismise bihAna
(फिसमिसे बिहान)

daydream, *n.* diwA swapna
(दिवास्वप्न)

daylight, *n.* din ko ujyAlo
(दिनको उज्यालो)

daylong, *n.* din bhari (दिनभरि)

daytime, *n.* diuso (दिउसो),
diuňso (दिउँसो)

dazzle, *v.* AṅkhA tirmirAunu (आँखा तिर्मिराउनु), chakAchak garnu (चकाचक गर्नु)

dead, *adj.* mareko (मरेको)

deadline, *n.* samaya sImA (समयसीमा)

deaf, *adj.* bahiro (बहिरो)

deal, *n.* bAñD (बाँड), *(bus.)* samjhautA (सम्झौता) *v. (cards)* bAñDnu (बाँड्नु), *(behave)* bartAw / wyawahAr garnu (बरताव/व्यवहार गर्नु)

dealing, *n.* wyawahAr (व्यवहार), bartAw (बरताव)

dear, *adj.* pyAro (प्यारो), *(cost)* mahaṅgo (महँगो)

dearness, *n.* mahaṅgAi (महँगाइ)

death, *n.* mrityu (मृत्यु), dehAnt (देहान्त)

death penalty, *n.* mrityu daND (मृत्युदण्ड)

debate, *n.* wAd wiwAd (वादविवाद), chhal phal (छलफल) *v.* wAd wiwAd/bahas garnu (वादविवाद/बहस गर्नु)

debt, *n.* rin (ऋन), riN (ऋण), karjA (कर्जा)

decade, *n.* das warsh ko samaya (दस वर्षको समय), dashak (दशक),

dashAbdI (दशाब्दी)

decay, *n.* kshaya (क्षय), jIrNa (जीर्ण) *v.* saDnu (सड्नु), galnu (गल्नु)

deceased, *adj.* mrit (मृत), mareko (मरेको), swargIya (स्वर्गीय)

deceit, *n.* kapaT (कपट), dhokhA (धोखा)

deceitful, *adj.* kapaTI (कपटी), dhokhe bAj (धोखेबाज)

deceive, *v.* dhokhA dinu (धोखा दिनु), chhalnu (छल्नु)

decent, *adj.* uchit (उचित), yogya (योग्य)

decide, *v.* phaisalA/nirNaya garnu (फैसला/निर्णय गर्नु)

deciduous, *adj.* pAt jharne (पात झर्ने)

decimal, *n.* dasamalab (दसमलब)

decision, *n.* phaisalA (फैसला), nirNaya (निर्णय)

declare, *v.* ghoshaNA garnu (घोषणा गर्नु), sunAunu (सुनाउनु)

decline, *v.* na mAnnu (नमान्नु), nAmanjur garnu (नामन्जुर गर्नु), *(volume)* ghaTnu (घट्नु)

decorate, *v.* siṅgArnu (सिँगार्नु), sajAunu (सजाउनु)

decoration, *n.* siṅgAr (सिँगार),
  shobhA (शोभा),
  sajAwaT (सजावट)

decrease, *n.* kamI (कमी),
  ghaTI (घटी), hrAs (ह्रास)
  v. ghaTnu (घट्नु),
  kam hunu (कम हुनु)

dedicate, *v.* arpaN/samarpaN
  garnu (अर्पण/समर्पण गर्नु)

dedication, *n.* lagan (लगन),
  arpAN (अर्पण),
  samarpaN (समर्पण)

deduct, *v.* kATnu (काट्नु),
  ghaTAunu (घटाउनु)

deed, *n.* kAm (काम), karma (कर्म)

deep, *adj.* gahiro (गहिरो),
  gambhIr (गम्भीर)

deeply, *adv.* gaDera (गडेर),
  gahirera (गहिरेर)

defeat, *n.* hAr (हार),
  parAjaya (पराजय)
  v. harAunu (हराउनु),
  parAjit garnu (पराजित गर्नु)

defeated, *adj.* hAreko (हारेको),
  parAjit (पराजित)

defecate, *v.* hagnu (हग्नु),
  disA garnu (दिसा गर्नु)

defect, *n.* dosh (दोष),
  wikAr (विकार), aib (ऐब)
  v. desh wa samUha chhaDnu
  (देश वा समूह छड्नु)

defective, *adj.* dosh bhaeko
  (दोष भएको),

dosh pUrN (दोषपूर्ण)

defence/defense, *n.* rakshA
  (रक्षा), prati rakshA (प्रतिरक्षा),
  bachAw (बचाव)

defend, *v.* rakshA garnu
  (रक्षा गर्नु)

defensive, *adj.* rakshAtmak
  (रक्षात्मक), niwArak (निवारक)

deficiency, *n.* kamI (कमी),
  abhAw (अभाव)

deficient, *adj.* kamI/abhAw
  bhaeko (कमी/अभाव भएको)

deficit, *n.* ghATA (घाटा),
  kamI (कमी)

defiled, *adj.* juTho (जुठो),
  biTulo (बिटुलो)

define, *v.* wyAkhyA /
  paribhAshit garnu
  (व्याख्या/परिभाषित गर्नु)

definite, *adj.* ThIk (ठीक),
  nishchaya (निश्चय),
  pakkA (पक्का)

definition, *n.* paribhAshA
  (परिभाषा)

deflection, *n.* mArg wichalan
  (मार्ग विचलन)

deft, *adj.* chatur (चतुर),
  sipAlu (सिपालु)

defy, *v.* wirodh garnu (विरोध
  गर्नु), na mAnnu (नमान्नु)

degrade, *v.* hochyAunu
  (होच्याउनु),
  apmAn garnu (अपमान गर्नु)

degree, *n. (rank, honour)*
darjA (दर्जा), padawI (पदवी),
upadhi (उपाधि)
(math., etc.) DigrI (डिग्री)

dehydration, *n.* pAnI ko kamI
(पानीको कमी),
wijalan (विजलन)

deity, *n.* dewI (देवी),
dewtA (देवता)

delay, *n.* DhilAi (ढिलाइ),
wilamb (विलम्ब)

delegate, *n.* pratinidhi
(प्रतिनिधि)
v. khaTAunu (खटाउनु),
niyukta garnu (नियुक्त गर्नु),
sumpanu (सुम्पनु)

delegation, *n.* pratinidhi
maNDal (प्रतिनिधि मण्डल),
khaTAune/sumpane kAm
(खटाउने/सुम्पने काम)

delete, *v.* nikAlnu (निकाल्नु),
meTnu (मेट्नु)

deliberate, *adj.* jAnera garieko
(जानेर गरिएको)

deliberately, *adv.* jAnI
jAnIkana (जानीजानीकन)

delicacy, *n.* swAdilo khAnA
(स्वादिलो खाना),
mAdhurya (माधुर्य)

delicate, *adj.* komal (कोमल),
kamalo (कमलो),
masino (मसिनो)

delicious, *adj.* mITho (मीठो),

swAdilo (स्वादिलो)

delight, *n.* khusI (खुसी),
Anand (आनन्द)

delighted, *adj.* khus (खुस),
Anandit (आनन्दित)

delirious, *adj.* achet awasthA
mA barbarAune (अचेत
अवस्थामा बर्बराउने)

deliver, *v.* puryAunu (पुर्‍याउनु),
chhoDnu (छोड्नु),
janmAunu (जन्माउनु)

demand, *n.* mAg (माग),
chAhA (चाहा)
v. mAg/chAhA garnu
(माग/चाहा गर्नु)

demeano(u)r, *n.* wyawahAr
(व्यवहार), AcharaN (आचरण),
Dhang (ढङ्ग)

demerit, *n.* baigun (बैगुन),
dosh (दोष)

demise, *n.* mrityu (मृत्यु),
maraN (मरण)

democracy, *n.* prajA tantra
(प्रजातन्त्र), lok rAj (लोकराज)

democratic, *adj.* prajA tAntrik
(प्रजातान्त्रिक)

demolish, *v.* bhatkAunu
(भत्काउनु)

demon, *n.* daitya (दैत्य),
dAnaw (दानव)

demonstrate, *v.* pradarshan
garnu (प्रदर्शन गर्नु),
dekhAunu (देखाउनु)

demonstration, *n.* pradarshan
(प्रदर्शन)

demoralize, *v.* bhrashT /
nirutsAhit garnu
(भ्रष्ट/निरुत्साहित गर्नु)

demotion, *n.* pad awanati
(पद अवनति)

den, *n.* guphA (गुफा),
oDAr (ओडार)

denote, *v.* batAunu (बताउनु),
janAunu (जनाउनु)

denounce, *v.* nindA garnu
(निन्दा गर्नु),
dhamkAunu (धम्काउनु)

dense, *adj.* ghanA (घना),
bAklo (बाक्लो)

dent, *n.* khopilTo (खोपिल्टो),
khADal (खाडल)

dental, *adj.* dAn̐t ko (दाँतको),
dAn̐t sambandhI (दाँतसम्बन्धी)

dentist, *n.* dAn̐t ko DAkTar
(दाँतको डाक्टर)

deny, *v.* inkAr garnu (इन्कार
गर्नु), na mAnnu (नमान्नु)

depart, *v.* ramAnA hunu
(रमाना हुनु),
prasthAn garnu (प्रस्थान गर्नु)

department, *n.* phAn̐T (फाँट),
wibhAg (विभाग)

departure, *n.* ramAnA (रमाना),
prasthAn (प्रस्थान)

depend, *v.* bhar garnu (भर गर्नु),
nirbhar hunu (निर्भर हुनु)

dependable, *adj.* bhar pardo
(भरपर्दो)

dependence, *n.* nirbhartA
(निर्भरता), adhIntA (अधीनता)

deplorable, *adj.* shochnIya
(शोचनीय)

deplore, *v.* aphsos garnu
(अफसोस गर्नु)

deploy, *v.* tainAth garnu
(तैनाथ गर्नु)

deployment, *n.* tainAthI
(तैनाथी)

deport, *v.* desh nikAlA garnu
(देश निकाला गर्नु)

deportation, *n.* desh nikAlA
(देशनिकाला)

deposit, *n.* jammA (जम्मा),
nikshep (निक्षेप)
v. jammA garnu (जम्मा गर्नु)

depot, *n.* bhaNDAr (भण्डार),
Dipo (डिपो)

depressed, *adj.* jhokrieko
(झोक्रिएको), khinna (खिन्न)

depth, *n.* gahirAi (गहिराइ),
gambhIrtA (गम्भीरता)

deputy, *n.* nAyab (नायब),
upa (उप)

derive, *v.* **(from)** bATa utpatti
hunu (बाट उत्पत्ति हुनु),
nikAlnu (निकाल्नु)

derogatory, *adj.* apmAn janak
(अपमानजनक),
badnAm garne (बदनाम गर्ने)

descend, *v.* orlanu (ओर्लनु),
tala jharnu (तल झर्नु)

describe, *v.* warNan/bayAn
garnu (वर्णन/बयान गर्नु)

description, *n.* warNan
(वर्णन), bayAn (बयान)

desert, *n.* maru bhUmi
(मरुभूमि), registAn (रेगिस्तान)
v. chhADnu (छाड्नु),
tyAgnu (त्याग्नु)

deserve, *v.* yogya/uchit hunu
(योग्य/उचित हुनु)

deserving, *adj.* yogya (योग्य)

design, *n. (scheme)* jukti
(जुक्ति), upAya (उपाय),
(intention) irAdA (इरादा),
(sketch) DijAin (डिजाइन),
(pattern) buTTA (बुट्टा)
v. yojanA/DijAin garnu
(योजना/डिजाइन गर्नु)

desirable, *adj.* wAñchhanIya
(वाञ्छनीय),
rahar lAgdo (रहरलाग्दो)

desire, *n.* ichchhA (इच्छा),
chAhanA (चाहना)
v. ichchhA/chAhanA garnu
(इच्छा/चाहना गर्नु)

desk, *n.* desk (डेस्क), Tebul (टेबुल)

desolate, *adj.* shUnya (शून्य),
nirjan (निर्जन)

despair, *n.* nirAshA (निराशा)

desperate, *adj.* nirAsh
(निराश)

despite, *n.* durAchAr (दुराचार),
abhimAn (अभिमान)
prep. tApani (तापनि),
taipani (तैपनि),
ko bawajUd (को बावजूद)

despot, *n.* prajA pIDak
shAsak (प्रजापीडक शासक),
tAnA shAh (तानाशाह)

dessert, *n.* bhojan pachhi
khAine miThAI Adi
(भोजनपछि खाइने मिठाई आदि)

destination, *n.* jAne ThAuñ
(जाने ठाउँ), mañjil (मंजिल)
gantawya (गन्तव्य)

destiny, *n.* bhAgya (भाग्य),
niyati (नियति)

destroy, *v.* nAsh/nashT garnu
(नाश/नष्ट गर्नु)

destruction, *n.* nAsh (नाश),
winAsh (विनाश)

detail, *n.* tapsil (तपसिल),
behorA (बेहोरा),
v. wiwaraN dinu
(विवरण दिनु),
warNan garnu (वर्णन गर्नु)

detain, *v.* roknu (रोक्नु), thunA
mA rAkhnu (थुनामा राख्नु)

detect, *v.* pattA lAunu (पत्ता
लाउनु), khoj talAsh garnu
(खोजतलाश गर्नु)

detective, *n.* jAsUs (जासूस)
adj./n. gupt char (गुप्तचर)
khuphiyA (खुफिया)

detente, *n.* tanAu ko kamI (तनाउको कमी)

detention, *n.* rok (रोक), thunA (थुना)

deter, *v.* roknu (रोक्नु)

deteriorate, *v.* bigranu (बिग्रनु), hrAs hunu (ह्रास हुनु)

determination, *n.* driDhtA (दृढता), sankalpa (संकल्प)

determine, *v.* AñTnu (आँट्नु), nirUpaN garnu (निरूपण गर्नु)

develop, *v.* wikAs garnu (विकास गर्नु), baDhnu (बढ्नु)

development, *n.* wikAs (विकास), pragati (प्रगति)

device, *n.* tarikA (तरिका), sAdhan (साधन)

devil, *n.* saitAn (सैतान), daitya (दैत्य)

devise, *v.* upAya/jukti garnu (उपाय/जुक्ति गर्नु)

devote, *v.* datta chitta hunu (दत्तचित्त हुनु), man lagAunu (मन लगाउनु), arpaN garnu (अर्पण गर्नु)

devotee, *n.* bhakta (भक्त)

devotion, *n.* bhakti (भक्ति), AsthA (आस्था)

devour, *v.* hasurnu (हसुर्नु), khAnu (खानु)

devout, *adj.* dhArmik (धार्मिक), samarpit (समर्पित)

dew, *n.* os (ओस), shIt (शीत)

diabetes, *n.* madhu meh (मधुमेह)

diagnose, *v.* rog pattA lAunu (रोग पत्ता लाउनु), rog chinnu (रोग चिन्नु)

diagnosis, *n.* rog ko nidAn (रोगको निदान)

diagram, *n.* rekhA chitra (रेखाचित्र)

dial, *v.* ghumAunu (घुमाउनु)

dialect, *n.* bhAshA (भाषा), bolI (बोली)

dialog(ue), *n.* wArtA (वार्ता), samwAd (संवाद)

diamond, *n.* hIrA (हीरा)

diarrh(o)ea, *n.* pakhAlA (पखाला), atisAr (अतिसार)

diary, *n.* dainik wiwaraN (दैनिक विवरण), DayarI (डायरी)

dice, *n.* pAsA (पासा)

dictate, *v.* Adesh dinu (आदेश दिनु), lekhAunu (लेखाउनु)

dictator, *n.* tAnA shAh (तानाशाह), nirankush shAsak (निरङ्कुश शासक)

dictionary, *n.* shabd kosh (शब्दकोश)

die, *v.* marnu (मर्नु)

diet, *n.* AhAr (आहार), bhojan (भोजन), khAnA (खाना)

diesel, *n.* Dijel (डिजेल)

differ, v. pharak/alag hunu (फरक/अलग हुनु)

difference, n. pharak (फरक), bhinnatA (भिन्नता)

different, adj. pharak (फरक), bhinna (भिन्न)

difficult, adj. gAhro (गाह्रो), kaThin (कठिन)

dig, v. khannu (खन्नु)

digest, n. sArAmsh (सारांश), nichoD (निचोड) v. pachAunu (पचाउनु)

digestion, n. pAchan kriyA (पाचनक्रिया)

dignify, v. sammAn dinu (सम्मान दिनु), mAn baDhAunu (मान बढाउनु)

dignity, n. mAn (मान), maryAdA (मर्यादा)

dilemma, n. dodhAr (दोधार), dubidhA (दुबिधा)

diligent, adj. udyogI (उद्योगी), parishramI (परिश्रमी)

dim, adj. dhamilo (धमिलो), madhuro (मधुरो)

dimension, n. AyAm (आयाम), parimAN (परिमाण)

diminish, v. ghaTAunu (घटाउनु), kam hunu/garnu (कम हुनु/गर्नु)

dimple, n. hAँsdA gAlA mA parne khADal (हाँस्दा गालामा पर्ने खाडल)

din, n. hallA (हल्ला), kolAhal (कोलाहल)

dine, v. khAnu (खानु), bhojan garnu (भोजन गर्नु)

dinner, n. rAt ko khAnA (रातको खाना), rAtri bhoj (रात्रिभोज)

dip, v. DubAunu (डुबाउनु), chopnu (चोप्नु)

diplomacy, n. kUT nIti (कूटनीति)

diplomat, n. kUT nItigyǎ (कूटनीतिज्ञ)

diplomatic, adj. kUT naitik (कूटनैतिक)

direct, v. nirdesh dinu (निर्देश दिनु), arAunu (अराउनु) adj. sojho (सोझो), pratyaksha (प्रत्यक्ष)

direction, n. dishA (दिशा), (act) nirdeshan (निर्देशन), Adesh (आदेश)

director, n. nirdeshak (निर्देशक)

dirt, n. phohor mailo (फोहोर मैलो)

dirty, adj. phohorI (फोहोरी)

disabled, adj. apAṅg (अपाङ्ग)

disadvantage, n. hAni (हानि), bephAidA (बेफाइदा)

disagree, v. nAmanjur /aswIkAr garnu (नामन्जुर/अस्वीकार गर्नु)

disappear, v. alpanu (अल्पनु), bilAunu (बिलाउनु), harAunu (हराउनु)

disappoint, *v.* nirAsh garnu
(निराश गर्नु),
AshA toDnu (आशा तोड्नु)

disappointment, *n.* nirAshA
(निराशा), nairAshya (नैराश्य)

disapprove, *v.* na mAnnu
(नमान्नु), aswIkAr garnu
(अस्वीकार गर्नु)

disaster, *n.* Apat (आपत्),
wipat (विपत्)

disc, *n.* golo chepTo wastu
(गोलो चेप्टो वस्तु)

discard, *v.* tyAgnu (त्याग्नु),
haTAunu (हटाउनु)

discharge, *n.* chhuTkArA
(छुट्कारा)
v. chhoDnu (छोड्नु),
haTAunu (हटाउनु), kAm
pUrA garnu (काम पूरा गर्नु)

disciple, *n.* chelA (चेला),
shishya (शिष्य)

discipline, *n.* anushAsan
(अनुशासन)

disclose, *v.* prakaT garnu
(प्रकट गर्नु)

discontinue, *v.* roknu (रोक्नु),
thAmnu (थाम्नु),
sthagit garnu (स्थगित गर्नु)

discount, *n.* chhUT (छूट),
kaTanI (कटनी)
v. chhUT dinu (छूट दिनु),
kaTanI kATnu
(कटनी काट्नु)

discourage, *v.* nirutsAhit
garnu (निरुत्साहित गर्नु)

discover, *v.* pattA lAunu
(पत्ता लाउनु),
khoj garnu (खोज गर्नु)

discovery, *n.* khoj (खोज),
anweshaN (अन्वेषण)

discriminate, *v.* bhed bhAw
garnu (भेदभाव गर्नु), antar
batAunu (अन्तर बताउनु)

discrimination, *n.* bhed bhAw
(भेदभाव), antar (अन्तर)

discuss, *v.* chhal phal garnu
(छलफल गर्नु)

discussion, *n.* chhal phal
(छलफल), bahas (बहस)

disease, *n.* rog (रोग)

disembark, *v.* utranu (उत्रनु),
orlanu (ओर्लनु)

disgrace, *n.* apmAn
(अपमान), anAdar (अनादर)
v. helA/apmAn garnu
(हेला/अपमान गर्नु)

disguise, *n.* chhadma bhesh
(छद्मभेष)
v. bhesh badalnu (भेष बदल्नु)

dish, *n.* thAl (थाल), thAlI
(थाली), khAnA (खाना),
parikAr (परिकार)
v. paskinu (पस्किनु),
paskanu (पस्कनु)

dishonest, *adj.* beimAn
(बेइमान), kapaTI (कपटी)

dislike, *n.* ghin (घिन),
aruchi (अरुचि)
v. man naparAunu
(मन नपराउनु)

dislodge, *v.* haTAunu
(हटाउनु), ukhelnu (उखेल्नु)

dismantle, *v.* bhatkAunu
(भत्काउनु),
phukAlnu (फुकाल्नु)

dismiss, *v.* khosnu (खोस्नु),
nikAlnu (निकाल्नु),
khArej garnu (खारेज गर्नु)

disobey, *v.* na Ternu (नटेर्नु),
na mAnnu (नमान्नु)

disorder, *n.* hohallA (होहल्ला),
gaDbaD (गडबड),
laThibajra (लठिबज्र), *(med.)*
rog (रोग), wyAdhi (व्याधि)

dispatch/despatch, *n.* sandesh
(सन्देश)
v. chalAn garnu (चलान गर्नु),
paThAunu (पठाउनु),
(fig.) mArnu (मार्नु),
jyAn linu (ज्यान लिनु)

displace, *v.* haTAunu
(हटाउनु), sArnu (सार्नु)

display, *n.* pradarshan (प्रदर्शन)
v. dekhAunu (देखाउनु),
pradarshan garnu (प्रदर्शन गर्नु)

displeasure, *n.* nArAjI
(नाराजी), khed (खेद)

dispute, *n.* jhagaDA (झगडा),
wiwAd (विवाद)

v. jhagaDA/wirodh garnu
(झगडा/विरोध गर्नु)

disregard, *n.* anAdar (अनादर),
bewAstA (बेवास्ता)
v. bewAstA garnu
(बेवास्ता गर्नु), hepnu (हेप्नु)

disrespect, *n.* anAdar
(अनादर), apmAn (अपमान)

disseminate, *v.* prachAr garnu
(प्रचार गर्नु),
phailAunu (फैलाउनु)

distance, *n.* dUrI (दूरी)

distant, *adj.* TADhA (टाढा),
dUr (दूर)

distinct, *adj.* chhuTTai (छुट्टै),
alag (अलग)

distinguish, *v.* chhuTTyAunu
(छुट्ट्याउनु)

distinguished, *adj.* wishishT
(विशिष्ट), prasiddh (प्रसिद्ध)

distress, *n.* kashT (कष्ट),
duhkh (दुःख), markA (मर्का)
v. kashT dinu (कष्ट दिनु),
markA pArnu (मर्का पार्नु)

distribute, *v.* bAñDnu (बाँड्नु),
witaraN garnu (वितरण गर्नु)

distribution, *n.* witarAn
(वितरण)

district, *n.* jillA (जिल्ला)

distrust, *n.* awishwAs
(अविश्वास)
v. wishwAs na garnu
(विश्वास नगर्नु)

disturb, *v.* bAdhA dinu (बाधा दिनु), bighna pArnu (बिघ्न पार्नु)

disturbance, *n.* bAdhA (बाधा), bighna (बिघ्न)

ditch, *n.* khAlDo (खाल्डो), khopilTo (खोपिल्टो)

ditto, *n.* uhI (उही), aijan (ऐजन)

dive, *n.* gotA (गोता), DubulkI (डुबुल्की) *v.* gotA lAunu (गोता लाउनु), DubulkI mArnu (डुबुल्की मार्नु)

divert, *v.* bahalAunu (बहलाउनु), bATo badalnu (बाटो बदल्नु)

divide, bhAg garnu (भाग गर्नु), bAñDnu (बाँड्नु)

divorce, *n.* pArpAchuke (पारपाचुके) *v.* pArpAchuke garnu (पारपाचुके गर्नु)

dizzy, *adj.* riṅgaTA lAgeko (रिंगटा लागेको)

do, *v./aux.* garnu (गर्नु) *n.* (ditto) aijan (ऐजन) *adj.* please (कृपया)

doctor, *n.* DAkTar (डाक्टर), waidya (वैद्य)

doctrine, *n.* siddhAnt (सिद्धान्त), mat (मत)

document, *n.* kAgaj patra (कागजपत्र), kAgjAt (कागजात)

dodge, *n.* chhalne/chhakyAune

kAm (छल्ने/छक्याउने काम) *v.* chhalnu (छल्नु), chhakyAunu (छक्याउनु)

dog, *n.* kukur (कुकुर)

doll, *n.* putalI (पुतली)

dome, *n.* gumbaj (गुम्बज), burjA (बुर्जा)

domestic, *adj.* ghar pAlA (घरपाला), gharelu (घरेलु)

domicile, *n.* prabAs (प्रवास), niwAs (निवास)

dominate, *v.* dabAunu (दबाउनु), kajyAunu (कज्याउनु)

domination, *n.* prabhutwa (प्रभुत्व), kajyAi (कज्याइ), Adhipatya (आधिपत्य)

don, *v.* lAunu (लाउनु) *n.* shikshak (शिक्षक), dAdA (दादा)

donate, *v.* dAn/chandA dinu (दान/चन्दा दिनु)

donation, *n.* chandA (चन्दा), dAn (दान)

donkey, *n.* gadhA (गधा)

donor, *n.* dAtA (दाता), dAnI (दानी)

door, *n.* dailo (दैलो), DhokA (ढोका)

doorkeeper, *n.* pAle (पाले), Dhoke (ढोके)

dormitory, *n.* ThUlo sutne ThAuñ / koThA (ठूलो सुत्ने ठाउँ/कोठा)

dose, *n.* mAtrA (मात्रा), khurAk (खुराक)

dot, *n.* thoplo (थोप्लो),
   bindu (बिन्दु)

double, *adj.* dobbar (दोब्बर),
   dugunA (दुगुना), Dabal (डबल)
   v. dobbar/Dabal garnu
   (दोब्बर/डबल गर्नु)

doubt, *n.* shaṅkA (शंका),
   sandeh (सन्देह)
   v. shaṅkA garnu/mAnnu
   (शंका गर्नु/मान्नु)

doubtful, *adj.* shaṅkA janak
   (शंकाजनक),
   shaṅkAspad (शंकास्पद)

doubtless, *adj.* nissandeh
   (निस्सन्देह)

dove, *n.* Dhukur (ढुकुर)

down, *n.* tala (तल),
   uṅdho (उँधो)

downcast, *adj.* jhokrAeko
   (भोक्राएको), udAs (उदास)

downfall, *n.* patan (पतन),
   adho gati (अधोगति)

downhill, *n.* orAlo (ओरालो)

downpour, *n.* musaldhAr pAnI
   (मुसलधार पानी)

downstairs, *adv.* tala (तल),
   tala tira (तलतिर)

dowry, *n.* dAijo (दाइजो)

doze, *v.* uṅghnu (उँघ्नु)
   n. uṅgh (उँघ),
   jhapak (भपक)

dozen, *n.* darjan (दर्जन)

drag, *v.* tAnnu (तान्नु),

ghichyAunu (घिच्याउनु),
   lachhArnu (लछार्नु)

dragon, *n.* pwaṅkhe sarpa
   (प्वाँखे सर्प)

drain, *n.* nAl (नाल), Dhal (ढल)
   v. bahAunu (बहाउनु),
   nithArnu (निथार्नु)

drama, *n.* nATak (नाटक)

dramatic, *adj.* nATkIya
   (नाटकीय)

draw, *n.* khichAtAnI
   (खिचातानी)
   v. tAnnu (तान्नु),
   khichnu (खिच्नु), chitra
   banAunu (चित्र बनाउनु)

drawback, *n.* dosh (दोष),
   aw guN (अवगुण),
   asuwidhA (असुविधा)

drawer, *n.* gharrA (घर्रा),
   (person) tAnne (तान्ने),
   khichne (खिच्ने)

drawing, *n.* rekhA chitra
   (रेखाचित्र),
   chitra kalA (चित्रकला)

drawing room, *n.* baiThak
   (बैठक), basne koThA/hal
   (बस्ने कोठा/हल)

dreadful, *adj.* bhayAnak
   (भयानक),
   Dar lAgdo (डरलाग्दो)

dream, *n.* sapanA (सपना)
   v. sapanA dekhnu
   (सपना देख्नु)

drench, *v.* bhijnu (भिज्नु)

dress, *n.* lugA (लुगा),
poshAk (पोशाक)
v. lugA lAunu (लुगा लाउनु),
(wound) malam paTTI garnu
(मलमपट्टी गर्नु),
sajAunu (सजाउनु)

drill, *n.* kabAyat (कबायत),
kabAj (कबाज),
(tool) barmA (बर्मा)

drill, *v.* kabAj khelnu (कबाज
खेल्नु), pwAl pArnu (प्वाल पार्नु)

drink, *n.* peya (पेय), raksI (रक्सी)
v. piunu (पिउनु), khAnu (खानु)

drive, *n.* haṅkAi (हँकाइ),
hAwA khorI (हावाखोरी),
phUrti (फूर्ति), AṅT (आँट)
v. hAṅknu (हाँक्नु), chalAunu
(चलाउनु), dhapAunu
(धपाउनु), lagArnu (लगार्नु)

driver, *n.* chAlak (चालक),
DAibhar (डाइभर)

drizzle, *n.* simsim pAnI
(सिमसिम पानी)
v. simsim pAnI parnu
(सिमसिम पानी पर्नु)

drop, *n. (water)* thopA
(थोपा), chhiTA (छिटा),
(number) hrAs (ह्रास)
v. khasAunu (खसाउनु),
jhArnu (झार्नु),
ghaTAunu (घटाउनु)

drought, *n.* sukkhA (सुक्खा),

anAwrishti (अनावृष्टि),
khaDerI (खडेरी)

drown, *v.* Dubnu (डुब्नु)

drug, *n.* aushadhi (औषधि),
(narcotics) lAgU padArth
(लागू पदार्थ)

drugstore, *n.* aushadhi pasal
(औषधि पसल)

drum, *n.* Dhol (ढोल),
mAdal (मादल), *(container)*
DhwAṅg (ढ्वाङ्ग), dram (ड्रम)

drunkard, *n.* dherai raksI
khAne (धेरै रक्सी खाने),
jaṅDyAhA (जँड्याहा)

dry, *adj.* sukeko (सुकेको),
sukkhA (सुक्खा)

duck, *n.* hAṅs (हाँस)
v. DubkI mArnu (डुब्की मार्नु)

due, *adj.* uchit (उचित),
yogya (योग्य)

duel, *n.* duI janA ko bhiDant
(दुई जनाको भिडन्त)

dues, *n.* tiro (तिरो), riN (ऋण),
bAṅkI (बाँकी), shulk (शुल्क)

duet, *n.* yugal gAn (युगलगान)

dull, *adj.* mand (मन्द),
niras (निरस), bojhi (बोझिल)

dumb, *adj.* lATo (लाटो),
gUṅgo (गुँगो)

dump, *n.* thupro (थुप्रो),
mal khAlDo (मलखाल्डो)
v. thupArnu (थुपार्नु),
khAṅdnu (खाँद्नु)

duplicate, *adj.* dohoro (दोहोरो),
  n. nakkal (नक्कल),
  prati lipi (प्रतिलिपि)
  v. dohoryAunu (दोहोर्‍याउनु)

durable, *adj.* TikAu (टिकाउ)

duration, *n.* awadhi (अवधि),
  myAd (म्याद)

during, *prep.* mA (मा),
  tAkA (ताका), bhitra (भित्र)

dusk, *n.* godhUli (गोधूलि),
  sAñjha (साँझ)

dust, *n.* dhUlo (धूलो)
  v. dhUlo jhArnu (धूलो झार्नु)

dusty, *adj.* dhUle (धूले)

dutiful, *adj.* AgyA pAlak

(आज्ञापालक),
kartawyanishTh (कर्तव्यनिष्ठ)

duty, *n.* kAm (काम),
  kartawya (कर्तव्य)

dwarf, *n.* bAunne (बाउन्ने),
  puDke (पुड्के)

dwelling, *n.* ghar (घर),
  DerA (डेरा)

dye, *n.* rañg (रङ्ग)
  v. rañgAunu (रङ्गाउनु)

dynasty, *n.* wamsha (वंश),
  kul (कुल), khalak (खलक)

dysentery, *n.* Auñ (आउँ),
  ragat mAsI (रगतमासी)

E

each, *adj.* harek (हरेक),
  pratyek (प्रत्येक)

eager, *adj.* utsuk (उत्सुक),
  ichchhuk (इच्छुक)

eagle, *n.* chIl (चील)

ear, *n.* kAn (कान)

early, *adj.* saberai (सबेरै),
  chAñDo (चाँडो)

earmark, *v.* khAs kAm ko
  lAgI kosh chhuTTyAunu
  (खास कामको लागि कोष
  छुट्ट्याउनु)

earn, *v.* kamAunu (कमाउनु),
  Arjan garnu (आर्जन गर्नु)

earning, *n.* kamAi (कमाइ)

earth, *n.* prithwI (पृथ्वी),
  dhartI (धर्ती), mATo (माटो)

earthquake, *n.* bhuiñchAlo
  (भुइँचालो)

ease, *n.* ArAm (आराम),
  sukh (सुख)

easily, *adv.* sajilo sañga/garI
  (सजिलोसँग/गरी)

east, *n.* pUrwa (पूर्व)

eastern, *adj.* pUrwI (पूर्वी)

easy, *adj.* sajilo (सजिलो), saral (सरल)

eat, *v.* khAnu (खानु)

eatables, *n.* khAne kurA (खानेकुरा)

eccentric, *n.* jhakkI (झक्की), sankAhA (सन्काहा)

echo, *n.* pratidhwani (प्रतिध्वनि), phirtI AwAj (फिर्ती आवाज) *v.* ghankanu (घन्कनु), guñjnu (गुँज्नु)

eclipse, *n.* grahaN (ग्रहण), andhyAro (अँध्यारो) *v.* grAs garnu (ग्रास गर्नु), andhyAro pArnu (अँध्यारो पार्नु)

ecology, *n.* paryAwaraN (पर्यावरण), wAtAwaraN (वातावरण)

economic, *adj.* Arthik (आर्थिक)

economical, *adj.* kam kharchilo (कम खर्चिलो), mitwyayI (मितव्ययी)

economics, *n.* arth shAstra (अर्थशास्त्र)

economize, *v.* kam kharch / kiphAyat garnu (कम खर्च / किफायत गर्नु)

economy, *n.* arth tantra (अर्थतन्त्र)

eczema, *n.* dAd (दाद), dinAi (दिनाइ)

edge, *n.* chheu (छेउ), kinArA (किनारा), *(have the edge on)*, *phr.* lAbh dAyak sthiti mA (लाभदायक स्थितिमा)

edgy, *adj.* jhokI (झोकी), uttejit (उत्तेजित)

edible *adj.* khAna hune (खान हुने)

edifice, *n.* bhawan (भवन), mahal (महल), ghar (घर)

edit, *v.* sampAdan garnu (सम्पादन गर्नु)

editor, *n.* sampAdak (सम्पादक)

educate, *v.* shikshA dinu (शिक्षा दिनु), paDhAunu (पढाउनु)

education, *n.* shikshA (शिक्षा), paDhAi (पढाइ)

eel, *n.* bAm mAchhA (बाम माछा)

effect, *n.* asar (असर), phal (फल), pariNAm (परिणाम)

effects, *n.* jhiTI (झिटी), jethA (जेथा), dhan mAl (धनमाल)

effective, *adj.* rAmro asar pArne (राम्रो असर पार्ने), prabhAw kArI (प्रभावकारी)

efficiency, *n.* dakshatA (दक्षता), yogyatA (योग्यता)

efficient, *adj.* daksha (दक्ष), yogya (योग्य)

effigy, *n.* putalA (पुतला), mUrti (मूर्ति)

effort, *n.* mihinet (मिहिनेत),
kosis (कोसिस),
prayAs (प्रयास)

egalitarian, *n.* samatA wAdI
(समतावादी)

egg, *n.* phul (फुल),
aNDA (अण्डा), dimA (डिमा)

eggplant, *n.* bhaNTA (भण्टा),
baigan (बैगन)

ego, *n.* aham (अहम),
garwa (गर्व)

eight, *n.* ATh (आठ)

eighteen, *n.* aThAra (अठार)

eighth, *adj.* AThauṅ (आठौं)

eighty, *n.* asI (असी)

either, *adj./pron.* duI mA ek
(दुईमा एक), wA (वा)

ejaculate, *v.* sirkA chhoDnu
(सिर्का छोड्नु),
phyAṅknu (फ्याँक्नु)

ejaculation, *n.* skhalan (स्खलन)

eject, *v.* nikAlnu (निकाल्नु)

elaborate, *adj.* wistrit (विस्तृत),
sawistAr (सविस्तार)
v. sawistAr bhannu/garnu
(सविस्तार भन्नु/गर्नु)

elan, *n.* phUrti (फूर्ती),
josh (जोश)

elastic, *adj.* tankane (तन्कने),
tankine (तन्किने)

elated, *adj.* khus (खुस),
daṅg dAs (दङ्गदास)

elbow, *n.* kuhinA (कुहिना),

kuhuno (कुहुनो)

elder, *adj.* jeTho (जेठो)

elderly, *adj.* prauDh (प्रौढ),
adh baiṅse (अधबैंसे)

elect, *v.* chunnu (चुन्नु),
chhAnnu (छान्नु)

election, *n.* chunAu (चुनाउ),
nirwAchan (निर्वाचन)

electric, *adj.* bijulI ko
(बिजुलीको), bijulI le chalne
(बिजुलीले चल्ने)

electric shock, *n.* bijulI ko
kareNT ko dhakkA
(बिजुलीको करेण्टको धक्का)

electricity, *n.* bijulI (बिजुली)

electrocute, *v.* bijulI ko
kareNT lAgera marnu
(बिजुलीको करेण्ट लागेर मर्नु)

elegant, *adj.* sundar (सुन्दर),
rAmro (राम्रो)

element, *n.* tattwa (तत्त्व),
mUl kurA (मूल कुरा)

elephant, *n.* hAttI (हात्ती)

elevate, *v.* uchAlnu (उचाल्नु),
mAthi laijAnu (माथि लैजानु)

elevation, *n.* UñchAi (ऊँचाइ),
aglAi (अग्लाइ)

elevator, *n.* liphT (लिफ्ट)

eleven, *n.* eghAra (एघार)

eleventh, *adj.* eghArauṅ
(एघारौं)

elicit, *v.* nikAlnu (निकाल्नु),
jhiknu (झिक्नु)

eligible, *adj.* chhanna yogya (छान्नयोग्य), yogyatA bhaeko (योग्यता भएको)

eliminate, *v.* lop garAunu (लोप गराउनु), nAmeT garnu (नामेट गर्नु)

elite, *n.* kulIn/gaNya mAnya warg (कुलीन/गण्यमान्य वर्ग)

elixir, *n.* amrit (अमृत), mahaushadhi (महौषधि)

elope, *v.* champat hunu (चम्पत हुनु), bhAgnu (भाग्नु), poila jAnu (पोइल जानु)

eloquent, *adj.* rAmro bolne (राम्रो बोल्ने), wAk paTu (वाक्पटु)

else, *pron.* arko (अर्को) *adv.* natra (नत्र), anyathA (अन्यथा)

elsewhere, *adj.* antai (अन्तै), anyatra (अन्यत्र), anta katai (अन्त कतै)

emancipation, *n.* mukti (मुक्ति), uddhAr (उद्धार)

embargo, *n.* rokkA (रोक्का), nishedh (निषेध)

embark, *v.* jahAj chaDhnu (जहाज चढ्नु)

embarkation, *n.* ArohaN (आरोहण), chaDhAi (चढाइ)

embarrass, *v.* apThyAro mA pArnu (अप्ठ्यारोमा पार्नु), lAj lagAunu (लाज लगाउनु)

embarrassment, *n.* apThyAro (अप्ठ्यारो), asajilo (असजिलो)

embassy, *n.* dUtAwAs (दूतावास), rAj dUtAwAs (राजदूतावास)

embrace, *v.* aṅgAlo hAlnu (अँगालो हाल्नु), aṅkmAl garnu (अंकमाल गर्नु)

embroidery, *n.* kArchop (कार्चोप), buTTA (बुट्टा), jarIles (जरीलेस), kasidA (कसिदा)

emerald, *n.* pannA (पन्ना)

emerge, *v.* niklanu (निक्लनु), niskanu (निस्कनु)

emergency, *n.* saṅkaT (सङ्कट), Apat (आपत्)

emergent, *adj.* nawodit (नवोदित)

emigrant, *n.* prawAsI (प्रवासी)

émigre, *n.* prawAsI (प्रवासी), nirwAsit wyakti (निर्वासित व्यक्ति)

eminent, *adj.* nAmI (नामी), prakhyAt (प्रख्यात)

emissary, *n.* dUt (दूत), jAsUs (जासूस)

emotion, *n.* bhAw (भाव), Aweg (आवेग)

emperor, *n.* samrAT (सम्राट), mahArAjA (महाराजा)

emphasis, *n.* jor (जोर), bal (बल)

empire, *n.* sAmrAjya (साम्राज्य), rAjya (राज्य)

employ, v. kAm dinu (काम दिनु), kAm mA lagAunu (काममा लगाउनु)

employee, n. kAm garne (काम गर्ने), kAmdAr (कामदार)

employment, n. kAm (काम), rojgAr (रोजगार)

empty, adj. ritto (रित्तो), khAll (खाली)

enable, v. yogya/lAyak banAunu (योग्य/लायक बनाउनु)

encephalitis, n. mastishka jwar (मस्तिष्क ज्वर), mathiṅgal ko jalan (मथिङ्गलको जलन)

enchant, v. TunA/mohit garnu (टुना/मोहित गर्नु)

enchantment, n. moh (मोह), TunA munA (टुनामुना)

enclose, v. ghernu (घेर्नु), gAbhnu (गाभ्नु)

enclosure, n. gherA (घेरा), hAtA (हाता), gAbhieko kurA (गाभिएको कुरा)

encounter, v. laDnu (लड्नु), bhiDnu (भिड्नु) n. laDAiṅ (लडाई), bhiDant (भिडन्त)

encourage, v. uksAunu (उक्साउनु), hausalA dinu (हौसला दिनु)

encouragement, n. hausalA (हौसला), utsAh (उत्साह)

encyclop(a)edia, n. wishwa kosh (विश्वकोश)

end, n. Akhir (आखिर), ant (अन्त), chheu (छेउ) v. sakinu (सकिनु), khatam/samApt garnu (खतम/समाप्त गर्नु)

endeavo(u)r, n. prayatna (प्रयत्न), udyog (उद्योग) v. prayatna garnu (प्रयत्न गर्नु)

endorse, v. lekhera swIkAr/ darpITh garnu (लेखेर स्वीकार/दरपीठ गर्नु)

endurance, n. sahan shIltA (सहनशीलता), sahishNutA (सहिष्णुता)

endure, v. sahanu (सहनु)

enemy, n. shatru (शत्रु), dushman (दुश्मन)

energy, n. bal (बल), jAṅgar (जाँगर), shakti (शक्ति), UrjA (ऊर्जा)

enforce, v. kar lagAunu (कर लगाउनु), (law) lAgU garnu (लागू गर्नु)

enforcement, n. lAgU garne kAm (लागू गर्ने काम)

engage, v. kAm mA lAgnu (काममा लाग्नु), lagAunu (लगाउनु), nokarI mA lagAunu (नोकरीमा लगाउनु)

engaged, *adj.* kAm mA lAgeko/ wyasta (काममा लागेको/व्यस्त), bihA chhinieko (बिहा छिनिएको)

engagement, *n.* kAm (काम), niyukti (नियुक्ति), bihA ko chhino phAno (बिहाको छिनेफानो), magnI (मगनी), wiwAh prastAw (विवाहप्रस्ताव)

engine, *n.* kal (कल), yantra (यन्त्र), *(railway)* injin (इन्जिन)

engineer, *n.* injiniyar (इन्जिनियर)
v. rachnA/sañchAlan garnu (रचना/संचालन गर्नु)

England, *n.* belAyat (बेलायत)

English, *n. (person)* añgrej (अँग्रेज), *(thing)* belAyatI (बेलायती), *(lg.)* añgrejI (अँग्रेजी)

engrave, *v.* khopnu (खोप्नु), kATnu (काट्नु), kuñdnu (कुँद्नु)

engulf, *v.* grAs garnu (ग्रास गर्नु), nilnu (निल्नु)

enhance, *v.* baDhnu (बढ्नु), baDhAunu (बढाउनु)

enjoy, *v.* ramAunu (रमाउनु), Anand linu (आनन्द लिनु)

enjoyable, *adj.* Anand dine (आनन्द दिने),

ramAilo (रमाइलो)

enjoyment, *n.* majA (मजा), Anand (आनन्द)

enlarge, *v.* ThUlo garnu (ठूलो गर्नु), baDhAunu (बढाउनु)

enlighten, *v.* prakAsh pArnu (प्रकाश पार्नु), updesh dinu (उपदेश दिनु)

enlightenment, *n.* gyÃn (ज्ञान), diwya gyÃn (दिव्यज्ञान)

enough, *adv.* yatheshT (यथेष्ट), paryApt (पर्याप्त)

enquire, *v.* sodh puchh garnu (सोधपुछ गर्नु)

enquiry, *n.* sodh puchh (सोधपुछ)

en route, *adv.* bATo mA (बाटोमा)

entangle, *v.* phasnu (फस्नु), aljhinu (अल्झिनु)

entanglement, *n.* aljhAi (अल्झाइ), las pas (लसपस)

enter, *v.* pasnu (पस्नु), prawesh garnu (प्रवेश गर्नु)

enterprise, *n.* udyam (उद्यम), abhiyAn (अभियान)

enterprising, *adj.* udyamI (उद्यमी), sAhasI (साहसी)

entertain, *v.* man bahalAunu (मन बहलाउनु), manorañjan garnu (मनोरञ्जन गर्नु)

entertainment, *n.* manorañjan (मनोरञ्जन), ramitA (रमिता)

enthusiasm, *n.* josh (जोश),
utsAh (उत्साह)

enthusiast, *adj.* utsAhI
(उत्साही), joshilo (जोशिलो)

entice, *v.* phakAunu (फकाउनु)
phuslAunu (फुस्लाउनु)

entire, *adj.* sampUrN (सम्पूर्ण),
sabai (सबै), pUrA (पूरा)

entirely, *adv.* pUrN rUp le
(पूर्ण रूपले), purai (पुरै)
pUrA tawar le (पूरा तवरले)

entourage. *n.* dal bal (दलबल),
sah gAmI (सहगामी)

entrance, *n.* prawesh (प्रवेश),
DhokA (ढोका)

entreat, *v.* bintI/anurodh garnu
(बिन्ती/अनुरोध गर्नु)

entrepreneur, *n.* udyamI (उद्यमी)

entrust, *v.* sumpanu (सुम्पनु),
jimmA dinu (जिम्मा दिनु)

entry, *n.* prawesh (प्रवेश),
dartA (दर्ता)

envelop, *v.* ghernu (घेर्नु),
DhAknu (ढाक्नु)

envelope, *n.* khAm (खाम)

environment, *n.* wAtAwaraN
(वातावरण)

envoy, *n.* dUt (दूत),
rAj dUt (राजदूत)

envy, *n.* DAhA (डाहा), Ikh (ईख)
v. DAhA/Ikh garnu
(डाहा/ईख गर्नु)

epic, *n.* mahA kAwya
(महाकाव्य)

epidemic, *n.* mahA mArI
(महामारी),
saruwA rog (सरुवा रोग)

epilepsy, *n.* chhAre rog
(छारेरोग), mirgI (मिर्गी)

episode, *n.* prasaṅg (प्रसङ्ग),
kathA (कथा)

epoch, *n.* kAl (काल), yug (युग)

equal, *adj.* barAbar (बराबर),
samAn (समान)

equality, *n.* barAbarI (बराबरी),
samAntA (समानता)

equalize, *v.* barAbar garnu
(बराबर गर्नु)

equator, *n.* bhUmadhya rekhA
(भूमध्य रेखा)

equestrian, *n.* ghoD chaDhI
(घोड्चढी), sawAr (सवार)
adj. sawAr sambandhI
(सवारसम्बन्धी)

equip, *v.* sajAunu (सजाउनु),
laya hunu (लय हुनु)

equipment, *n.* upkaraN
(उपकरण), sar sAmAn (सरसामान)

equivalent, *adj.* barAbar
(बराबर), sam tulya (समतुल्य)

era, *n.* yug (युग), kAl (काल)

eradicate, *v.* nirmUl/unmUlan
garnu (निर्मूल/उन्मूलन गर्नु)

erase, *v.* meTnu (मेट्नु)

eraser, *n.* meTne rabar
(मेट्ने रबर)

erect, *v.* banAunu (बनाउनु), khaDA garnu (खडा गर्नु) *adj.* ThADo (ठाडो), khaDA (खडा)

erode, *v.* khyAunu (ख्याउनु), mAsnu (मास्नु)

erosion, *n.* kaTAn (कटान), bhU kshaya (भूक्षय)

erotic, *adj.* kAmuk (कामुक), uttejak (उत्तेजक)

errand, *n.* bAhir gaI garine kAm (बाहिर गई गरिने काम), matlab (मतलब)

error, *n.* galtI (गल्ती), bhUl (भूल)

escalate, *v.* baDhAunu (बढाउनु), charkAunu (चर्काउनु)

escalator, *n.* Aphai chalne bhareŋg (आफै चल्ने भरेङ्ग)

escape, *v.* phutkanu (फुत्कनु), bhAgnu (भाग्नु), *(accident)* bAñchnu (बाँच्नु), joginu (जोगिनु) *n.* bhagAi (भगाइ), palAyan (पलायन)

escort, *n.* sAth jAne/sawArI chalAune wyakti (साथ जाने/सवारी चलाउने व्यक्ति), ATh pahariyA (आठपहरिया) *v.* puryAunu (पुर्‍याउनु), sawArI chalAunu (सवारी चलाउनु)

especially, *adv.* wishesh garI (विशेषगरी), prAyah (प्राय:)

espionage, *n.* jAsUsI (जासूसी)

espouse, *v.* bihe garnu (बिहे गर्नु)

essay, *n.* nibandh (निबन्ध), rachnA (रचना) *v.* udyog garnu (उद्योग गर्नु)

essence, *n.* sAr (सार), sugandh (सुगन्ध)

essential, *adj.* jarurI (जरुरी), Awashyak (आवश्यक)

establish, *v.* sthApanA/khaDA garnu (स्थापना/खडा गर्नु)

establishment, *n.* sthApanA (स्थापना), pratishThAn (प्रतिष्ठान)

esteem, *n.* Adar (आदर), shraddhA (श्रद्धा) *v.* Adar/shraddhA garnu (आदर/श्रद्धा गर्नु)

estimate, *n.* lAgat (लागत), anumAn (अनुमान) *v.* anumAn garnu (अनुमान गर्नु), Añknu (आँक्नु)

et cetera (etc.), *adv.* ityAdi (इत्यादि), Adi (आदि)

eternal, *adj.* anant (अनन्त), nitya (नित्य), lagAtAr ko (लगातारको)

ethical, *adj.* naitik (नैतिक)

ethics, *n.* nIti shAstra (नीतिशास्त्र)

etiquette, *n.* kAidA (काइदा), somat (सोमत), shishTAchAr (शिष्टाचार)

evacuate, *v.* khAlI garnu (खाली गर्नु)

evaluate, *v.* mUlyAṅkan / pArakh garnu (मूल्याङ्कन / पारख गर्नु)

evaluation, *n.* mUlyAṅkan (मूल्याङ्कन), pArakh (पारख)

evaporate, *v.* bAph bannu (बाफ बन्नु), uDnu (उड्नु), suknu (सुक्नु)

even, *adv.* pani (पनि), *(level)* samma (सम्म), *(equal)* barAbar (बराबर), *(number)* jor (जोर)

evening, *n.* belukA (बेलुका), sAṅjha (साँझ), rAti (राति)

event, *n.* ghaTnA (घटना), *(sports)* khel (खेल), bAjI (बाजी)

eventual, *adj.* antim (अन्तिम), Akhir mA (आखिरमा)

ever, *adv.* sadhaiṅ (सधैँ), sadaiwa (सदैव)

evergreen, *adj.* sadAbahAr (सदाबहार) *n.* hariyAlI (हरियाली)

everlasting, *adj.* sadhaiṅ rahane (सधैँ रहने), akshaya (अक्षय), anant (अनन्त)

every, *adj.* harek (हरेक), pratyek (प्रत्येक)

everybody, *n.* har wyakti (हर व्यक्ति), jo pani (जो पनि)

everything, *n.* har chIj (हर चीज), harek wastu (हरेक वस्तु)

everywhere, *adv.* jahAṅ sukai (जहाँसुकै), jatA sukai (जतासुकै)

evidence, *n.* sAkshI (साक्षी), gawAhI (गवाही)

evident, *adj.* pratyaksha (प्रत्यक्ष), spashT (स्पष्ट), jAhir (जाहिर)

evil, *n.* kharAbI (खराबी), dushTatA (दुष्टता), anishT (अनिष्ट) *adj.* kharAb (खराब), dushT (दुष्ट), pApI (पापी)

evolution, *n.* wikAs (विकास), wistAr (विस्तार)

exact, *adj.* ThIk (ठीक), durust (दुरुस्त) *v.* upar/asul garnu (उपर/असुल गर्नु)

exactly, *adv.* ThIk saṅga (ठीकसँग), sahI (सही)

exaggeration, *n.* baDhAI chaDhAI gareko kurA (बढाई चढाई गरेको कुरा), atyukti (अत्युक्ति)

examination, *n.* jAṅch (जाँच), parIkshA (परीक्षा)

examine, *v.* jAṅchnu (जाँच्नु), parIkshA garnu (परीक्षा गर्नु)

example, *n.* udAharaN
(उदाहरण),
drishTAnt (दृष्टान्त),
(for example) jastai(जस्तै),
uDaharaN ko lAgi
(उदाहरणको लागि)

excavate, *v.* khanera nikAlnu
(खनेर निकाल्नु), utkhanan
garnu (उत्खनन गर्नु)

exceed, *v.* baDhnu (बढ्नु),
jyAdA hunu (ज्यादा हुनु)

excel, *v.* jitnu (जित्नु),
shreshTh hunu (श्रेष्ठ हुनु)

Excellency, *n.* mahA mahim
(महामहिम)

excellent, *adj.* uttam (उत्तम),
ekdam rAmro (एकदम राम्रो)

except, *prep.* siwAya (सिवाय),
bAhek (बाहेक)

exception, *n.* niyam bAhira ko
kurA (नियमबाहिरको कुरा),
apwAd (अपवाद)

excess, *n.* jyAdA (ज्यादा),
adhik (अधिक), prachur (प्रचुर)

excessive, *adj.* atyadhik
(अत्यधिक), jyAdA (ज्यादा),
baDhtA (बढ्ता)

exchange, *n.* sATA sAT
(साटासाट),
saTTA paTTA (सट्टापट्टा),
winimaya (विनिमय)
v. sATA sAT garnu
(साटासाट गर्नु),

sATnu (साट्नु)

excite, *v.* uttejit garnu
(उत्तेजित गर्नु),
uksAunu (उक्साउनु)

excitement, *n.* uttejanA
(उत्तेजना), Aweg (आवेग)

excursion, *n.* saphar (सफर),
yAtrA (यात्रा)

excuse, *n.* kshamA (क्षमा),
nihuň (निहुँ)
v. kshamA/mAph garnu
(क्षमा/माफ गर्नु)

execute, *v.* garnu (गर्नु),
(law) prAN daND dinu
(प्राण दण्ड दिनु)

executive, *n./adj.* kArya
kAriNI (कार्यकारिणी)

exempt, *v.* chhUT dinu
(छूट दिनु)

exemption, *n.* chhUT (छूट),
mAphI (माफी)

exercise, *n.* abhyAs (अभ्यास),
wyAyAm (व्यायाम),
kasrat (कसरत)
v. abhyAs / wyAyAm /
kasrat garnu (अभ्यास /
व्यायाम / कसरत गर्नु)

exhaust, *v.* siddhinu (सिद्धिनु),
siddhyAunu (सिद्ध्याउनु),
rittinu (रित्तिनु)
n. nikAs (निकास)

exhausted, *adj.* thAkeko
(थाकेको), thakit (थकित)

exhibit 66 **expire**

exhibit, *n.* pradarshan (प्रदर्शन)
v. dekhAunu (देखाउनु),
pradarshan garnu
(प्रदर्शन गर्नु)

exhibition, *n.* pradarshanI
(प्रदर्शनी)

exile, *n.* nishkAsan (निष्कासन),
desh nikAlA (देशनिकाला)
v. nikAlnu (निकाल्नु),
desh nikAlA garnu
(देश निकाला गर्नु)

exist, *v.* bAñchnu (बाँच्नु),
hunu (हुनु), rahanu (रहनु)

existence, *n.* astitwa
(अस्तित्व), satwa (सत्व)

exit, n. niskane bATo
(निस्कने बाटो)
v. niskanu (निस्कनु),
bAhira jAnu (बाहिर जानु)

exodus, *n.* prasthAn (प्रस्थान),
nirgaman (निर्गमन)

exorbitant, *adj.* jyAdai baDhI
(ज्यादै बढी), charko (चर्को)

exotic, *adj.* naulo (नौलो),
mohak (मोहक)

expand, *v.* wistAr garnu
(विस्तार गर्नु), phailanu
(फैलनु), phailAunu (फैलाउनु)

expansion, *n.* wistAr (विस्तार),
phailAwaT (फैलावट)

expect, *v.* AshA / anumAn /
apekshA garnu
(आशा/अनुमान/अपेक्षा गर्नु),

(*woman*) garbh watI
hunu (गर्भवती हुनु)

expectant, *adj.* AshA garne
(आशा गर्ने), (*woman*) garbh
wati (गर्भवती)

expectation, *n.* AshA (आशा),
apekshA (अपेक्षा),
AkAñkshA (आकांक्षा)

expedite, *v.* chAñDo / tAkitA
garnu (चाँडो/ताकिता गर्नु)

expedition, *n.* yAtrA (यात्रा),
abhiyAn (अभियान)

expel, *v.* nikAlnu (निकाल्नु)

expenditure, *n.* kharch (खर्च)

expense, *n.* kharch (खर्च)

expensive, *adj.* mahañgo
(महङ्गो), kharchilo (खर्चिलो)

experience, *n.* anubhaw
(अनुभव)

experienced, *adj.* anubhawI
(अनुभवी), pAko (पाको)

experiment, *n.* prayog (प्रयोग),
parIkshaN (परीक्षण)
v. prayog garnu (प्रयोग गर्नु),
jAñchnu (जाँच्नु)

expert, *adj.* sipAlu (सिपालु),
nipuN (निपुण)
n. sipAlu mAnis
(सिपालु मानिस),
wisheshagña (विशेषज्ञ)

expire, *v.* marnu (मर्नु),
miti pugnu (मिति पुग्नु),
myAd saknu (म्याद सक्नु)

explain, *v.* bataunu (बताउनु),
wyAkhyA garnu
(व्याख्या गर्नु)

explanation, *n.* wyAkhyA
(व्याख्या),
spashTIkaraN (स्पष्टीकरण)

explode, *v.* paDkanu (पड्कनु),
wishphoT hunu (विस्फोट हुनु)

explore, *v.* khoj/anweshaN
garnu (खोज/अन्वेषण गर्नु)

explosion, *n.* wishphoTan
(विष्फोटन)

export, *n.* niryAt nikAsI garnu
(निर्यात निकासी गर्नु)

express, *v.* bolnu (बोल्नु),
prakaT garnu (प्रकट गर्नु)

expression, *n.* abhiwyakti
(अभिव्यक्ति)

expulsion, *n.* nikAlA (निकाला),
nishkAsan (निष्कासन)

exquisite, *adj.* uttam (उत्तम),
sundar (सुन्दर)

extempore, *adj.* binA tayArI/
TipoT boleko (बिना तयारी/
(टिपोट बोलेको)

extend, *v.* phailAunu (फैलाउनु),
phiṅjAunu (फिंजाउनु)

exterior, *adj.* bAhirI (बाहिरी)

external, *adj.* bAhirI (बाहिरी)

extinct, *adj.* bilAeko (बिलाएको),
lop bhaeko (लोप भएको),
lupt (लुप्त)

extinguish, *v.* nibhAunu

(निभाउनु)

extra, *adj.* atirikta (अतिरिक्त),
baDhtA (बढ्ता),
jageDA (जगेडा)

extradite, *v.* (*criminal*)
sumpanu (सुम्पनु),
bujhAunu (बुझाउनु)

extradition, *n.* supurdagI
(सुपुर्दगी)

extraordinary, *adj.* asAdhAraN
(असाधारण),
achamma ko (अचम्मको)

extravagant, *adj.* kharchilo
(खर्चिलो),
phajul kharchI (फजुलखर्ची)

extreme, *adj.* ugra (उग्र),
charam (चरम),
(*edge*) chheu (छेउ)

eye, *n.* AṅkhA (आँखा),
netra (नेत्र),
v. hernu (हेर्नु),
drishTi dinu (दृष्टि दिनु)

eyeball, *n.* AṅkhI geDI
(आँखीगेडी), AṅkhA ko nAnI
(आँखाको नानी)

eyebrow, *n.* AṅkhI bhauṅ
(आँखीभौँ)

eyeglasses, *n.* chasmA (चस्मा)

eyelash, *n.* parelA (परेला)

eyesight, *n.* drishTi (दृष्टि),
najar (नजर)

eyewitness, *n.* pratyaksha
darshI (प्रत्यक्षदर्शी)

F

fable, *n.* kathA (कथा),
nIti kathA (नीति कथा)

fabric, *n.* kapaDA (कपडा),
(structure) rachnA (रचना)

fabricate, *v.* banAunu
(बनाउनु), rachnu (रच्नु)

fabulous, *adj.* prakhyAt
(प्रख्यात),
akalpanIya (अकल्पनीय)

face, *n.* mukh (मुख),
anuhAr (अनुहार)
v. sAmnA garnu (सामना गर्नु)

facility, *n.* suwidhA (सुविधा),
sahuliyat (सहुलियत)

fact, *n.* kurA (कुरा),
sAñcho/pakkA kurA
(साँचो/पक्का कुरा),
tathya (तथ्य)

faction, *n.* guT (गुट), dal (दल)

factor, *n.* tattwa (तत्त्व), *(math.)*
guNan khaND (गुणनखण्ड),
(bus.) pratinidhi
(प्रतिनिधि), ghaTak (घटक)

factory, *n.* kAr khAnA
(कारखाना)

faculty, *n.* *(univ.)* sañkAya
(सङ्काय), *(skill)* sIp (सीप),
sAmarthya (सामर्थ्य)

fad, *n.* dhun (धुन),
sanak (सनक), lahaD (लहड)

fade, *v.* khuilanu (खुइलनु),
harAunu (हराउनु)

f(a)eces, *n.* disA (दिसा)

feather, *n.* pwAňkh (प्वाँख)

fail, *v.* phel/nishphal hunu
(फेल/निष्फल हुनु)

failure, *n.* asaphaltA
(असफलता), chUk (चूक)

faint, *adj.* mUrchhit (मूर्छित),
ashakta (अशक्त),
phIkA (फीका)
v. mUrchhA parnu (मूर्छा पर्नु),
behosh hunu (बेहोश हुनु)

fair, *n.* melA (मेला),
jAtrA (जात्रा)
adj. goro (गोरो), rAmro (राम्रो),
(bus.) supath (सुपथ),
(decision, etc.) nishpaksha
(निष्पक्ष)

fairy, *n.* parI (परी)

faith, *n.* wishwAs (विश्वास),
imAn (इमान), AsthA (आस्था),
nishThA (निष्ठा)

faithful, *adj.* imAndAr
(इमान्दार),
wishwAsI (विश्वासी)

fake, *n.* nakkalI wastu (नक्कली वस्तु), kirte (किर्ते) *v.* nakkalI mAl banAunu (नक्कली माल बनाउनु), chhalnu (छल्नु)

falcon, *n.* bAj (बाज)

fall, *v.* khasnu (खस्नु), laDnu (लड्नु) *n.* patan (पतन), khasAi (खसाइ), *(season)* sharad (शरद)

false, *adj.* jhUTo (झूटो), nakkalI (नक्कली)

fame, *n.* kIrti (कीर्ति), prasiddhi (प्रसिद्धि)

familiar, *adj.* chine jAneko (चिनेजानेको), parichit (परिचित)

family, *n.* pariwAr (परिवार), jahAn (जहान), *(lineage)* santAn (सन्तान), khAndAn (खानदान)

famine, *n.* anikAl (अनिकाल), akAl (अकाल)

famous, *adj.* prasiddha (प्रसिद्ध), nAmI (नामी)

fan, *n.* paṅkhA (पङ्खा), *(person)* bhakta (भक्त)

fanatic, *n./adj.* dharmAndh (धर्मान्ध), kaTTar (कट्टर)

fanfare, *n.* dhUm dhAm (धूमधाम), saṅkshipta samAroh (संक्षिप्त समारोह)

fang, *n.* DarhA (दाह्रा),

baṅgArA (बङ्गारा)

fantastic, *adj.* wilakshAN (विलक्षण), lahaDI (लहडी)

far, *adj.* TADhA (टाढा), dUr (दूर)

far away, *adj.* TADhA (टाढा)

farewell, *n.* bidAi (बिदाइ), bidA (बिदा)

farm, *n.* khet (खेत)

farmer, *n.* kisAn (किसान), khetI wAl (खेतीवाल)

fascinate, *v.* mohit/Akarshit garnu (मोहित/आकर्षित गर्नु)

fashion, *n.* chalan (चलन), pheshan (फेशन)

fast, *adj.* chhiTo (छिटो), tej (तेज), *(colour)* gADhA (गाढा), pakkA (पक्का) *v.* upwAs garnu (उपवास गर्नु), wrat basnu (व्रत बस्नु)

fasten, *v.* bAňdhnu (बाँध्नु), kasnu (कस्नु)

fat, *n.* chillo (चिल्लो), boso (बोसो) *adj.* moTo (मोटो)

fatal, *adj.* jyAn jAne (ज्यान जाने), ghAtak (घातक)

fate, *n.* bhAgya (भाग्य)

father, *n.* bAbu (बाबु), bubA (बुबा), pitA (पिता)

father-in-law, *n.* sasurA (ससुरा)

fatigue, *n.* thakAi (थकाइ), thakAwaT (थकावट)

fault, *n.* galtI (गलती), kasUr (कसूर)

fauna, *n.* prANI harU (प्राणीहरू)

favo(u)r, *n.* kripA (कृपा), nigAh (निगाह) *v.* kripA/nigAh garnu (कृपा/निगाह गर्नु)

favo(u)rable, *adj.* anukUl (अनुकूल)

favo(u)rite, *n.* pyAro (प्यारो), man pareko (मन परेको)

fear, *n.* Dar (डर), bhaya (भय) *v.* DarAunu (डराउनु), Dar mAnnu (डर मान्नु)

fearless, *adj.* niDar (निडर), na DarAune (नडराउने)

fearful, *adj.* Dar lAgdo (डरलाग्दो), bhayAnak (भयानक)

feasible, *adj.* sambhaw (सम्भव)

feast, *n.* bhoj (भोज), bhater (भतेर)

feat, *n.* ThUlo kAm (ठूलो काम), kamAl (कमाल)

fee, *n.* shulka (शुल्क),

feeble, *adj.* kamjor (कमजोर), nirbal (निर्बल)

feed, *v.* khwAunu (ख्वाउनु), *n.* dAnA (दाना), chArA (चारा)

feel, *v.* chAl pAunu (चाल पाउनु), anubhaw/mahsus garnu (अनुभव/महसुस गर्नु) chhAmnu (छाम्नु), (*sense*)

lAgnu (लाग्नु), ThAnnu (ठान्नु) *n.* sparsh (स्पर्श)

feeling, *n.* bhAw (भाव), bhAwanA (भावना)

feet, *n. (body)*, pAu/khuTTA haru (पाउ/खुट्टाहरू), *(measure)* phIT (फीट)

felicitate, *v.* badhAI dinu (बधाई दिनु), sammAn garnu (सम्मान गर्नु)

felicitation, *n.* badhAI (बधाई)

fell, *v.* rUkh kATnu (रूख काट्नु), DhAlnu (ढाल्नु)

fellow, *n.* sAthI (साथी), sańgI (सँगी), *(colloq.)* mAnchhe (मान्छे)

female, *n.* strI (स्त्री), nArI (नारी), pothI (पोथी)

feminine, *adj.* strI liṅg (स्त्रीलिङ्ग)

fence, *n.* bAr (बार), gherA (घेरा) *v.* chhekru (छेक्नु), bArnu (बार्नु)

fenugreek, *n.* methI (मेथी)

fern, *n.* unyU (उन्यू)

ferocious, *adj.* Dar lAgdo (डरलाग्दो)

ferry, *n.* DuṅgA (डुङ्गा), pherI (फेरी) *v.* DuṅgA mA tarnu / tArnu (डुङ्गामा तर्नु/तार्नु)

fertile, *adj.* ubjAu (उब्जाउ), malilo (मलिलो)

fertilizer, *n.* mal (मल),
khAd (खाद)

fervo(u)r, *n.* josh (जोश),
umaṅg (उमङ्ग)

fervent, *adj.* wyagra (व्यग्र),
tIwra (तीव्र)

festival, *n.* chAd (चाड),
parwa (पर्व), jAtrA (जात्रा)

festive, *adj.* ramAilo (रमाइलो),
majA ko (मजाको)

fetch, *v.* liera Aunu
(लिएर आउनु)

feud, *n.* jhagaDA (झगडा)

fever, *n.* jaro (जरो), jwar (ज्वर)

feverish, *adj.* jwar grast
(ज्वरग्रस्त)

few, *adj.* ali kati (अलिकति),
thorai (थोरै)

fiction, *n.* kAlpanik bayAn
(काल्पनिक बयान),
kathA (कथा)

fictitious, *adj.* kAlpanik
(काल्पनिक), kritrim (कृत्रिम)

fiddle, *n.* sAraṅgI (सारङ्गी)
v. sAraṅgI bajAunu
(सारङ्गी बजाउनु)

field, *n.* khet (खेत), bArI (बारी),
(sports) maidAn (मैदान)
v. khelADI/ummed wAr
prastut garnu
(खेलाडी/उम्मेदवार प्रस्तुत गर्नु)

fierce, *adj.* Dar lAgdo
(डरलाग्दो),

bhayaṅkar (भयङ्कर)

fifteen, *n.* pandhra (पन्ध्र)

fifth, *adj.* pAñchauṅ (पाँचौं)

fifty, *n.* pachAs (पचास)

fig, *n.* anjIr (अन्जीर)

fight, *n.* laDant (लडन्त),
bhiDant (भिडन्त),
v. laDnu (लड्नु),
bhiDnu (भिड्नु)

fighting, *n.* laDAiṅ (लडाई)

figure, *n. (math.)* aṅk (अङ्क),
(sketch) chitra (चित्र),
(external form) bAnkI
(बान्की), rUp (रूप)
v. kalpanA/chitrit garnu
(कल्पना/चित्रित गर्नु)

file, *n. (tool)* retI (रेती), ret
(रेत), *(folder)* phAil (फाइल)
v. ret lagAunu (रेत लगाउनु),
(law) phAil garnu (फाइल गर्नु),
muddA hAlnu (मुद्दा हाल्नु)

fill, *v.* bharnu (भर्नु)

film, *n.* chal chitra (चलचित्र),
cinemA (सिनेमा), *(eye)* jhillI
(झिल्ली), jAlo (जालो),
(photo) tasbir khichne philm
(तस्विर खिच्ने फिल्म)

filter, *n.* philTar (फिल्टर)
v. chhAnnu (छान्नु)

filth, *n.* phohor (फोहोर),
mailA (मैला)

filthy, *adj.* phohorI (फोहोरी),
gandA (गन्दा)

fin, *n.* mAchhA ko pakheTA (माछाको पखेटा)

final, *adj.* antim (अन्तिम) *n. (sports)* phAinal khel (फाइनल खेल)

finally, *adv.* ant mA (अन्तमा)

find, *v.* phelA pArnu (फेला पार्नु), bheTTAunu (भेट्टाउनु) *n.* pattA (पत्ता), barAmad (बरामद)

fine, *adj.* asal (असल), rAmro (राम्रो), *(greetings)* bes (बेस), *(quality)* masino (मसिनो), mihin (मिहिन), *(law, etc.)* daND (दण्ड), jarimAnA (जरिमाना) *v.* jarimAnA garnu (जरिमाना गर्नु)

finger, *n.* auñlA (औंला) *v.* chhunu (छुनु)

fingernail, *n.* nañ (नङ)

fingerprint, *n.* lyApche (ल्याप्चे), auñThA chhAp (औंठाछाप)

finish, *v.* siddhyAunu (सिद्ध्याउनु), khatam garnu (खतम गर्नु) *n.* ant (अन्त), samApti (समाप्ति)

fire, *n.* Ago (आगो), agni (अग्नि), *(fervour)* josh (जोश) *v.* bAlnu (बाल्नु),

(gun) hAnnu (हान्नु), chalAunu (चलाउनु), *(employer)* barkhAst garnu (बखास्त गर्नु)

fire brigade, *n.* damkal (दमकल), wAruN yantra (वारुणयन्त्र)

fire engine, *n.* damkal (दमकल)

firefly, *n.* jUn kIrI (जूनकीरी)

fireman, *n.* Ago nibhAune mAnis (आगो निभाउने मानिस), damkal ko sipAhI (दमकलको सिपाही)

fireplace, *n.* agenu (अगेनु), Atash khAn (आतशखान)

firewood, *n.* dAurA (दाउरा)

fireworks, *n.* Atash bAjI (आतशबाजी), paTAkA (पटाका)

firm, *n. (bus.)* kampanI (कम्पनी), samsthA (संस्था) *adj.* kaDA (कडा), sthir (स्थिर)

first, *adj.* pahilo (पहिलो) *adv.* pahile (पहिले)

fiscal year, *n.* Arthik warsh (आर्थिक वर्ष)

fish, *n.* mAchhA (माछा), mAchho (माछो) *v.* mAchhA mArnu (माछा मार्नु)

fisherman, *n.* mallAh (मल्लाह), machhuwA (मछ्वा), mAjhI (माझी)

fist, *n.* muTThI (मुट्ठी),
  muDkI (मुड्की)

fit, *adj.* lAyak (लायक),
  suhAuṅdo (सुहाउँदो)
  v. ThIk hunu (ठीक हुनु),
  milnu (मिल्नु)

fitness, *n.* yogyatA (योग्यता)

five, *n.* pAñch (पाँच)

fix, *n.* dodhAr (दोधार),
  anyol (अन्योल)
  v. (tool) jaDnu (जड्नु),
  lagAunu (लगाउनु),
  (make firm) daro pArnu
  (दरो पार्नु), kasnu (कस्नु),
  (charge) ThaharAunu
  (ठहराउनु),
  (price, time) toknu (तोक्नु),
  kiTAn garnu (किटान गर्नु)

flag, *n.* jhaNDA (झण्डा)

flagrant, *adj.* spashT
  (स्पष्ट), jwalant (ज्वलन्त)

flame, *n.* jwAlA (ज्वाला),
  Ago ko lapkA
  (आगोको लप्का)
  v. rankinu (रन्किनु),
  jalnu (जल्नु)

flank, *n.* chheu (छेउ),
  pAkho (पाखो), bagal (बगल)

flannel, *n.* phalATin (फलाटिन)

flap, *n.* phaDphaDAhat
  (फडफडाहट),
  thapthapAhaT (थपथपाहट)
  v. thapthapAunu

  (थपथपाउनु),
  dhapAunu (धपाउनु)

flare, *n.* jwAlA (ज्वाला),
  masAl (मसाल)
  v. dankanu (दन्कनु),
  dan dan balnu (दनदन बल्नु)

flash, *n.* jhilko (झिल्को),
  chamak damak (चमकदमक)
  v. jhilikka chamkanu
  (झिलिक्क चम्कनु)

flashlight, *n.* Tarch lAiT
  (टर्चलाइट)

flat, *adj. (surface)* samma
  (सम्म), *(shape)* chyApTo
  (च्याप्टो), chepTo (चेप्टो)
  (taste) khallo (खल्लो)
  n. phlyAT (फ्ल्याट),
  talA (तला)

flatly, *adv.* spashT saṅga
  (स्पष्टसंग),
  khullam khullA (खुल्लमखुल्ला)

flatter, *v.* baDhAi garnu (बढाइ
  गर्नु), chiplo ghasnu (चिप्लो
  घस्नु), khusAmad/chAkDI
  garnu (खुसामद/चाकडी गर्नु)

flattery, *n.* khusAmad
  (खुसामद), chAplusI (चापलुसी),
  jhUTo tAriph (भूटो तारिफ)

flavo(u)r, *n.* swAd (स्वाद),
  sugandh (सुगन्ध)

flaw, *n.* khoT (खोट), dosh (दोष)

flawless, *adj.* nirdosh (निर्दोष),
  chokho (चोखो)

flea, *n.* upiyAn̐ (उपियाँ)

flee, *v.* bhAgnu (भाग्नु)

flesh, *n. (body)* mAsu (मासु),
(fruit) gudI (गुदी),
(non-spiritual) sharIr (शरीर)

flexible, *adj.* lachkine (लच्किने),
lachilo (लचिलो)

flight, *n.* uDAn (उडान),

flirt, *n.* nAThI (नाठी),
nakhar mAulI (नखरमाउली)
v. prem gare jasto garnu
(प्रेम गरेजस्तो गर्नु), nakkalI
mAyA garnu (नक्कली माया
गर्नु), nakharA garnu (नखरा गर्नु)

float, *n.* pAnI mA utrane
wastu (पानीमा उत्रने वस्तु),
ryAphT (र्‍याफ्ट)
v. pAnI mA utranu (पानीमा
उत्रनु), tairanu (तैरानु)

flock, *n.* bathAn (बथान),
bagAl (बगाल)
v. jhumminu (झुम्मिनु),
jammA hunu (जम्मा हुनु)

flog, *v.* korrA hAnnu
(कोर्रा हान्नु), kuTnu (कुट्नु)

flood, *n.* bADhI (बाढी),
bhal (भल)
v. urlanu (उर्लनु),
bADhI Aunu (बाढी आउनु),
jalthal hunu (जलथल हुनु)

flooded, *adj.* bADhI Aeko
(बाढी आएको),
bADhI grast (बाढीग्रस्त)

floor, *n.* koThA ko bhuin̐
(कोठाको भुईं), talA (तला),
sadan (सदन),
bolne maukA (बोल्ने मौका)
v. pachhArnu (पछार्नु),
laDAunu (लडाउनु)

flora, *n.* wanaspati (वनस्पति)

florist, *n.* mAlI (माली), phUl ko
wyApArI (फूलको व्यापारी)

flour, *n.* pITho (पीठो),
An̐TA (आँटा), *(fine)* maidA
(मैदा), *(gram)* besan (बेसन)

flourish, *v.* maulAunu
(मौलाउनु), sapranu (सप्रनु),
phasTAunu (फस्टाउनु)

flow, *n.* prawAh (प्रवाह),
dhArA (धारा)
v. bagnu (बग्नु),
bahanu (वहनु)

flower, *n.* phUl (फूल),
pushpa (पुष्प)
v. phulnu (फुल्नु),
phakranu (फक्रनु)

flowerpot, *n.* gamlA (गमला)

flu, *n.* flu (फ्लु),
rughA, khokI, jwaro Adi
(रुघा, खोकी, ज्वरो आदि)

fluent, *adj.* pharra bolne (फर्र
बोल्ने), wAk paTu (वाक्पटु)

fluid, *n.* taral wastu (तरल
वस्तु), ras (रस),
adj. (state) taral (तरल)
asthAyI (अस्थायी)

flush, *n.* mukh ko lAlI
(मुखको लाली), kAnti (कान्ति)
v. bahanu (बहनु), mukh rAto
hunu (मुख रातो हुनु), *(bath)*
pAnI hAlera pakhAlnu
(पानी हालेर पखाल्नु)

flustered, *adj.* haDbaDAeko
(हडबडाएको),
hatpatAeko (हतपताएको)

flute, *n.* bAñsurI (बाँसुरी),
murlI (मुरली)

fly, *n.* jhiñgA (भिँगा),
mAkho (माखो)
v. uDnu (उड्नु),
akAsinu (अकासिनु)

foam, *n.* phIñj (फीँज),
(pad) gaddA (गद्दा)

fog, *n.* kuiro (कुइरो),
kuhiro (कुहिरो), hussu (हुस्सु)
v. dhamilyAunu
(धमिल्याउनु),
dhumminu (धुम्मिनु)

foggy, *adj.* kuhiro lAgeko
(कुहिरो लागेको),
kuhiro le DhAkeko
(कुहिरोले ढाकेको)

fold, *n. (sheep)* khor (खोर),
(herd) bathAn (बथान),
(cloth) mujA (मुजा)
v. paTyAnunu (पट्याउनु),
moDnu (मोड्नु)

folk, *n. (colloq.)* sAthI (साथी)
adj. jAti (जाति), jan (जन),

lok (लोक)

folklore, *n.* jan shruti
(जनश्रुति)

folk music, *n.* lok sañgIt
(लोकसंगीत)

folk song, *n.* lok gIt (लोकगीत)

follow, *v.* pachhi lAgnu
(पछिलाग्नु),
pachhyAunu (पछ्याउनु),
lakheTnu (लखेट्नु),
(order) mAnnu (मान्नु)

follower, *n.* samarthak
(समर्थक), anugAmI (अनुगामी)

fond, *adj.* mAyA garne
(माया गर्ने), Asakta (आसक्त)

fondle, *v.* sum sumyAunu
(सुमसुम्याउनु), musArnu (मुसार्नु)

food, *n.* khAne kurA (खानेकुरा),
khAnA (खाना)

foodstuff, *n.* khAne kurA
(खानेकुरा),
khAdya wastu (खाद्यवस्तु)

fool, *n./adj.* mUrkh (मूर्ख),
bekuph (बेकुफ)

foolish, *adj.* mUrkh (मूर्ख),
hussU (हुस्सू),
nAsamajh (नासमझ)

foot, *n.* pAu (पाउ), khuTTA
(खुट्टा), *(step)* kadam (कदम),
pAilA (पाइला), *(hill)* phedI
(फेदी), *(tree)* phed (फेद),
(measure) phuT (फुट)
v. tirnu (तिर्नु)

football, *n.* bhakuNDo
(भकुण्डो), *(Am.)* sakar (सकर)

footpath, *n.* peTI (पेटी),
goreTo (गोरेटो)

footprint, *n.* pAilA (पाइला),
pad chinha (पदचिन्ह)

footstep, *n.* kadam (कदम)

footwear, *n.* juttA (जुत्ता)

for, *prep.* lAI (लाई),
lAgi (लागि), nimti (निम्ति)
conj. kinaki (किनकि)

forbid, *v.* roknu (रोक्नु),
manAhI garnu (मनाही गर्नु)

forbidden, *adj.* manAhI
garieko (मनाही गरिएको)

force, *n.* bal (बल), shakti
(शक्ति), *(mil.)* senA (सेना)
v. jor lagAunu (जोर लगाउनु),
bal/kar garnu (बल/कर गर्नु)

forearm, *n.* pAkhurA (पाखुरा),
hAt (हात)

forefinger, *n.* chor auñlA
(चोरऔंला)

forecast, *n.* bhawishya wANI
(भविष्यवाणी), anumAn (अनुमान)
v. bhawishya wANI garnu
(भविष्यवाणी गर्नु)

forefather, *n.* purkhA (पुर्खा),
pUrwaj (पूर्वज)

forehead, *n.* nidhAr (निधार),
purpuro (पुर्पुरो)

foreign, *adj.* wideshI (विदेशी),
birAno (बिरानो)

foreign country, *n.* widesh
(विदेश), pardesh (परदेश)

foreigner, *n.* wideshI (विदेशी),
pardeshI (परदेशी)

foremost, *adj.* sab bhandA
pahilo (सबभन्दा पहिलो),
agADi ko (अगाडिको)

forest, *n.* ban (बन), jañgal (जंगल)

forever, *adv.* hameshA ko lAgi
(हमेशाको लागि),
sadhain (सधैं), sadA (सदा)

forfeit, *v.* gumAunu (गुमाउनु),
japhat garnu (जफत गर्नु)
n. japhatI (जफती)

forgery, *n.* kirte (किर्ते),
phareb (फरेब)

forget, *v.* birsanu (बिर्सनु),
bhulnu (भुल्नु)

forgetful, *adj.* besudhI (बेसुधी),
birsane (बिर्सने),
bhulakkaD (भुलक्कड)

forgive, *v.* mAph/kshamA
garnu (माफ/क्षमा गर्नु)

fork, *n.* *(utensil)* kAñTA (काँटा),
(snake) jibro (जिब्रो), *(tree, leg)*
kAp (काप), *(road)* dobATo (दोबाटो)
v. hAñgA hAlnu (हाँगा हाल्नु),
chhuTTinu (छुट्टिनु)

form, *n.* AkAr (आकार), rUp (रूप),
(office) phArAm (फाराम)
v. rachnu (रच्नु), banAunu
(बनाउनु), DhAlnu (ढाल्नु),
hunu (हुनु), bannu (बन्नु)

formal, *adj.* niyamAnusAr (नियमानुसार), aupchArik (औपचारिक)

formality, *n.* aupchAriktA (औपचारिकता), wyawahAr (व्यवहार)

former, *adj.* aghi ko (अघिको), bhUt pUrwa (भूतपूर्व), sAbik (साबिक)

formerly, *adv.* uhile (उहिले), paile paile (पैले पैले)

formidable, *adj.* bhayaṅkar (भयङ्कर), bhayAnak (भयानक)

fort, *n.* killA (किल्ला), gaDh (गढ)

forthcoming, *adj.* AgAmI (आगामी), Auṅdo (आउँदो)

fortitude, *n.* dhairya (धैर्य), sahishNutA (सहिष्णुता)

fortnight, *n.* chaudha din (चौध दिन), paksha (पक्ष)

fortress, *n.* killA (किल्ला), gaDh (गढ)

fortunate, *adj.* bhAgya mAnI (भाग्यमानी), bhAgya shAlI (भाग्यशाली)

fortunately, *adv.* bhAgya was (भाग्यवश)

fortune, *n.* bhAgya (भाग्य), takdIr (तकदीर)

fortune teller, *n.* jyotishI (ज्योतिषी)

forty, *n.* chAlIs (चालीस)

forum, *n.* mañch (मञ्च), sabhA sthal (सभास्थल)

forward, *adj.* agADi ko (अगाडिको), *adv.* agADi (अगाडि), aghil tira (अघिल्तिर), *v.* baDhnu/baDhAunu (बढ्नु/बढाउनु), chalAn garnu (चलान गर्नु)

foster, *v.* pAlnu (पाल्नु), hurkAunu (हुर्काउनु)

foster parents, *n.* pAlne bAbu AmA (पाल्ने बाबुआमा)

foul, *adj.* durgandhI (दुर्गन्धी), mailo (मैलो), galat (गलत)

found, *v.* pAyo (पायो), sthApanA garnu (स्थापना गर्नु)

foundation, *n.* jag (जग), samsthApan (संस्थापन)

founder, *n.* samsthApak (संस्थापक)

fountain, *n.* jharnA (झर्ना), phohrA (फोहरा)

four, *n.* chAr (चार), chaukA (चौका)

four-footed, *adj.* chAr khuTTe (चारखुट्टे)

fourth, *adj.* chArauṅ (चारौँ), chautho (चौथो)

fowl, *n.* kukhurA (कुखुरा)

fox, *n.* phyAuro (फ्याउरो), *v.* chalAkI garnu (चलाकी गर्नु), chhalnu (छल्नु)

fraction, *n.* amsh (अंश),
  khaND (खण्ड)

fracture, *n.* bhang (भङ्ग)
  v. bhAnchinu (भाँचिनु),
  TuTnu (टुट्नु)

fragment, *n.* TukrA (टुक्रा),
  khaND (खण्ड)

fragmentation, *n.* wikhaNDan
  (विखण्डन)

fragrant, *adj.* sugandhit
  (सुगन्धित),
  bAsnA Aune (बास्ना आउने)

frame, *n.* gherA (घेरा),
  (door) chaukhaT (चौखट),
  chaukas (चौकस),
  phrem (फ्रेम)
  v. rachnu (रच्नु),
  banAunu (बनाउनु)

frank, *adj.* pharAsilo (फरासिलो),
  khulast (खुलस्त),
  spashT waktA (स्पष्टवक्ता)

frankly, *adv.* khulast sanga
  (खुलस्तसँग), khulera (खुलेर)

fraternal, *adj.* bhAi chArA ko
  (भाइचाराको), dAju bhAi jasto
  (दाजुभाइजस्तो),
  bhrAtritwa purN (भातृत्वपूर्ण)

fraternity, *n.* bhAi chArA
  (भाइचारा), bhrAtritwa (भ्रातृत्व),
  (orgn.) samAj (समाज)

fraud, *n.* dhokA (धोका),
  chhal (छल), kapaT (कपट)

freak, *n.* lahaD (लहड),

taranga (तरङ्ग)

free, *adj.* swatantra (स्वतन्त्र),
  AjAd (आजाद),
  phukkA (फुक्का)
  v. mukta/rihA hunu
  (मुक्त/रिहा हुनु),
  chhuTnu (छुट्नु), chhuTkArA
  dinu (छुट्कारा दिनु)

freedom, *n.* swatantratA
  (स्वतन्त्रता), AjAdI (आजादी)

freely, *adv.* swatantra rUp le
  (स्वतन्त्र रूपले)

free of cost, *adj.* sittai (सित्तै),
  binA mUlya (बिनामूल्य),
  nihshulk (निःशुल्क)

freeze, *v.* jamnu (जम्नु),
  kaThAngrinu (कठाङ्ग्रिनु)

freight, *n.* mAl DhuwAnI
  bhADA (मालढुवानी भाडा),
  DhuwAnI (ढुवानी)

freight train, *n.* mAl gADI
  (मालगाडी)

frequent, *adj.* barAbar/
  bArambAr bhai Aeko
  (बराबर/बारम्बार भइ आएको)

frequently, *adv.* gharI gharI
  (घरीघरी),
  bArambar (बारम्बार)

fresh, *adj.* tAjA (ताजा)

fret, *v.* piralnu (पिरल्नु),
  jharkinu (झर्किनु)

friction, *n.* ragaD (रगड),
  gharshaN (घर्षण)

Friday, *n.* shukra wAr (शुक्रवार)

friend, *n.* sAthI (साथी),
mitra (मित्र)

friendly, *adj.* milan sAr
(मिलनसार), mitrawat (मित्रवत्)

friendship, *n.* mitratA (मित्रता),
maitrI (मैत्री), dostI (दोस्ती)

frighten, *v.* tarsAunu (तर्साउनु)

frog, *n.* bhyAguto (भ्यागुतो)

from, *prep.* bATa (बाट),
dekhi (देखि)

front, *adj.* agADi ko (अगाडिको)
n. morchA (मोर्चा)

frontier, *n.* simAnA (सिमाना),
sImAnt (सीमान्त)

frost, *n.* tusAro (तुसारो),
pAlA (पाला)

frostbite, *n.* hiuṅ le khAeko
ghAu (हिउँले खाएको घाउ)

frugal, *adj.* kiphAyatI
(किफायती), kanjus (कन्जुस)

fruit, *n.* phal (फल),
phal phUl (फलफूल),
(result) natIjA (नतीजा),
pariNAm (परिणाम)
v. phal lAgnu (फल लाग्नु)

fruitful, *adj.* lAbh dAyak
(लाभदायक),
phal dAyak (फलदायक)

frustrate, *v.* nirAsh/hatotsAh
garAunu (निराश/हतोत्साह
गराउनु)

frustrated, *adj.* nirAsh

(निराश), hatAs (हतास)

fry, *v.* bhuTnu (भुट्नु),
tArnu (तार्नु)

fuel, *n.* indhan (इन्धन)
v. dAurA/indhan hAlnu
(दाउरा/इन्धन हाल्नु)

fugitive, *n.* bhaguwA (भगुवा),
pharAr (फरार)

fulfi(l)l, *v.* pUrA/tAmel garnu
(पूरा/तामेल गर्नु)

fulfil(l)ment, *n.* siddhi (सिद्धि),
tAmelI (तामेली), pUrti (पूर्ति)

full, *adj.* bharieko (भरिएको),
pUrN (पूर्ण), pUrA (पूरा)

fun, *n.* tamAsA (तमासा),
majA (मजा)

function, *n.* kAm (काम)

fund, *n.* kosh (कोष),
rakam (रकम)
v. kosh juTAunu (कोष जुटाउनु)

fundamental, *adj.* AdhAr bhUt
(आधारभूत), maulik (मौलिक)

funeral, *n.* malAmI (मलामी)

funnel, *n.* solI (सोली)

funny, *adj.* ramAilo (रमाइलो),
majA ko (मजाको),
hAṅso uThne (हाँसो उठ्ने)

fur, *n.* bhuwA (भुवा),
bhutlA (भुत्ला)

furious, *adj.* ris le chUr
(रिसले चूर), kruddha (क्रुद्ध)

furniture, *n.* Tebul, kurchI,
Adi (टेबुल, कुर्ची, आदि)

further, *adv.* para (पर),
agADi (अगाडि)
v. madat garnu (मदत गर्नु),
baDhAunu (बढाउनु)

fury, *n.* ris (रिस), krodh (क्रोध)

fuse, *n.* *(wire)* phyuj (फ्युज)
v. paglanu (पग्लनु),
galnu (गल्नु), joDinu (जोडिनु)

fuss, *n.* khalbal (खलबल),

kachiṅgal (कचिङ्गल)
v. pirnu (पिर्नु), pirolnu (पिरोल्नु)

fussy, *adj.* nATIkuTI garne
(नाटीकुटी गर्ने),
sagsage (सगसगे)

futile, *adj.* wyartha (व्यर्थ),
nirarthak (निरर्थक)

future, *n.* bhawishya (भविष्य),
(in future) AindA (आइन्दा)

G

gag, *n.* bujo (बुजो)
v. bujo lAunu (बुजो लाउनु),
bolna na dinu (बोल्न नदिनु)

gain, *n.* phAidA (फाइदा),
lAbh (लाभ)
v. phAidA/lAbh garnu
(फाइदा/लाभ गर्नु)

gainsay, *v.* wirodh garnu
(विरोध गर्नु),
kurA kATnu (कुरा काट्नु)

gait, *n.* chAl (चाल), gati (गति)

galaxy, *n.* AkAsh gaṅgA
(आकाशगङ्गा),
tArA puñj (तारापुञ्ज)

gale, *n.* AṅdhI (आँधी),
batAs (बतास)

gall, *n.* pitta (पित्त)

gallant, *adj.* bIr (वीर), sUro (सूरो)

gallery, *n.* baranDA (बरन्डा),
poTI (पोटी), *(art)* kalA
shAlA (कलाशाला),
gyAlarI (ग्यालरी)

gallon, *n.* *(measure, etc.)*
gyAlan (ग्यालन)

gallop, *n.* paiyAṅ (पैयाँ)
v. paiyAṅ mArnu (पैयाँ मार्नु),
chhiTo jAnu (छिटो जानु)

galore, *adj.* prachur (प्रचुर),
prashast (प्रशस्त)

gamble, *v.* jUwA khelnu
(जूवा खेल्नु),
bAjI thApnu (बाजी थाप्नु)

gambling, *n.* jUwA (जूवा)

gambler, *n.* juwADI (जुवाडी),
juwADe (जुवाडे),
bArha mAse (बाह्रमासे)

game, *n.* khel (खेल),
(*hunting*) shikAr (शिकार)

gamine, *n. (fem.)* dublI ra
Akarshak keTI
(दुब्ली र आकर्षक केटी),
keTA jhaiñ dhekhine keTI
(केटाभैं देखिने केटी)

gamut, *n.* sabai (सबै),
sampUrN amsh (सम्पूर्ण अंश)

gang, *n.* dal (दल), hUl (हूल)
v. hUl bAñdhnu (हूल बाँध्नु),
sAth dinu (साथ दिनु)

gap, *n.* chhidra (छिद्र),
khAlI ThAuñ (खाली ठाउँ)

garage, *n.* moTar kArkhAnA
(मोटर कारखाना),
gyArej (ग्यारेज)

garb, *n.* lugA (लुगा),
poshAk (पोशाक)
v. lugA lAunu (लुगा लाउनु)

garbage, *n.* phohar mailA
(फोहरमैला)

garden, *n.* bagaiñchA (बगैंचा),
bArI (बारी)

gardener, *n.* bagaiñche (बगैंचे),
mAlI (माली)

gargantuan, *adj.* wishAl
(विशाल), bhIm kAya (भीमकाय)

gargle, *v.* kullA garnu
(कुल्ला गर्नु)

garland, *n.* mAlA (माला),
v. mAlA lAi dinu
(माला लाइदिनु)

garlic, *n.* lasun (लसुन)

garment, *n.* lugA (लुगा),
poshAk (पोशाक)

gas, *n.* wAyu (वायु), gyAñs (ग्याँस)

gasbag, *n.* gaphI (गफी),
dherai bolne mAnchhe
(धेरै बोल्ने मान्छे)

gash, *n.* gahiro ghAu
(गहिरो घाउ)
v. gahiro ghAu pArnu
(गहिरो घाउ पार्नु)

gasoline, *n.* peTrol (पेट्रोल)

gasp, *v.* hAñphnu (हाँफ्नु),
swAñ swAñ garnu
(स्वाँ स्वाँ गर्नु)
n. dam (दम)

gastric, *adj.* peT ko (पेटको)

gate, *n.* DhokA (ढोका),
phATak (फाटक), dailo (दैलो)

gatecrasher, *n.* nimtA binA ko
pAhunA (निम्तिबिनाको
पाहुना), TikaT bina ko
darshak (टिकटबिनाको दर्शक)

gatekeeper, *n.* Dhoke (ढोके),
pAle (पाले)

gather, *v.* jammA garnu
(जम्मा गर्नु), thupArnu (थुपार्नु)

gathering, *n.* jamghaT (जमघट),
jamAt (जमात)

gaudy, *adj.* bhaDkilo (भड्किलो)

ga(u)ge, *n.* nApne DanDI
(नाप्ने डन्डी)
v. nApnu (नाप्नु)

gay, *adj.* ramAilo (रमाइलो),
khus (खुस), sam liṅgI (समलिङ्गी)

gaze, *n.* ek Tak ko herAi
(एकटकको हेराइ)
v. ek Tak hernu
(एकटक हेर्नु),
AṅkhA tarnu (आँखा तर्नु)

gazelle, *n.* sAno sundar hariN
(सानो सुन्दर हरिण)

gazette, *n.* rAj patra
(राजपत्र), gajeT (गजेट)

gear, *n.* sajjA (सज्जा), upkaraN
(उपकरण), dAṅtI wAl
chakkA (दाँतीवाल चक्का)
v. ghoDA kasnu (घोडा कस्नु),
sAj hAlnu (साज हाल्नु)

geese, *n.* rAj hAṅs harU
(राजहाँसहरू)

gem, *n.* ratna (रत्न), maNi (मणि)

gemini, *n.* mithun rAshi
(मिथुन राशि)

gender, *n.* liṅg (लिङ्ग)

general, *n.* jarNel (जर्नेल),
janral (जनरल)
adj. sAmAnya (सामान्य),
goswArA (गोस्वारा)

general knowledge, *n.*
sAmAnya gỹAn
(सामान्य ज्ञान)

general post office, *n.*
goswArA hulAk
(गोस्वारा हुलाक)

generation, *n.* pustA (पुस्ता),

waṃsh (वंश)

generosity, *n.* udArtA
(उदारता)
dAnshIltA (दानशीलता)

generous, *adj.* udAr (उदार),
dAnI (दानी)

genius, *n.* pratibhA (प्रतिभा),
pratibhA shAlI wyakti
(प्रतिभाशाली व्यक्ति)

gentle, *adj.* naram (नरम),
sajjan (सज्जन)

gentleman, *n.* bhalAdmI
(भलादमी), sajjan (सज्जन)

gently, *adv.* halukA dhaṅg le
(हलुका ढङ्गले), prem pUrwak
(प्रेमपूर्वक) sustarI (सुस्तरी)

genuine, *adj.* sakkalI (सक्कली),
asalI (असली)

geodesy, *n.* bhU gaNit
(भूगणित)

geography, *n.* bhUgol (भूगोल)

geology, *n.* bhU garbh shAstra
(भूगर्भशास्त्र)

geometry, *n.* rekhA gaNit
(रेखागणित), jyAmiti (ज्यामिति)

georgette, *n.* pAtalo resamI
kapaDa (पातलो रेसमी कपडा)
jarjeT (जर्जेट)

geriatrics, *n.* buDhyaulI rog
sambandhI shAstra
(बुढ्यौली रोगसम्बन्धी शास्त्र)

germ, *n.* kITANu (कीटाणु),
aṅkur (अँकुर)

germinate, *v.* umranu (उम्रनु),
TusAunu (टुसाउनु)

gerrymander, *v.* chunAu mA
anuchit Dhaṅg le phAidA
uThaunu (चुनाउमा अनुचित
ढङ्गले फाइदा उठाउनु)

gestation, *n.* garbh dharaN
(गर्भधारण)

gesticulate, *v.* hAw bhAw
garnu (हावभाव गर्नु)

gesture, *n.* ishArA (इशारा),
hAw bhAw (हावभाव),
cheshtA (चेष्टा)
v. hAw bhAw garnu
(हावभाव गर्नु)

get, *v.* pAunu (पाउनु),
lyAunu (ल्याउनु)

get away, *v.* bhAgnu (भाग्नु)

get out of, *v.* haTnu (हट्नु),
bhAgnu (भाग्नु)

get ready, *v.* tayAr hunu
(तयार हुनु)

get-together, *n.* sAmAjik
jamghaT (सामाजिक जमघट)

get up, *v.* uThnu (उठ्नु)

gha(u)t, *n.* ghAT (घाट)

ghetto, *n.* *(town)* garib bastI
(गरिब बस्ती)

ghost, *n.* bhUt (भूत),
pret (प्रेत)

giant, *n.* dAnaw (दानव),
daitya (दैत्य),
aglo mAnis (अग्लो मानिस)

adj. ThUlo (ठूलो),
baDemAn ko (बडेमानको)

giddiness, *n.* riṅgaTA (रिंगटा),
chakkar (चक्कर)

gift, *n.* koselI (कोसेली),
uphAr (उपहार), dAn (दान)

gigantic *adj.* jyAdai ThUlo
(ज्यादै ठूलो), wishAl (विशाल)

giggle, *v.* swAṅg pArera
hAnsñu (स्वाङ्ग पारेर हाँस्नु)
n. swAṅge hAñso
(स्वाङ्गे हाँसो)

ginger, *n.* aduwA (अदुवा)

girdle, *n.* peTI (पेटी),
paTukA (पटुका)
v. bernu (बेर्नु), parikramA
garnu (परिक्रमा गर्नु)

girl, *n.* keTI (केटी),
ThiTI (ठिटी), kanyA (कन्या)

girlfriend, *n.* premIkA (प्रेमिका)

gist, *n.* sAr (सार),
tAtparya (तात्पर्य)

give, *v.* dinu (दिनु),
sumpanu (सुम्पनु)

give and take, *n.* AdAn
pradAn (आदानप्रदान),
lenA denA (लेनादेना)

give away, *n. (bus.)* sittai
dieko (सित्तै दिएको)
adj. (inf.) ati sasto
(अति सस्तो)

give away, *v.* dinu (दिनु),
sumpanu (सुम्पनु)

give in, v. Atma samarpaN garnu (आत्मसमर्पण गर्नु)

give out, v. siddhinu (सिद्धिनु)

give up, v. chhoDnu (छोड्नु)

give way, v. dabAb mA hAr mAnnu (दबाबमा हार मान्नु)

glacier, n. him nadI (हिमनदी)

glad, adj. khush (खुश)

glance, n. jhalak (झलक), drishTi pAt (दृष्टिपात) v. pulukka hernu (पुलुक्क हेर्नु)

gland, n. girkhA (गिर्खा)

glare, n. Talak (टलक), tej (तेज) v. Talkanu (टल्कनु), ek Tak hernu (एकटक हेर्नु)

glass, n. (material) kAñch (काँच), sisA (सिसा), (utensil) gilAs (गिलास), (mirror) ainA (ऐना)

glaucoma, n. (med.) drishTi kam hune rog (दृष्टि कम हुने रोग)

glaze, n. Talak (टलक) v. TalkAunu (टल्काउनु)

gleam, n. chamak (चमक), dhip dhipe ujyAlo (धिपधिपे उज्यालो)

glen, n. upatyakA (उपत्यका) v. chamkanu (चम्कनु)

glide, v. chiplanu (चिप्लनु), uDnu (उड्नु)

glimpse, n. jhalak (झलक) v. jhalakka hernu (झलक्क हेर्नु)

glitter, v. chamkanu (चम्कनु), Talkanu (टल्कनु)

globe, n. prithwI (पृथ्वी), golo wastu (गोलो वस्तु)

globetrotter, n. wibhinna desh ko yAtra gardai hiñdne (विभिन्न देशको यात्रा गर्दै हिंड्ने)

gloom, n. andhkAr (अन्धकार), añdhyAro (अँध्यारो)

gloomy, adj. malin (मलिन), añdhyAro (अँध्यारो)

glorify, v. guNgAn garnu (गुणगान गर्नु)

glorious, adj. tejaswI (तेजस्वी), mahAn (महान)

glory, n. yash (यश), jas (जस) pratAp (प्रताप), gauraw (गौरव)

glove, n. panjA (पन्जा)

glow, n. jhalak (झलक), chamak (चमक) v. Talkanu (टल्कनु), chamkanu (चम्कनु)

glow-worm, n. jUn kIrI (जूनकीरी)

glue, n. guñd (गुँद), sares (सरेस)

glutton, n. dherai khAne (धेरै खाने), khanchuwA (खन्चुवा)

go, v. jAnu (जानु), hiñDnu (हिंड्नु), bATo lAgnu (बाटो लाग्नु)

go down, *v.* orlanu (ओर्लनु),
jharnu (झर्नु)

go off, *v.* paDkanu (पड्कनु),
phuTnu (फुट्नु)

go under, *v.* nishphal/parAjit
hunu (निष्फल/पराजित हुनु),
Dubnu (डुब्नु)

goal, *n.* uddeshya (उद्देश्य),
lakshya (लक्ष्य)

goat, *n. (mas.)* boko (बोको),
bokA (बोका),
(fem.) bAkhrI (बाख्री),
(castrated) khasI (खसी)

gobble, *v.* khapAkhap khAnu
(खपाखप खानु),
hasurnu (हसुर्नु)

go-between, *n.* bIch ko
mAnchhe (बीचको मान्छे),
lamI (लमी)

God/god, *n.* Ishwar (ईश्वर),
parmeshwar (परमेश्वर),
dewtA (देवता)

goddess, *n.* dewI (देवी)

godown, *n.* godAm (गोदाम)

go-getter, *n.* udyogI (उद्योगी),
sAhasI wyakti (साहसी व्यक्ति)

goggles, *n.* ghAm mA lAune
kAlo chasmA (घाममा लाउने
कालो चस्मा)

goitre, *n.* gAňD (गाँड),
galgaND (गलगण्ड)

gold, *n.* sun (सुन)

golden, *adj.* sunaulo (सुनौलो)

goldsmith, *n.* sunAr (सुनार),
bAňDA (बाँडा)

gonorrh(o)ea, *n.* sujAk
(सुजाक), dhAtu rog (धातुरोग)

good, *adj.* asal (असल),
rAmro (राम्रो), bhalo (भलो)
n. kalyaN (कल्याण),
bhalAi (भलाइ)

goodbye, *n.* namaste(नमस्ते),
bidA (बिदा)

goods, *n.* mAl (माल),
sAmAn (सामान)

goose, *n.* rAj hAňs (राजहाँस)

gorge, *n.* khoňch (खोंच)

gorgeous, *adj.* bhawya (भव्य),
bhaDkilo (भड्किलो)

go-slow, *v.* wirodh janAuna
mand gati mA kAm garnu
(विरोध जनाउन मन्द गतिमा
काम गर्नु)

gossip, *n.* gaph (गफ),
bakbake (बकबके)
v. gaph garnu (गफ गर्नु),
gaph chuTnu (गफ चुट्नु)

gourd, *n.* laukA (लौका)

gout, *n.* bAth (बाथ),
bAth rog (बाथरोग)

govern, *v.* shAsan chalAunu
(शासन चलाउनु),
rAj kAj garnu
(राजकाज गर्नु)

government, *n.* sarkAr
(सरकार), rAj (राज)

governor, n. (state) rAjya pAl
(राज्यपाल),
(bank) gabharnar (गभर्नर)

gown, n. phariyA (फरिया),
lahaṅgA (लहङ्गा)

grab, v. khosnu (खोस्नु)

grace, n. kripA (कृपा),
anugraha (अनुग्रह)
v. shobhA baDhAunu (शोभा
बढाउनु), pratishThit garnu
(प्रतिष्ठित गर्नु)

graceful, adj. rAmro (राम्रो),
manohArI (मनोहारी)

gracious, adj. dayAlu (दयालु),
kripAlu (कृपालु)

grade, n. darjA (दर्जा),
mUlya (मूल्य)
v. darjA chhuTTyAunu
(दर्जा छुट्ट्याउनु)

gradually, adv. ali ali garI
(अलि अलि गरी),
kramik rUp le (क्रमिक रूपले)

graduate, n. snAtak (स्नातक)

graffitti, n. bhittA mA koriekA
chitra wA lekh (भित्तामा
कोरिएका चित्र वा लेख)

graft, n. (plant) kalam (कलम),
(bribe) ghUs (घूस)
v. kalam sArnu (कलम सार्नु)

grain, n. anna (अन्न),
anAj (अनाज)

gram, n. chanA (चना),
(measure) grAm (ग्राम)

graminivorous, adj. ghAṅs
khAne jantu (घाँस खाने जन्तु),
triNAhArI (तृणाहारी)

grammar, n. wyAkaraN
(व्याकरण)

granary, n. bhakArI (भकारी),
bhaNDAr (भण्डार)

grand, adj. bhawya (भव्य),
ThUlo (ठूलो)

granddaughter, n. nAtinI
(नातिनी)

grandeur, n. raunak (रौनक),
sAn (सान)

grandfather, n. bAje (बाजे)

grandmother, n. bajai (बजै)

grandson, n. nAti (नाति)

grant, n. anudAn (अनुदान),
dAn (दान)
v. manjur garnu (मन्जुर गर्नु),
anudAn dinu (अनुदान दिनु)

granule, n. dAnA (दाना)

grape, n. aṅgur (अङ्गुर),
dAkh (दाख)

grapevine, n. aṅgur ko laharA
(अङ्गुरको लहरा), (fig.) hallA
(हल्ला), ghuiro (घुइरो)

grasp, n. muThI (मुठी),
chaṅgul (चङ्गुल)
v. pakranu (पक्रनु),
samAunu (समाउनु)

grass, n. ghAṅs (घाँस)

grasshopper, n. phaTeṅgro
(फटेङ्ग्रो)

grateful, *adj.* AbharI (आभारी), guN mAnne (गुण मान्ने)

gratify, *v.* khusI pArnu (खुसी पार्नु), santushT pArnu (सन्तुष्ट पार्नु)

gratis, *adv.* sittai (सित्तै), muphta (मुफ्त)

gratitude, *n.* AbhAr (आभार), kritagÿatA (कृतज्ञता)

grave, *adj.* gambhIr (गम्भीर) *n.* chihAn (चिहान)

gravity, *n.* gurutwAkarshaN (गुरुत्वाकर्षण), gambhIrtA (गम्भीरता), mahattwa (महत्त्व)

gravy, *n.* ledo (लेदो), jhol (भोल)

graze, *v.* charnu (चर्नु), charAunu (चराउनु)

grease, *n.* chillo (चिल्लो), boso (बोसो) *v.* chillo pArnu (चिल्लो पार्नु), *(office)* ghUs khwAunu/dinu (घूस ख्वाउनु/दिनु)

greasy, *adj.* chillo (चिल्लो)

great, *adj.* ThUlo (ठूलो), mahAn (महान)

great granddaughter, *n.* panAtinI (पनातिनी)

great grandfather, *n.* jiju bAje (जिजु बाजे)

great grandmother, *n.* jiju bajai (जिजु बजै)

great grandson, *n.* panAti (पनाति)

greatly, *adv.* besarI (बेसरी), bichhaTTa (बिच्छट्ट)

greatness, *n.* mahAntA (महानता), mahattwa (महत्त्व)

greed, *n.* lobh (लोभ), lAlach (लालच)

greedy, *adj.* lobhI (लोभी), lAlchI (लालची)

green, *adj.* hariyo (हरियो)

greenhouse, *n.* biruwA ghar (बिरुवाघर)

greenery, *n.* hariyo pariyo (हरियोपरियो), sAg pAt (सागपात), hariyAlI (हरियाली)

greet, *v.* abhinandan/salAm garnu (अभिनन्दन/सलाम गर्नु)

greetings, *n.* bandanA (बन्दना), shubh kAmnA (शुभकामना)

grenade, *n.* hAt golA (हातगोला), hAte bam (हाते बम)

grey, *adj.* kharAnI raṅga ko (खरानी रङ्गको), *(sky)* dhumma (धुम्म), *(hair)* phuleko (फुलेको)

grief, *n.* duhkh (दुःख), shok (शोक), surtA (सुर्ता)

grievance, *n.* ujUr (उजूर), gunAso (गुनासो)

grieve, *v.* dhukh mAnnu (दुःख मान्नु), shok garnu (शोक गर्नु)

griffin, n. (myth.) chIl ko TAuko ra pakheTA, simha ko sharIr bhaeko paurANik jantu (चीलको टाउको र पखेटा, सिंहको शरीर भएको पौराणिक जन्तु)

grill(e), n. gril (ग्रिल)

grim, adj. bhayAnak (भयानक), wikaT (विकट), udAs (उदास)

grind, v. piňdhnu (पिँध्नु), dalnu (दल्नु)

grip, n. pakaD (पकड) v. pakranu (पक्रनु), joD le samAtnu (जोडले समात्नु)

groan, v. khyAr khyAr garnu (ख्यारख्यार गर्नु), sAno swar mA runu karAunu (सानो स्वरमा रुनु कराउनु)

grocer, n. kirAnA pasale (किराना पसले)

grocery, n. kirAnA pasal (किराना पसल)

groom, n. (horse) sais (सइस), dulahA (दुलहा) v. tAlim dinu (तालिम दिनु), tayAr pArnu (तयार पार्नु)

groove, n. khoňch (खोंच), kholsA (खोल्सा) v. koparnu (कोपर्नु)

gross, n. bArha darjan (बाह्र दर्जन) adj. ThUlo (ठूलो), ghor (घोर)

ground, n. jamIn (जमीन), maidAn (मैदान), bhuiň (भुईं)

groundless, adj. nirAdhAr (निराधार)

groundnut, n. badAm (बदाम)

groundwork, n. AdhAr (आधार)

group, n. DaphphA (डफ्फा), samUh (समूह), dal (दल) v. dal bAňdhnu (दल बाँध्नु), juTnu (जुट्नु)

grow, v. umranu (उम्रनु), baDhnu (बढ्नु)

growl, v. jharkanu (झर्कनु), ňAr ňur garnu (झरदुर गर्नु)

grudge, n. DAh (डाह), Ikh (ईख) v. DAh/Ikh garnu (डाह/ईख गर्नु)

grumble, v. asantosh dekhAunu (असन्तोष देखाउनु), gangan garnu (गनगन गर्नु)

guarantee, n. gyAraNTI (ग्यारण्टी) v. gyAraNTI garnu (ग्यारण्टी गर्नु)

guard, n. pAle (पाले), paharedAr (पहरेदार) v. rakhwArI garnu (रखवारी गर्नु), paharA dinu (पहरा दिनु)

guardian, n. abhibhAwak (अभिभावक), rakhwAlA (रखवाला)

guava, n. ambA (अम्बा)

guess, n. andAj (अन्दाज), aDkal (अड्कल), lakh (लख) v. andAj/aDkal garnu (अन्दाज/अड्कल गर्नु), lakh kATnu (लख काट्नु)

guest, *n.* pAhunA (पाहुना), atithi (अतिथि)

guide, *n.* mArg darshak (मार्ग दर्शक), pradarshak (प्रदर्शक) *v.* bATo dekhAunu (बाटो देखाउनु), nirdeshan dinu (निर्देशन दिनु)

guilt, *n.* dosh (दोष), aprAdh (अपराध)

guilty, *adj.* doshI (दोषी), aprAdhI (अपराधी)

guinea, *n.* ginnI (गिन्नी)

guinea pig, *n.* chaugaDA (चौगडा)

guitar, *n.* gitAr (गितार)

gulp, *n.* gAňs (गाँस), ghuTko (घुट्को) *v.* nilnu (निल्नु), ghuTkAunu (घुट्काउनु)

gum, *n. (tooth)* gijA (गिजा), *(glue)* khoTo (खोटो), guňd (गुँद)

v. guňd lAunu (गुँद लाउनु)

gun, *n.* banduk (बन्दुक), top (तोप)

gunpowder, *n.* bArUd (बारूद)

guru, *n.* guru (गुरु), shikshak (शिक्षक)

gust, *n.* hAwA ko jhokkA (हावाको भोक्का)

gut, *n.* AndrA bhuňDI (आन्द्राभुँडी)

gutter, *n.* kulo (कुलो), rachhAn (रछान)

gymnasium, *n.* wyAyAm shAlA (व्यायामशाला)

gymnast, *n.* wyAyAmI (व्यायामी), kasratI (कसरती)

gymnastics, *n.* kasrat (कसरत), wyAyAm (व्यायाम)

gyn(a)ecologist, *n.* strI rog wisheshgỹa (स्त्रीरोग विशेषज्ञ)

gyn(a)ecology, *n.* strI rog shAstra (स्त्रीरोग शास्त्र)

H

habit, *n.* bAnI (बानी)

habitable, *adj.* basna/bAs yogya (बस्न/बासयोग्य)

habitual, *adj.* bAnI pareko (बानी परेको), niyamit (नियमित), palke (पल्के)

habituated, *adj.* bAnI pareko (बानी परेको), abhyast (अभ्यस्त)

hag, *n.* bUDhI AimAI (बूढी आइमाई), boksI (बोक्सी)

haggle, *v.* jhagaDA garnu (झगडा गर्नु), mol molAi

garnu (मोलमोलाइ गर्नु)

hail, *v.* namaskAr/swAgat garnu (नमस्कार/स्वागत गर्नु), asinA parnu (असिना पर्नु)

hail(stone), *n.* asinA (असिना)

hair, *n.* *(sing)* rauň (रौँ), *(head)* kapAl (कपाल), kesh (केश), *(pubic)* jAňThA (जाँठा), *(plant, insect)* jhus (भुस)

haircut, *n.* kapAl kaTAi (कपाल कटाइ)

hairdo, *n.* kesh sajjA (केश सज्जा)

hairpin, *n.* kapAl ko kAňTA (कपालको काँटा)

hair'sbreadth, *n.* dherai nikaT/kam (धेरै निकट/कम)

hairy, *adj.* dherai rauň bhaeko (धेरै रौँ भएको), bhutle (भुत्ले)

hale, *adj.* swasth (स्वस्थ), tandurust (तन्दुरुस्त)

half, *n.* AdhA (आधा)

half-brother, *n.* sautinI dAju/bhAi (सौतिनी दाजु/भाइ)

half-hearted, *adj.* kam AňTilo (कम आँटिलो)

half mast, *adj.* *(at)* *(flag)* AdhA jhukeko (आधा भुकेको)

half-moon, *n.* ardh chandra (अर्धचन्द्र), ashTamI ko chandramA (अष्टमीको चन्द्रमा)

half past, *n.* sADhe (साढे)

half-time, *n.* madhyAntar

(मध्यान्तर)

hall, *n.* baiThak (बैठक), dalAn (दलान), hal (हल)

hallmark, *n.* *(gold, silver)* nambarI sun chAňdI (नम्बरी सुन चाँदी)

halo, *n.* tej maNDal (तेजमण्डल), prabhA maNDal (प्रभामण्डल)

halt, *n.* bAs (बास), bisaunI (बिसौनी), mukAm (मुकाम) *v.* roknu (रोक्नु), aDnu (अड्नु), aDAunu (अडाउनु)

ham, *n.* *(pig)* jAňgh (जाँघ), sapeTo (सपेटो)

hamlet, *n.* gAuň (गाउँ)

hammer, *n.* ghan (घन), hathauDA (हथौडा) *v.* Thoknu (ठोक्नु)

hammock, *n.* jholuňgo (भोलुङ्गो), dolA (दोला), DolA (डोला)

hamper, *v.* bAdhA pArnu (बाधा पार्नु)

hand, *n.* hAt (हात), *(clock)* suI (सुई), *(by hand)* haste (हस्ते)

hand in hand, *adv.* hAtemAlo (हातेमालो)

handbag, *n.* hAte byAg (हाते ब्याग)

handbill, *n.* parchA (पर्चा)

handbook, *n.* nirdeshikA (निर्देशिका)

handcuffs, *n.* hatkaDI (हतकडी)

handful, *n.* muTThI bhar (मुट्ठीभर)

handicap, *n.* asuwidhA (असुविधा), bAdhA (बाधा)

handicapped, *adj.* apAṅg (अपाङ्ग)

handicraft, *n.* hast kalA (हस्तकला)

handout, *n.* parchA (पर्चा)

handover, *v.* sumpanu (सुम्पनु), bujhAunu (बुझाउनु)

handkerchief, *n.* rumAl (रुमाल)

handle, *n.* bIṇD (बीँड), hyANDal (ह्याण्डल) *v.* hAt lAunu (हात लाउनु), samAtnu (समात्नु), *(bus., etc.)* prabandh garnu (प्रबन्ध गर्नु)

handmaid, *n.* nokarnI (नोकर्नी)

hand-picked, *adj.* rAmrarI chhAnieko (राम्ररी छानिएको)

handsome, *adj.* rAmro (राम्रो), sundar (सुन्दर)

hand-to-mouth, *adj.* kamAune bittikai kharcha garnu parne (कमाउने बित्तिकै खर्च गर्नु पर्ने)

handwriting, *n.* hastAkshar (हस्ताक्षर)

handy, *adj.* sajilo (सजिलो)

hang, *v.* jhuNDyAunu (झुण्ड्याउनु), phAnsI dinu (फाँसी दिनु), jhuNDinu (झुण्डिनु), jhumirahnu (झुमिरहनु)

hang around, *v.* dherai TADhA na jAnu (धेरै टाढा नजानु)

hang up, *v.* kurA sake pachhi Teliphon rAknu (कुरा सकेपछि टेलिफोन राख्नु)

hanger, *n.* lugA Adi jhuNDyAune hyAṅgar (लुगा आदि झुण्ड्याउने ह्याङ्गर)

hangover, *n.* raksI Adi ko pachhi samma rahane asar (रक्सी आदिको पछिसम्म रहने असर)

hanky, *n.* paket rumAl (पकेट रुमाल)

hanky-panky, *n.* gol mAl (गोलमाल)

haphazar, *adj.* jathA bhAbI (जथाभावी), laTar paTar (लटरपटर)

hapless, *adj.* abhAgI (अभागी)

happen, *v.* hunu (हुनु)

happily, *adv.* khushI le (खुशीले), khusI sAth (खुशीसाथ)

happiness, *n.* khushI (खुशी), sukh (सुख), Anand (आनन्द)

happy, *adj.* khush (खुश)

harass, *v.* satAunu (सताउनु), pirolnu (पिरोल्नु)

harbinger, *n.* aguwA (अगुवा)

harbo(u)r, *n.* bandar gAh (बन्दरगाह) *v.* sharaN/Ashraya dinu (शरण/आश्रय दिनु)

hard, *adj.* sArho (साह्रो), kaDA (कडा), kaThin (कठिन)

hard and fast, *adj.* kaDA (कडा), sakht (सख्त)

hard cash, *n.* nagad (नगद)

hard-headed, *adj.* wyAwhArik (व्यावहारिक)

hardliner, *n.* kaTTar (कट्टर), siddhAnt wAdI (सिद्धान्तवादी)

hard-pressed, *adj.* kAm baDhI tara paisA, samaya kam bhaeko (काम बढी तर पैसा, समय कम भएको)

hardship, *n.* kashT (कष्ट), kaThinAi (कठिनाइ)

hardware, *n.* mesin ra dhAtu kA sAmAn harU (मेसिन र धातुका सामानहरू)

hardy, *adj.* baliyo (बलियो), majbUt (मजबूत)

hare, *n.* kharAyo (खरायो)

harem, *n.* janAnA ghar (जनानाघर), antahpur (अन्तःपुर)

harlot, *n.* weshyhAh (वेश्याः), raNDI (रण्डी)

harm, *n.* hAni (हानि), noksAn (नोक्सान) *v.* nAsnu (नास्नु), hAni puryAunu (हानि पुर्‍याउनु)

harmful, *adj.* hAni kArak (हानिकारक)

harmless, *adj.* hAni rahit (हानिरहित)

harmonious, *adj.* mildo (मिल्दो), mel khAne (मेलखाने)

harmony, *n.* mel (मेल), milAp (मिलाप)

harsh, *adj.* kaDA (कडा), kaThor (कठोर)

harvest, *n.* bAlI (बाली), bAlI nAlI (बालीनाली) *v.* bAlI bhitryAunu (बाली भित्र्याउनु)

hashish, *n.* chares (चरेस)

haste, *n.* hatAr (हतार), jaldI bAjI (जल्दीबाजी)

hasten, *v.* hatAr garnu (हतार गर्नु), hattArinu (हत्तारिनु)

hasty, *adj.* hatpate (हतपते), haDbaDe (हडबडे)

hat, *n.* Top (टोप)

hatch, *n.* jahAj ko DhokA (जहाजको ढोका) *v.* koralnu (कोरल्नु), challA/bachchA kADhnu (चल्ला/बच्चा काढ्नु)

hatchet, *n.* sAno bancharo (सानो बन्चरो)

hate, *n.* ghriNA (घृणा), ghIn (घीन) *v.* ghriNA garnu (घृणा गर्नु)

hatred, *n.* ghriNA (घृणा)

haughty, *adj.* ahaṅkArI (अहङ्कारी), ghamaNDI (घमण्डी)

haul, *v.* tAnnu (तान्नु), ghichchhyAunu (घिच्च्याउनु)

haunt, *v.* barAbar dimAg mA Aunu (बराबर दिमागमा आउनु), man mai basnu (मनमै बस्नु), man mA Airahnu (मनमा आइरहनु), tarsAunu (तर्साउनु)

have, *v./aux.* saṅga hunu (सँग हुनु), rAkhnu (राख्नु)

haven, *n.* Ashraya (आश्रय), sharaN (शरण)

havoc, *n.* winAsh (विनाश), nAsh (नाश)

hawk, *n.* bAj (बाज)

hawker, *n.* pherI wAlA (फेरीवाला)

hay, *n.* parAl (पराल), sukeko ghAṅs (सुकेको घाँस)

haystack, *n.* parAl ko kunyU (परालको कुन्यू)

hazard, *n.* saṅkaT (सङ्कट), khatarA (खतरा)

hazardous, *adj.* khatar nAk (खतरनाक), hAni kArak (हानिकारक)

haze, *n.* tuwAṅlo (तुवाँलो)

he, *pron.* tyo (त्यो), U (ऊ), unI (उनी), uhAṅ (उहाँ)

head, *n.* TAuko (टाउको), shir (शिर)

headache, *n.* kapAl dukhAi (कपाल दुखाइ), shir dard (शिरदर्द)

headdress, *n.* TopI (टोपी), shir posh (शिरपोश)

headlight, *n.* *(vehicle)* agAdi ko battI (अगाडिको बत्ती)

headline, *n.* shIrshak (शीर्षक)

headlong, *adv.* Tauko Thokine garI (टाउको ठोकिने गरी), homiera (होमिएर)

headmaster, *n.* pradhAnAdhyApak (प्रधानाध्यापक)

headquarters, *n.* mukhya kAryAlaya (मुख्य कार्यालय)

headway, *n.* pragati (प्रगति)

heal, *v.* niko hunu (निको हुनु)

health, *n.* swAsthya (स्वास्थ्य), tandurustI (तन्दुरुस्ती)

healthy, *adj.* swasth (स्वस्थ), tandurust (तन्दुरुस्त), nirogI (निरोगी)

heap, *n.* thupro (थुप्रो), khAt (खात), *v.* thupryAunu (थुप्र्याउनु), thupArnu (थुपार्नु)

hear, *v.* sunnu (सुन्नु)

hearing, *n.* sunwAi (सुनवाइ), tArikh (तारिख)

hearsay, *n.* suneko kurA (सुनेको कुरा), jan shruti (जनश्रुति)

heart, *n.* muTu (मुटु), dil (दिल), man (मन), hridaya (हृदय), *(by heart)* kaNThastha (कण्ठस्थ)

heart attack, *n.* hridayA ghAt (हृदयाघात)

heartbeat, *n.* muTu ko DhukDhukI (मुटुको ढुकढुकी)

heartbreaking, *adj.* chitta dukhAune (चित्त दुखाउने), marm bhedI (मर्मभेदी)

heartburn, *n.* chhAtI polne rog (छाती पोल्ने रोग), amal pitta (अमलपित्त)

heartfelt, *adj.* sachchA (सच्चा), wishuddha (विशुद्ध)

heart-rending, *adj.* hridaya widArak (हृदयविदारक)

hearts, *n. (cards)* pAn (पान)

heart-throb, *n.* mAyAlu (मायालु), premI (प्रेमी), prasiddha kalA kAr (प्रसिद्ध कलाकार)

heart-to-heart, *adj.* khulast (खुलस्त)

hearty, *adj.* hArdik (हार्दिक)

heat, *n.* garmI (गर्मी), tAp (ताप), rAp (राप) *v.* tatAunu (तताउनु)

heat rash, *n.* ghamaurA (घमौरा)

heatstroke, *n.* baDhI garmI bATa hune bimArI (बढी गर्मी बाट हुने बिमारी), lU (लू)

heatwave, *n.* tAp lahar (ताप लहर), lU (लू)

heaven, *n.* swarg (स्वर्ग)

heavenly, *adj.* swargIya (स्वर्गीय)

heavy, *adj.* garhuṅgo (गहुँगो), gahrauṅ (गहौँ), bhArI (भारी)

heavy-duty, *adj.* kaDA prayog ko lAgi banAieko (कडा प्रयोगको लागि बनाइएको)

heavy industry, *n.* bhArI udyog (भारी उद्योग)

heavyweight, *n.* baDhI mahattwa pUrn wyakti (बढी महत्त्वपूर्ण व्यक्ति), *(boxing)* baDhI taul samUh ko mukkewAj (बढी तौल समूहको मुक्केवाज)

heed, *v.* dhyAn dinu (ध्यान दिनु), wAstA garnu (वास्ता गर्नु) *n.* wAstA (वास्ता), dhyAn (ध्यान)

heel, *n.* kurkuchchA (कुर्कुच्चा)

height, *n.* uchAi (उचाइ), aglAi (अग्लाइ)

heinous, *adj.* ghor (घोर), ghriNit (घृणित)

heir, *n.* hakdAr (हकदार), wAris (वारिस)

heir apparent, *n.* yuwarAj (युवराज), uttarAdhikArI (उत्तराधिकारी)

heiress, *n.* yuwarAgyI (युवराज्ञी), uttarAdhikAriNI (उत्तराधिकारिणी)

hell, *n.* narak (नरक), nark (नर्क)

hello, *n./excl. (for.)* helo (हेलो), namaste (नमस्ते)

helmet, *n.* phalAme Top
(फलामे टोप)

help, *n.* madat (मदत),
sahAyatA (सहायता)
v. madat/sahAyatA garnu
(मदत/सहायता गर्नु)

helpful, *adj.* upkArI (उपकारी),
sahyogI (सहयोगी),
sahAyatA garne (सहायता गर्ने)

helpless, *adj.* asahAya
(असहाय), nihsahAya (निःसहाय)

helter-skelter, *adv.* haDbaD
mA (हडबडमा),
yatra tatra (यत्रतत्र)

hemp, *n.* gAñjA (गाँजा),
bhAṅ (भाङ)

hen, *n.* kukhurI (कुखुरी),
pothI (पोथी)

hence, *adv.* atah (अतः),
tasarth (तसर्थ),
yahAṅ bATa (यहाँबाट)

henceforth, *adv.* aba dekhi
(अबदेखि)

henpecked, *adj.* joi Tiṅgre
(जोइटिङ्ग्रे),
swAsnI ko wash mA rahane
(स्वास्नीको वशमा रहने)

her, *pron.* un ko (उनको),
un lAI (उनलाई),
unI lAI (उनीलाई)

herald, *n.* dUt (दूत),
sandesh wAhak (सन्देशबाहक)
v. Aune kurA ghoshaNA

garnu (आउने कुरा घोषणा गर्नु)

herb, *n.* jaDI butI (जडीबुटी),
jhAr (झार)

herd, *n.* bagAl (बगाल),
bathAn (बथान)
v. bathAn banAunu (बथान
बनाउनु), baTulnu (बटुल्नु)

herdsman, *n.* goThAlo
(गोठालो)

here, *adv.* yahAṅ (यहाँ)

hereby, *adv.* yas le (यसले)

heredity, *n.* waṃshAgat/bAbu
bAje ko guN
(वंशागत/बाबुबाजेको गुण)

heresy, *n.* nAstiktA
(नास्तिकता),
widharm (विधर्म)

heritage, *n.* bapautI (बपौती)

hermit, *n.* sAdhu (साधु),
sannyAsI (सन्न्यासी),
jogI (जोगी)

hero, *n.* wIr (वीर),
yoddhA (योद्धा),
(film) nAyak (नायक)

heroine, *n.* wIrAṅganA
(वीराङ्गना), nAyikA (नायिका)

heron, *n.* bakullo (बकुल्लो)

herpes, *n.* luto (लुतो), dAd (दाद)

herself, *pron.* unI Aphai
(उनी आफै)

hesitate, *v.* hichkichAunu
(हिचकिचाउनु),
ankanAunu (अनकनाउनु)

hesitation, *n.* hichkichAhaT (हिचकिचाहट), AnA kAnI (आनाकानी)

hew, *v.* bancharo le kATnu (बन्चरोले काट्नु)

heyday, *n.* saphaltA kA din (सफलताका दिन), khAňdo jAgeko awasthA (खाँदो जागेको अवस्था)

hi, *n./excl. (inf.)* hAi (हाइ), namaste (नमस्ते)

hiccup/hiccough, *n.* bADulI (बाडुली), hikkA (हिक्का) *v.* bADulI lAgnu (बाडुली लाग्नु)

hidden, *adj.* lukeko (लुकेको), adrishya (अदृश्य)

hide, *v.* luknu (लुक्नु), lukAunu (लुकाउनु) *n.* chhAlA (छाला), chamaDA (चमडा)

hide-and-seek, *n.* lukAmArI (लुकामारी)

hideous, *adj.* ghin lAgdo (घिनलाग्दो)

hideout, *n.* lukne ThAuň (लुक्ने ठाउँ)

high, *adj.* aglo (अग्लो), Uňcho (ऊंचो), *(voice)* charko (चर्को), *(price)* mahaňgo (महंगो)

high court, *n.* uchcha nyAyAlaya (उच्च न्यायालय)

high-handed, *adj.*

swechchhAchArI (स्वेच्छाचारी)

high-level, *adj.* uchchastarIya (उच्चस्तरीय)

highlight, *n. (news, etc.)* mukhya amsh (मुख्य अंश) *v.* mukhya rUp le prakAsh mA lyAunu (मुख्य रूपले प्रकाशमा ल्याउनु)

high-rise, *adj.* dherai talA bhaeko (धेरै तला भएको), dherai aglo (धेरै अग्लो)

highway, *n.* rAj mArg (राजमार्ग)

hijack, *v.* wimAn apharaN garnu (विमान अपहरण गर्नु)

hike, *n.* paidal saphar/yAtrA (पैदल सफर/यात्रा), *v.* paidal yAtrA garnu (पैदल यात्रा गर्नु)

hilarious, *adj.* ullAs pUrN (उल्लासपूर्ण), ramAilo (रमाइलो)

hill, *n.* DAňDA (डाँडा), pahAD (पहाड)

hillock, *n.* thumko (थुम्को), Dhisko (ढिस्को)

hilly, *adj.* pahADI (पहाडी)

him, *pron.* us lAI (उसलाई), un lAI (उनलाई)

himself, *pron.* U Aphai (ऊ आफै), unI Aphai (उनी आफै)

hind, *adj.* pachhillo (पछिल्लो), pachhADi (पछाडि) *n.* muDulI mirga (मुडुली मिर्ग)

hindrance, *n.* bAdhA (बाधा),
aDko (अड्को)

hinge, *n.* kabjA (कब्जा),
chukul (चुकुल)

hint, *n.* suiṅko (सुइँको),
saṅket (संकेत)
v. saṅket/sUchanA dinu
(संकेत/सूचना दिनु)

hip, *n.* puTThA (पुट्ठा),
nitamb (नितम्ब), kaTi (कटि)

hire, *n.* bhADA (भाडा),
kirAyA (किराया)
v. bhADA mA linu
(भाडामा लिनु)

his, *pron.* us ko (उसको),
un ko (उनको)

His Majesty's Government,
n. (Nepal) shrI pAṅch ko
sarkAr (श्री पाँचको सरकार)

historian, *n.* itihAs kAr
(इतिहासकार)

historical, *adj.* aitihAsik
(ऐतिहासिक)

history, *n.* itihAs (इतिहास)

hit, *n.* mAr (मार),
(suceess) saphaltA (सफलता)
v. hirkAunu (हिर्काउनु), piTnu
(पिट्नु), Thoknu (ठोक्नु)

hitch, *n.* dhakkA (धक्का),
aDko (अड्को)
v. jhaTkArnu (भट्कार्नु)

hitch-hike, *v.* arkA ko moTar
mA ThAuṅ mAgI yAtrA

garnu (अर्काको मोटरमा ठाउँ
मागी यात्रा गर्नु)

hitherto, *adv.* ahile samma
(अहिलेसम्म)

hoard, *n.* bhaNDAr (भण्डार),
thupro (थुप्रो)
v. thupArnu (थुपार्नु),
jammA garnu (जम्मा गर्नु)

hoarse, *adj.* dhotro (धोत्रो),
dhokro (धोक्रो)

hobby, *n.* sokh (सोख)

hoe, *n.* kodAlo (कोदालो),
kuTo (कुटो)
v. khannu (खन्नु),
goDnu (गोड्नु)

hog, *n.* suṅgur (सुँगुर)

hogwash, *n.* kAm na lAgne
wastu (काम नलाग्ने वस्तु)

hoist, *v.* uchAlnu (उचाल्नु),
uThAunu (उठाउनु)

hold, *n.* pakaD (पकड),
muTThI (मुट्ठी)
v. pakranu (पक्रनु),
samAunu (समाउनु),
aTAunu (अटाउनु)

hold out, *v.* pratirodh kAyam
garnu (प्रतिरोध कायम गर्नु)

holdall, *n.* gunTA kasne byAg
(गुन्टा कस्ने ब्याग)

holder, *n.* bIñD (बींड)

hold-up, *n.* DakaitI (डकैती),
lUT (लूट), awrodh (अवरोध)

hole, *n.* pwAl (प्वाल), dulo (दुलो)

holiday, *n.* bidA (बिदा),
chhuTTI (छुट्टी)

hollow, *adj.* khokro (खोक्रो)

holy, *adj.* pawitra (पवित्र),
shuddha (शुद्ध)

homage, *n.* shraddhAñjalI
(श्रद्धाञ्जली), sewA (सेवा)

home, *n.* ghar (घर),
swadesh (स्वदेश)

homeless, *adj.* ghar na bhaeko
(घर नभएको)

homesick, *adj.* ghar samjhi
rahane (घर सम्झिरहने)

homework, *n.* grih kArya
(गृहकार्य)

homicide, *n.* nar hatyA
(नरहत्या)

homosexual, *adj.* sam liṅgI
(समलिङ्गी)

honest, *adj.* imAndAr (इमान्दार)

honesty, *n.* imAndArI
(इमान्दारी)

honey, *n.* maha (मह),
(person) priye (प्रिये)

honeymoon, *n.* Anand mAS
(आनन्दमास), hanI mUn (हनीमून)

honorarium, *n.* pArishramik
(पारिश्रमिक)

honorary, *adj.* mAnArth
(मानार्थ),
awaitnik (अवैतनिक),
talab na line (तलब नलिने)

hono(u)r, *n.* mAn (मान),

ijjat (इज्जत)
v. mAn/ijjat garnu
(मान/इज्जत गर्नु)

hono(u)rable, *adj.* mAn nIya
(माननीय),
Adar NIya (आदरणीय)

hoof, *n.* khur (खुर)

hook, *n.* aṅkush (अंकुश),
(fishing) balchhI (बल्छी)
v. aṅkuse le samAunu
(अंकुसेले समाउनु)

hookah, *n.* hukkA (हुक्का)

hooligan, *n.* badmAs
(बदमास), guNDA (गुण्डा)

hoop, *n.* chakra (चक्र),
chakkA (चक्का)

hoot, *v. (horn)* bajAunu
(बजाउनु), bajnu (बज्नु),
(protest) wirodh mA
karAunu (विरोधमा कराउनु)

hop, *v.* ek khuTTA mA
uphranu (एक खुट्टामा उफ्रनु)

hope, *n.* AshA (आशा), Ash (आश)
v. Ash garnu (आश गर्नु)

hopeful, *adj.* AshA janak
(आशाजनक),
AshA pUrN (आशापूर्ण)

hopeless, *adj.* nirAsh (निराश),
hatAsh (हताश),
(derog.) nikammA (निकम्मा)

horizon, *n.* kshitij (क्षितिज)

horizontal, *adj.* terso (तेर्सो)

horn, *n.* siṅ (सिङ),

(rhino) khAg (खाग),
(motor) harn (हर्न)

hornbill, *n.* dhanesh charA
(धनेश चरा)

hornet, *n.* ariṅgAl (अरिङ्गाल),
bArulo (बारुलो)

horoscope, *n.* chinA (चिना),
janma patrikA (जन्मपत्रिका),
kuNDalI (कुण्डली)

horrible, *adj.* bhayAnak
(भयानक), apriya (अप्रिय)

horror, *n.* Dar (डर), trAs (त्रास)

horse, *n.* ghoDA (घोडा)

horse laugh, *n.* charko
bhaddA hAṅso
(चर्को भद्दा हाँसो)

horsepower, *n.* kAm garne
darko yuniT (काम गर्ने दरको
युनिट), ashwa shakti (अश्वशक्ति)

horseshoe, *n.* nAl (नाल)

horticulture, *n.* bAgwAnI
(बागवानी),
udyAn widyA (उद्यानविद्या)

hospitable, *adj.* satkArshIl
(सत्कारशील),
Atithya pUrN (आतिथ्यपूर्ण)

hospital, *n.* aspatAl (अस्पताल)

hospitality, *n.* Atithya
(आतिथ्य), satkAr (सत्कार)

host, *n.* ThUlo saṅkhyA
(ठूलो संख्या), *(party)* Atitheya
(आतिथेय), mejmAn (मेजमान)

hostage, *n. (pol.)* bandhak

(बन्धक)

hostel, *n.* chhAtrAwAs
(छात्रावास)

hostess, *n.* mahilA mejmAn
(महिला मेजमान)

hostile, *adj.* wipakshI
(विपक्षी), pratikUl (प्रतिकूल)

hot, *adj.* tAto (तातो),
garam (गरम),
(weather) garmI (गर्मी),
(taste) piro (पिरो)

hotchpotch/hodgepodge, *n.*
laThibajra (लठिबज्र),
lathAliṅg (लथालिङ्ग)

hotel, *n.* hoTel (होटेल)

hot-headed, *adj.* garam mijAs
ko (गरम मिजासको)

hotline, *n.* TADhA kA ThAuṅ
harU bIch sidhA sañchAr
sampark (टाढाका ठाउँहरू बीच
सिधा संचार सम्पर्क)

hound, *n.* shikArI kukur
(शिकारी कुकुर)
v. lakheTnu (लखेट्नु)

hour, *n.* ghaNTA (घण्टा)

house, *n.* ghar (घर),
(bus.) koThI (कोठी)

house arrest, *n.* najar bandI
(नजरबन्दी)

household, *n.* ghar pariwAr
(घरपरिवार)

housemaid, *n.* nokarnI
(नोकर्नी)

house-warming, *n.* grih prawesh samAroh (गृहप्रवेश समारोह)

housewife, *n.* grihiNI (गृहिणी)

housing, *n.* AwAs nirmAN (आवास निर्माण)

hover, *v.* ekai ThAuň mA uDi rahanu (एकै ठाउँमा उडिरहनु)

how, *adv.* kasarI (कसरी), kasto (कस्तो)

however, *adv.* taipani (तैपनि), tyaso bhae tA pani (त्यसो भए तापनि)

howl, *v.* garjanu (गर्जनु), karAunu (कराउनु)

hubbub, *n.* hallA (हल्ला), gol mAl (गोलमाल)

hue, *n.* rañg (रङ्ग)

hue and cry, *n.* hallA (हल्ला)

hug, *n.* añgAlo (अङ्गालो) *v.* añgAlo hAlnu (अङ्गालो हाल्नु)

huge, *adj.* dherai ThUlo (धेरै ठूलो), wishAl (विशाल), bhawya (भव्य)

hullabaloo, *n.* hohallA (होहल्ला), kolAhal (कोलाहल)

hum, *v.* gun gunAunu (गुनगुनाउनु)

human, *adj.* mAnawIya (मानवीय)

human (being), *n.* mAnaw (मानव)

human nature, *n.* mAnaw swabhAw (मानव स्वभाव)

human rights, *n.* mAnaw adhikAr (मानव अधिकार)

humane, *adj.* dayAlu (दयालु), kripAlu (कृपालु)

human interest, *n.* jan abhiruchi (जन अभिरुचि)

humanity, *n.* mAnawtA (मानवता)

humble, *adj.* namra (नम्र), winIt (विनीत)

humbug, *n.* chhal (छल), dhokA (धोका)

humid, *adj.* osieko (ओसिएको), Ardra (आर्द्र)

humidity, *n.* ArdratA (आर्द्रता)

humiliate, *v.* apmAn/khisI garnu (अपमान/खिसी गर्नु)

humiliation, *n.* apmAn (अपमान), mAn bhañg (मानभङ्ग)

humo(u)r, *n.* lahaD (लहड), ThaTTA (ठट्टा)

humorous, *adj.* lahaDI (लहडी), haňsAune (हँसाउने)

hunchback, *n.* kUňjo (कूँजो)

hundred, *n.* saya (सय), shaya (शय)

hundred percent, *n.* saya prati shat (सय प्रतिशत)

hundred thousand, *n.* lAkh (लाख)

hunger, n. bhok (भोक)

hungry, adj. bhoko (भोको),
bhokAeko (भोकाएको)

hunt, v. shikAr khelnu
(शिकार खेल्नु)

hunter, n. shikArI (शिकारी)

hurdle, n. bAdhA (बाधा),
awrodh (अवरोध)

hurl, v. phyAňknu (फ्याँक्नु),
hutyAunu (हुत्याउनु)

hurricane, n. AňdhI (आँधी),
tUphAn (तूफान)

hurry, n. hatAr (हतार)
v. hatAr garnu (हतार गर्नु)

hurt, v. choT lAgnu (चोट
लाग्नु), bijhnu (बिभ्नु)

husband, n. logne (लोग्ने),
poi (पोइ), pati (पति)

husbandry, n. khetI (खेती)

hush, n. maun (मौन),
shAnti (शान्ति)

v. chup lagAunu (चुप लगाउनु)
adj. gopya (गोप्य)

hush money, n. pol na kholna
diine ghUs (पोल नखोल्न दिइने
घूस)

husk, n. chokar (चोकर),
khosTA (खोस्टा)

hut, n. chhApro (छाप्रो),
jhupaDI (भुपडी)

hygiene, n. swAsthya wigỹAn
(स्वास्थ्य विज्ञान)

hydroelectricity, n.
jal widyut/shakti
(जलविद्युत/शक्ति)

hydrophobia, n. pAnI dekhI
Dar (पानीदेखि डर),
bahulaTTIpan ko lakshaN
(बहुलट्टीपनको लक्षण)

hymn, n. bhajan (भजन)

hypocrisy, n. pAkhaND
(पाखण्ड), ADambar (आडम्बर)

I

I, pron. ma (म), maile (मैले)

ice, n. baraph (बरफ), hiuň (हिउँ)
v. jamnu (जम्नु)

ice cream, n. Ais krIm
(आइस्क्रीम)

icon, n. mUrti (मूर्ति),

pratimA (प्रतिमा)

idea, n. wichAr (विचार),
tarkanA (तर्कना),
akkal (अक्कल)

ideal, adj. Adarsh (आदर्श),
kAlpanik (काल्पनिक)

identical, *adj.* ustai (उस्तै),
uhI (उही),
ekai nAs ko (एकैनासको)

identification, *n.* pahichAn
(पहिचान), sanAkhat (सनाखत)

identify, *v.* pahichAn garnu
(पहिचान गर्नु), chinnu (चिन्नु)

identity, *n.* wyaktitwa (व्यक्तित्व),
parichaya (परिचय)

identity (ID) card, *n.* parichaya
patra (परिचयपत्र)

ideology, *n.* wichAr dhArA
(विचारधारा),
siddhAnt (सिद्धान्त)

ideosyncrasy, *n.* lahaD (लहड),
sanak (सनक),
baulaTTI (बौलट्टी)

idiot, *n.* paT mUrkh
(पटमूर्ख), lamphU (लम्फू),
swAñTh (स्वाँठ)

idle, *adj.* alchhI (अल्छी),
sust (सुस्त)
v. alchhI garnu (अल्छी गर्नु)

idol, *n.* mUrti (मूर्ति),
pratimA (प्रतिमा)

if, *conj.* yadi (यदि),
kadAchit (कदाचित्),
(emph.) uso bhae (उसो भए)

ignorance, *n.* agyÅn (अज्ञान),
agyÅntA (अज्ञानता)

ignorant, *adj.* agyÅnI (अज्ञानी),
abodh (अबोध), anjAn
(अन्जान), nirbuddhi (निर्बुद्धि)

ignore, *v.* bewAstA/upekshA
garnu (बेवास्ता/उपेक्षा गर्नु)

ill, *adj.* birAmI (बिरामी)

ill-advised, *adj.* na rAmro
sallAh pAeko (नराम्रो सल्लाह
पाएको), anupyogI (अनुपयोगी)

ill-bred, *adj.* asabhyA (असभ्य)

illegal, *adj.* gair kAnUnI
(गैरकानूनी), awaidh (अवैध)

illegible, *adj.* paDhna na
sakine (पढ्न नसकिने),
na bujhine (नबुझिने)

illegitimate, *adj.* ain le na
dieko (ऐनले नदिएको),
(child) ThamyAhA (ठम्याहा),
maThyAha (मठ्याहा)

ill-gotten, *adj.* anyAya pUrwak
prApt gareko (अन्यायपूर्वक
प्राप्त गरेको)

illicit, *adj.* gair kAnUnI
(गैरकानूनी),
nishiddha (निषिद्ध)

illiterate, *adj.* nirakshar
(निरक्षर), apaDh (अपढ)

illness, *n.* rog (रोग),
bimArI (बिमारी)

ill-tempered, *adj.* risAhA
(रिसाहा), jhagaDAlu (झगडालु)

ill-treatment, *n.* durwyawahAr
(दुर्व्यवहार)

illuminate, *v.* ujyAlo/jhilimilI
pArnu (उज्यालो/झिलिमिली
पार्नु)

illusion, *n.* bhram (भ्रम),
chhal (छल), mAyA (माया)

illustrate, *v.* chitrit/wyAkhyA
garnu (चित्रित/व्याख्या गर्नु)

illustration, *n.* udAharaN
(उदाहरण), chitra (चित्र),
drishTAnt (दृष्टान्त)

ill will, *n.* dwesh (द्वेष),
ris (रिस), DAh (डाह)

image, *n.* chhawi (छवि),
mUrti (मूर्ति)

imaginary, *adj.* manchinte
(मनचिन्ते),
kAlpanik (काल्पनिक)

imagination, *n.* kalpanA
(कल्पना)

imagine, *v.* kalpanA/wichAr
garnu (कल्पना/विचार गर्नु)

imitate, *v.* nakkal/dekhA sikI
garnu (नक्कल/देखासिकी गर्नु)

imitation, *n.* nakkal (नक्कल)
adj. nakkalI (नक्कली)

immature, *adj.* kAñcho
(काँचो),
aparipakwa (अपरिपक्व)

immediate, *adj.* tatkAl
(तत्काल),
turnta hune (तुरुन्त हुने)

immediately, *adv.* jhaTTai
(झट्टै), turuntai (तुरुन्तै)

immense, *adj.* jyAdai ThUlo
(ज्यादै ठूलो),
baDemAn (बडेमान)

immerse, *v.* Dubnu (डुब्नु),
DubAunu (डुबाउनु),
chopalnu (चोपल्नु)

immigrant, *n.* AprawAsI
(आप्रवासी)

imminent, *adj.* najik ko
(नजिकको),
huna AñTeko (हुन आँटेको)

immoral, *adj.* anaitik (अनैतिक),
pApI (पापी)

immortal, *adj.* amar (अमर)

immovable, *adj.* achal (अचल),
aTal (अटल)

immune, *adj.* rakshit (रक्षित),
surakshit (सुरक्षित)

immunity, *n.* rog pratirodh
kshamatA (रोग प्रतिरोध
क्षमता),
(pol.) kUTnaitik chhuT
(कूटनैतिक छुट)

impact, *n.* ghAt (घात),
prabhAw (प्रभाव)

impart, *v.* dinu (दिनु),
pradAn garnu (प्रदान गर्नु)

impartial, *adj.* nishpaksha
(निष्पक्ष)

impartiality, *n.* nishpakshatA
(निष्पक्षता)

impasse, *n.* gati rodh (गतिरोध)

impediment, *n.* bAdhA
(बाधा), awrodh (अवरोध)

imperfect, *adj.* apUrN
(अपूर्ण), dosh yukta (दोषयुक्त)

imperialism, *n.* sAmrAjya wAd (साम्राज्यवाद)

imperialist, *n.* sAmrAjya wAdI (साम्राज्यवादी)

impertinent, *adj.* aTerI (अटेरी), mukhAle (मुखाले)

impetus, *n.* preraNA (प्रेरणा), gati shakti (गति शक्ति)

implement, *n.* sAdhan (साधन), aujAr (औजार)
v. kAryAnwit garnu (कार्यान्वित गर्नु)

implicate, *v.* sarik garAunu (सरिक गराउनु), muchhnu (मुछ्नु)

implore, *v.* bintI/prArthanA garnu (बिन्ती/प्रार्थना गर्नु)

imply, *v.* matlab bujhAunu (मतलब बुझाउनु), sañket garnu (सङ्केत गर्नु)

import, *v.* AyAt/paiThArI garnu (आयात/पैठारी गर्नु)
n. AyAt (आयात), paiThArI (पैठारी)

important, *adj.* mahattwa pUrN (महत्त्वपूर्ण)

impose, *v.* lAdnu (लादनु), bhiDAunu (भिडाउनु)

impossible, *adj.* asambhaw (असम्भव), huna na sakne (हुन नसक्ने)

impotent, *adj.* nAmard (नामर्द), napuñsak (नपुङ्सक)

impractical, *adj.* asAdhya (असाध्य), awyAwhArik (अव्यावहारिक)

impress, *v.* prabhAw pArnu (प्रभाव पार्नु), chhAp lAunu (छाप लाउनु)

impression, *n.* prabhAw (प्रभाव), anubhaw (अनुभव)

impressive, *adj.* prabhAw shAlI (प्रभावशाली), Akarshak (आकर्षक)

imprison, *v.* jel hAlnu (जेल हाल्नु), kaid garnu (कैद गर्नु)

imprisonment, *n.* kaid (कैद), thunA (थुना)

improbable, *adj.* asambhaw (असम्भव)

impromptu, *adj.* tAtkAlik (तात्कालिक)
adv. tatkAl (तत्काल), tyati kherai (त्यतिखेरै)
n. (speech) tayArI binA ko bhAshaN (तयारी बिनाको भाषण)

improper, *adj.* anuchit (अनुचित)

improve, *v.* sudhArnu (सुधार्नु), unnati garnu (उन्नति गर्नु)

improvement, *n.* unnati (उन्नति), sudhAr (सुधार), tarakkI (तरक्की)

impulse, *n.* samweg (संवेग), Aweg (आवेग)

impure, *adj.* biTulo (बिटुलो), apawitra (अपवित्र)

in, *prep.* mA (मा), bhitra (भित्र)

inability, *n.* asAmarthya (असामर्थ्य)

inaccessible, *adj.* durgam (दुर्गम), agamya (अगम्य)

inaccurate, *adj.* beThIk (बेठीक), ashuddha (अशुद्ध)

inadequate, *adj.* kam (कम), na pug (नपुग), aparyApt (अपर्याप्त)

inalienable, *adj.* haraN garna na milne (हरण गर्न नमिल्ने)

inappropriate, *adj.* anuchit (अनुचित), anupayukta (अनुपयुक्त)

inasmuch as, *adv.* kina bhane (किनभने)

inattentive, *adj.* asAwdhAn (असावधान), hussU (हुस्सू)

inaudible, *adj.* na sunine (नसुनिने), sunna na sakine (सुन्न नसकिने)

inaugurate, *v.* udghATan garnu (उद्घाटन गर्नु)

inauguration, *n.* udghATan (उद्घाटन), pratisthApan (प्रतिस्थापन)

inauspicious, *adj.* ashubh (अशुभ), ashakun (अशकुन)

incapable, *adj.* ayogya (अयोग्य), ashakta (अशक्त)

incapacitate, *v.* ayogya banAunu (अयोग्य बनाउनु)

incarnation, *n.* awtAr (अवतार), junI (जुनी), chhawi (छवि)

incense, *n.* dhUp (धूप), agar battI (अगरबत्ती)

incentive, *n.* protsAhan (प्रोत्साहन, utpreraNA (उत्प्रेरणा)

incest, *n.* hAD nAtA karaNI (हाडनाता करणी)

inch, *n.* inchI (इन्ची)

incident, *n.* ghaTanA (घटना)

incidental, *adj.* Akasmik (आकस्मिक)

inclination, *n.* prawritti (प्रवृत्ति), jhukAw (भुकाव)

inclined, *adj.* jhukeko (भुकेको), Dhalkeko (ढल्केको)

include, *v.* gAbhnu (गाभ्नु), samAwesh garnu (समावेश गर्नु)

including, *prep.* samet (समेत), lagAyat (लगायत)

incognito, *adv./adj.* nAm chhalera (नाम छलेर), chhadma bhesh mA (छद्म भेषमा), gupt (गुप्त)

income, *n.* AmdAnI (आम्दानी), Aya (आय)

income tax, *n.* Aya kar (आयकर)

incommunicable, *adj.* bhanna na sakine (भन्न नसकिने)

incomparable, *adj.* atulnIya
(अतुलनीय)

incompetent, *adj.* ayogya
(अयोग्य), asaksham (असक्षम)

incomplete, *adj.* apUro
(अपूरो), adhUro (अधुरो)

incomprehensible, *adj.* na
bujhine (नबुझिने),
agamya (अगम्य)

inconvenient, *adj.* asuwidhA
janak (असुविधाजनक)

incorrect, *adj.* ashuddha
(अशुद्ध), galat (गलत)

increase, *v.* baDhnu (बढ्नु),
baDhAunu (बढाउनु)
n. wriddhi (वृद्धि), unnati (उन्नति)

incredible, *adj.* patyAuna na
sakine (पत्याउन नसकिने),
awishwasnIya (अविश्वसनीय)

increment, *n.* wriddhi (वृद्धि),
thap (थप)

incubate, *v.* othAro basnu
(ओथारो बस्नु), koralnu (कोरल्नु)

inculcate, *v.* Agraha garnu
(आग्रह गर्नु), man mA
basAlnu (मनमा बसाल्नु)

incumbent, *adj.* bahAl wAlA
(बहालवाला)

incurable, *adj.* niko na hune
(निको नहुने), asAdhya (असाध्य)

indebted, *adj.* riNI (ऋणी),
anugrihIt (अनुगृहीत)

indeed, *adv.* wastaw mA

(वास्तवमा), sAñchchai (साँच्चै)

independence, *n.* swatantratA
(स्वतन्त्रता),
swDhIntA (स्वाधीनता)

independent, *adj.* swatantra
(स्वतन्त्र), swDhIn (स्वाधीन),
phukkA (फुक्का)

indestructible, *adj.* nAsh huna
na sakne (नाश हुन नसक्ने),
akshaya (अक्षय),
awinAshI (अविनाशी)

index finger, *n.* chor auñlA
(चोरऔंला)

indicate, *v.* dekhAunu (देखाउनु),
darshAunu (दर्शाउनु)

indication, *n.* sañket (सङ्केत),
sUchanA (सूचना)

indifference, *n.* lAparbAhI
(लापर्बाही), bewAstA (बेवास्ता)

indifferent, *adj.* udAsIn
(उदासीन)

indigestion, *n.* apach (अपच),
ajIrNa (अजीर्ण)

indignation, *n.* krodh (क्रोध),
ris (रिस)

indirect, *adj.* paroksha (परोक्ष),
apratyaksha (अप्रत्यक्ष)

indiscriminate, *adj.* jathA
bhAbI (जथाभावी),
andhA dhundh (अन्धाधुन्ध)

indiscriminately, *adv.* andhA
dhundh (अन्धाधुन्ध),
jathA bhAbI (जथाभावी)

indispensable, *adj.* na bhai na hune (नभै नहुने), aparihArya (अपरिहार्य)

individual, *n.* wyakti (व्यक्ति) *adj.* janahI (जनही, wyaktigat (व्यक्तिगत)

indivisible, *adj.* bhAg garna/lAuna na sakine (भाग गर्न/लाउन नसकिने)

indomitable, *adj.* himmat na hArne (हिम्मत नहार्ने), adamya (अदम्य)

indoor, *adj.* bhitrI (भित्री), antaraṅg (अन्तरङ्ग)

indoors, *adv.* ghar bhitra (घरभित्र, chhAnA muni (छानामुनि)

induce, *v.* manAunu (मनाउनु), phakAunu (फकाउनु)

indulge, *v.* nirdhakka sita Anand manAunu (निर्धक्कसित आनन्द मनाउनु), Ashakta hunu (आशक्त हुनु)

industrious, *adj.* parishramI (परिश्रमी), mehnatI (मेहनती)

industry, *n.* udyog (उद्योग), wyawasAya (व्यवसाय)

inept, *adj.* ayogya (अयोग्य), bekuph (बेकुफ)

ineffective, *adj.* asar na parne (असर नपर्ने), prabhAw hIn (प्रभावहीन)

inefficient, *adj.* ayogya

(अयोग्य), asaksham (असक्षम)

inequality, *n.* asamAntA (असमानता)

inevitable, *adj.* aniwArya (अनिवार्य), aparihArya (अपरिहार्य)

inexperienced, *adj.* anubhaw na bhaeko (अनुभव नभएको), anabhigỹa (अनभिज्ञ)

infamous, *adj.* badnAm (बदनाम), kukhyAt (कुख्यात)

infancy, *n.* shaishaw kAl (शैशव काल)

infant, *n.* shishu (शिशु), bachchA (बच्चा)

infatuated, *adj.* mohit (मोहित), prem le unmatta (प्रेमले उन्मत्त)

infection, *n.* saruwA rog (सरुवा रोग), saṅkrAmak rog (सङ्क्रामक रोग)

infectious, *adj.* saruwA (सरुवा), sarne (सर्ने)

inferior, *adj.* tallo (तल्लो), kamsal (कमसल), ghaTiyA (घटिया)

inferiority, *n.* hIntA (हीनता)

infidel, *n.* nAstik (नास्तिक), adharmI (अधर्मी)

infidelity, *n.* wishwAs ghAt (विश्वासघात)

infiltrate, *v.* pasnu (पस्नु), chhirnu (छिर्नु), ghusnu (घुस्नु)

infiltration, *n.* ghus paiTh
(घुसपैठ),
atikramaN (अतिक्रमण)

infinity, *n.* anant (अनन्त),
anantatA (अनन्तता)

inflammation, *n.* suj (सुज),
sujan (सुजन), jalan (जलन)

inflation, *n.* mudrA sphIti
(मुद्रास्फीति),
mUlya wriddhi (मूल्यवृद्धि)

inflict, *v.* kashT dinu
(कष्ट दिनु)

influence, *n.* prabhAw (प्रभाव)

influential, *adj.* prabhaw shAlI
(प्रभावशाली), ThUlo prabhAw
bhaeko (ठूलो प्रभाव भएको)

influenza, *n.* kaDA rughA
(कडा रुघा), rughA ko jwaro
(रुघाको ज्वरो)

influx, *n.* antar Agaman
(अन्तर आगमन),
antar prawAh (अन्तरप्रवाह)

inform, *v.* thAhA dinu
(थाहा दिनु),
sUchit garnu (सूचित गर्नु)

information, *n.* sUchanA
(सूचना), samAchAr (समाचार)

infrastructure, *n.* pUrwAdhAr
(पूर्वाधार)

ingenious, *adj.* prawIN (प्रवीण),
daksha (दक्ष)

ingredient, *n.* aṅg (अङ्ग),
awayaw (अवयव),

sAmAgrI (सामाग्री)

inhabit, *v.* bAs garnu
(बास गर्नु), basnu (बस्नु)

inhabitable, *adj.* bAs garna
yogya (बास गर्न योग्य)

inhabitant, *n.* bAsindA
(बासिन्दा), niwAsI (निवासी)

inhale, *v.* sAs linu (सास लिनु)

inherit, *v.* purkhA Adi bATa
pAunu (पुर्खा आदिबाट पाउनु)

inheritance, *n.* amsh (अंश),
adhikAr (अधिकार)

inhuman, *adj.* nirdayI (निर्दयी),
amAnwIya (अमानवीय)

initial, *n.* nAm ko pahilo
akshar (नामको पहिलो अक्षर)
adj. pahilo (पहिलो),
suru ko (सुरुको)

initiative, *n.* pahal (पहल),
upkram (उपक्रम)

injection, *n.* suI (सुई)

injure, *v.* choT lagAunu
(चोट लगाउनु)

injurious, *adj.* hAni kArak
(हानिकारक), choT puryAune
(चोट पुर्‍याउने)

injury, *n.* choT (चोट),
hAni (हानि),
choT paTak (चोटपटक)

injustice, *n.* anyAya (अन्याय)

ink, *n.* masI (मसी)

inkling, *n.* saṅket (सङ्केत),
sUchanA (सूचना)

ink-pot, *n.* masI dAnI (मसीदानी)

inlaid, *adj.* buTTA jaDieko (बुट्टा जडिएको)

in-laws, *n.* sasurAlI khalak (ससुराली खलक)

inmate, *n. (house, prison, etc.)* bAsindA (बासिन्दा)

inn, *n.* pATI (पाटी), saraya (सराय), bhaTTI (भट्टी)

inner, *adj.* bhitrI (भित्री), Antarik (आन्तरिक)

innocent, *adj.* nirdosh (निर्दोष)

innovation, *n.* nawIn prawartan (नवीन प्रवर्तन)

innuendo, *n.* chheD (छेड), chheD pech (छेडपेच)

innumerable, *adj.* angintI (अनगिन्ती), asaṅkhya (असङ्ख्य)

inoculate, *v.* suI dinu (सुई दिनु), khopnu (खोप्नु)

inoculation, *n.* suI (सुई), khop (खोप)

inquest, *n.* lAsh jAñch (लाश जाँच), adAlatI jAñch (अदालती जाँच)

inquiry, *n.* sodh puchh (सोधपुछ), jAñch bujh (जाँचबुझ)

inroad, *n.* dhAbA (धाबा), hamlA (हमला)

insane, *adj.* baulAhA (बौलाहा), pAgal (पागल)

inscription, *n.* lekh (लेख), shilA lekh (शिलालेख)

insect, *n.* kIrA (कीरा)

insecticide, *n.* kIT nAshak (कीटनाशक), kIrA mArne aushadhi (कीरामार्ने औषधि)

inseparable, *adj.* alag na hune (अलग नहुने)

inside, *prep.* bhitra (भित्र)

insight, *n.* antar drishTi (अन्तरदृष्टि)

insignificant, *adj.* nirarthak (निरर्थक), thorai (थोरै)

insipid, *adj.* khallo (खल्लो), alino (अलिनो)

insist, *v.* joD dinu (जोड दिनु), haTh garnu (हठ गर्नु)

insolent, *adj.* be adab (बेअदब), apmAn garne (अपमान गर्ने)

insomnia, *n.* anidrA (अनिद्रा), nidrA na lAgne (निद्रा नलाग्ने)

inspect, *v.* jAñchnu (जाँच्नु), nirIkshaN garnu (निरीक्षण गर्नु)

inspection, *n.* jAñch (जाँच), nirIkshaN (निरीक्षण)

inspector, *n.* nirIkshak (निरीक्षक), jAñchKI (जाँचकी)

inspiration, *n.* preraNA (प्रेरणा)

inspire, *v.* prerit garnu (प्रेरित गर्नु), sAs linu (सास लिनु)

install, *v.* sthApit garnu (स्थापित गर्नु), jaDnu (जड्नु)

instal(I)ment, *n.* kistA (किस्ता),
kistA bandI (किस्ताबन्दी)

instance, *n.* udAharaN
(उदाहरण),
drishTant (दृष्टान्त)

instant, *n.* tAtkAlik kshaN
(तात्कालिक क्षण)

instantly, *adv.* turunt (तुरुन्त),
jhaTTa (भट्ट)
adj. tAtkAlik (तात्कालिक),
(food) chhito pAkne
(छिटो पाक्ने)

instead of, *adv.* badlA mA
(बदलामा), sATo mA (साटोमा)

instigate, *v.* uksAunu
(उक्साउनु), bhAǎDnu (भाँड्नु)

institute, *n.* samsthAn(संस्थान),
widyAlaya (विद्यालय)
v. thAlnu (थाल्नु),
niyukta garnu (नियुक्त गर्नु)

institution, *n.* samsthA(संस्था),
samsthAn (संस्थान),
pratishThAn (प्रतिष्ठान)

instruct, *v.* sikAunu (सिकाउनु),
shikshA dinu (शिक्षा दिनु)

instruction, *n.* Adesh (आदेश),
updesh (उपदेश),
shikshA (शिक्षा)

instructor, *n.* guru (गुरु),
shikshak (शिक्षक)

instrument, *n.* aujAr (औजार),
hatiyAr (हतियार), bAjA gAjA
(बाजागाजा), wAdya wAdan

(वाद्यवादन), *(mus.)* sAj (साज)

insufficient, *adj.* kam (कम),
ghaTI (घटी),
aparyApt (अपर्याप्त)

insulator, *n.* bijulI ko kareNT
Adi chhekne wastu (बिजुलीको
करेण्ट आदि छेक्ने बस्तु)

insult, *n.* apmAn (अपमान),
beijjatI (बेइज्जती)
v. apmAn/beijjat garnu
(अपमान/बेइज्जत गर्नु)

insurance, *n.* bImA (बीमा)

insure, *v.* bImA/pakkA garnu
(बीमा/पक्का गर्नु)

insurrection, *n.* widroh (विद्रोह)

integral, *adj.* abhinna (अभिन्न)

integrity, *n.* pUrNtA (पूर्णता),
akhaNDatA (अखण्डता)

intellect, *n.* buddhi (बुद्धि),
dimAg (दिमाग)

intellectual, *n.* buddhi jIwI
(बुद्धिजीवी), paThit (पठित)

intelligence, *n.* buddhi (बुद्धि),
jehen (जेहेन)

intelligent, *adj.* buddhi mAn
(बुद्धिमान), chalAkh (चलाख),
bATho (बाठो),
jehendAr (जेहेन्दार)

intend, *v.* chitAunu (चिताउनु),
ichchhA garnu (इच्छा गर्नु)

intense, *adj.* tIwra (तीव्र),
charko (चर्को),
ati tej (अति तेज)

intensity, *n.* tIwratA (तीव्रता),
pragADhtA (प्रगाढता)

intention, *n.* ichchhA (इच्छा),
irAdA (इरादा)

intentional, *adj.* jAnA jAnI
(जानाजानी)

intercept, *v.* bIchai mA
roknu/samAunu
(बीचैमा रोक्नु/समाउनु)

intercourse, *n.* sampark
(सम्पर्क), wArtA (वार्ता), *(sex)*
maithun (मैथुन), rati kriyA
(रतिक्रिया), sambhog (सम्भोग)

interest, *n.* ruchi (रुचि),
chAkh (चाख),
(eco.) byAj (ब्याज)

interesting, *adj.* rahar/chAkh
lAgdo (रहर/चाखलाग्दो)

interfere, *v.* bAdhA dinu
(बाधा दिनु), hastakshep garnu
(हस्तक्षेप गर्नु)

interference, *n.* hastakshep
(हस्तक्षेप), bAdhA (बाधा)

interim, *adj.* antarim (अन्तरिम)

interior, *adj.* bhitrI (भित्री)

intermediate, *adj.* bIch ko
(बीचको),
antarwartI (अन्तरवर्ती)

internal, *adj.* bhitrI (भित्री),
Antarik (आन्तरिक)

international, *adj.* antar
rAshtriya (अन्तर्राष्ट्रिय)

interpret, *v.* arth batAunu

(अर्थ बताउनु),
wyAkhyA garnu (व्याख्या गर्नु)

interpreter, *n.* do bhAshe
(दोभाषे)

interrogate, *v.* prashna garnu
(प्रश्न गर्नु), sodhnu (सोध्नु)

interrogation, *n.* prashna
(प्रश्न), sawAl (सवाल),
sodh pUchh (सोधपुछ)

interrupt, *v.* bitholnu (बिथोल्नु),
bighna puryAunu
(बिघ्न पुर्‍याउनु)

interruption, *n.* awrodh
(अवरोध), bighna (बिघ्न)

intersection, *n.* chaubATo
(चौबाटो)

interval, *n.* madhyAntar
(मध्यान्तर), wirAm (विराम)

interview, *n.* antar wArtA
(अन्तरवार्ता)
v. antar wArtA garnu
(अन्तरवार्ता गर्नु)

intestine, *n.* Andro (आन्द्रो)

intimate, *adj.* ghanishTh
(घनिष्ठ)

intimation, *n.* janAu (जनाउ),
sUchanA (सूचना)

intimidate, *v.* dhamkyAunu
(धम्क्याउनु), tarsAunu (तर्साउनु)

into, *prep.* mA (मा), bhitra (भित्र)

intolerable, *adj.* sahana na
sakine (सहन नसकिने),
asahya (असह्य)

intoxicate, *v.* mAt lagAunu
(मात लगाउनु),
laTTha pArnu (लट्ठ पार्नु)

intoxicated, *adj.* mAt lAgeko
(मात लागेको),
mAttieko (मात्तिएको)

intrepid, *adj.* niDar (निडर),
nirbhayI (निर्भयी),
sUro (सूरो)

intricate, *adj.* jaTil (जटिल),
pechilo (पेचिलो),
masino (मसिनो)

intrigue, *n.* dAu pech
(दाउपेच), jAl (जाल),
chhal kapaT (छलकपट)

introduce, *v.* chin jAn /
parichaya garAunu
(चिनजान/परिचय गराउनु)

introduction, *n.* chin jAn
(चिनजान),
parichaya (परिचय)

intrusion, *n.* jabarjastI
prawesh (जबर्जस्ती प्रवेश)

invade, *v.* hamlA/AkramaN
garnu (हमला/आक्रमण गर्नु)

invalid, *adj.* nAkAm (नाकाम),
khArij (खारिज)
n. rogI (रोगी), birAmI (बिरामी)

invaluable, *adj.* anmol
(अनमोल), amUlya (अमूल्य)

invasion, *n.* hamlA (हमला),
AkramaN (आक्रमण)

invent, *v.* AwishkAr garnu

invention, *n.* AwishkAr
(आविष्कार), rachnA (रचना)

invest, *v.* lagAnI garnu
(लगानी गर्नु)

investigate, *v.* khojI/jAňch
paDtAl garnu
(खोजी/जाँचपडताल गर्नु)

investigation, *n.* jAňch
paDtAl (जाँचपडताल),
chhAn bin (छानबिन)

invincible, *adj.* ajeya (अजेय),
adamya (अदम्य)

invisible, *adj.* na dekhine
(नदेखिने), adrishya (अदृश्य)

invitation, *n.* nimto (निम्तो),
nimtA (निम्ता),
nimantraNA (निमन्त्रणा)

invite, *v.* nimto dinu
(निम्तो दिनु),
nimtyAunu (निम्त्याउनु)

invoice, *n.* bil (बिल),
hisAb (हिसाब)

involve, *v.* sarik/samAwesh
garnu (सरिक/समावेश गर्नु)

involvement, *n.* saṁlagnatA
(संलग्नता)

inward, *adj.* bhitra ko (भित्रको),
bhitra tira (भित्रतिर)

iron, *n.* phalAm (फलाम),
lohA (लोहा), istrI (इस्त्री)
v. istrI garnu (इस्त्री गर्नु)

ironical, *adj.* wiDambanA pUrN (विडम्बनापूर्ण)

ironmonger, *n.* phalAme bhAñDA wA aujAr ko kArobAr garne (फलामे भाँडा वा औजारको कारोबार गर्ने)

irony, *n.* wiDambanA (विडम्बना)

irrational, *adj.* tark hIn (तर्कहीन), yukti hIn (युक्तिहीन)

irregular, *adj.* na milne (नमिल्ने), aniyamit (अनियमित)

irrelevant, *adj.* asambaddh (असम्बद्ध), asañgat (असङ्गत)

irreparable, *adj.* marammat garna na sakine (मरम्मत गर्न नसकिने)

irresistible, *adj.* wirodh garna na sakine (विरोध गर्न नसकिने), durdhar (दुर्धर)

irrigate, *v. (field)* paTAunu (पटाउनु), siñchnu (सिँच्नु)

irrigation, *n.* siñchAi (सिँचाइ)

irritate, *v.* ris uThAunu (रिस उठाउनु),

irritation, *n.* ris (रिस), jhok (भोक), jharko (भर्को)

is, *v./aux.* chha (छ), ho (हो)

island, *n.* TApu (टापु), dwIp (द्वीप)

isolate, *v.* alagyAunu (अलग्याउनु)

issue, *n. (offspring)* santAn (सन्तान), *(journal)* añk (अङ्क), *(question)* prashna (प्रश्न) *v.* niskanu (निस्कनु), prakAsh hunu (प्रकाश हुनु)

it, *pron.* yo (यो)

itch, *n.* chilAi (चिलाइ), luto (लुतो) *v.* chilAunu (चिलाउनु)

item, *n.* wishaya (विषय), wiwraN (विवरण), goTA (गोटा)

itinerary, *n.* saphar/yAtrA tAlikA (सफर/यात्रा तालिका)

its, *pron.* yas ko (यसको)

itself, *pron.* yo Aphai (यो आफै)

ivory, *n.* hasti hAD (हस्तिहाड)

J

jack, *n.* moTar uchAlne aujAr (मोटर उचाल्ने औजार), *(cards)* gulAm (गुलाम)

jackal, *n.* syAl (स्याल)

jack in office, *n.* rawAphilo karmchArI (रवाफिलो कर्मचारी)

jack of all trades, *n.* sabai wishaya ali ali jAnne (सबै विषय अलि अलि जान्ने)

jackass, *n.* bhAle gadhA (भाले गधा)

jacket, *n.* koT (कोट), jyAkeT (ज्याकेट), *(book)* khol (खोल)

jackfruit, *n.* rUkh kaThar (रूखकटहर)

jackknife, *n.* ThUlo chakku (ठूलो चक्कु)

jade, *n.* thAkeko ghoDA (थाकेको घोडा), *(stone)* harit maNi (हरितमणि)

jail, *n.* jel (जेल), jhyAl khAnA (भ्यालखाना) *v.* thunnu (थुन्नु), kaid garnu (कैद गर्नु)

jailor, *n.* jelar (जेलर), jhyAl khAnA ko hAkim (भ्यालखानाको हाकिम)

jam, *n.* rukAwaT (रुकावट), bhID (भीड), *(fruit)* jAm (जाम), phal phUl ra chinI pakAera banAeko bAklo ledo (फलफूल र चिनी पकाएर बनाएको बाक्लो लेदो)

jamboree, *n.* keTA skAuT harU ko bhelA (केटा स्काउटहरूको भेला), samAroh (समारोह)

jar, *n.* *(glass)* ThUlo sisI (ठूलो सिसी), *(metal)* ghalchhA (गल्छा), gAgro (गाग्रो), gAgrI (गाग्री), *(pottery)* ghaiñTo (घैँटो), hAñDo (हाँडो)

jargon, *n.* bakwAs (बकवास), wishisT bolI (विशिष्ट बोली)

jasmine, *n.* chamelI (चमेली)

jasper, *n.* sUrya kAnt maNi (सूर्यकान्त मणि)

jaundice, *n.* kamal pitta (कमलपित्त)

javelin, *n.* bhAlA (भाला), barchhA (बर्छा)

jaw, *n.* bañgAro (बङ्गारो), bañgarA (बङ्गारा)

jazz, *n.* jyAj saṅgIt (ज्याज
सङ्गीत), amerikI habsI mUl
ko saṅgIt (अमेरिकी हब्सी
मूलको सङ्गीत)

jazzy, *adj.* chaDkA (चड्का)

jealous, *adj.* ikhAlu (इखालु),
DAhA garne (डाहा गर्ने)

jealousy, *n.* DahA (डाहा),
Ikh (ईख), IrshyA (ईर्ष्या)

jean, *n.* jIn kapaDA
(जीन कपडा)

jeep, *n. (vehicle)* jIp (जीप)

jeer, *v.* gijyAunu (गिज्याउनु),
khisI garnu (खिसी गर्नु)

jelly, *n.* jeli (जेलि), phal phUl
bATa baneko thalthale wastu
(फलफूलबाट बनेको थलथले
वस्तु)

jeopardy, *n.* shaṅkA (शङ्का),
bhaya (भय), Dar (डर)

jerk, *n.* jhaTkA (झट्का),
jhokka (झोक्का)
v. jhaTkA dinu (झट्का दिनु)

jerkin, *n.* bAhulA na bhaeko
kasieko jyAkeT (बाहुला
नभएको कसिएको ज्याकेट)

jersey, *n.* ganjI (गन्जी)

jest, *n.* ThaTTA (ठट्टा),
dillagI (दिल्लगी)
v. ThaTTA garnu (ठट्टा गर्नु)

jester, *n.* ThaTTA garne (ठट्टा
गर्ने), widUshak (विदूषक)

jet, *n.* chhirkA (चिर्का),

sirkA (सिर्का), *(plane)* jeT
wimAn (जेटविमान)
v. sirkA chhuTnu
(सिर्का छुट्नु)

jet-black, *adj.* gADhA kAlo
(गाढा कालो)

jet engine, *n.* sirkA ko joD le
chalne injin (सिर्कको जोडले
चल्ने इन्जिन)

jet lag, *n.* lAmo uDAn pachhi
lAgne thakAi
(लामो उडान पछि लाग्ने थकाइ)

jet plane, *n.* jeT wimAn
(जेटविमान)

Jew, *n.* yahUdI (यहूदी)

jewel, *n.* ratna (रत्न),
juhArat (जुहारत)

jeweller, *n.* juhArI (जुहारी),
jauharI (जौहरी)

jewellery, *n.* gahnA (गहना),
juhArAt (जुहारात)

jingle, *n.* sAnA ghaNTI ko
TanTan AwAj (साना घण्टीको
टनटन आवाज)

jinx, *n.* alachchhinA wyakti
wA wastu (अलच्छिना व्यक्ति
वा वस्तु)

job, *n.* kAm (काम),
nokarI (नोकरी)

jobless, *adj.* DhAkre (ढाक्रे),
be rojgAr (बेरोजगार)

jockey, *n.* ghoD dauD ko
sabAr (घोडदौडको सबार)

jocular, *adj.* ThaTyaulo
(ठट्यौलो), hañsilo (हँसिलो)

jog, *v.* ghach ghachyAunu
(घचघच्याउनु),
dhakkA dinu (धक्का दिनु),
(exercise) wistArai dauDanu
(विस्तारै दौडनु)

join, *v.* jornu (जोर्नु),
gAñsnu (गाँस्नु),
(group) sañga lAgnu (सँग
लाग्नु), *(orgn., etc.)* bharnA
hunu (भर्ना हुनु), prawesh
garnu (प्रवेश गर्नु), sadasyatA
linu (सदस्यता लिनु)

joint, *adj.* samyukta (संयुक्त)
n. jornI (जोर्नी)

joke, *n.* ThaTTA (ठट्टा), dillagI
(दिल्लगी), ThaTeulI (ठटेउली)
v. ThaTTA/khyAl khyAl
garnu (ठट्टा/ख्यालख्याल गर्नु)

jolly, *adj.* khush (खुश),
majA ko (मजाको)

jolt, *n.* dhakkA (धक्का)
v. dhakkA dinu (धक्का दिनु),
ghach ghachyAunu
(घचघच्याउनु)

jot, *n.* thorai (थोरै), sAnu (सानु)
v. (write) lekhnu (लेख्नु),
Tipnu (टिप्नु)

journal, *n.* patrikA (पत्रिका),
bahi khAtA (बहिखाता)

journalism, *n.* patra kAritA
(पत्रकारिता)

journalist, *n.* patra kAr
(पत्रकार)

journey, *n.* yAtrA (यात्रा),
saphar (सफर),
v. yAtrA/saphar garnu
(यात्रा/सफर गर्नु)

jovial, *adj.* AnandI (आनन्दी),
maujI (मौजी)

joy, *n.* khushI (खुशी),
harsh (हर्ष)

jubilant, *adj.* dañg (दङ्ग),
dañg dAs (दङ्गदास)

jubilation, *n.* harsh (हर्ष),
harshollAs (हर्षोल्लास)

jubilee, *n.* jayantI (जयन्ती)

judge, *n.* nyAyAdhIsh
(न्यायाधीश)
v. nyAya/phaislA garnu
(न्याय/फैसला गर्नु), *(estimate)*
anumAn garnu (अनुमान गर्नु)

judg(e)ment, *n.* insAph (इन्साफ),
nyAya (न्याय), wiwek (विवेक)

judicial, *adj.* adAlatI (अदालती),
nyAyik (न्यायिक)

judiciary, *n.* nyAya pAlikA
(न्यायपालिका)

judicious, *adj.* wiwekI (विवेकी),
pakkA wichAr bhaeko
(पक्का विचार भएको)

judo, *n.* jApAnI kustI
(जापानी कुस्ती), judo (जुडो)

jug, *n.* jag (जग), surAhI (सुराही),
kalash (कलश)

juggler, *n.* jAdugar (जादुगर), chaTkI (चटकी)

juice, *n.* ras (रस), jhol (झोल)

juicy, *adj.* rasilo (रसिलो), rasdAr (रसदार)

jumble, *n.* thupro (थुप्रो), misAwaT (मिसावट)
v. pasAro garnu (पसारो गर्नु), misAunu (मिसाउनु)

jumbo, *adj.* baDemAn (बडेमान), ati ThUlo (अति ठूलो)

jumbo jet, *n.* ati ThUlo jeT wimAn (अति ठूलो जेटविमान)

jump, *n.* phAl (फाल), uphrAi (उफ्राइ)
v. uphranu (उफ्रनु), phAl hAlnu (फाल हाल्नु)

jump the gun, *v.* belA na bhaI suru garnu (बेला नभई सुरु गर्नु)

jump jet, *n.* ThADai uDne ra orlane jeT wimAn (ठाडै उड्ने र ओर्लने जेटविमान)

jumpsuit, *n. (woman)* sabai sharIr DhAkne euTA singai sUT (सबै शरीर ढाक्ने एउटा सिङ्गै सूट)

jumper, *n.* UnI suiTar (ऊनी सुइटर)

junction, *n.* jornI (जोर्नी), sangam (सङ्गम)

juncture, *n.* sankaT ko sthiti (सङ्कटको स्थिति)

jungle, *n.* ban (बन), wan (वन), jangal (जङ्गल)

junior, *n.* nAyab (नायब), kAnchho (कान्छो), sAnu (सानु)

Jupiter, *n.* wrihaspati graha (वृहस्पति ग्रह)

jury, *n.* jurI (जुरी), phaislA garna sahayog garne bArha janA ko samUh (फैसला गर्न सहयोग गर्ने बाह्र जनाको समूह)

just, *adj.* nyAyI (न्यायी), yogya (योग्य), uchit (उचित)

just before, *adv.* ali aghi (अलि अघि)

just now, *adv.* bharkharai (भखरै)

justice, *n.* nyAya (न्याय), insAph (इन्साफ)

justify, *v.* auchitya dekhAunu (औचित्य देखाउनु), uchit dekhAunu (उचित देखाउनु)

jut, *n.* chuchcho (चुच्चो), Tuppo (टुप्पो)

jute, *n.* san (सन), san pAT (सनपाट)

juvenile, *adj.* taruN (तरुण), kishor sambandhI (किशोरसम्बन्धी)

juvenile delinquency, *n.* nAbAlig aprAdh (नाबालिग अपराध)

K

kaleidoscope, n. barAbar badli rahane drishya (बराबर बदलिरहने दृश्य)

keen, adj. TATho (ठाठो), tej (तेज), tIwra (तीव्र)

keenness, n. tIwratA (तीव्रता)

keep, v. rAkhnu (राख्नु), rakshA garnu (रक्षा गर्नु), *(for keeps)*, sadhaiñ ko lAgi (सधैंको लागि)

keepsake, n. chinu (चिनु), samjhauTo (सम्झौटो)

kennel, n. kukur khor (कुकुर खोर)

kerchief, n. majetro (मजेत्रो), rumAl (रुमाल)

kernel, n. gudI (गुदी)

kerosene, n. maTTI tel (मट्टीतेल)

ketchup, n. gol bheñDA Adi ko ras bATa baneko sas (गोलभेंडा आदिको रसबाट बनेको सस)

kettle, n. pAnI tatAune bhAñDo (पानी तताउने भाँडो), kitlI (किट्ली)

key, n. sAñcho (साँचो), kUñjI (कुञ्जी), *(geo.)* hocho TApu

(होचो टापु), *(word, etc.)* wyAkhyA (व्याख्या)

keynote, n. pramukh wichAr (प्रमुख विचार)

keyring, n. sAñcho harU hAlne riñ (साँचोहरू हाल्ने रिङ), jhutto (भुत्तो)

keyhole, n. sAñcho chhirAune pwAl (साँचो छिराउने प्वाल)

khaki, n. khAkI kapaDA (खाकी कपडा)

kick, n. lAt (लात), lAttI (लात्ती) v. lAt hAnnu (लात हान्नु), latyAunu (लत्याउनु)

kick out, n. nikAli dinu (निकालिदिनु)

kickback,n. kamisan (कमिसन)

kick-off, n. khel Adi shuru (खेल आदि शुरु)

kid, n. keTA keTI (केटाकेटी), bachchA (बच्चा) v. chhalnu (छल्नु), chhakAunu (छकाउनु)

kidnap, v. apa haraN garnu (अपहरण गर्नु)

kidney, n. mirgaulA (मिर्गौला)

kill, v. mArnu (मार्नु), khatam garnu (खतम गर्नु)

killer, *n.* hatyArA (हत्यारा),
jyAn mArA (ज्यानमारा)

kiln, *n.* awAl (अवाल),
bhaTTA (भट्टा)

kilogram(me), *n.* hajAr grAm
(हजार ग्राम), kilo (किलो)

kin, *n.* nAtA dAr (नातादार)

kind, *adj.* dayAlu (दयालु),
kripAlu (कृपालु)
n. kisim (किसिम),
Dhaṅg (ढङ्ग),
prakAr (प्रकार), tharI (थरी)

kindergarten, *n.* shishu
widyAlaya (शिशु विद्यालय)

kindle, *v.* bAlnu (बाल्नु),
salkAunu (सल्काउनु)

kindly, *adv.* dayA/kripA
pUrwak (दया/कृपापूर्वक)

kindness, *n.* dayA (दया),
kripA (कृपा)

king, *n.* rAjA (राजा),
mahArAjA (महाराजा),
(Nepal) mahA rAjAdhirAj
(महाराजाधिराज)

kingdom, *n.* adhirAjya
(अधिराज्य), rAjya (राज्य)

kingpin, *n.* Awashyak wyakti
(आवश्यक व्यक्ति)

kingship, *n.* rAjA ko pad
(राजाको पद)

kiosk, *n.* akhbAr ra khAn pin
kA wastu bechne sAnu
khulA pasal (अखबार र
खानपिनका वस्तु बेच्ने सानु
खुला पसल)

kiss, *n.* mwAIṅ (म्वाई),
chumban (चुम्बन)
v. mwAIṅ khAnu (म्वाई खानु),
chumban garnu (चुम्बन गर्नु)

kit, *n.* sAmAn (सामान)

kitchen, *n.* bhAnsA koThA
(भान्साकोठा)

kitchen garden, *n.* karesA
bArI (करेसाबारी)

kite, *n.* chaṅgA (चङ्गा),
(bird) chIl (चील)

kitten, *n.* birAlo ko bachchA
(बिरालोको बच्चा)

kleptomania, *n.* chorI garna
lAlAyit hune rog
(चोरी गर्न लालायित हुने रोग)

knack, *n.* sIp (सीप), yukti (युक्ति)

knapsack, *n.* pachhil tira
bokne TAT wA chhAlA ko
byAg (पछिल्तिर बोक्ने टाट वा
छालाको ब्याग)

knave, *n./adj.* dhUrt (धूर्त),
swAṅTh (स्वाँठ)

knead, *v.* piTho/mATo
muchhnu (पिठो/माटो मुछ्नु)

knee, *n.* ghuṅDA (घुँडा)

kneecap, *n.* ghuṅDA ko
chakkA (घुँडाको चक्का)

knee-deep, *adj.* ghuṅDA
samma ko gahiro
(घुँडासम्मको गहिरो)

kneel, *v.* ghuñDA Teknu (घुँडा टेक्नु)

knife, *n.* chakku (चक्कु), chhurA (छुरा)

knit, *v.* bunnu (बुन्नु)

knob, *n.* gaTTA (गट्टा), gAñTho (गाँठो)

knock, *n.* danak (दनक), jhApaT (झापट) *v.* ghach ghachyAunu (घचघच्याउनु), khaT khaTAunu (खटखटाउनु)

knock down, *v.* pachhArnu (पछार्नु), bhatkAunu (भत्काउनु)

knoll, *n.* Dhisko (ढिस्को), thumko (थुम्को)

knot, *n.* gAñTho (गाँठो), kATh ko Añkho (काठको आँखो)

knotty, *adj.* gaThilo (गठिलो), kaThin (कठिन), jaTil (जटिल)

know, *v.* chinnu (चिन्नु), jAnnu (जान्नु), thAhA hunu (थाहा हुनु)

know-how, *n.* sIp (सीप), jAnkArI (जानकारी)

knowingly, *adv.* jAnI jAnI (जानीजानी)

knowledge, *n.* gỹAn (ज्ञान), ilam (इलम)

known, *adj.* thAhA bhaeko (थाहा भएको), gỹAt (ज्ञात)

knuckle, *n.* auñlA ko jornI (औंलाको जोर्नी)

knuckle down, *v.* man diyera kAm mA lAgnu (मन दिएर काममा लाग्नु)

knuckle under, *v.* hAr mAnnu (हार मान्नु), dabnu (दब्नु)

L

lab, *n. (abb.)* prayog shAlA (प्रयोगशाला), lyAb (ल्याब)

label, *n.* chinha patra (चिन्हपत्र), lebul (लेबुल) *v.* TAñsnu (टाँस्नु), chipkAunu (चिप्काउनु), nAm karaN garnu (नामकरण गर्नु)

laboratory, *n.* prayog shAlA (प्रयोगशाला)

laborious, *adj.* parishramI (परिश्रमी), mehnatI (मेहनती)

labo(u)r, *n.* kAm (काम), shram (श्रम), mehnat (मेहनत) *v.* mehnat/parishram garnu (मेहनत/परिश्रम गर्नु)

labo(u)rer, *n.* jyAmI (ज्यामी), majdUr (मजदूर)

lace, *n.* phittA (फित्ता),
tunA (तुना), les (लेस)
v. phittA bAndhnu (फित्ता बाँध्नु),
kinArA hAlnu (किनारा हाल्नु)

lack, *n.* kamI (कमी), abhAw
(अभाव), khAncho (खाँचो)
v. kam hunu (कम हुनु),
na pugnu (नपुग्नु)

lackadaisical, *adj.* shithil
(शिथिल), phurtilo na bhaeko
(फुर्तिलो नभएको)

lackey, *n.* nokar (नोकर),
TahaluA (टहलुआ)

ladder, *n.* bharyAn̐ (भर्‍याङ),
sin̐DhI (सिँढी), lisnu (लिस्नु)

ladle, *n.* DADu (डाडु)
v. DADu le hAlnu
(डाडुले हाल्नु),
khanyAunu (खन्याउनु)

lady, *n.* mahilA (महिला),
strI (स्त्री), *(young)*
tarunI (तरुनी), keTI (केटी)

lady's finger, *n.* rAm toriyAn̐
(रामतोरियाँ)

lag, *v.* pachhi parnu (पछि पर्नु)

laissez-faire, *n.* wyApAr mA
hastakshep na garne nIti
(व्यापारमा हस्तक्षेप नगर्ने नीति)

lake, *n.* tAl (ताल), daha (दह),
jhIl (झील)

lamb, *n.(sheep)* pATho (पाठो)

lame, *adj.* lan̐gaDo (लङ्गडो),
khoraNDo (खोरण्डो)

lame duck, *n.* shakti hIn
wyakti (शक्तिहीन व्यक्ति),
diwAliyA saṃsthA
(दिवालिया संस्था)

lament, *v.* shok/wilAp garnu
(शोक/विलाप गर्नु)

lamp, *n.* battI (बत्ती),
diyo (दियो), pAnas (पानस)

land, *n.* jamIn (जमीन),
jaggA (जग्गा), desh (देश)
v. utranu (उत्रनु), orlanu (ओर्लनु)

landholder, *n.* jaggA dhanI
(जग्गाधनी)

landlady, *n.* ghar paTinI
(घरपटिनी), sAhunI (साहुनी)

landlocked, *adj.* bhU
pariweshTit (भूपरिवेष्टित)

landlord, *n.* *(house)* ghar paTI
(घरपटी),
(land) jamindAr (जमिनदार)

landmark, *n.* sarahd (सरहद),
sImA chinha (सीमाचिन्ह),
(his.) mahattwa pUrN
ghaTnA (महत्त्वपूर्ण घटना)

landmine, *n.* jamIn muni
rAkhieko wisphoTak
(जमीनमुनि राखिएको
विस्फोटक)

landscape, *n.* bhU drishya
(भूदृश्य)

landslide, *n.* pahiro (पहिरो),
(election) atyadhik bahumat
(अत्यधिक बहुमत)

landowner, *n.* jaggA dhanI
(जग्गाधनी),
jaggA wAl (जग्गावाल)

lane, *n.* gallI (गल्ली),
sA̐guro bATo (साँगुरो बाटो)

language, *n.* bhAshA (भाषा),
bolI (बोली)

languish, *v.* shithil / durbal
hunu (शिथिल/दुर्बल हुनु)

lanky, *adj.* aglo ra dublo
(अग्लो र दुब्लो)

lantern, *n.* lAlTin (लालटिन),
battI (बत्ती)

lap, *n.* kAkh (काख)
v. (cat, etc.) chATnu (चाट्नु)

lapel, *n.* kaThAlo (कठालो)

lapse, *n.* bhUl chUk (भूलचूक),
sAnu galtI (सानु गल्ती)
v. gujranu (गुज्रनु),
myAd nAghnu (म्याद नाघ्नु)

larceny, *n.* chorI (चोरी)

large, *adj.* ThUlo (ठूलो),
(at large), *phr.* mukta (मुक्त),
pharAr (फरार)

largely, *adv.* dherai had samma
(धेरै हदसम्म),
dherai jaso (धेरैजसो)

lascivious, *adj.* kAmuk
(कामुक), wyasanI (व्यसनी)

laser, *n.* ekai dishA mA jAne
shakti shAlI wikiraN paidA
garne upkaraN
(एकै दिशामा जाने शक्तिशाली
विकिरण पैदा गर्ने उपकरण)

lash, *n.* korrA (कोर्रा)
v. korrA hAnnu (कोर्रा हान्नु)

last, *adj.* antim (अन्तिम),
AkhirI (आखिरी)
v. aDnu (अड्नु),
pugnu (पुग्नु), thegnu (थेग्नु),
(at last), *phr.* Akhir mA
(आखिरमा)

last night, *n.* pachhillo rAt
(पछिल्लो रात)

last time, *n.* pachhillo paTak
(पछिल्लो पटक)

last year, *n.* pohor (sAl)
(पोहोर (साल))

lasting, *adj.* TikAu (टिकाउ),

lastly, *adv.* Akhir mA
(आखिरमा), khapne (खप्ने)

latch, *n.* chukul (चुकुल),
gajbAr (गजबार),
chheskinI (छेस्किनी)

late, *n.* abelA (अबेला),
aber (अबेर), Dhilo (ढिलो)
adj. (dead) swargIya
(स्वर्गीय), *(of late),* *phr.* hAlai
ko (हालैको)

lately, *adv.* hAlai (हालै)

later, *adj.* pachhi (पछि),
bhare (भरे)

lather, *n.* sAbun ko phIñj
(साबुनको फीँज)

latitude, *n.* akshAmsh (अक्षांश)

latrine, *n.* charpI (चर्पी)

latter, *adj.* pachhillo
(पछिल्लो), dosro (दोस्रो)

laugh, *n.* hAǹso (हाँसो)
v. hAǹsnu (हाँस्नु),
(to make laugh), phr.
haǹsAunu (हँसाउनु),
(to laugh at), phr. khisI
garnu (खिसी गर्नु)

laughing gas, *n.* haǹsAune
gyAǹs (हँसाउने ग्याँस)
[*nAiTras aksAiD* (नाइट्रस
अक्साइड)]

laughing stock, *n.* majAk wA
ThaTTA ko pAtra
(मजाक वा ठट्टाको पात्र)

laughter, *n.* hAǹso (हाँसो)

launch, *v.* chhoDnu (छोड्नु),
prakshepaN garnu
(प्रक्षेपण गर्नु)
n. jahAj ko DuǹgA
(जहाजको डुङ्गा)

laundry, *n.* dhobI ko ghar
(धोबीको घर), lugA dhune
pasal (लुगा धुने पसल),
(clothes) dhune lugA ko
Daǹgur (धुने लुगाको डङ्गुर)

lavatory, *n.* charpI (चर्पी),
shauchAlaya (शौचालय)

lavish, *adj.* man phukAera
kharch garnu
(मन फुकाएर खर्च गर्नु),
ati udAr (अति उदार)

law, *n.* kAnUn (कानून), ain (ऐन)

lawful, *adj.* kAnUnI (कानूनी),
nyAya pUrN (न्यायपूर्ण)

lawless, *adj.* man parI garne
(मनपरी गर्ने),
anAchArI (अनाचारी)

lawn, *n.* chaur (चौर),
maidAn (मैदान)

lawsuit, *n.* muddA (मुद्दा),
mAmilA (मामिला)

lawyer, *n.* wakIl (वकील),
kAnUn wettA (कानूनवेत्ता)

lay, *v.* bichhAunu (बिछ्याउनु,
rAkhnu (राख्नु),
ochhyAunu (ओछ्याउनु),
(eggs) phul pArnu (फुल पार्नु)

lay aside, *v.* alag rAkhnu
(अलग राख्नु),
chuTTyAunu (छुट्ट्याउनु)

lay down, *v.* bujhAunu
(बुझाउनु), tyAgnu (त्याग्नु)

lay waste, *v.* nAsh garnu
(नाश गर्नु)

layer, *n.* tah (तह)

layman, *n.* Am/sAdharAN
wyakti (आम/साधारण व्यक्ति)

lay-off, *n.* asthAyI khArejI ko
awadhi (अस्थायी खारेजीको
अवधि), kAm na hune/garne
awasthA (काम नहुने/गर्ने
अवस्था)

layout, *n.* sajAwaT (सजावट)

laziness, *n.* Alasya (आलस्य)

lazy, *adj.* alchhI (अल्छी),
alsI (अल्सी), alse (अल्से)

lead, *n. (metal)* sisA (सिसा),
(leash) DorI (डोरी),
dAmlo (दाम्लो),
(role, etc.) pramukh (प्रमुख)
v. DoryAunu (डोर्‍याउनु),
bATo dekhAunu
(बाटो देखाउनु),
netritwa garnu (नेतृत्व गर्नु)

leader, *n.* netA (नेता), nAike
(नाइके), aguwA (अगुवा)

leading, *adj.* pramukh (प्रमुख),
pahilo (पहिलो)

leaf, *n.* pAt (पात), pAnA (पाना)

leaflet, *n.* sAnu pAt (सानु पात),
parchA (पर्चा),
patrikA (पत्रिका)

leak, *n.* chuhAwaT (चुहावट)
v. chuhunu (चुहुनु),
khulnu (खुल्नु)

leakage, *n.* chuhAwaT (चुहावट)

leaky, *adj.* chuhine (चुहिने)

lean, *adj.* dublo (दुब्लो),
pAtalo (पातलो)
v. Dhessinu (ढेस्सिनु),
aDes lAunu (अडेस लाउनु),
Dhalkanu (ढल्कनु)

leap, *n.* chhalAṅg (छलाङ्ग),
uphryAi (उफ्राइ)
v. uphranu (उफ्रनु),
phAl hAlnu (फालहाल्नु)

(by leaps and bounds), *phr.*
dherai chhiTTo (धेरै छिट्टो)

learn, *v.* siknu (सिक्नु),

paDhnu (पढ्नु), jAnnu (जान्नु)

learned, *adj.* widwAn (विद्वान),
paDhe lekheko (पढेलेखेको)

learning, *n.* widyA (विद्या),
gyAn (ज्ञान)

leash, *n.* DorI (डोरी),
dAmlo (दाम्लो), sikrI (सिक्री)

least, *adj.* sabai bhandA thorai
(सबैभन्दा थोरै), ***(at least),*** *phr.*
kamtI mA (कम्तीमा)

leather, *n.* chhAlA (छाला),
chamaDA (चमडा)

leave, *n.* bidA (बिदा),
chhuTTI (छुट्टी)
v. chhoDnu (छोड्नु),
chhADnu (छाड्नु),
(to take one's leave of), *phr.*
bidA hunu (बिदा हुनु)

leave off, *v.* chhoDnu (छोड्नु)

lecture, *n.* bhAshaN (भाषण)
v. bhAshaN dinu
(भाषण दिनु)

lecturer, *n.* up prAdhyApak
(उपप्राध्यापक)

ledger, *n.* bahI khAtA
(बही खाता)

leech, *n.* jukA (जुका),
jugA (जुगा)

left, *adj.* debre (देब्रे),
bAyAṅ (बायाँ)

leftist, *n.* wAm panthI
(वामपन्थी)

leftover, *adj.* ubrieko (उब्रिएको)

left wing, *n.* wAm panthI dal (वामपन्थी दल)

lefty, *adj.* debre hAt chalne (देब्रे हात चल्ने)

leg, *n.* goDA (गोडा), khuTTA (खुट्टा) *v.* khuTTA lAunu (खुट्टा लाउनु)

legacy, *n.* bapautI (बपौती), wirAsat (विरासत)

legal, *adj.* kAnUnI (कानूनी)

legend, *n.* dantya/paurANik kathA (दन्त्य/पौराणिक कथा)

legible, *adj.* paDhna sakine (पढ्न सकिने)

legislation, *n.* ain (ऐन), kAnUn (कानून), widhAn (विधान)

legislative, *adj.* wyawasthApikA (व्यवस्थापिका)

legislature, *n.* widhAn sabhA (विधानसभा), wyawasthApikA (व्यवस्थापिका)

legitimate, *adj.* waidh (वैध), kAnUnI (कानूनी), jAyaj (जायज)

legume, *n.* geDA guDI (गेडागुडी)

leisure, *n.* phursat (फुर्सत), ArAm (आराम)

leisurely, *adv.* phursat mA/sa\nga (फुर्सतमा/सँग)

lemon, *n.* kAgatI (कागती), nibuwA (निबुवा)

lend, *v.* sApaT/riN dinu (सापट/ऋण दिनु)

length, *n.* lamAi (लमाइ), lambAi (लम्बाइ)

lengthy, *adj.* lAmo (लामो)

lens, *n.* chasmA ko ainA (चस्माको ऐना), lens (लेन्स)

lentil, *n.* dAl (दाल)

leopard, *n.* chituwA (चितुवा)

leper, *n.* korI (कोरी)

leprosy, *n.* kushTh rog (कुष्ठ रोग), kor (कोर)

lesbian, *n.* samli\ngI strI (समलिङ्गी स्त्री)

less, *adj.* kam (कम), thorai (थोरै)

lesson, *n.* pATh (पाठ), sabak (सबक)

let, *v.* garna dinu (गर्न दिनु), *(flat, etc.)* bahAl mA dinu (बहालमा दिनु)

let alone, *v.* chhoDi dinu (छोडिदिनु), hastakshep na garnu (हस्तक्षेप नगर्नु)

let down, *v.* dhokA dinu (धोका दिनु)

let go, *v.* chhodnu (छोड्नु)

let in, *v.* prawesh garna dinu (प्रवेश गर्न दिनु)

let in for, *v.* samlagna garAunu (संलग्न गराउनु)

let loose, *v.* rihA garnu
(रिहा गर्नु),
chhADi dinu (छाडिदिनु)

let on, *v.* gopya/kurA kholnu
(गोप्य/कुरा खोल्नु)

let up, *v.* kam/shithil hunu
(कम/शिथिल हुनु)

lethal, *adj.* ghAtak (घातक),
mArne khAle (मार्ने खाले)

lethargy, *n.* udAsIntA
(उदासीनता), jAñgar nahune
awasthA (जाँगर नहुने अवस्था)

letter, *n.* chiThI (चिठी),
patra (पत्र),
(alphabet) akshar (अक्षर)

letter box, *n.* patra mañjUshA
(पत्रमञ्जूषा)

letterhead, *n.* nAm ra
ThegAna chhApieko lekhne
pyAD (नाम र ठेगाना
छापिएको लेख्ने प्याड)

lettuce, *n.* jirI ko sAg
(जिरीको साग)

let-up, *n.* wirAm (विराम),
sthagan (स्थगन)

leuk(a)emia, *n.* ragat mA setA
rakta kaN hune rog (रगतमा
सेता रक्त कण हुने रोग)

level, *n.* tah (तह), star (स्तर)
adj. (ground) samma (सम्म),
(even) barAbar (बराबर)

lever, *n.* gal (गल),
uttolak (उत्तोलक)

lever up, *v.* ukkAunu
(उक्काउनु)

liability, *n.* dAyitwa (दायित्व)

liable, *adj.* jawAph deh
(जबाफदेह),
jimmewAr (जिम्मेवार)

liaison, *n.* sampark (सम्पर्क),
samsarg (संसर्ग)

liaison officer, *n.* sampark
adhikrit (सम्पर्क अधिकृत)

liar, *n.* jhUTo bolne (झूटो
बोल्ने), phaTAhA (फटाहा)

liberal, *adj.* udAr (उदार)

liberate, *v.* mukta garnu
(मुक्त गर्नु)

liberation, *n.* mukti (मुक्ति),
chhuTkArA (छुट्कारा)

liberty, *n.* swAdhIntA (स्वाधीनता),
swatantratA (स्वतन्त्रता)

libra, *n.* tulA rAshi (तुला राशि)

librarian, *n.* pustakAdhyaksha
(पुस्तकाध्यक्ष)

library, *n.* pustakAlaya
(पुस्तकालय)

lice, *n.* jumrA harU (जुम्राहरू)

licence, *n.* AgyÃ/anumati
patra (आज्ञा/अनुमति पत्र)

license, *v.* AgyÃ dinu
(आज्ञा दिनु)

lichen, *n.* jhyAu (भ्याउ)

lick, *v.* chATnu (चाट्नु)

lid, *n.* birko (बिर्को),
DhakanA (ढकना)

lie, *n.* jhUTo kurA (भूटो कुरा)
    v. (lie) jhUTo bolnu (भूटो
    बोल्नु), *(rest)* leTnu (लेट्नु)

lie down, *v.* sutnu (सुत्नु),
    Dhalkanu (ढल्कनु)

lie flat, *v.* pasrinu (पस्रिनु),
    lampasAr parnu (लम्पसार पर्नु)

life, *n.* jIwan (जीवन),
    jindagI (जिन्दगी)

lifeblood, *n.* jIwan dhAnne
    wastu (जीवन धान्ने वस्तु)

life cycle, *n.* jIwan chakra
    (जीवनचक्र)

life expectancy, *n.* AyurAshA
    (आयुराशा),
    Ausat Ayu (औसत आयु)

life insurance, *n.* jIwan bImA
    (जीवनबीमा)

lifeless, *adj.* be jAn (बेजान),
    nirjIw (निर्जीव)

lifeline, *n.* jyAn bachAuna
    prayog hune DorI (ज्यान
    बचाउन प्रयोग हुने डोरी)

lifelong, *adj.* AjIwan (आजीवन),
    jIwan bhar (जीवनभर)

life-size(d), *adj.* pUrn kad
    (पूर्णकद)

lifetime, *n.* junI (जुनी),
    jindagI (जिन्दगी)

lift, *n. (elevator)* liphT (लिफ्ट),
    uttolak (उत्तोलक)
    v. uchAlnu (उचाल्नु),
    uThAunu (उठाउनु)

light, *n.* prakAsh (प्रकाश),
    ujyAlo (उज्यालो), battI (बत्ती)
    adj. haluṅgo (हलुङ्गो)
    v. bAlnu (बाल्नु),
    salkAunu (सल्काउनु)

light bulb, *n.* bijulI ko gulup
    (बिजुलीको गुलुप)

light-colo(u)red, *adj.* phIkA
    raṅg ko (फीका रङ्गको)

light-fingered, *adj.* hAt pherne
    (हात फेर्ने), chorne (चोर्ने)

light-headed, *adj.* chapal
    (चपल), chañchal (चञ्चल)

light-hearted, *adj.* AnandI
    (आनन्दी),
    prasanna chitta (प्रसन्नचित्त)

light industry, *n.* sAnu udyog
    (सानु उद्योग)

lightning, *n.* chaTyAṅ (चट्याङ)

lightweight, *n.* kam mahattwa
    ko (कम महत्त्वको), *(boxing)*
    sAThI kejI samma ko taul
    (साठी केजीसम्मको तौल)

like, *adj.* jasto (जस्तो),
    saraha (सरह)
    v. ruchAunu (रुचाउनु),
    man parAunu (मन पराउनु)

likelihood, *n.* sambhAwanA
    (सम्भावना)

likely, *adj./adv.* sambhaw
    (सम्भव),
    sambhaw hune (सम्भव हुने),
    sambhawtah (सम्भवतः)

likeness, *n.* samAntA
(समानता),
prati rUp (प्रतिरूप)

likewise, *adv.* tyasai garI
(त्यसैगरी)

liking, *n.* ruchi (रुचि),
ichchhA (इच्छा)

lily, *n.* nalinI (नलिनी),
shwet kamal (श्वेतकमल)

limb, *n.* aṅg (अङ्ग),
hAt khuTTA (हातखुट्टा)

lime, *n.* (*citrus fruit*)
kAgatI (कागती),
(*chemical*) chUn (चून)

limestone, *n.* chUn DhuṅgA
(चूनढुङ्गा)

limit, *n.* sImA (सीमा), had (हद)
v. sImit garnu (सीमित गर्नु),
roknu (रोक्नु)

limitation, *n.* sImittA
(सीमितता),
niyantraN (नियन्त्रण)

limited, *adj.* sImit (सीमित),
(*company*) sImit saṃsthAn
(सीमित संस्थान)

limitless, *adj.* sImA rahit
(सीमारहित), asIm (असीम)

limousine, *n.* band moTar
gADI (बन्द मोटरगाडी)

limp, *adj.* lulo (लुलो)
v. khochyAunu (खोच्याउनु)

line, *n.* rekhA (रेखा),
dharko (धर्को), Doro (डोरो),

(*people, writing*)
paṅkti (*पङ्क्ति*),
(*lineage*) khalak (खलक),
wamsh (वंश)
v. rekhA kornu (रेखा कोर्नु)
dharko tAnnu (धर्को तान्नु)

lineage, *n.* kul (कुल),
khalak (खलक),
gharAnA (घराना)

linen, *n.* sutI kapaDA
(सुती कपडा), tannA (तन्ना)

line-up, *n.* paṅkti (पङ्क्ति)
v. paṅktibaddh garnu/hunu
(पङ्क्तिबद्ध गर्नु/हुनु)

linguist, *n.* bhAshA wid
(भाषाविद्)

liniment, *n.* mAlis (मालिस),
lep (लेप)

lining, *n.* lugA ko bhitrI
(लुगाको भित्री)

link, *n.* joD (जोड),
jornI (जोर्नी), kaDI (कडी)
v. jornu (जोर्नु)

linkage, *n.* sambaddhtA
(सम्बद्धता), saṃyojan (संयोजन)

linseed, *n.* Alas (आलस),
tisI (तिसी)

lion, *n.* simha (सिंह)

lioness, *n.* simhinI (सिंहिनी)

lip, *n.* oTh (ओठ), adhar (अधर)

lip-service, *n.* chepAre bolI
(चेपारे बोली),
chAplusI (चापलुसी)

lipstick, *n.* lAlI (लाली),
lipisTik (लिपिस्टिक)

liquid, *n.* taral (तरल),
jhol (झोल)

liquidate, *v.* mArnu (मार्नु),
sidhyAunu (सिध्याउनु)

liquor, *n. (Am.)* raksI (रक्सी)

list, *n.* sUchI (सूची),
phirist (फिरिस्त)
v. sUchI banAunu
(सूची बनाउनु), phirist lekhnu
(फिरिस्त लेख्नु)

listen, *v.* sunnu (सुन्नु),
kAn thApnu (कान थाप्नु)

listener, *n.* sunne wyakti
(सुन्ने व्यक्ति)

literal, *adj.* aksharashah
(अक्षरशः), shAbdik (शाब्दिक)

literary, *adj.* sAhityik
(साहित्यिक)

literate, *adj.* lekh paDh garna
jAnne (लेखपढ गर्न जान्ने),
sAkshar (साक्षर)

literature, *n.* sAhitya (साहित्य)

litre/liter, *n.* liTar (लिटर)

litter, *n.* phohar mailA
(फोहरमैला), sotar (सोतर)

little, *adj.* sAnu (सानु),
sAno (सानो)
(a little), *adv.* ali (अलि),
ali kati (अलिकति)

live, *adj.* jIuÑdo (जिउँदो),
sajIw (सजीव),

(wire) kareNt bhaeko/nAÑgo
(करेण्ट भएको/नाङ्गो)
v. basnu (बस्नु), rahanu
(रहनु), bAÑchnu (बाँच्नु),
jiunu (जिउनु)

livelihood, *n.* jIwikA (जीविका),
gujArA (गुजारा)

lively, *adj.* phurtilo (फुर्तिलो),
sajIw (सजीव)

liver, *n.* kalejo (कलेजो)

livestock, *n.* gAI wastu
(गाईवस्तु)

living, *adj.* jIwikA (जीविका),
rahan sahan (रहनसहन)

Living Goddess, *n. (Nepal)*
kumArI (कुमारी)

living room, *n.* baiThak (बैठक)

lizard, *n.* chhepAro (छेपारो)

load, *n.* bhArI (भारी),
bojh (बोझ)
v. lAdnu (लादनु), bokAunu
(बोकाउनु), bharnu (भर्नु)

loaf, *n.* pAu roTI (पाउरोटी)
v. alchhI garnu (अल्छी गर्नु),
rallinu (रल्लिनु)

loafer, *n.* AwArA (आवारा)

loan, *n.* riN (ऋण),
painÑcho (पैंचो)

lobe, *n.* kAn ko lotI
(कानको लोती)

lobster, *n.* Thulo chiÑgDI
mAchhA (ठूलो चिङ्गडी माछा)

local, *adj.* sthAnIya (स्थानीय)

locality, *n*. Tol (टोल), thalo (थलो)

location, *n*. sthAn (स्थान), ThegAnA (ठेगाना)

lock, *n*. tAlchA (ताल्चा), *(hair)* chulTho (चुल्ठो), julphI (जुल्फी)
v. tAlchA mArnu (ताल्चा मार्नु), band garnu (बन्द गर्नु)

lock up, *v*. thankyAunu (थन्क्याउनु)

locust, *n*. salaha (सलह)

lodge, *n*. DerA (डेरा), laj (लज)
v. rAkhnu (राख्नु), bAs dinu (बास दिनु)

lodging, *n*. bAs (बास), DerA (डेरा)

lofty, *adj*. aglo (अग्लो), Uncho (ऊँचो)

log, *n*. kATh ko muDhA (काठको मुढा)

logic, *n*. tark (तर्क)

logical, *adj*. manAsib (मनासिब), tark sangat (तर्कसङ्गत)

loin, *n*. kammar (कम्मर), kaTi (कटि)

loincloth, *n*. kachhAD (कछाड), langauTI (लँगौटी)

loiter, *v*. bhauntArinu (भौंतारिनु), hallinu (हल्लिनु)

lone, *adj*. eklo (एक्लो), nirjan (निर्जन)

loneliness, *n*. eklo pan (एक्लोपन)

lonely, *adj*. ekAnt (एकान्त), sunsAn (सुनसान)

long, *adj*. lAmo (लामो)
v. chAhanA garnu (चाहना गर्नु), *(for a long time)* dherai ber samma (धेरै बेरसम्म), *(in the long run)* Akhir mA (आखिरमा)

long ago, *adv*. dherai aghi (धेरैअघि)

long distance, *adj*. lAmo dUrI ko (लामो दुरीको)

longevity, *n*. dIrghAyu (दीर्घायु)

long face, *n*. andhyAro mukh (अँध्यारो मुख)

longitude, *n*. deshAntar (देशान्तर)

long jump, *n*. lAmo dUrI ko uphrAi (लामो दूरीको उफ्राइ)

long life, *n*. lAmo Ayu (लामो आयु), dIrghAyu (दीर्घायु)

long range, *adj*. dherai dUrI ko (धेरै दूरीको), dIrgh kAlik (दीर्घकालिक)

long shot, *n*. andAj (अन्दाज)

long-term, *adj*. dIrgh kAlIn (दीर्घकालीन)

look, *n*. herAi (हेराइ), rUp (रूप), *(gaze)* najar (नजर)
v. hernu (हेर्नु)

look after, *v*. her wichAr/syAhAr garnu (हेरविचार/स्याहार गर्नु)

look for, *v.* khojnu (खोज्नु)

look forward to, *v.* apekshA garnu (अपेक्षा गर्नु)

look into, *v.* khoj talAs / chhAn bin garnu (खोजतलास/छानबिन गर्नु)

look like, *v.* jasto dekhinu (जस्तो देखिनु)

look out, *n.* rakhbArI garne ThAuṅ/mAnis (रखबारी गर्ने ठाउँ/मानिस)

look up, *v.* hernu (हेर्नु), bheTnu (भेट्नु)

loom, *n.* lugA bunne tAn (लुगा बुन्ने तान)
v. aspashT saṅga dekhinu (अस्पष्टसँग देखिनु)

loop, *n.* gAṅTho (गाँठो), surkenI (सुर्केनी), pAso (पासो)
v. surkenI pArnu (सुर्केनी पार्नु)

loophole, *n.* niyam bhaṅg garne upAya (नियम भङ्ग गर्ने उपाय), bhittA ko chyAune pwAl (भित्ताको च्याउने प्वाल)

loose, *adj.* lulo (लुलो), khukulo (खुकुलो), holo (होलो), *(soil, flour)* phukA (फुका), *(person)* chhADA (छाडा), swatantra (स्वतन्त्र)
v. phukAunu (फुकाउनु), phuskAunu (फुस्काउनु)

loosen, *v.* phukAunu (फुकाउनु), phuskAunu (फुस्काउनु),

khukulo pArnu (खुकुलो पार्नु)

loot, *n.* luTeko mAl (लुटेको माल), lUT (लूट)
v. luTnu (लुट्नु)

looting, *n.* lUT lAT (लूटलाट)

lord, *n.* mAlik (मालिक), Ishwar (ईश्वर)
v. haikam dekhAunu (हैकम देखाउनु)

lose, *v.* *(game)* hArnu (हार्नु), *(thing)* harAunu (हराउनु), *(money)* TuTTA parnu (टुट्टा पर्नु)

loser, *n.* haruwA (हरुवा), **(lose the way)** bATo birAunu (बाटो बिराउनु), **(lose weight)** dublAunu (दुब्लाउनु)

loss, *n.* noksAn (नोक्सान), hAni (हानि), khati (खति), *(bus.)* TuTTA (टुट्टा)

loss of face, *n.* mAn hAni (मानहानि)

lost, *adj.* harAeko (हराएको)

lot, *n.* bhAgya (भाग्य), **(a lot)** dherai (धेरै), thupro (थुप्रो)

lot(s) of, *adj.* dherai (धेरै)

lotion, *n.* ras (रस), jhol (झोल), losan (लोसन)

lottery, *n.* chiTThA (चिट्ठा)

lotus, *n.* kamal ko phUl (कमलको फूल)

loud, *adj.* charko (चर्को),
ThUlo (ठूलो)

loudly, *adv.* ThUlo AwAj le
(ठूलो आवाजले)

loudspeaker, *n.* AwAj ThUlo
pArne yantra (आवाज ठूलो
पार्ने यन्त्र)

louse, *n.* jumro (जुम्रो)

love, *n.* prem (प्रेम),
mAyA (माया), piratI (पिरती)
v. mAyA/prem garnu
(माया/प्रेम गर्नु),
(to fall in love), *phr.* prem
mA phasnu (प्रेममा फस्नु),
Ashakta hunu (आशक्त हुनु),
(to make love), *phr.* sahwAs
garnu (सहवास गर्नु)

love affair, *n.* mAyA prItI
(मायाप्रीती)

lovebirds, *n.* chakhewA
chakhewI (चखेवाचखेवी)

lovelorn, *adj.* wirahI (विरही)

lovely, *adj.* sundar (सुन्दर),
rAmro (राम्रो)

love marriage, *n.* prem wiwAh
(प्रेमविवाह)

lover, *n.* premI (प्रेमी)

lovesick, *n.* wirahI premI
(विरही प्रेमी)

loving, *adj.* mAyA garne
(माया गर्ने), mAyAlu (मायालु)

low, *adj.* *(height)* hocho
(होचो), tala (तल), muni

(मुनि), *(price)* kamtI (कम्ती),
(character) nIch (नीच),
(light, sound) madhuro (मधुरो)

lower, *adj.* tallo (तल्लो)
v. tala orlanu (तल ओर्लनु),
jhArnu (झार्नु)

lowly, *adj.* namra (नम्र),
sushIl (सुशील)

loyal, *adj.* baphAdAr
(बफादार), bhakta (भक्त)

loyalty, *n.* baphAdArI
(बफादारी), bhakti (भक्ति)

lubricate, *v.* tel lagAunu
(तेल लगाउनु),
chiplo pArnu (चिप्लो पार्नु)

luck, *n.* bhAgya (भाग्य)

luckily, *adv.* bhAgya wash
(भाग्यवश)

lucky, *adj.* bhAgya mAnI
(भाग्यमानी)

lucrative, *adj.* lAbh dAyak
(लाभदायक),
Akarshak (आकर्षक)

luggage, *n.* mAl (माल),
jhiTI miTI (फिटीमिटी)

lukewarm, *adj.* man tAto
(मनतातो)

lull, *n.* shAnti (शान्ति),
wishrAm (विश्राम)

lullaby, *n.* lorI (लोरी)

luminous *adj.* prakAsh yukta
(प्रकाशयुक्त),
tejomaya (तेजोमय)

lump, *n.* DhikA (ढिका),
  Dallo (डल्लो)

lunar, *adj.* chandramA ko
  (चन्द्रमाको)

lunatic, *n.* pAgal (पागल),
  baulAhA (बौलाहा)

lunch, *n.* diuso ko khAnA
  (दिउसोको खाना),
  diwA bhoj (दिवाभोज)

luncheon, *n.* diwA bhoj
  (दिवाभोज)

lung, *n.* phokso (फोक्सो)

lure, *v.* lobhyAunu (लोभ्याउनु)

luscious, *adj.* mITho (मीठो),
  swAdishT (स्वादिष्ट)

lust, *n.* wAsnA (वासना),

bhog wilAs (भोगविलास)

lustre, *n.* chamak (चमक),
  shobhA (शोभा)

lustrous, *adj.* jhalkan (झल्कने),
  ujjwal (उज्ज्वल)

luxuriant, *adj.* dherai (धेरै),
  prachur (प्रचुर)

luxurious, *adj.* sokh sayal
  garne (सोख सयल गर्ने),
  wilAsI (विलासी)

luxury, *n.* sokh (सोख),
  sayal (सयल),
  aish ArAm (ऐशआराम),
  wilAsitA (विलासिता)

lyric, *n.* gIt (गीत),
  kawitA (कविता)

M

machine, *n.* kal (कल),
  masin (मसिन), yantra (यन्त्र)

mackintosh, *n.* barsAdI (बर्सादी)

mad, *adj.* baulAhA (बौलाहा),
  pAgal (पागल)

madam, *n.* mahodayA
  (महोदया), mAliknI (मालिकनी),
  myAdam (म्याडम)

madcap, *adj.* lAparbAh
  (लापरबाह), sankI (सनकी)

magazine, *n.* patrikA (पत्रिका)

magic, *n.* jAdu (जादु),

jAdugarI (जादुगरी)

magical, *adj.* jAdu ko (जादुको),
  indrajAlI (इन्द्रजाली)

magician, *n.* jAdugar (जादुगर)

magnet, *n.* chumbak (चुम्बक)

magnificient, *adj.* bhawya
  (भव्य), shAndAr (शान्दार)

magnify, *v.* baDhAunu
  (बढाउनु),
  ThUlo pArnu (ठूलो पार्नु)

magnitude, *n.* mAtrA (मात्रा),
  rAshi (राशि), mahattwa (महत्त्व)

magnolia, *n.* thal kamal ko phUl (थलकमलको फूल)

maid, *n.* nokarnI (नोकर्नी), susAre (सुसारे)

maiden, *n.* kumArI keTI (कुमारी केटी), taruNI (तरुणी)

maiden speech, *n.* pahilo bhAshaN (पहिलो भाषण)

maidservant, *n.* nokarnI (नोकर्नी)

mail, *n.* DAňk (डाँक), hulAk (हुलाक), chiThI patra (चिठीपत्र)

mailbox, *n.* patra mañjUshA (पत्रमञ्जूषा)

mailman, *n.* hulAkI (हुलाकी)

main, *adj.* mukhya (मुख्य), mUl (मूल)

mainly, *adv.* prAyaḥ (प्रायः), mukhya rUp le (मुख्य रूपले)

mainstay, *n.* mukhya sahArA (मुख्य सहारा), mukhya AdhAr (मुख्य आधार)

mainstream, *n.* mUl prawAh (मूलप्रवाह)

maintain, *v.* sambhAr/her chAh/kAyam garnu (सम्भार/हेरचाह/कायम गर्नु)

maintenance, *n.* sambhAr (सम्भार), her chAh (हेरचाह)

maize, *n.* makai (मकै)

majestic, *adj.* prabhAw shAlI (प्रभावशाली)

majesty, *n.* *(Royal)* mausuph (मौसुफ), rAj shrI (राजश्री)

major, *n.* senAnI (सेनानी), mejar (मेजर) *adj.* mukhya (मुख्य)

majority, *n.* bahumat (बहुमत)

make, *v.* banAunu (बनाउनु)

make-up, *n.* shriňgAr (श्रृङ्गार), siňgAr paTAr (सिंगारपटार)

malady, *n.* bimArI (बिमारी), rog (रोग)

malaria, *n.* aulo (औलो)

male, *n.* logne mAnchhe (लोग्नेमान्छे), bhAle (भाले), purush (पुरुष)

malice, *n.* DAhA (डाहा), ris (रिस)

malignant, *adj.* hAni kArak (हानिकारक)

mallet, *n.* muňgro (मुड्ग्रो), hathauDA (हथौडा)

malnutrition, *n.* kuposhaN (कुपोषण)

malpractice, *n.* durwyawahAr (दुर्व्यवहार), durAchAr (दुराचार)

maltreatment, *n.* durwyawahAr (दुर्व्यवहार)

mammal, *n.* stanpAyI jantu (स्तनपायी जन्तु)

man, *n.* mAnchhe (मान्छे), mAnis (मानिस), logne mAnchhe (लोग्नेमान्छे)

manage, *v.* sañchAlan garnu (सञ्चालन गर्नु), sambhAlnu (संभाल्नु)

management, *n.* wyawasthApan (व्यवस्थापन)

manager, *n.* wyawsthApak (व्यवस्थापक)

mane, *n.* ghoDA ko jagar (घोडाको जगर), yAl (याल)

mango, *n.* Amp/Aँp (आँप)

manhandle, *v.* hAt hAlnu (हात हाल्नु), kuTnu (कुट्नु)

manipulate, *v.* chalAkhI saṅga kAm chalAunu (चलाखीसँग काम चलाउनु)

mankind, *n.* manushya jAti (मनुष्यजाति), mAnaw jAti (मानवजाति)

manly, *adj.* baliyo (बलियो), wIr (वीर), sAhasI (साहसी)

manner, *n.* kAiDA (काइदा), tarIkA (तरीका), rIti (रीति)

manners, *n.* adab (अदब), shishTAchAr (शिष्टाचार)

manpower, *n.* kAmdAr harU ko Thulo jamAt (कामदारहरूको ठूलो जमात)

mansion, *n.* bhawan (भवन), mahal (महल)

manslaughter, *n.* nar hatyA (नरहत्या)

manual, *n.* wiwaraN pustikA (विवरणपुस्तिका) *adj.* hAt le garne (हातले गर्ने)

manufacture, *n.* utpAdan garnu (उत्पादन गर्नु)

manure, *n.* mal (मल), khAd (खाद)

manuscript, *n.* pANDulipi (पाण्डुलिपि), hast likhit pustak /lekh (हस्तलिखित पुस्तक/लेख)

many, *adj.* dherai (धेरै), anek (अनेक)

map, *n.* naksA (नक्सा)

mar, *v.* bigArnu (बिगार्नु), hAni garnu (हानि गर्नु)

marathon, *n.* ati lAmo dauD (अति लामो दौड), dherai aDna sakne shakti (धेरै अड्न सक्ने शक्ति)

marble, *n.* *(stone)* saṅg marmar (सङ्गमरमर), *(plaything)* guchchA (गुच्चा)

march, *n.* hiṅDAi (हिँडाइ), chAl (चाल), kUch (कूच) *v.* yAtrA / kUch garnu (यात्रा/कूच गर्नु)

mare, *n.* ghoDI (घोडी)

margarine, *n.* wanaspati bATa baneko makkhan (वनस्पतिबाट बनेको मक्खन)

margin, *n.* chheu (छेउ), kinArA (किनारा)

marigold, *n.* saya patrI phUl (सयपत्री फूल)

marijuana, *n.* gAṅjA (गाँजा)

marine, *adj.* sAmudrik (सामुद्रिक), nau sainik (नौसैनिक)

marionette, *n.* kaTh putalI
(कठपुतली)

marital, *adj.* dAmpatya (दाम्पत्य),
waiwAhik (वैवाहिक)

mark, *n.* chino (चिनो), chinha
(चिन्ह), nisAnA (निसाना)
v. chino lAunu (चिनो लाउनु),
dhyAn saṅga hernu
(ध्यानसंग हेर्नु)

market, *n.* bajAr (बजार),
hAT (हाट)
v. bech bikhan/kinmel garnu
(बेचबिखन/किनमेल गर्नु)

marketing, *n.* bech bikhan
(बेचबिखन), kin mel (किनमेल)

marketplace, *n.* chok bajAr
(चोकबजार),
hAT bajAr (हाटबजार)

marriage, *n.* bihe (बिहे),
wiwAh (विवाह)

marriageable, *adj.* wiwAh
yogya (विवाहयोग्य)

married, *adj.* wiwAhit (विवाहित)

marry, *v.* bihe/wiwAh garnu
(बिहे/विवाह गर्नु)

Mars, *n.* maṅgal graha
(मङ्गल ग्रह)

marsh, *n.* dhAp (धाप),
daldal (दलदल)

martial law, *n.* jaṅgI ain
(जङ्गी ऐन)

martyr, *n.* shahId (शहीद)

marvel(l)ous, *adj.* wichitra

(विचित्र)

Marxism, *n.* mArks wAd
(मार्क्सवाद)

masculine, *n.* puliṅg (पुलिङ्ग),
bhAle jAti (भाले जाति)

mask, *n.* makuNDo (मकुण्डो)
v. mukh DhAknu (मुख
ढाक्नु), chhopnu (छोप्नु)

mason, *n.* DakarmI (डकर्मी)

mass, *n.* rAshi (राशि),
piND (पिण्ड),
puñj (पुञ्ज), bhelA (भेला)
v. jammA garnu/hunu
(जम्मा गर्नु/हुनु)

massacre, *n.* kATmAr
(काटमार), hatyA (हत्या),
saṃhAr (संहार)

massage, *n.* mAlis (मालिस)
v. mAlis garnu (मालिस गर्नु),
Aṅg michnu (आँग मिच्नु)

massive, *adj.* ThUlo (ठूलो),
bhArI (भारी), brihat (बृहत्)

mass media, *n.* Am sañchAr kA
sAdhan (आमसञ्चारका साधन)

mass movement, *n.* jan
Andolan (जनआन्दोलन)

mass production, *n.* bahu
utpAdan (बहुउत्पादन)

master, *n.* mAlik (मालिक),
guru (गुरु), mAsTar (मास्टर),
shikshak (शिक्षक)
v. adhikAr/gyĀn hunu
(अधिकार/ज्ञान हुनु)

mastermind, *n.* asAdhAraN gyÄn (असाधारण ज्ञान) *v.* kunai kAm ko nirdeshan ra yojanA garnu (कुनै कामको निर्देशन र योजना गर्नु)

masterpiece, *n.* utkrishT kriti (उत्कृष्ट कृति)

master plan, *n.* guru yojanA (गुरुयोजना)

masturbation, *n.* hast maithun (हस्तमैथुन)

mat, *n.* chaTAI (चटाई), sukul (सुकुल), gundrI (गुन्द्री)

match, *n.* *(light)* salAI (सलाई), *(equal)* joDA (जोडा), samAn (समान), *(game)* pratiyogitA (प्रतियोगिता), *(marriage)* wiwAh sambandh (विवाहसम्बन्ध) *v.* dAñjnu (दाँज्नु), milnu (मिल्नु), suhAunu (सुहाउनु)

matchbox, *n.* salAI ko baTTA (सलाईको बट्टा)

matchless, *adj.* be joD (बेजोड)

matchmaker, *n.* lamI (लमी)

matchstick, *n.* salAI ko kAñTI (सलाईको काँटी)

mate, *n.* sAthI (साथी), joDA (जोडा), *(chess)* mAth (माथ) *v.* sAthI banAunu (साथी बनाउनु), bihe garnu (बिहे गर्नु), *(chess)* mAth garnu

(माथ गर्नु)

material, *n.* mAl (माल), sAmAn (सामान), chIj bIj (चीजबीज)

maternal, *adj.* AmA paTTi ko (आमापट्टिको)

maternal uncle, *n.* mAmA (मामा)

maternity hospital, *n.* prasUti griha (प्रसूतिगृह)

maternity leave, *n.* sutkerI bidA (सुत्केरी बिदा)

mathematics, *n.* gaNit (गणित)

matricide, *n.* mAtri hatyA (मातृहत्या)

matrimonial, *adj.* bihe ko (बिहेको), waiwAhik (वैवाहिक)

matrimony, *n.* bihe (बिहे), wiwAh (विवाह)

matron, *n.* ghar kI mAliknI (घरकी मालिक्नी), *(hospital, etc.)* mukhya parichArikA (मुख्य परिचारिका)

matter, *n.* wastu (वस्तु), kurA (कुरा), wishaya (विषय), padArth (पदार्थ) *v.* mahattwa ko hunu (महत्त्वको हुनु), *(as a matter of fact)* wAstaw mA (वास्तवमा)

matter of fact, *n.* wAstawik kuro (वास्तविक कुरो), tathya (तथ्य),

matter-of-fact, *adj.*
wyAwhArik (व्यावहारिक)

mattress, *n.* DasnA (डसना),
gaddA (गद्दा)

mature, *adj.* pAko (पाको),
pakwa (पक्व)
v. pAko/paripakwa hunu
(पाको/परिपक्व हुनु)

maturity, *n.* paripakwatA
(परिपक्वता),
prauDhtA (प्रौढता)

mauve, *n.* phIkA baijanI rang
(फीका बैजनी रङ्ग)

mausoleum, *n.* samAdhi
(समाधि), chihAn (चिहान),
makbarA (मकबरा)

maximum, *adj.* adhiktam
(अधिकतम), sab bhandA
baDhI (सबभन्दा बढी)

may, *mod.* saknu (सक्नु)

maybe, *adv.* huna sakchha
(हुनसक्छ), shAyad (शायद)

mayor, *n.* nagar pramukh
(नगरप्रमुख),
nagar pitA (नगरपिता)

me, *pron.* ma lAI (मलाई)

meadow, *n.* chaur (चौर),
gauchar (गौचर)

meagre/meager, *adj.* kamsal
(कमसल), mAtrA mA thorai
(मात्रामा थोरै)

meal, *n.* khAnA (खाना),
chhAk (छाक)

mean, *adj.* chhuchcho (छुच्चो),
nIch (नीच), tuchchha (तुच्छ)
n. (math.) ausat (औसत)
v. mAne dinu (माने दिनु),
arth hunu (अर्थ हुनु),
bujhinu (बुझिनु)

meaning, *n.* mAne (माने),
arth (अर्थ), matlab (मतलब)

meaningful, *adj.* arth pUrN
(अर्थपूर्ण)

meaningless, *adj.* arth hIn
(अर्थहीन),
be matlab ko (बेमतलबको)

means, *n.* jukti (जुक्ति),
upAya (उपाय), dhan (धन),
(by all means), *phr.* awashya
nai (अवश्य नै),
nishchaya nai (निश्चय नै),
(by no means), *phr.* kadApi
huñdaina (कदापि हुँदैन),
ekdam huñdaina (एकदम हुँदैन)

meantime, *adv.* yasai bIch mA
(यसैबीचमा)

meanwhile, *adv.* yasai bIch
mA (यसैबीचमा)

measles, *n.* dAdurA (दादुरा)

measure, *n.* nAp (नाप)
v. nApnu (नाप्नु)

measurement, *n.* nAp (नाप),
nApo (नापो)

meat, *n.* mAsu (मासु)

mechanic, *n.* mistrI (मिस्त्री),
kAligaD (कालिगड)

mechanical, *adj.* kal purjA sambandhI (कलपुर्जासम्बन्धी), yAntrik (यान्त्रिक)

mechanism, *n.* kal purjA ko rachnA widhi (कलपुर्जाको रचनाविधि), tarIkA (तरीका)

medal, *n.* padak (पदक), takmA (तक्मा)

medi(a)eval, *adj.* madhya yugI (मध्ययुगी)

mediate, *v.* madhyasth hunu (मध्यस्थ हुनु)

mediator, *n.* milAp garAune (मिलाप गराउने), madhyasth (मध्यस्थ)

medical, *adj.* DAkTarI (डाक्टरी), aushadhi ko (औषधिको)

medicine, *n.* okhatI (ओखती), aushadhi (औषधि)

mediocre, *adj.* sAdhAraN (साधारण), mAmulI (मामुली), madhyam (मध्यम)

meditate, *v.* dhyAn/chintan garnu (ध्यान/चिन्तन गर्नु)

meditation, *n.* dhyAn (ध्यान), chintan manan (चिन्तनमनन)

medium, *n.* madhyam (मध्यम), *(means)* mAdhyam (माध्यम) *adj.* majhyaulA (मभ्यौला)

meek, *adj.* namra (नम्र), sojho (सोभ्फो)

meet, *n.* jamghaT (जमघट)

v. bheTnu (भेट्नु), milnu (मिल्नु)

meeting, *n.* bheT (भेट), *(assembly)* sabhA (सभा), sammelan (सम्मेलन), baiThak (बैठक)

melancholy, *n./adj.* udAsIntA (उदासीनता), udAs (उदास), chintA magna (चिन्तामग्न)

melee, *n.* bhiDant (भिडन्त), bhID bhAD (भिडभाड), jhagaDA (भ्फगडा)

melodious, *adj.* madhur (मधुर), manohar (मनोहर)

melody, *n.* madhur gIt/saṅgIt (मधुर गीत/संगीत)

melon, *n.* kharbujA (खर्बुजा)

melt, *v.* paglanu (पग्लनु), pagAlnu (पगाल्नु), galnu (गल्नु)

melting point, *n.* kunai padArth pagAlne tAp kram bindu (कुनै पदार्थ पगाल्ने तापक्रम बिन्दु), drawaN bindu (द्रवणबिन्दु)

melting pot, *n.* dherai jan jAti misiera basobAs garne ThauṅTh (धेरै जनजाति मिसिएर बसोबास गर्ने ठाउँ)

member, *n.* sadasya (सदस्य)

memento, *n.* samjhAune wastu (सम्फ्फाउने वस्तु), samjhauTo (सम्फ्फौटो)

memorable, *adj.* samjhana lAyak ko (सम्झन लायकको), na birsine (नबिर्सिने)

memo(randum), *n.* lekhoT (लेखोट), TippaNI (टिप्पणी), gȳApan patra (ज्ञापनपत्र)

memorial, *n.* smArak (स्मारक)

memorize, *v.* yAd garnu (याद गर्नु), samjhanu (सम्झनु)

memory, *n.* samjhanA (सम्झना), smaraN (स्मरण)

men, *n.* logne mAnchhe harU (लोग्नेमान्छेहरू), mAnis harU (मानिसहरू)

menace, *n.* dhamkI (धम्की), trAs (त्रास)

mend, *v.* marmat garnu (मर्मत गर्नु), banAunu (बनाउनु)

meningitis, *n.* mastishka ra DaṇDAlnu rankAune jaro (मस्तिष्क र डँडाल्नु रन्काउने जरो), gardan toD jaro (गर्दन-तोड जरो), dhanush TaṅkAr (धनुष्टङ्कार)

menstruate, *v.* na chhune hunu (नछुने हुनु), para sarnu (पर सर्नु)

menstruation, *n.* na chhune (नछुने), rajaswalA (रजस्वला)

mental, *adj.* mAnsik (मानसिक), man ko (मनको)

mention, *n.* ullekh (उल्लेख), charchA (चर्चा)

v. ullekh garnu (उल्लेख गर्नु), janAunu (जनाउनु)

menu, *n.* khAne kurA ko sUchI (खानेकुराको सूची), khAdya sUchI (खाद्यसूची)

merchandise, *n.* wyApAr kA mAl sAmAn (व्यापारका मालसामान), saudA (सौदा)

merchant, *n.* wyApArI (व्यापारी), mahAjan (महाजन)

merciful, *adj.* dayAlu (दयालु), dayA wAn (दयावान)

merciless, *adj.* nishThur (निष्ठुर), nirdayI (निर्दयी)

mercury, *n.* pAro (पारो)

Mercury, *n.* budh graha (बुध ग्रह)

mercy, *n.* dayA (दया), kripA (कृपा)

mercy killing, *n.* birAmI ko asahya pIDA samApt garna garine hatyA (बिरामीको असह्य पीडा समाप्त गर्न गरिने हत्या)

mere, *n.* pokharI (पोखरी), tAl (ताल)

adj. mAtra (मात्र), khAli (खालि)

merely, *adv.* mAtra (मात्र), mAtrai (मात्रै)

merge, *v.* gAbhnu (गाभ्नु), misinu (मिसिनु)

merger, *n.* misine kAm (मिसिने काम), wilayan (विलयन)

merit, *n.* guN (गुण),
yogyatA (योग्यता)
v. yogya hunu (योग्य हुनु)

meritorious, *adj.* yogya (योग्य),
lAyak (लायक),
guN wAn (गुणवान)

merriment, *n.* khusIyAlI
(खुसीयाली),
ramAilo (रमाइलो)

merry, *n.* harsh (हर्ष),
Anand (आनन्द)

mess, *n.* laThI bajra (लठीबज्र),
alpatra (अलपत्र), mismAs
(मिसमास), *(hostel)* dherai
janA khAne bhAnsA (धेरैजना
खाने भान्सा)

message, *n.* sandesh (सन्देश),
samAchAr (समाचार)

messenger, *n.* sandesh
puryAune (सन्देश पुर्याउने)

metal, *n.* dhAtu (धातु)

meteor, *n.* ulkA (उल्का),
khasne tArA (खस्ने तारा)

method, *n.* upAya (उपाय),
tarIkA (तरीका)

meticulous, *adj.* ati sAwdhAn
(अति सावधान)

metre/meter, *n. (measure)*
miTar (मिटर)

metropolis, *n.* mahA nagar
(महानगर)

mew, *n.* myAu myAu
(म्याउम्याउ)

v. myAu myAu garnu
(म्याउम्याउ गर्नु)

mica, *n.* abhrak (अभ्रक)

mice, *n.* mUsA harU (मूसाहरू)

microcphone/mic/mike, *n.*
mAik (माइक)

microscope, *n.* sUksham
darsak (सूक्ष्मदर्शक),
mAikro skop (माइक्रोस्कोप)

midday, *n.* madhyAnha
(मध्यान्ह)

middle, *adj.* mAjh (माझ),
bIch (बीच)

middle age, *n.* adhbaiňse umer
(अधबैँसे उमेर)

Middle Ages, *n.* madhya yug
(मध्ययुग)

middle class, *n.* madhyam
warg (मध्यम वर्ग)

middleweight, *n. (boxing)*
pachhattar kejI samma ko
taul (७५ केजीसम्मको तौल)

midnight, *n.* AdhA rAt (आधारात),
madhya rAtri (मध्यरात्रि)

midwife, *n.* suňDenI (सुँडेनी)

might, *n.* shakti (शक्ति), bal (बल)
mod. huna saknu (हुन सक्नु)

mighty, *adj.* baliyo (बलियो),
shakti shAlI (शक्तिशाली)

migrant, *n.* prawAsI (प्रवासी)

migration, *n.* prawAs (प्रवास),
basAi sarne kAm
(बसाइ सर्ने काम)

mild, *adj.* naram (नरम),
sojho (सोझो)

mile, *n.* mAil (माइल)

milestone, *n.* kose DhuṅgA
(कोसेढुङ्गा), *(fig.)* mahattwa
pUrN ghaTnA (महत्त्वपूर्ण घटना)

military, *n.* senA (सेना),
phauj (फौज)
adj. jaṅgI (जङ्गी),
phaujI (फौजी)

milk, *n.* dUdh (दूध)
v. dUdh duhunu (दूध दुहुनु)

milkman, *n.* gwAlA (ग्वाला)

milky, *adj.* dUdh jasto (दूधजस्तो)

Milky Way, *n.* AkAsh gaṅgA
(आकाशगंगा)

mill, *n.* kAr khAnA (कारखाना),
mil (मिल), ghaTTa (घट्ट)

millennium, *n.* hajAr warsh ko
awadhi (हजार वर्षको अवधि)

millet, *n.* kodo (कोदो)

million, *n.* das lAkh (दस लाख)

millionaire, *n.* lakh pati
(लखपति)

millstone, *n.* jAṅto (जाँतो)

mind, *n.* man (मन), chitta (चित्त)
(be in two minds), *phr.*
hichkichAunu (हिचकिचाउनु),
(change one's mind), *phr.*
man phernu (मन फेर्नु)
v. dhyAn dinu (ध्यान दिनु),
hosh garnu (होश गर्नु),
(worry) phikrI garnu (फिक्री गर्नु)

garnu (गर्नु), gAhro mannu (गाह्रो मान्नु),
her wichAr garnu (हेरविचार गर्नु)

mindful, *adj.* wichAr shIl
(विचारशील)

mine, *pron.* mero (मेरो)
n. khAnI (खानी), *(explosive)*
jamIn muni wA pAnI bhitra
rAkhine bishphoTak wastu
(जमीनमुनि वा पानीभित्र राखिने
विष्फोटक वस्तु)
v. khAnI khannu (खानी खन्नु)

mineral, *n.* khanij padArth
(खनिज पदार्थ)

mingle, *v.* misinu (मिसिनु),
milnu (मिल्नु)

miniature, *n.* sAnu AkAr ko
wastu (सानु आकारको वस्तु)

minimum, *n.* sab bhandA kam
(सबभन्दा कम)

mining, *n.* khanI khanne kAm
(खानी खन्ने काम)

minister, *n.* mantrI (मन्त्री)
v. sewA/upchAr garnu
(सेवा/उपचार गर्नु)

ministry, *n.* mantrAlaya
(मन्त्रालय)

minority, *n.* alp saṅkhyA
(अल्पसङ्ख्या),
nabAligpan (नाबालिगपन)

mint, *n.* Tak sAr (टकसार),
(plant) bAbarI (बाबरी),
pudinA (पुदिना)
v. Tak mArnu (टक मार्नु)

minus, *n.* ghaTAu (घटाउ),
(sign) riN chinha (ऋण चिन्ह)
prep. ghaTAera (घटाएर),
kam garera (कम गरेर)

minute, *n. (time)* mineT
(मिनेट), *(meeting, etc.)*
mAinyuT (माइन्युट)
adj. ati sAnu (अति सानु)

minutely, *adv.* ThIk hisAb le
(ठीक हिसाबले)

miracle, *n.* chamatkAr
(चमत्कार),
karAmat (करामत)

miraculous, *adj.* chamatkAr
pUrN (चमत्कारपूर्ण),
adbhut (अद्भुत)

mirror, *n.* ainA (ऐना)

misadventure, *n.* durbhAgya
(दुर्भाग्य)

miscalculate, *v.* galat andAj
garnu (गलत अन्दाज गर्नु)

miscarriage, *n.* tuhine kAm
(तुहिने काम),
garbh pAt (गर्भपात)

miscellaneous, *adj.* wiwidh
(विविध), mishrit (मिश्रित)

mischief, *n.* upadro (उपद्रो),
utpAt (उत्पात)

mischievous, *adj.*
upadhryAhA (उपद्र्याहा),
utpAte (उत्पाते)

misconception, *n.* galat
dhArNA (गलत धारणा),

bhram (भ्रम)

misconduct, *n.* durAchAr
(दुराचार), anAchAr (अनाचार)

miscreant, *adj.* dushTa (दुष्ट)

misdeed, *n.* kharAb kAm
(खराब काम), kukarm (कुकर्म)

miser, *n.* kanjUs (कन्जूस)

miserable, *adj.* duhkhI (दुःखी)

misery, *n.* duhkh (दुःख),
Apat (आपत्)

misfortune, *n.* Apat (आपत्),
wipad (विपद्)

misgiving, *n.* shaṅkA (शंका),
sandeh (सन्देह)

misguide, *v.* bahkAunu
(बहकाउनु), barAlnu (बरालनु)

mishap, *n.* durghaTnA
(दुर्घटना)

mishmash, *n.* mismAs
(मिसमास)

misinform, *v.* galat sUchanA
dinu (गलत सूचना दिनु)

misinterpret, *v.* galat arth
lagAunu (गलत अर्थ लगाउनु)

mislead, *v.* kubATo laijAnu
(कुबाटो लैजानु),
barAlnu (बरालनु)

mismanage, *v.* kharAb
bandobast garnu
(खराब बन्दोबस्त गर्नु)

mismanagement, *n.* kharAb
intjAm (खराब इन्तजाम),
kuwyawasthA (कुव्यवस्था)

misrule, *n.* ku shAsan
(कुशासन)
v. kharAb shAsan garnu
(खराब शासन गर्नु)

miss, *n. (girl)* kumArI
(कुमारी), sushrI (सुश्री),
shikshikA (शिक्षिका)
v. nishAnA chuknu
(निशाना चुक्नु),
birAunu (बिराउनु)

missile, *n.* kshepyAstra
(क्षेप्यास्त्र)

mission, *n.* khaTAeko kAm
(खटाएको काम), *(diplomacy)*
abhiyAn (अभियान),
niyog (नियोग)

mist, *n.* kuhiro (कुहिरो)

mistake, *n.* bhUl (भूल),
wirAm (विराम), galtI (गल्ती)
v. bhulnu (भुल्नु),
galtI garnu (गल्ती गर्नु)

mistaken, *adj.* bhUl/bhram
mA pareko (भूल/भ्रममा परेको)

mister/Mr, *n.* mahAshaya
(महाशय), misTar (मिस्टर),
shrI (श्री), shrI mAn (श्रीमान्)

mistress, *n.* mAliknI(मालिक्नी),
guru mA (गुरुमा),
rakhauTI (रखौटी)

mistrust, *n.* awishwAs
(अविश्वास)
v. wishwAs na garnu
(विश्वास नगर्नु)

misunderstand, *v.* galat
samjhanu (गलत सम्फनु)

misunderstanding, *n.* galat
phahamI (गलतफहमी)

misuse, *n.* durupyog
(दुरुपयोग)
v. durupayog garnu
(दुरुपयोग गर्नु)

mix, *v.* misAunu (मिसाउनु),
misinu (मिसिनु)

mixture, *n.* mishraN (मिश्रण)

moan, *v.* wilAp garnu
(विलाप गर्नु)

mob, *n.* hUl (हूल)
v. hUl garnu (हूल गर्नु),
ghernu (घेर्नु)

mobile, *adj.* halchal garna
sakne (हलचल गर्न सक्ने),
ghumtI (घुम्ती)

mock, *n.* nakkal (नक्कल)
v. gijyAunu (गिज्याउनु),
khisI garnu (खिसी गर्नु)

mode, *n.* kAida (काइदा),
tarIkA (तरीका)

model, *n.* namUnA (नमूना),
nakkal (नक्कल)

moderate, *adj.* Thikai ko
(ठिकैको), madhyam khAl ko
(मध्यम खालको)

modern, *adj.* Adhunik (आधुनिक),
hAlsAl ko (हालसालको)

modernize, *v.* Adhunik
banAunu (आधुनिक बनाउनु)

modest, *adj.* sekhI na garne
(सेखी नगर्ने),
sankochI (सङ्कोची),
winamra (विनम्र)

modesty, *n.* namratA (नम्रता),
lAj(लाज), sankoch (सङ्कोच)

moist, *adj.* bhijeko (भिजेको),
osieko (ओसिएको)

moisture, *n.* os (ओस),
shIt (शीत), ArdratA (आर्द्रता)

mole, *n.* *(rodent)* chhuchundro
(छुचुन्द्रो),
(birthmark) koThI (कोठी)

molest, *v.* satAunu (सताउनु),
hairAn garnu (हैरान गर्नु)

molten, *adj.* pagleko(पग्लेको)

moment, *n.* chhin (छिन),
kshaN (क्षण)

momentous, *adj.* gahkilo
(गहकिलो),
mahattwa pUrN (महत्त्वपूर्ण)

momentum, *n.* gati (गति),
Aweg (आवेग)

monarch, *n.* rAjA (राजा)

monarchy, *n.* rAj tantra
(राजतन्त्र)

monastery, *n.* maTh (मठ),
gumbA (गुम्बा)

Monday, *n.* som wAr(सोमवार)

monetary, *adj.* Arthik
(आर्थिक), wittIya (वित्तीय)

money, *n.* dhan (धन),
dAm (दाम), paisA (पैसा),

drawya (द्रव्य)

moneylender, *n.* rin dine sAhu
(रिन दिने साहु),
mahAjan (महाजन)

money order, *n.* hulAk bATa
paisA paThAune prabandh
(हुलाकबाट पैसा पठाउने
प्रबन्ध), dhanAdesh (धनादेश)

mongoose, *n.* nyAurI mUso
(न्याउरी मूसो)

monk, *n.* yogI (योगी),
mahant (महन्त),
gumbA mA basne bhikshu
(गुम्बामा बस्ने भिक्षु),
lAmA (लामा)

monkey, *n.* bAndar (बाँदर)

monopoly, *n.* ekAdhikAr
(एकाधिकार)

monotonous, *adj.* nyAsro
(न्यास्रो), ek sure (एकसुरे),
urАТh lAgdo (उराठलाग्दो)

monsoon, *n.* barkhA (बर्खा),
warshA (वर्षा), barsAt (बर्सात)

monster, *n.* rAkshas (राक्षस),
daitya (दैत्य)

month, *n.* mahinA (महिना)

monthly, *adj.* mAsik (मासिक)

monument, *n.* smArak
(स्मारक)

mood, *n.* man ko awasthA
(मनको अवस्था)

moody, *adj.* udAs (उदास),
jhokrAeko (भोक्राएको)

moon, *n.* chandramA (चन्द्रमा),
jUn (जून),
(full moon) purNe (पूर्ण),
pUrNimA (पूर्णिमा),
(new moon) auñsI (औंसी),
(once in a blue moon),
phr. kahile kAhiñ (कहिलेकाहीं)

moonlight, *n.* jUn (जून),
junelI (जुनेली)

mop, *v.* puchhnu (पुछ्नु)

moral, *n.* nIti siikshA
(नीतिशिक्षा),
updhesh (उपदेश)
adj. naitik (नैतिक)

moral courage, *n.* naitik
sAhas (नैतिक साहस)

morale, *n.* hausalA (हौसला)

moral force, *n.* naitik bal
(नैतिक बल)

morality, *n.* naitiktA (नैतिकता)

morally, *adv.* naitik Dhaṅg le
(नैतिक ढङ्गले)

more, *adj.* baDhI (बढ़ी),
arU (अरू), baDhtA (बढ्ता)

moreover, *adv.* ajha (अझ),
usmA pani (उसमा पनि)

morning, *n.* bihAna (बिहान),
(this morning) Aja bihAna
(आज बिहान)

morning star, *n.* shukra tArA
(शुक्रतारा), bihAna dekhine
tArA (बिहान देखिने तारा)

morsel, *n.* gAñs (गाँस)

mortal, *adj.* maraN shIl
(मरणशील), nashwar (नश्वर)

mortgage, *n.* bandhakI
(बन्धकी), dharoT (धरोट)
v. bandhak rAkhnu
(बन्धक राख्नु)

mosquito, *n.* lAm khuTTe
(लाम्खुट्टे)

mosquito net, *n.* jhUl (झूल)

moss, *n.* kAI (काई),
jhyAu (भ्याउ)

most, *adj./adv.* sab bhandA
(सबभन्दा), audhI (औधी)

mostly, *adv.* dherai jaso
(धेरैजसो)

mother, *n.* AmA (आमा),
mAtA (माता)

mother-in-law, *n.* sAsU (सासू)

motherly, *adj.* AmA ko guN
bhaekI (आमाको गुण भएकी)

mother-of-pearl, *n.* sipI (सिपी)

mother tongue, *n.* mAtri
bhAshA (मातृभाषा)

motion, *n.* chAl (चाल),
gati (गति)
v. isArA garnu (इसारा गर्नु)

motionless, *adj.* sthir (स्थिर),
nishchal (निश्चल)

motion picture, *n.* chal chitra
(चलचित्र), sinemA (सिनेमा)

motor, *n.* moTar (मोटर)

motor car, *n.* moTar kAr
(मोटरकार), gADI (गाडी)

motorcade, *n.* moTar gAdI harU ko lAm (मोटर-गाडीहरूको लाम)

motorcycle, *n.* moTar sAikal (मोटरसाइकल)

motto, *n.* siddhAnt (सिद्धान्त)

mould, *v.* DhAlnu (ढाल्नु) *n.* sAñcho (साँचो), DhAñchA (ढाँचा)

mound, *n.* Dhisko (ढिस्को), thupro (थुप्रो)

mount, *v.* ghoDA chaDhnu (घोडा चढ्नु), uklanu (उक्लनु)

mountain, *n.* pahAD (पहाड), parwat (पर्वत), DAñDA (डाँडा)

mountaineer, *n.* parwatArohI (पर्वतारोही)

mountainous, *adj.* pahADI (पहाडी)

mourn, *v.* shok manAunu (शोक मनाउनु), juTho bArnu (जुठो बार्नु)

mourning, *n.* Ashauch (आशौच)

mouse, *n.* mUsA (मूसा), mUso (मूसो)

m(o)ustache, *n.* juñgA (जुँगा)

mouth, *n.* mukh (मुख)

mouthful, *n.* mukh bhari (मुखभरि), gAñs (गाँस)

movable, *adj.* chalne (चल्ने), sarne (सर्ने), chal (चल)

move, *n.* chAl (चाल), hal chal (हलचल)

v. chalnu (चल्नु), chAlnu (चाल्नु), sarnu (सर्नु), sArnu (सार्नु)

movement, *n.* chAl (चाल), Andolan (आन्दोलन)

movie, *n.* chal chitra (चलचित्र)

Mr, *n.* shrI (श्री), shrI mAn (श्रीमान्)

Mrs, *n.* shrI matI (श्रीमती)

much, *adj.* dherai (धेरै),

mucus, *n.* (*nose*) siñgAn (सिँगान), (*stool*) Auñ (आउँ)

mud, *n.* hilo (हिलो)

muddy, *adj.* hile (हिले)

muffler, *n.* gal bandI (गलबन्दी)

mug, *n.* gilAs (गिलास), mag (मग)

mulberry, *n.* kimbu (किम्बु)

mule, *n.* khachchar (खच्चर)

multi-colo(u)red, *adj.* bahu rañgI (बहुरङ्गी), rañgI chañgI (रङ्गीचङ्गी)

multiply, *v.* gunnu (गुन्नु), guNan garnu (गुणन गर्नु)

multi-purpose, *adj.* bahu mukhI (बहुमुखी), bahuddeshyIya (बहुउद्देश्यीय)

multitude, *n.* ghuiñcho (घुइँचो), thupro (थुप्रो)

mumps, *n.* hAñDe rog (हाँडे रोग)

munch, *v.* chapAunu (चपाउनु)

mundane, *adj.* sAṃsArik (सांसारिक)

municipality, *n.* nagar pAlikA (नगरपालिका)

murder, *n.* hatyA (हत्या)
v. mArnu (मार्नु),
hatyA garnu (हत्या गर्नु)

murderer, *n.* hatyArA (हत्यारा),
jyAn mArA (ज्यानमारा)

murky, *adj.* aňdhyAro (अँध्यारो), dhamilo (धमिलो)

murmur, *v.* gun gunAunu (गुनगुनाउनु),
phat phatAunu (फतफताउनु)

muscle, *n.* sumlo (सुम्लो),
mAñs peshI (मांसपेशी)

muscular, *adj.* pushT (पुष्ट),
mAñsal (मांसल),
(strong) baliyo (बलियो)

museum, *n.* myujiyam (म्युजियम),
saňgrahAlaya (संग्रहालय)

mushroom, *n.* chyAu (च्याउ)
v. chyAu jhaiň umranu (च्याउभैँ उम्रनु)

music, *n.* saňgIt (सङ्गीत),
gAnA bajAnA (गानाबजाना)

musical, *adj.* saňgIt sambandhI (सङ्गीतसम्बन्धी)

musical instrument, *n.* sAj bAj (साजबाज)

musician, *n.* saňgIt kAr (सङ्गीतकार)

musk, *n.* kastUrI (कस्तूरी)

musk deer, *n.* kastUrI mriga (कस्तूरी मृग)

Muslim, *n.* musalmAn (मुसलमान)

muslin, *n.* malmal kapaDA (मलमल कपडा)

must, *mod.* parchha (पर्छ)

mustard green, *n.* torI/rAyo ko sAg (तोरी/रायोको साग)

mustard seed, *n.* torI (तोरी)

mute, *adj.* lATo (लाटो),
maun (मौन)

mutiny, *n.* sainik widroh (सैनिक विद्रोह)

mutter, *v.* gangan garnu (गनगन गर्नु),
phat phatAunu (फतफताउनु)

mutton, *n.* khasI/bheDA ko mAsu (खसी/भेडाको मासु)

mutual, *adj.* Apas ko (आपसको), ApasI (आपसी)

mutually, *adv.* Apas mA (आपसमा), paraspar (परस्पर)

muzzle, *n. (animal)* thutunu (थुतुनु), *(gun)* nAl (नाल)
v. bolna na dinu (बोल्न नदिनु)

my, *pron.* mero (मेरो)

myriad, *n.* ThUlo saňkhyA (ठूलो संख्या), asaňkhya (असंख्य)

myself, *pron. (emph.)* ma Aphaiň (म आफैँ)

mysterious, *adj.* rahasya maya (रहस्यमय), gUDh (गूढ)

mystery, *n.* rahasya (रहस्य)

myth, n. paurANik kathA (पौराणिक कथा), galat dhArNA (गलत धारणा)

mythology, n. paurANik kathA mAlA (पौराणिक कथामाला)

N

nab, v. samAtnu (समात्नु), pakranu (पक्रनु)

nail, n. (spike) kilA (किला), (finger) nan̄ (नङ), (animal) nan̄grA (नङ्ग्रा) v. kilA Thoknu (किला ठोक्नु)

naive, adj. sojho (सोझो), sIdha (सीधा)

naked, adj. nAn̄go (नाङ्गो)

name, n. nAun̄ (नाउँ), nAm (नाम), (fig.) ijjat (इज्जत), mAn (मान) v. nAm rAkhnu (नाम राख्नु) **(loose one's name)**, phr. ijjat jAnu (इज्जत जानु)

nameless, adj. nAm na bhaeko (नाम नभएको), be nAmI (बेनामी)

namely, adv. arthAt (अर्थात्), yAne (याने)

named, adj. nAun̄ gareko (नाउँ गरेको), nAmak (नामक)

namesake, n. ustai nAm bhaeko wyakti (उस्तै नाम भएको व्यक्ति)

nanny, n. dhAI (धाई)

nap, n. chhoTo nidrA (छोटो निद्रा) v. jhapakka sutnu (झपक्क सुत्नु)

napkin, n. hAt puchhne rumAl (हात पुछ्ने रुमाल), nyApkin (न्याप्किन)

narcotic, n. mAdak/lAgU padArth (मादक/लागू पदार्थ) adj. mAdak (मादक), lAgU (लागू)

narrate, v. warNan garnu (वर्णन गर्नु), wiwaraN sunAunu (विवरण सुनाउनु)

narration, n. warNan (वर्णन), bayAn (बयान)

narrow, adj. sAn̄ghuro (साँघुरो) v. sAn̄ghurinu (साँघुरिनु), **(have a narrow escape)**, phr. bAl bAl bAn̄chnu (बाल बाल बाँच्नु), jhanDai marnu (झण्डै मर्नु)

narrow-minded, adj. anudAr (अनुदार), san̄kIrN (सङ्कीर्ण)

nasal, *adj.* nAke (नाके)

nasty, *adj.* phohor (फोहोर), kharAb (खराब)

nation, *n.* rAshtra (राष्ट्र), jAti (जाति)

national, *adj.* rAshtriya (राष्ट्रिय) *n.* nAgrik (नागरिक)

nationalism, *n.* rAshtra wAd (राष्ट्रवाद)

nationality, *n.* rAshtriyatA (राष्ट्रियता), nAgriktA (नागरिकता)

native, *n.* bAsindA (बासिन्दा) *adj.* deshI (देशी), raithAne (रैथाने)

natural, *adj.* prAkritik (प्राकृतिक), swabhAwik (स्वाभाविक)

naturalize, *v.* nAgrikta dinu (नागरिकता दिनु), rAshtriyakaraN garnu (राष्ट्रियकरण गर्नु)

naturally, *adv.* swabhAwai le (स्वभावैले)

nature, *n.* prakriti (प्रकृति), swabhAw (स्वभाव)

naughty, *adj.* dushT (दुष्ट), upadryAhA (उपद्रयाहा)

nausea, *n.* wAk wAkI (वाकवाकी), ghin (घिन)

navel, *n.* naiTo (नाइटो)

near, *adv.* najik (नजिक),

nikaT (निकट)
v. najik Aunu (नजिक आउनु)

nearby, *adj.* najikai ko (नजिकैको)

nearly, *adv.* lag bhag (लगभग), karIb (करीब)

near-sighted, *adj.* nikaT darshI (निकटदर्शी)

neat, *adj.* saphA (सफा)

neat and clean, *adj.* saphA sugghar (सफा–सुग्घर)

neatly, *adv.* saphA saṅga (सफासँग)

necessaries, *n.* bAňchhne sAmagrI (बाँच्ने सामग्री)

necessary, *adj.* jarurI (जरुरी), Awashyak (आवश्यक)

necessity, *n.* jarurat (जरुरत), AwashyaktA (आवश्यकता)

neck, *n.* gardan (गर्दन), ghichro (घिच्रो), *(nape)* ghuchchuk (घुच्चुक), *(throat)* ghAňTI (घाँटी)

necklace, *n.* hAr (हार), mAlA (माला)

necktie, *n.* nekTAi (नेकटाइ)

need, *n.* khAňcho (खाँचो)

needful, *adj.* Awashyak (आवश्यक)

needle, *n.* siyo (सियो), suI (सुई), suiro (सुइरो)

needless, *adj.* anAwashyak (अनावश्यक)

needlework, *n.* silAi (सिलाइ)

neglect, *n.* bewAstA (बेवास्ता),
upekshA (उपेक्षा)
v. bewAstA garnu
(बेवास्ता गर्नु), hepnu (हेप्नु)

negligence, *n.* lAparbAhI
(लापर्बाही),
bewAstA (बेवास्ता)

negligent, *adj.* asAwdhAn
(असावधान),
lAparbAh (लापर्बाह)

negligible, *adj.* nagaNya
(नगण्य)

negotiation, *n.* wArtA (वार्ता),
kurA kAnI (कुराकानी)

neighbo(u)r, *n.* chhimekI
(छिमेकी)

neighbo(u)rhood, *n* chhimek
(छिमेक)

neighbo(u)ring, *adj.* chhimek/
AspAs ko (छिमेक/आसपासको)

neither, *adj./adv./conj.* na (न),
pani (पनि)

nephew, *n.* bhatijA (भतिजा),
bhAnjA (भान्जा),
bhadA (भदा)

Neptune, *n.* waruN graha
(वरुण ग्रह)

nerve, *n.* snAyu (स्नायु),
nADI (नाडी), nasA (नसा),
(loose one's nerve), *phr.*
hos uDnu (होस उड्नु)

nervous, *adj.* Attieko

(आत्तिएको)

nervous system, *n.* snAyu
praNAlI (स्नायु प्रणाली)

nest, *n.* guňD (गुँड)

net, *n.* jAl (जाल), jAlI (जाली),
v. jAl mA pArnu
(जालमा पानुं)

nettle, *n.* sisnu (सिस्नु),
v. satAunu (सताउनु)

network, *n.* jAlo (जालो),
sanjAl (सञ्जाल)

never, *adv.* kahile pani hoina
(कहिले पनि होइन)

never mind, *v.* kehI chhaina
(केही छैन), phikrI na linos
(फिक्री नलिनोस्)

nevertheless, *adv.* tyaso bhae
tApani (त्यसो भए तापनि),
tathApi (तथापि)

new, *adj.* nayAñ (नयाँ)

newcomer, *n.* nawAgantuk
(नवागन्तुक)

newly, *adj.* hAl ko (हालको),
ahile ko (अहिलेको)

newly-wed, *n./adj.* hAl bihe
bhaeko (हाल बिहे भएको)

new moon, *n.* auñsI (औंसी)

news, *n.* khabar (खबर),
samAchAr (समाचार)

newspaper, *n.* akhbAr (अखबार),
samAchAr patra (समाचारपत्र)

news-stand, *n.* akhbAr pasal
(अखबार पसल)

newsworthy, *adj.* samAchAr
yogya (समाचारयोग्य)

new year, *n.* nayAǹ/nawa
warsh (नयाँ/नव वर्ष),

next, *adj.* arko (अर्को),
AgAmI (आगामी)

nib, *n.* nib (निब), Tuppo (टुप्पो)

nice, *adj.* rAmro (राम्रो)

nickel, *n.* nikal (निकल),
gilTI (गिल्टी)

nickname, *n.* bolAune nAm
(बोलाउने नाम), upnAm (उपनाम)

niece, *n.* bhatijI (भतिजी),
bhAnjI (भान्जी), bhadinI (भदिनी)

night, *n.* rAt (रात), rAti (राति),
(*all night*) rAt bhar (रातभर),
(*at night*) rAt mA (रातमा),
(*last night*) hijo rAti
(हिजो राति)

nightingale, *n.* jurelI (जुरेली),
bulbul (बुलबुल)

nightlife, *n.* rAt ko manorañjan
(रातको मनोरञ्जन)

nightmare, *n.* Dar lAgdo
sapanA (डरलाग्दो सपना)

nightshirt, *n.* sutne belA mA
lAune kamij (सुत्ने बेलामा
लाउने कमिज)

nightsoil, *n.* rAt ko disA
pisAb (रातको दिसापिसाब)

nil, *n.* shUnya (शून्य),
phussA (फुस्सा)

nimble, *adj.* chhiTo (छिटो),

phurtilo (फुर्तिलो)

nine, *n.* nau (नौ)

nineteen, *n.* unnAis (उन्नाइस)

ninety, *n.* nabbe (नब्बे)

ninth, *n.* nawauǹ (नवौं)

nipple, *n.* munTo (मुन्टो),
munTI (मुन्टी)

no, *adv.* ahaǹ (अहँ),
huǹdaina (हुँदैन), nAiǹ (नाई)

noble, *adj.* udAr (उदार),
shreshtha (श्रेष्ठ)

nobody, *n.* kohI hoina
(कोही होइन), nagaNya
wyakti (नगण्य व्यक्ति)

nod, *v.* TAuko hallAunu
(टाउको हल्लाउनु)

no doubt, *n.* nissandeh
(निस्सन्देह)

noise, *n.* AwAj (आवाज),
khailA bailA (खैलाबैला)

noisy, *adj.* ThUlo Awaj hune
(ठूलो आवाज हुने),
kolAhal pUrN (कोलाहलपूर्ण)

nominal, *adj.* nAuǹ ko (नाउँको),
nAm mAtra ko (नाम मात्रको)

nominate, *v.* nAuǹ toknu
(नाउँ तोक्नु),
manonIt garnu (मनोनीत गर्नु)

nomination, *n.* manonayan
(मनोनयन), niyukti (नियुक्ति)

none, *pron./adv.* kehI/kohI
pani hoina (केही/कोही पनि
होइन)

non-existent, *adj.* kAlpanik (काल्पनिक), astitwa na bhaeko (अस्तित्व नभएको)

nonsense, *n.* be matlab ko kuro (बेमतलबको कुरो), aNT saNT (अण्टसण्ट), wAhiyAt (वाहियात)

non-smoker, *n.* dhUmra pAn na garne (धूम्रपान नगर्ने)

non-stop, *adj.* na rokine (न रोकिने), awirAm (अविराम)

nook, *n.* kunA (कुना), kuno (कुनो)

noon, *n.* madhyAnha (मध्यान्ह)

no one, *pron.* kohI pani hoina (कोही पनि होइन)

noose, *n.* pAso (पासो), phandA (फन्दा)

normal, *adj.* sAmAnya (सामान्य)

normally, *adv.* sAmAnya tawar le (सामान्यतवरले)

north, *n.* uttar (उत्तर)

northern, *adj.* uttarI (उत्तरी)

north pole, *n.* uttarI dhruwa (उत्तरी ध्रुव)

north star, *n.* dhruwa tArA (ध्रुवतारा)

northward, *adv.* uttar tira (उत्तरतिर)

nose, *n.* nAk (नाक)

nose jewel, *n.* phUlI (फूली)

nose ring, *n.* bulAkI (बुलाकी)

nostri, *n.* nAk ko pwAl (नाकको प्वाल), poro (पोरो)

not, *adv.* hoina (होइन), nAiñ (नाईं), chhaina (छैन)

notable, *adj.* samjhana lAyak ko (सम्झन लायकको) *n.* ThUlA baDA (ठूलाबडा)

note, *n.* TipoT (टिपोट), TippaNI (टिप्पणी), *(currency)* noT (नोट) *v.* Tipnu (टिप्नु), janAunu (जनाउनु), yAd garnu (याद गर्नु)

notebook, *n.* sAnu kApI (सानु कापी), noT buk (नोटबुक)

noted, *adj.* prakhyAt (प्रख्यात), nAmud (नामुद)

nothing, *adj.* kehI hoina (केही होइन)

notice, *n.* sUchanA (सूचना), janAu (जनाउ) *v.* dekhnu (देख्नु), chAl pAunu (चाल पाउनु)

notify, *v.* sUchit garnu (सूचित गर्नु), janAunu (जनाउनु)

notion, *n.* wichAr (विचार), siddhAnt (सिद्धान्त)

notorious, *adj.* kukhyAt (कुख्यात), badnAm (बदनाम)

notwithstanding, *adv.* tApani (तापनि), tathApi (तथापि)

nourish, *v.* posnu (पोस्नु)

nourishment, *n.* poshaN (पोषण), paushTik khurAk (पौष्टिक खुराक)

novel, *n.* upanyAs (उपन्यास)
    adj. nayAঁ (नयाঁ), naulo (नौलो)

novelist, *n.* upanyAs kAr
    (उपन्यासकार),
    kathA kAr (कथाकार)

novice, *n.* anADI (अनाडी),
    sikAru (सिकारु)

now, *adv.* ahile (अहिले),
    aba (अब)

nowadays, *adv.* Aj kal
    (आजकल), hijo Aja (हिजोआज)

nowhere, *adv.* kahIঁ katai pani
    hoina (कहीঁ कतै पनि होइन)

nuclear, *adj.* ANwik (आण्विक)

nuclear energy, *n.* ANwik
    shakti (आण्विक शक्ति)

nuclear family, *n.* sAnu/ekal
    pariwAr (सानु/एकल परिवार)

nuclear power, *n.* ANwik
    shakti (आण्विक शक्ति)

nude, *adj.* nAঁgo (नाङ्गो)

nuisance, *n.* jhanjhaT
    (फन्फट), markA (मर्का)

numb, *adj.* lATieko (लाटिएको),
    nidAeko (निदाएको)

number, *n.* gantI (गन्ती),
    hisAb (हिसाब), aঁk (अङ्क),
    saঁkhyA (संख्या)
    v. gannu (गन्नु)

number one, *adj.* ek nambar
    ko (एक नम्बरको)
    pron. (oneself) AphU (आफू)

numeral, *n.* aঁk (अङ्क)

numerous, *adj.* dherai (धेरै),
    asaঁkhya (असङ्ख्य)

nun, *n.* joginI (जोगिनी),
    bhikshuNI (भिक्षुणी)

nuptial, *n.* wiwAh (विवाह)
    adj. waiwAhik (वैवाहिक),
    biheko (बिहेको)

nurse, *n. (home)* dhAI (धाई),
    (hospital, clinic) nars (नर्स)
    parichArikA (परिचारिका)
    v. syAhArnu (स्याहार्नु),
    posnu (पोस्नु)

nursery, *n. (orgn.)* sAnA
    bachchA harU padhne
    koThA wA widyAlaya
    (साना बच्चाहरू पढ्ने कोठा वा
    विद्यालय),
    (plants) narsarI (नर्सरी)

nursing home, *n.* narsiঁ hom
    (नर्सिङ होम)

nurture, *v.* pAlnu (पाल्नु),
    posnu (पोस्नु)

nut, *n.* supArI (सुपारी),
    kaDA biyaঁ bhaeko phal
    (कडा बियाঁ भएको फल)

nutcracker, *n.* sarautA (सरौता)

nutmeg, *n.* jAiphal (जाइफल)

nutrition, *n.* poshaN (पोषण)

nutritious, *adj.* paushTik
    (पौष्टिक)

nylon, *n.* nAilan (नाइलन)

nymph, *n.* parI (परी),
    apsarA (अप्सरा)

oat, *n.* jai (जै)

oath, *n.* kiriyA (किरिया),
kasam (कसम),
shapath (शपथ)

obedience, *n.* AgỹA pAlan
(आज्ञापालन)

obedient, *adj.* AgỹA kArI
(आज्ञाकारी)

obesity, *n.* moTopan (मोटोपन)

obey, *v.* AgỹA pAlan garnu
(आज्ञा पालन गर्नु), bhaneko
mAnnu (भनेको मान्नु)

object, *n.* wastu (वस्तु),
chIj (चीज)
v. wirodh garnu (विरोध गर्नु)

objection, *n.* wirodh (विरोध),
Apatti (आपत्ति)

objective, *n.* laksha (लक्ष),
uddeshya (उद्देश्य)
adj. wastu gat (वस्तुगत),
wishaya parak (विषयपरक)

obligation, *n.* kartawya
(कर्तव्य), dAyitwa (दायित्व)

obligatory, *adj.* kar/bAdhya
garAune (कर/बाध्य गराउने)

oblige, *v.* bAdhya/kritagỹa
garAunu (बाध्य/कृतज्ञ गराउनु)

oblique, *adj.* terso (तेर्सो),

chhaDke (छड्के)

oblong, *adj.* lAmcho (लाम्चो)

obliterate, *v.* meTnu (मेट्नु),
nAmeT garnu (नामेट गर्नु)

obscene, *adj.* ashlIl (अश्लील),
phohorI (फोहोरी)

obscure, *adj.* dhamilo (धमिलो)
v. dhamilo parnu (धमिलो पर्नु),
chheknu (छेक्नु)

observation, *n.* awlokan
(अवलोकन), herAi (हेराइ)

observatory, *n.* wedh shAlA
(वेधशाला)

observe, *v.* hernu (हेर्नु),
awlokan garnu
(अवलोकन गर्नु)

observer, *n.* darshak (दर्शक),
paryawekshak (पर्यवेक्षक)

obsolete, *adj.* be chaltI ko
(बेचल्तीको), purAno (पुरानो)

obstacle, *n.* tagAro (तगारो),
aDko (अड्को)

obstinate, *adj.* jiddI wAl
(जिद्दीवाल), jirAhA (जिराहा)

obstruct, *v.* bAdhA dinu
(बाधा दिनु), chheknu (छेक्नु)

obstruction, *n.* aljho (अल्झो),
aDko (अड्को)

obtain, v. pAunu (पाउनु),
juTAunu (जुटाउनु)

obtainable, adj. pAine (पाइने),
pAuna sakne (पाउन सक्ने)

obvious, adj. spashT (स्पष्ट),
jhaTTa bujhine (झट्ट बुझिने)

occasion, n. ausar (औसर),
awsar (अवसर)

occasional, adj. kahile kAhiĬ
hune (कहिलेकाहीँ हुने)

occasionally, adv. kahile
kahĬ (कहिलेकहीँ)

Occident, n. pashchim
(पश्चिम), pashchim yurop
(पश्चिम युरोप)

occupation, n. dakhal (दखल),
peshA (पेशा), kAm (काम)

occupy, v. dakhal garnu (दखल
गर्नु), ogaTnu (ओगट्नु)

occur, v. hunu (हुनु),
man mA parnu (मनमा पर्नु)

occurrence, n. ghaTnA (घटना)

ocean, n. mahA sAgar
(महासागर)

o'clock, n. baje (बजे)

octogenarian, n. asI dekhi
unAnabbe warsh samma ko
umer bhaeko mAnis (८० देखि
८९ वर्षसम्मको उमेर भएको
मानिस)

odd, adj. (thing, event)
anauTho (अनौठो),
(number) bijoD (बिजोड)

odds, n. pharak (फरक),
asamAn (असमान), mat bhed
(मतभेद), (at odds), phr. mat
bhed/kalah bahaeko
(मतभेद/कलह भएको)

odds and ends, n. chhUT
phUT (छुटफुट),
chAn chun (चानचुन)

odo(u)r, n. (smell) gandh
(गन्ध), bAsnA (बास्ना)

of, prep. ko (को)

off, adv. TADhA (टाढा), alag
(अलग), rokieko (रोकिएको)
prep. bATa (बाट)
adj. TADhA (टाढा), para (पर)

off and on, adv. belA belA
mA (बेलाबेलामा)

offbeat, adj. asAmAnya
(असामान्य),
asAdhAraN (असाधारण)

off chance, n. kam
sambhAwanA (कम सम्भावना)

off colo(u)r, adj. aswasth
(अस्वस्थ)

offence, n. AkrAmak kArya
(आक्रामक कार्य), kasur (कसुर)

offend, v. ris uThAunu
(रिस उठाउनु),
apmAn garnu (अपमान गर्नु)

offender, n. aprAdhI (अपराधी),
kasur wAlA (कसुरवाला)

offensive, n. hamlA (हमला)
adj. AkrAmak (आक्रामक),

apmAn janak (अपमानजनक)

offer, *n.* prastAw (प्रस्ताव)
v. chaDhAunu (चढाउनु),
prastAw garnu (प्रस्ताव गर्नु)

offering, *n.* saugAt (सौगात),
naiwedya (नैवेद्य),
bheTI (भेटी)

offhand, *adj.* binA tayArI
(बिनातयारी), jhaTTa (झट्ट)

office, *n.* aDDA (अड्डा),
kAryAlaya (कार्यालय),
aphis (अफिस)

officer, *n.* adhikrit (अधिकृत),
aphisar (अफिसर)

official, *n.* adhikrit (अधिकृत),
adhikArI (अधिकारी),
padAdhikArI (पदाधिकारी)
adj. sarkArI (सरकारी),
aupchArik (औपचारिक)

offshoot, *n.* hAṅgA (हाँगा),
shAkhA (शाखा)

offspring, *n.* santAn (सन्तान),
bAl bachchA (बालबच्चा)

often, *adv.* aksar (अक्सर),
bArambAr (बारम्बार)

oil, *n.* tel (तेल)
v. tel hAlnu (तेल हाल्नु),
tel lAunu (तेल लाउनु)

oilcake, *n.* pinA (पिना)

oil colo(u)r, *n.* tel raṅg (तेल रङ्ग)

oilfield, *n.* tel khAnI (तेल खानी)

oil painting, *n.* tail chitra
(तैलचित्र)

oil well, *n.* tel ko kUwA
(तेलको कूवा)

oily, *adj.* chillo (चिल्लो)

ointment, *n.* malam (मलम),
lep (लेप)

okay (OK), *n.* swIkriti
(स्वीकृति), swIkAr (स्वीकार)
adv. sab ThIk (सब ठीक)
v. hunchha (हुन्छ)

okra, *n.* rAm toriyAṅ
(रामतोरियाँ)

old, *adj. (age)* bUDho (बूढो),
(time) purAno (पुरानो)

old age, *n.* buDhes kAl
(बुढेसकाल)

oldest, *adj.* sab bhandA jeTho
/ bUDho (सबभन्दा जेठो/बूढो)

old-fashioned, *adj.* purAno
DhAṅchA ko (पुरानो ढाँचाको)

old hand, *n.* anubhawI mAnis
(अनुभवी मानिस)

old hat, *adj.* purAno DharrA
ko (पुरानो ढर्राको), *(derog.)*
ghise piTeko (घिसेपिटेको)

olive, *n.* jaitUn (जैतून)

olive branch, *n.* shAnti ko
pratIk (शान्तिको प्रतीक)

omelet(te), *n.* amleT
(अम्लेट)

omen, *n.* shakun (शकुन),
sAit (साइत)

ominous, *adj.* aphAp (अफाप),
bichchhukI (बिच्छुकी)

omit, *v.* chhoDnu (छोड्नु)

on, *prep.* mA (मा),
mAthi (माथि)

once, *adv.* ek choTi (एक
चोटि), ek palTa (एकपल्ट),
(at once) turunt (तुरुन्त),
ekai palTa (एकैपल्ट)

once upon a time, *adv.* ekA
desh mA (एकादेशमा)

oncoming, *adj.* Auñdo (आउँदो)

one, *n.* ek (एक), euTA (एउटा)

one by one, *adv.* ek ek garera
(एकएक गरेर)

one-eyed, *adj.* kAno (कानो)

one-sided, *adj.* ek tarphI
(एकतर्फी)

onion, *n.* pyAj (प्याज)

onlooker, *n.* tamAse (तमासे),
darshak (दर्शक)

only, *adj.* kewal (केवल),
mAtra (मात्र), sirph (सिर्फ)

onset, *n.* *(attack)* dhAwA
(धावा), hamlA (हमला),
(beginning) shuru (शुरु),
Arambh (आरम्भ)

onward, *adv.* aghi aghi
(अघिअघि)

opaque, *adj.* apArdarshI
(अपारदर्शी)

open, *adj.* khulA (खुला)
v. kholnu (खोल्नु)

open-air, *adj.* khulA (खुला),
bAhirI (बाहिरी)

open-handed, *adj.* udAr (उदार),
dAnI (दानी)

opening, *n.* *(hole)* pwAl (प्वाल),
(for.) udghATan (उद्घाटन),
(opportunity) awsar
(अवसर), maukA (मौका)

openly, *adv.* khulast (खुलस्त)

open-minded, *adj.* khulA man
ko (खुला मनको), udAr (उदार)

operate, *v.* chalAunu (चलाउनु),
sañchAlan garnu
(सञ्चालन गर्नु)

operation, *n.* *(med.)* chir
phAr (चिर फार), kAm
(काम), abhiyAn (अभियान),
sañchAlan (सञ्चालन)

operator, *n.* sañchAlak
(सञ्चालक)

opinion, *n.* wichAr (विचार),
mantawya (मनतव्य)

opium, *n.* aphIm (अफीम)

opponent, *n.* wipakshI
(विपक्षी), wirodhI (विरोधी)

opportunity, *n.* awsar
(अवसर), maukA (मौका)

oppose, *v.* wirodh garnu
(विरोध गर्नु)

opposite, *adj.* ulTo (उल्टो),
(facing) sAmunne (सामुन्ने)

opposition, *n.* wirodh (विरोध)

opposition, *n.* *(pol.)* wipaksha
(विपक्ष),
prati paksha (प्रतिपक्ष)

oppress, *v.* thicho micho / atyAchAr garnu (थिचोमिचो / अत्याचार गर्नु)

optician, *n.* chasmA banAune (चस्मा बनाउने)

optimist, *n.* AshA wAdI (आशावादी)

option, *n.* rojI (रोजी), chhanoT (छनोट)

optional, *adj.* ichchhA dhIn (इच्छाधीन)

or, *conj.* athawA (अथवा), arthAt (अर्थात्)

oral, *adj.* mukh ko (मुखको), maukhik (मौखिक)

orange, *n.* suntalA (सुन्तला)

orbit, *n.* kaksha (कक्ष) *v.* ghumnu (घुम्नु)

orchard, *n.* bagaiñchA (बगैंचा)

orchid, *n.* sunAkharI (सुनाखरी), sungAbhA (सुनगाभा)

ordeal, *n.* kaThin parIkshA (कठिन परीक्षा)

order, *n.* urdI (उर्दी), hukum (हुकुम), Adesh (आदेश), *(sequence)* kram (क्रम), silsilA (सिलसिला) *v.* arhAunu (अह्राउनु), *(bus.)* magAunu (मगाउनु)

orderly, *n.* ardalI (अर्दली) *adv.* kAidA sita (काइदासित) *adj.* milAeko (मिलाएको)

ordinance, *n.* sarkArI Adesh (सरकारी आदेश), adhyAdesh (अध्यादेश)

ordinary, *adj.* sAdhAraN (साधारण), mAmulI (मामुली)

ore, *n.* dhAu (धाउ), kachchA dhAtu (कच्चा धातु)

organ, *n. (music)* bAjA (बाजा), *(body)* añg (अङ्ग), indriya (इन्द्रिय)

organization, *n.* sañgaThan (सङ्गठन), samsthA (संस्था)

organize, *v.* sañgaThan / bandobast garnu (सङ्गठन / बन्दोबस्त गर्नु)

orient, *n.* pUrwa (पूर्व)

oriental, *adj.* pUrwIya (पूर्वीय)

origin, *n.* mUl (मूल), utpatti (उत्पत्ति)

original, *adj.* sakkalI (सक्कली), maulik (मौलिक), shuru ko (शुरुको)

originate, *v.* paidA garAunu / hunu (पैदा गराउनु/हुनु) prArambh hunu (प्रारम्भ हुनु)

ornament, *n.* gahanA (गहना)

orphan, *n.* Tuhuro (टुहुरो), anAth (अनाथ)

orphanage, *n.* anAthAlaya (अनाथालय)

orthodox, *adj.* kaTTar (कट्टर)

other, *adj.* arko (अर्को), arU (अरू)

otherwise, *conj.* natra (नत्र), anyathA (अन्यथा)

ounce, *n.* auns (औंस)

our, *pron.* hAmro (हाम्रो), hAmI harU ko (हामीहरूको)

out, *n./v.* bAhira (बाहिर)

out-and-out, *adv.* harek tabar le (हरेक तबरले)

outbreak, *n.* danga phasAd (दङ्गाफसाद), *(disease)* phailAw (फैलाव)

outcast, *n.* samAj le nikAleko mAnis (समाजले निकालेको मानिस)

outcome, *n.* natijA (नतिजा), phal (फल)

outdoor, *adj.* bAhirI (बाहिरी)

outdoors, *adv.* bAhira (बाहिर)

outer, *adj.* bAhirI (बाहिरी)

outfit, *n.* lugA phATA (लुगाफाटा), upkaraN (उपकरण)

outing, *n.* saphar (सफर), sayar (सयर)

outlaw, *n.* nirwAsit (निर्वासित)

outlet, *n.* nikAs (निकास)

outline, *n.* rUp rekhA (रूपरेखा)

outlook, *n.* drishTi koN (दृष्टिकोण), wichAr (विचार)

outnumber, *v.* sankhyA baDhI hunu (सङ्ख्या बढी हुनु)

out of date, *adj.* gujreko (गुज्रेको), chaltI na bhaeko (चल्ती नभएको), purAno (पुरानो)

out of order, *adj.* bigreko (बिग्रेको), be chaltI ko (बेचल्ती को)

outpost, *n.* chaukI (चौकी)

output, *n.* upaj (उपज), utpAdan (उत्पादन)

outrage, *n.* arkA ko adhikAr ko hanan (अर्काको अधिकारको हनन), *(fury)* krodh (क्रोध)

outright, *adj./adv.* spashT (स्पष्ट), turunt (तुरुन्त)

outset, *n.* shuru (शुरु), prArambh (प्रारम्भ)

outside, *adv.* bAhira paTTi (बाहिरपट्टि) *n.* bAhira (बाहिर)

outskirts, *n.* shahar ko bAhirI bhAg (शहरको बाहिरी भाग), kAnTh (काँठ)

outspoken, *adj.* khulast kurA garne (खुलस्त कुरा गर्ने), spashT waktA (स्पष्टवक्ता)

outward, *adv.* bAhira tira ko (बाहिरतिरको), bAhirI (बाहिरी)

outworn, *adj.* purAno (पुरानो), be chaltI ko (बेचल्तीको)

oval, *adj.* aNDAkAr (अण्डाकार)

oven, *n.* chUlo (चूलो)

over, *prep.* mAthi (माथि) *adv.* dherai jyAdA (धेरै ज्यादा), *(end)* samApt (समाप्त)

over and over, *adv.* bArambAr (बारम्बार)

overall, *adj.* samast (समस्त)
  n. bAhirI lugA (बाहिरी लुगा)

overbearing, *adj.* ghamaNDI
  (घमण्डी), ahaṅkArI (अहङ्कारी)

overcast, *adj.* bAdal/badalI
  lAgeko (बादल/बदली लागेको),

overcome, *v.* jitnu (जित्नु),
  wijaya pAunu (विजय पाउनु)

overdue, *adj.* myAd nAgheko
  (म्याद नाघेको)

overflow, *n.* chhaTA chhulla
  hune awasthA
  (छताछुल्ल हुने अवस्था)
  v. pokhinu (पोखिनु),
  rasAunu (रसाउनु)

overhear, *v.* thAhA nadikana
  sunnu (थाहा नदिकन सुन्नु)

overlap, *v.* khapTinu (खप्टिनु)

overload, *n.* baDhI bhAr
  (बढी भार)
  v. baDhI bhAr lAdnu
  (बढी भार लाद्नु)

overlook, *v.* dekhna na saknu
  (देख्न नसक्नु),
  bewAstA garnu (बेवास्ता गर्नु)

overnight, *adv.* rAt bhari (mA)
  (रातभरि(मा))

overpower, *v.* jitnu (जित्नु),
  kAbu garnu (काबु गर्नु)

overrule, *v.* badar/khArej

garnu (बदर/खारेज गर्नु)

overseas, *adj.* samudra pAr
  (समुद्रपार)
  adv. smudra pAri (समुद्रपारी)

oversight, *n.* bhUl (भूल),
  lAparbAhI (लापरबाही)

overt, *adj.* khulast (खुलस्त),
  na lukAune (नलुकाउने)

overtake, *v.* uchhinnu (उछिन्नु)

overthrow, *v.* ulTai dinu
  (उल्टाइदिनु),
  palTAunu (पल्टाउनु)

overtime, *adj.* baDhI samaya
  ko (बढी समयको)

overturn, *v.* palTAunu
  (पल्टाउनु)

overwhelm, *v.* DhAknu (ढाक्नु),
  bhakran pArnu (भक्रन पार्नु)

owe, *v.* riNI hunu (ऋणी हुनु)

owl, *n.* lATo kosero
  (लाटोकोसेरो)

own, *adj.* Aphno (आफ्नो),
  Aphnai (आफ्नै)
  v. upbhog garnu (उपभोग
  गर्नु), swAmitwa mA lyAunu
  (स्वामित्वमा ल्याउनु),
  sanga hunu (सँग हुनु)

owner, *n.* mAlik (मालिक),
  dhanI (धनी)

ox, *n.* goru (गोरु), bayal (बयल)

P

pace, *n.* kadam (कदम),
(*speed*) gati (गति)

pack, *n.* poko (पोको),
gaTharI (गठरी),
jholA (झोला),
(*cards*) gaDDI (गड्डी)
v. poko pArnu (पोको पार्नु)

package, *n.* poko (पोको),
kumlo (कुम्लो),
pulindA (पुलिन्दा)

packet, *n.* poko (पोको),
pyAkeT (प्याकेट)

pact, *n.* sandhi (सन्धि),
samjhautA (सम्झौता)

pad, *n.* gaddA (गद्दा),
(*writing*) lekhne pyAD
(लेख्ने प्याड)

paddy, *n.* dhAn (धान)

padlock, *n.* tAlchA (ताल्चा)

page, *n.* pAnA (पाना),
patra (पत्र),
(*servant*) nokar (नोकर)

pageant, *n.* tamAshA (तमाशा)

pagoda, *n.* mandir (मन्दिर),
nepAlI shailI ko mandir
(नेपाली शैलीको मन्दिर)

pail, *n.* bAITI (बाल्टी),
ThekI (ठेकी)

pain, *n.* duhkh (दुःख),
pIDA (पीडा),
v. dukhnu (दुख्नु),
duhkh dinu (दुःख दिनु)

painful, *adj.* pIDA dAyI
(पीडादायी),
kashT kar (कष्टकर)

painless, *adj.* pIDA rahit
(पीडारहित),
kashT hIn (कष्टहीन)

paint, *n.* raṅg (रङ्ग), rogan (रोगन)
v. chitra kornu (चित्र कोर्नु),
raṅg lagAunu (रङ्ग लगाउनु)

painter, *n.* chitra kAr
(चित्रकार), chitra banAune
(चित्र बनाउने)

painting, *n.* chitra kArI
(चित्रकारी), taswIr (तस्वीर)

pair, *n.* jor (जोर), joDA (जोडा),
(*family*) joDI (जोडी),
dampatI (दम्पती)

pal, *n.* sAthI (साथी)

palace, *n.* darbAr (दरबार),
mahal (महल)

palatable, *adj.* swAdilo
(स्वादिलो), mITho (मीठो)

pale, *adj.* phikkA paheñlo
(फिक्का पहेँलो)

palm, *n. (hand)* hatkelA (हत्केला), *(tree)* khajur ko rUkh (खजुरको रूख)

palpitation, *n.* kampan (कम्पन), *(heart)* dhuk dhuk (ढुकढुक), swAň swAň (स्वाँस्वाँ)

palsy, *n.* pakshAghAt (पक्षाघात)

pamper, *v.* pul pulyAunu (पुलपुल्याउनु)

pamphlet, *n.* parchA (पर्चा), *(booklet)* pustikA (पुस्तिका)

pan, *n.* karAhI (कराही), tAwA (तावा)

panacea, *n.* sarwaushadhi (सर्वोषधि), rAm bAN (रामबाण)

pancake, *n.* mAl puwA (मालपुवा)

pang, *n.* pIDA (पीडा), wedanA (वेदना)

panic, *n.* Dar (डर), trAs (त्रास) *v.* Attinu (आत्तिनु)

panorama, *n.* manoram (मनोरम), khulA drishya (खुला दृश्य)

pant, *v.* swAň swAň garnu (स्वाँ स्वाँ गर्नु), hAňpnu (हाँप्नु)

pants, *n.* pyAnT (प्यान्ट), pAinT (पाइन्ट)

papa, *n.* bubA (बुबा), bA (बा)

papaya, *n.* mewA (मेवा)

paper, *n.* kAgaj (कागज), *(papers)* kAgaj patra (कागजपत्र), *(newspaper)* akhbAr (अखबार)

paperback, *n.* kAgaj ko jillA bhaeko kitAb (कागजको जिल्ला भएको किताब)

paperwork, *n.* aphis kA likhit kAm harU (अफिसका लिखित कामहरू)

par, *n.* barAbarI (बराबरी), *(above par)* baDhI mUlya mA (बढी मूल्यमा), *(at par)* barAbar mUlya mA (बराबर मूल्यमा), *(below par)* kam mUlya mA (कम मूल्यमा), *(par excellence)* shresTh (श्रेष्ठ)

parachute, *n.* pyArAsuT (प्यारासुट)

parade, *n.* kabAj (कबाज), *(pol.)* julus (जुलुस) *v.* kabAj khelnu (कबाज खेल्नु), julus mA hiňDnu (जुलुसमा हिंड्नु)

paradise, *n.* swarg (स्वर्ग)

paragraph, *n.* anuchchhed (अनुच्छेद)

paralysis, *n.* pakshAghAt (पक्षाघात), paksh wAt (पक्ष वात)

paramount, *adj.* sarwochcha (सर्वोच्च), sarwa pramukh (सर्वप्रमुख)

paramour, *n.* jAr (जार)

parapet, *n.* bArdalI (बार्दली),
kausI (कौसी),
hocho parkhAl (होचो पर्खाल)

parasite, *n.* arU ko mukh
tAkne (अरूको मुख ताक्ने),
bhatuwA (भतुवा),
parjIwI (परजीवी)

parcel, *n.* pulindA (पुलिन्दा),
poko (पोको),
(part) bhAg (भाग)
v. bhAg lAunu (भाग लाउनु)

pardon, *n.* kshamA (क्षमा),
mAphI (माफी)
v. mAph/kshamA garnu
(माफ/क्षमा गर्नु)

parents, *n.* AmA bAbu
(आमाबाबु),
mAtA pitA (मातापिता)

park, *n.* pArk (पार्क),
udyAn (उद्यान)
v. (vehicles) chheu mA
rAkhnu (छेउमा राख्नु),
pArk garnu (पार्क गर्नु)

parliament, *n.* saṃsad (संसद)

parlo(u)r, *n.* baiThak (बैठक)

parrot, *n.* sugA (सुगा)

part, *n.* bhAg (भाग),
hissA (हिस्सा), khaND (खण्ड),
(role) abhinaya (अभिनय)
v. bhAg lAunu (भाग लाउनु),
(take part) bhAg linu
(भाग लिनु)

part and parcel, *n.* Awashyak
bhAg (आवश्यक भाग)

partial, *adj.* Aṃshik (आंशिक),
(attitude) paksh pAtI
(पक्षपाती)

partiality, *n.* paksh pAt
(पक्षपात)

participant, *n.* sah bhAgI
(सहभागी)

participate, *v.* bhAg linu
(भाग लिनु)

particle, *n.* kaN (कण),
ati sAnu TukrA
(अति सानु टुक्रा)

particular, *adj.* khAs (खास),
wishesh (विशेष)

particularly, *adv.* khAs /
wishesh garI (खास/विशेषगरी)

particulars, *n.* wiwaraN harU
(विवरणहरू)

parting, *n. (departure)*
bidAi (बिदाइ),
(hair) siuṇdo (सिउँदो)

partition, *n.* wibhAjan
(विभाजन)
v. wibhAjan garnu
(विभाजन गर्नु)

partly, *adv.* Aṃshik rUp mA
(आंशिक रूपमा)

partner, *n.* sAthI (साथी),
(bus.) hissedAr (हिस्सेदार),
sAjhedAr (साझेदार)

partridge, *n.* titrA (तित्रा)

part-time, adj./adv. Aṃshik samaya ka lAgi (आंशिक समयका लागि)

part with, v. chhoDnu (छोड्नु), tyAgnu (त्याग्नु)

party, n. pArTI (पार्टी), utsaw (उत्सव), (pol.) dal (दल), pArTI (पार्टी)

pass, n. (mt.) bhanjyAṅ (भन्ज्याङ), (exam.) pAs (पास), (permit) pAs (पास) v. uchhinnu (उछिन्नु), pAs hunu/garnu (पास हुनु/गर्नु), (time) kATnu (काट्नु), bitAunu (बिताउनु), (proceed) baDhnu (बढ्नु), **(make a pass at)** AṅkhA karkyAunu (आँखा कर्क्याउनु)

passage, n. bATo (बाटो), maTAn (मटान), yAtrA (यात्रा), (writing) parichchhed (परिच्छेद)

pass away, v. marnu (मर्नु), bitnu (बित्नु)

passenger, n. yAtrI (यात्री), musAphir (मुसाफिर)

passion, n. ris (रिस), josh (जोश), prem (प्रेम), anurAg (अनुराग)

passionate, adj. risAhA (रिसाहा), joshilo (जोशिलो), kAmuk (कामुक)

passport, n. rAh dAnI (राहदानी), pAspoT (पास्पोट)

past, n. (gram.) bhUt kAl (भूतकाल), atIt (अतीत) adj. biteko (बितेको) prep. (via) bATo bhaera (बाटो भएर)

paste, n. mAD (माड), ledo (लेदो) v. TAṅsnu (टाँस्नु)

pastime, n. manorañjan (मनोरञ्जन), Amod (आमोद)

pasture, n. kharak (खर्क), charan (चरन), chaur (चौर)

pat, n. dhAp (धाप) v. thapthapAunu (थपथपाउनु)

patch, n. (land) jamIn ko TukrA (जमीनको टुक्रा), (cloth) TAlo (टालो) v. TAlnu (टाल्नु)

patch pocket, n. TAleko jasto khaltI (टालेको जस्तो खल्ती)

patch up, v. milAunu (मिलाउनु), sapArnu (सपार्नु)

patchwork, n. TAlTul garne kAm (टालटुल गर्ने काम)

paternal, adj. bAbu ko (बाबुको), bAbu paTTi ko (बाबुपट्टिको), paitrik (पैतृक)

path, n. bATo (बाटो), peTI (पेटी)

pathetic, adj. dayA mAyA lAgdo (दया मायालाग्दो)

patience, *n.* dhairya (धैर्य), sahan shIltA (सहनशीलता)

patient, *n.* birAmI (बिरामी), rogI (रोगी)
adj. dhairya wAn (धैर्यवान), dhIr (धीर)

patriot, *n.* desh bhakta (देशभक्त)

patron, *n.* samrakshak (संरक्षक)

patronize, *v.* samrakshaN dinu (संरक्षण दिनु)

pattern, *n.* buTTA (बुट्टा), bAnkI (बान्की)

pauper, *n.* kaňgAl (कङ्गाल), garIb mAnis (गरीब मानिस)

pause, *n.* wirAm (विराम) *v.* thAmnu (थाम्नु), thAminu (थामिनु)

pave, *v.* DhuňgA chhApnu (ढुङ्गा छाप्नु)

pavement, *n.* saDak ko peTI (सडकको पेटी)

paw, *n.* pañjA (पञ्जा)

pay, *n.* talab (तलब), mahinA wArI (माहिनावारी) *v.* paisA tirnu (पैसा तिर्नु)

payable, *adj.* tirnu parne (तिर्नु पर्ने), bhuktAn hune (भुक्तान हुने)

payload, *n.* paisA tirera rAkhine bhArI (पैसा तिरेर राखिने भारी)

payment, *n.* tiro (तिरो), bhuktAnI (भुक्तानी), chuktA (चुक्ता)

pay off, *v.* rAmro natijA lyAunu (राम्रो नतिजा ल्याउनु)

pay-off, *n.* ghUs (घूस)

payroll, *n.* talabI sUchI (तलबी सूची)

pea, *n.* kerAu (केराउ), maTar (मटर)

peace, *n.* shAnti (शान्ति)

peaceful, *adj.* shAnti pUrN (शान्तिपूर्ण)

peaceful coexistence, *n.* shAnti pUrN sah astitwa (शान्तिपूर्ण सह-अस्तित्व)

peach, *n.* Aru (आरु)

peacock, *n.* mujur (मुजुर), mayUr (मयूर)

peahen, *n.* pothI mujur (पोथी मुजुर)

peak, *n.* chuchuro (चुचुरो), shikhar (शिखर), chullI (चुली)

peal, *n.* gaD gaDAhaT (गडगडाहट), guňjan (गुञ्जन)

pear, *n.* nAspAtI (नास्पाती)

pearl, *n.* motI (मोती), *(mother of pearl)* sipI (सिपी)

pearl button, *n.* sipI ko TAňk (सिपीको टाँक)

pearl onion, *n.* chhyApI (छ्यापी)

peasant, *n.* kisAn (किसान), khetI wAl (खेतीवाल)

peasantry, *n.* kisAn warg
(किसानवर्ग)

pebble, *n.* roDA (रोडा),
golo sAnu DhuṅgA
(गोलो सानु ढुङ्गा)

peck, *v.* Thuñnu (ठुङ्नु),
kotarnu (कोतर्नु)

peculiar, *adj.* anauTho
(अनौठो), wichitra (विचित्र)

pedestrian, *n.* baTuwA (बटुवा),
peTI bATa hiñDne
(पेटीबाट हिँड्ने)

peel, *n.* bokrA (बोक्रा),
chhAlA (छाला)
v. tAchhnu (ताछ्नु),
chhoDAunu (छोडाउनु)

peep, *v.* chyAunu (च्याउनु)

peephole, *n.* chyAune pwAl
(च्याउने प्वाल)

peepshow, *n.* chyAera herne
chitra pradarshan (च्याएर हेर्ने
चित्र प्रदर्शन)

peerless, *adj.* tulnA garna na
sakine (तुलना गर्न नसकिने),
be joD (बेजोड)

peg, *n.* kilA (किला), kAñTA
(काँटा), *(off the peg)*
tayArI (तयारी)

pen, *n.* kalam (कलम),
(animal) khor (खोर)
v. lekhnu (लेख्नु)

penalty, *n.* daND (दण्ड),
jaribAnA (जरिबाना)

pencil, *n.* sisA kalam
(सिसाकलम), pensil (पेन्सिल)

pending, *adj.* Tuṅgo na
lAgeko (टुङ्गो नलागेको)

penetrate, *v.* pasAunu (पसाउनु),
chhirAunu (छिराउनु)

penetration, *n.* chhirAi (छिराइ),
prawesh (प्रवेश)

penfriend, *n.* patra mitra
(पत्रमित्र)

penicillin, *n.* pensilin (पेन्सिलिन)

penis, *n.* liṅg (लिङ्ग)

penknife, *n.* sAnu chakku
(सानु चक्कु)

pen-name, *n.* up nAm
(उपनाम)

pen pal, *n.* patra mitra (पत्रमित्र)

pension, *n.* pensan (पेन्सन),
niwritti bharaN (निवृत्तिभरण)

peon, *n.* piun (पिउन),
chaprAsI (चपरासी)

people, *n.* jantA (जनता),
jAti (जाति),
mAnis harU (मानिसहरू)

pepper, *n.* marIch (मरीच),
(red) khorsAnI (खोर्सानी),
(long) piplA (पिपला)

per annum, *adj.* prati warsh
(प्रतिवर्ष)

per capita, *adj.* prati wyakti
(प्रतिव्यक्ति)

per cent, *adj.* sayakaDA
(सयकडा)

perception, *n.* gÁÅAn (ज्ञान),
dhArNA (धारणा)

perfect, *adj.* bilkul ThIk
(बिलकुल ठीक), pUrN (पूर्ण)

perfectly, *adv.* pUrA tawar le
(पूरातवरले),
pUrN rUp le (पूर्ण रूपले)

perform, *v.* kAm garnu (काम
गर्नु), *(play)* abhinaya garnu
(अभिनय गर्नु)

performance, *n.* kAm garAi
(काम गराइ),
(play) pradarshan (प्रदर्शन)

perfume, *n.* attar (अत्तर)

perhaps, *adv.* sAyad (सायद)

period, *n. (time)*
awadhi (अवधि), *(women)*
na chhune hune (नछुने हुने),
rajo dharm (रजो धर्म), *(gram.)*
pUrN wirAm (पूर्णविराम)

periodical, *adj.* samaya
samaya mA hune
(समय समयमा हुने)
n. patrikA (पत्रिका)

perish, *v.* nAsinu (नासिनु),
nAsh hunu (नाश हुनु)

perishable, *adj.* bigrane
(बिग्रने), nAsine (नासिने)

permanent, *adj.* sthAyI (स्थायी)

permission, *n.* anumati
(अनुमति), AgyÁÅA (आज्ञा)

permit, *n.* anumati patra
(अनुमति पत्र)

v. anumati dinu (अनुमति दिनु)

perplexed, *adj.* jilla (जिल्ल),
rumallieko (रुमल्लिएको)

persecute, *v.* satAunu (सताउनु)

persecution, *n.* julum (जुलुम),
sAstI (सास्ती)

perseverance, *n.* lagan (लगन),
parishram (परिश्रम)

persimmon, *n.* haluwA bed
(हलुवाबेद)

persist, *v.* joD garnu (जोड गर्नु),
hatte hAlnu (हत्ते हाल्नु)

person, *n.* wyakti (व्यक्ति)

personal, *adj.* nijI (निजी),
wyaktigat (व्यक्तिगत)

personality, *n.* wyaktitwa
(व्यक्तित्व)

personally, *adv.* Aphai (आफै)

persona non grata, *n.* swIkAr
na garieko wyakti (स्वीकार
नगरिएको व्यक्ति)

personnel, *n.* karm chArI/
kAmdAr harU
(कर्मचारी/कामदारहरू)

perspective, *n.* paripreksha
(परिप्रेक्ष),
drishTi koN (दृष्टिकोण)

perspiration, *n.* pasinA (पसिना)

perspire, *v.* pasinA Aunu
(पसिना आउनु)

persuade, *v.* manAunu (मनाउनु),
samjhAunu (सम्झाउनु),
phakAunu (फकाउनु)

persuasion, *n.* bintI bhAu
(बिन्तीभाउ), anunaya (अनुनय)

pertinent, *adj.* suhAuñdo
(सुहाउँदो),
prAsaṅgik (प्रासङ्गिक)

pessimism, *n.* nirAshA wAd
(निराशावाद)

pest, *n.* nAsh kArI
wyakti/janAwar/wastu
(नाशकारी व्यक्ति/जनवार/वस्तु)

pet, *n.* pAleko pashu/charA
(पालेको पशु/चरा),
pyAro wastu (प्यारो वस्तु)

petal, *n.* phUl ko pAt/patra
(फूलको पात/पत्र), dal (दल)

petition, *n.* bintI patra
(बिन्तीपत्र), niwedan (निवेदन)
v. bintI lAunu (बिन्ती लाउनु),
niwedan garnu (निवेदन गर्नु)

pet name, *n.* bolAune 'pyAro'
nAm (बोलाउने 'प्यारो' नाम)

petrol, *n.* tel (तेल),
peTrol (पेट्रोल)

petroleum, *n.* khanij/kachchA
tel (खनिज/कच्चा तेल)

petticoat, *n.* peTI koT
(पेटीकोट), fariyA (फरिया)

petty, *adj.* sAnu (सानु),
jAbo (जाबो)

petty cash, *n.* dainik kharch
kA lAgi chhuTTyAieko sanu
rakam (दैनिकखर्चका लागि
छुट्ट्याइएको सानु रकम)

phantom, *n.* bhUt (भूत),
pret (प्रेत)

pharmacy, *n.* aushadhi pasal
(औषधि पसल)

phase, *n.* charaN (चरण),
(moon) kalA (कला)

pheasant, *n.* kAlij (कालिज)

pheasant impeyan, *n.* DAñphe
(डाँफे)

phial, *n.* sAnu sisI (सानु सिसी)

philanthropy, *n.* lok hit
(लोकहित),
mAnaw prem (मानवप्रेम),
paropkAr (परोपकार)

philosopher, *n.* dArshanik
(दार्शनिक)

philosophy, *n.* darshan
shAstra (दर्शनशास्त्र)

phlegm, *n.* khakAr (खकार)

phone, *n.* Teli phon (टेलिफोन)

phony, *adj.* nakkalI (नक्कली),
jhuTTA (झुट्टा)

photo, *n.* phoTo (फोटो),
taswIr (तस्वीर)

photocopy, *n.* phoTo kApI
(फोटोकापी)

photograph, *n.* taswIr
(तस्वीर), phoTo (फोटो)
v. phoTo/taswIr khichnu
(फोटो/तस्वीर खिच्नु)

phrase, *n.* chhoTo wAkya
(छोटो वाक्य),
wAkyAṁsh (वाक्यांश)

physical, *adj.* shArIrik
(शारीरिक)

physical exercise, *n.* kasrat
(कसरत), wyAyAm (व्यायाम)

physician, *n.* DAkTar
(डाक्टर), waidya (वैद्य)

physics, *n.* bhautik shAstra
(भौतिकशास्त्र)

piano, *n.* pyAno (प्यानो)

pick, *v.* koTyAunu (कोट्याउनु)
n. (tool) pik (पिक),
khantI (खन्ती)

pick up, *v.* Tipnu (टिप्नु)

pick-up, *n.* pachhADi khulA
bhaeko sAno gADI (पछाडि
खुला भएको सानो गाडी)

picket, *v.* rok TolI rAkhnu
(रोक टोली राख्नु)
n. rok TolI (रोक टोली)

pickle, *n.* achAr (अचार)

pickpocket, *n.* baglI mArA
(बगलीमारा)

picnic, *n.* piknik (पिक्निक),
wan bhoj (वनभोज)

picture, *n.* taswIr (तस्वीर),
chitra (चित्र),
(movie) sinemA (सिनेमा)

picturesque, *adj.* Akarshak
(आकर्षक), manohar (मनोहर)

piece, *n.* TukrA (टुक्रा),
chauTA (चौटा),
(section) khaND (खण्ड),
hissA (हिस्सा), *(in pieces)*

Tute phuTeko (टुटेफुटेको),
(to pieces) TukrA TukrA
(टुक्राटुक्रा)

piecemeal, *adv.* ek ek garera
(एक-एक गरेर)
adj. ek ek garera garieko
(एक-एक गरेर गरिएको)

pierce, *v.* chheDnu (छेड्नु),
ghopnu (घोप्नु),
pwAl pArnu (प्वाल पार्नु)

pig, *n. (domestic)* suṅgur
(सुँगुर), *(wild)* baṅdel (बँदेल)

pigeon, *n.* parewA (परेवा),
(wild) malewA (मलेवा),
Dhukur (ढुकुर)

pig-headed, *adj.* jiddI (जिद्दी)

pigtail, *n.* TupI (टुपी)

pike, *n.* bhAlA (भाला)

pile, *n.* thupro (थुप्रो),
(books) ThelI (ठेली),
(orderly) chAṅ (चाङ),
v. thupArnu (थुपार्नु)

piles, *n.* alkAI (अलकाई)

pilgrim, *n.* yAtru (यात्रु),
tIrth yAtrI (तीर्थयात्री)

pill, *n.* chakkI (चक्की), golI
(गोली), *(the pill)* garbh rokne
chakkI (गर्भ रोक्ने चक्की)

pillage, *n.* nAsh (नाश)

pillar, *n.* khambA (खम्बा),
thAm (थाम)

pillow, *n.* takiyA (तकिया),
sirAnI (सिरानी)

pilot, *n.* wimAn chAlak
(विमानचालक)

pimp, *n.* dalAl (दलाल)

pimple, *n.* DanDI phor
(डन्डीफोर)

pin, *n.* pin (पिन),
Alpin (आलपिन)
v. siurinu (सिउरिनु),
ghopnu (घोप्नु)

pincers, *n.* chimTA (चिम्टा),
sanAso (सनासो)

pinch, *n.* chimTI (चिम्टी),
chiuňTI (चिउँटी)
v. chimaTnu (चिमट्नु)

pin down, *v.* wiwash garnu
(विवश गर्नु)

pine, *n.* sallo (सल्लो)
v. pIr le dublAunu
(पीरले दुब्लाउनु)

pineapple, *n.* bhuiň kaThar
(भुइँकटहर)

pine cone, *n.* simTA (सिम्टा)

pingpong, *n.* Tebul Tenis
(टेबुलटेनिस)

pink, *adj.* gulAphI (गुलाफी)

pinpoint, *v.* kiTnu (किट्नु)

pint, *n.* taral wastu ko nAp
(तरल वस्तुको नाप),
lag bhag AdhA liTar
(लगभग आधा लिटर)

pinprick, *n.* ghoch pech
(घोचपेच)

pioneer, *n.* aguwA (अगुवा)

adj. agra gAmI (अग्रगामी)
v. nayAň kAm thAlnu
(नयाँ काम थाल्नु)

pious, *adj.* dharmAtmA
(धर्मात्मा)

pipe, *n.* *(water)* pAip
(पाइप), *(gen.)* nalI (नली)

pipedream, *n.* asambhaw
ichchhA (असम्भव इच्छा)

piping hot, *adj.* *(food, water)*
ati tAto (अति तातो)

Pisces, *n.* mIn rAshi
(मीन राशि)

piss, *v.* mutnu (मुत्नु),
pisAb garnu (पिसाब गर्नु)

pistachio, *n.* pestA (पेस्ता)

pistol, *n.* pistol (पिस्तोल)

pit, *n.* khADal (खाडल),
khAlTo (खाल्टो)

pitch, *n.* *(tar)* alkatrA (अलकत्रा)
v. pAl TAňnu/khaDA garnu
(पाल टाङ्नु/खडा गर्नु)

pitch-dark, *adj.* chak manna
aňdhyAro (चकमन्न अँध्यारो)

pitcher, *n.* surAhI (सुराही),
gAgro (गाग्रो), ghaDA (घडा)

pitfall, *n.* fandA (फन्दा)

pitiless, *adj.* nirdayI (निर्दयी)

pity, *n.* dayA (दया),
(what a pity) kaThai (कठै)
v. dayA garnu (दया गर्नु)

placard, *n.* ple kArD (प्लेकार्ड),
parchA (पर्चा)

place, *n.* ThAuṅ (ठाउँ),
sthAn (स्थान),
(all over the place) ast wyast
(अस्तव्यस्त), lathAliṅg
(लथालिङ्ग), *(in place of)*
saTTA mA (सट्टामा),
(out of place) na suhAune
(नसुहाउने), *(take place)* hunu
(हुनु), ghaTnA ghaTnu
(घटना घट्नु)
v. rAkhnu (राख्नु)

placid, *adj.* shAnt (शान्त)

plaque, *n.* ghar ko gAro mA
TAṅsne dhAtu wA patthar
ko pAtA (घरको गारोमा टाँस्ने
धातु वा पत्थरको पाता)

plain, *n.* samtal maidAn
(समतल मैदान), phAṅT (फाँट)
adj. sAdA (सादा),
saral (सरल), spashT (स्पष्ट)

plain sailing, *n.* saral kArya
(सरल कार्य)

plainspoken, *adj.* spashT
waktA (स्पष्टवक्ता)

plan, *n.* yojanA (योजना)
v. yojanA garnu (योजना गर्नु)

plane, *n.* hawAI jahAj
(हवाईजहाज),
(level) talA (तला),
(tool) randA (रन्दा)
v. samma pArnu (सम्म पार्नु),
(wood) randA lAunu
(रन्दा लाउनु)

planet, *n.* graha (ग्रह)

plank, *n.* phalyAk (फल्याक),
phalek (फलेक)

planning, *n.* yojanA (योजना)

plant, *n.* biruwA (बिरुवा),
boT (बोट), *(factory)* kAr
khAnA (कारखाना)
v. ropnu (रोप्नु)

plantain, *n.* kerA (केरा)

plantation, *n.* boT wiruwA
lagAeko jaggA (बोट बिरुवा
लगाएको जग्गा), bAg (बाग),
bATikA (बाटिका),
bagAn (बगान)

plaster, *n.* plAsTar (प्लास्टर),
bajra (बज्र)
v. plAsTar garnu (प्लास्टर
गर्नु), liun lAunu (लिउन लाउनु)

plastic, *n.* plAsTik (प्लास्टिक)

plate, *n.* thAl (थाल),
rikAbI (रिकाबी), pleT (प्लेट),
(metal) pAtA (पाता)

platform, *n.* mañch (मञ्च)

play, *n.* nATak (नाटक),
khel (खेल)
v. khelnu (खेल्नु),
(music) bajAunu (बजाउनु)

playboy, *n.* moj majA mA
lAgne dhanI yuwak (मोज
मजामा लाग्ने धनी युवक)

play down, *v.* mahatthwa kam
garnu (महत्त्व कम गर्नु)

player, *n.* khelADI (खेलाडी)

playful, *adj.* ThaTyaulo (ठट्चौलो),
winod pUrN (विनोदपूर्ण)

playground, *n.* khel maidAn (खेल मैदान)

playing card, *n.* tAs (तास)

playmate, *n.* sAthI (साथी), dauṅtarI (दौंतरी)

play-off, *n.* atirikta samaya ko khel (अतिरिक्त समयको खेल)

playwright, *n.* nATak kAr (नाटककार)

plea, *n.* bintI (बिन्ती), prArthanA (प्रार्थना)

plead, *v.* bintI garnu (बिन्ती गर्नु), *(law)* bahas garnu (बहस गर्नु)

pleader, *n.* wakIl (वकील), adhiwaktA (अधिवक्ता)

pleasant, *adj.* ramAilo (रमाइलो)

please, *v.* rijhAunu (रिझाउनु), khush pArnu (खुश पार्नु)
adv./inter. kripA garera (कृपा गरेर), kripayA (कृपया)

pleased, *adj.* khush (खुश), rijhieko (रिझिएको)

pleasing, *adj.* rochak (रोचक), manohar (मनोहर)

pleasure, *n.* Anand (आनन्द), khushI (खुशी)

pledge, *n.* wAchA (वाचा), pratigỹA (प्रतिज्ञा)
v. wAchA/pratigỹA garnu

(वाचा/प्रतिज्ञा गर्नु),
wachan dinu (वचन दिनु)

plenty, *n.* prashast (प्रशस्त), yathesT (यथेष्ट)

plight, *n.* hAlat (हालत), sthiti (स्थिति)

plot, *n. (land)* jaggA (जग्गा), *(conspiracy)* shaDyantra (षड्यन्त्र)
v. jAl rachnu (जाल रच्नु), shaDyantra garnu (षड्यन्त्र गर्नु)

plough/plow, *n.* halo (हलो)

pluck, *v.* Tipnu (टिप्नु), *(exam.)* phel garAunu (फेल गराउनु)

plum, *n.* Alu bakhDA (आलुबखडा), bayar (बयर)

plumber, *n.* dhArA mistrI (धारामिस्त्री), palambar (पलम्बर), nal sAj (नलसाज)

plume, *n.* pwAṅkh (प्वाँख)

plunder, *n.* lUT (लूट), lUT ko mAl (लूटको माल)
v. luTnu (लुट्नु)

plunderer, *n.* luTerA (लुटेरा), luTAhA (लुटाहा)

plunge, *v.* Dubnu (डुब्नु), DubkI lagAunu (डुब्की लगाउनु)
n. DubkI (डुब्की), gotA (गोता)

plural, *n.* bahu wachan (बहुवचन), anek (अनेक)

plus, *n. (math.)* dhan chinha,
+ (धन चिन्ह, +), thap (थप)
adj. thap (थप),
atirikta (अतिरिक्त)

Pluto, *n.* yam graha (यम ग्रह)

ply, *n.* patra (पत्र),
moTAi (मोटाइ)
v. (vehicles) chalnu (चल्नु)

plywood, *n.* plAi uD (प्लाइउड)

pneumonia, *n.* nimoniyA
(निमोनिया), phokso ko suj
(फोक्सोको सुज)

pocket, *n.* khaltI (खल्ती),
gojI (गोजी), baglI (बगली)
v. khaltI mA hAlnu/rAkhnu
(खल्तीमा हाल्नु/राख्नु),
(out of pocket), phr. noksAn
(नोक्सान), kharch (खर्च)

pocketbook, *n.* khaltI mA
rAkhne sAnu kitAb
(खल्तीमा राख्ने सानु किताब),
pAkeT buk (पाकेटबुक)

pod, *n.* kosA (कोसा),
khol (खोल)
v. kosA lAgnu (कोसा लाग्नु)

poem, *n.* kawitA (कविता),
shlok (श्लोक)

poet, *n.* kawi (कवि)

poetess, *n.* mahilA kawi
(महिला कवि),
kawayitrI (कवयित्री)

poetry, *n.* kawitA (कविता),
shlok (श्लोक)

poinsettia, *n.* lAlu pAte
(लालुपाते)

point, *n.* chuchcho (चुच्चो),
Tuppo (टुप्पो), *(dot)* thoplo
(थोप्लो), bindu (बिन्दु)
(on the point of) najIk
(नजीक), nikaT (निकट)
v. tikho pArnu (तिखो पार्नु),
tikhArnu (तिखार्नु),
(point out), phr. dekhAunu
(देखाउनु), auñlyAunu (औंल्याउनु)

point-blank, *adj.* sojhai (सोझै),
sAph sAph (साफ साफ)
adv. atyant najIk bATa
(अत्यन्त नजीकबाट)

pointed, *adj.* tIkho (तीखो),
chuchcho (चुच्चो)

point of view, *n.* wichAr
(विचार),
drishTi koN (दृष्टिकोण)

poise, *n.* DhAñchA (ढाँचा),
santulan (सन्तुलन)

poison, *n.* wish (विष),
bikh (बिख)
v. bikh hAlnu/dinu
(बिष हाल्नु/दिनु)

poisonous, *adj.* wishAlu
(विषालु), wishAdI (विषादी)

poke, *v.* ghochnu (घोच्नु)

poke fun at, *phr.* ThaTTA
garnu (ठट्टा गर्नु),
uDAunu (उडाउनु)

polar, *adj.* dhruwIya (ध्रुवीय)

pole, *n. (earth)* dhruwa (ध्रुव), khambA (खम्बा)

Pole Star, *n.* dhruwa tArA (ध्रुवतारा)

police, *n.* pulis (पुलिस), praharI (प्रहरी)

policeman, *n.* pulis (पुलिस), pulis ko jawAn (पुलिसको जवान)

police station, *n.* thAnA (थाना), chaukI (चौकी)

policy, *n.* nIti (नीति)

polish, *n.* pAlis (पालिस) *v.* pAlis lAunu (पालिस लाउनु), TalkAunu (टल्काउनु)

polite, *adj.* namra (नम्र), mijAsilo (मिजासिलो)

political, *adj.* rAj naitik (राजनैतिक)

politician, *n.* rAj nItigỹa (राजनीतिज्ञ)

politics, *n.* rAj nIti (राजनीति)

poll, *n.* mat dAn (मतदान), chunAu (चुनाउ), *(opinion poll)* mat sankalan (मत संकलन) *v.* mat dinu (मत दिनु)

polling booth, *n.* mat dAn sthal (मतदानस्थल)

pollution, *n.* pradUshaN (प्रदूषण)

pomegranate, *n.* anAr (अनार), dArim (दारिम)

pomp, *n.* rabAph (रबाफ), bhaDak (भडक)

pompous, *adj.* bhaDkilo (भड्किलो)

pond, *n.* pokharI (पोखरी), talAu (तलाउ)

ponder, *v.* sochnu (सोच्नु), ghorinu (घोरिनु)

pony, *n.* TaTTu (टट्टू)

pool, *n.* pokharI (पोखरी), talAu (तलाउ)

poor, *adj.* garIb (गरीब), nirdhan (निर्धन), *(pitiful)* bicharA (बिचरा)

poor man, *inter.* bicharA (बिचरा), kaThai (कठै)

poppy, *n.* aphim ko boT (अफिमको बोट)

populace, *n.* Am janatA (आमजनता)

popular, *adj.* prachalit (प्रचलित), *(admired)* lok priya (लोकप्रिय)

popularity, *n.* lok priyatA (लोकप्रियता)

population, *n.* jan sankhyA (जनसङ्ख्या)

populous, *adj.* ghanA AwAdI bhaeko (घना आवादी भएको)

porcelain, *n.* chinI mATo (चिनीमाटो), chinI mATA kA wastu (चिनीमाटाका वस्तु)

porch, *n.* DyauDhI (डचौढी)

porcupine, *n.* dumsI (दुम्सी)

pore, *n.* rauň ko pwAl (रौंको
प्वाल), chhidra (छिद्र)

porous, *adj.* chhidra bhaeko
(छिद्र भएको), sosne (सोस्ने)

port, *n.* bandar gAh
(बन्दरगाह),
jahAj ghAT (जहाजघाट)

portable, *adj.* sajilo saňga
laijAna sakine (सजिलोसँग
लैजान सकिने),
bokna hune (बोक्न हुने)

porter, *n.* bhariyA (भरिया)

portfolio, *n.* mantrI ko wibhAg
(मन्त्रीको विभाग)

portico, *n.* bAhirI baraNDA
(बाहिरी बरण्डा)

portion, *n.* bhAg (भाग)

portrait, *n.* chitra (चित्र),
mUrti (मूर्ति)

portray, *v.* chitra banAunu
(चित्र बनाउनु)

pose, *n.* (posture) hAu bhAu
(हाउभाउ), mudrA (मुद्रा)
v. mudrA banAunu
(मुद्रा बनाउनु),
DhAňchA garnu(ढाँचा गर्नु)

position, *n.* (stance) DhAňchA
(ढाँचा), (state) hAlat (हालत),
sthiti (स्थिति), (rank) padwI
(पदवी), darjA (दर्जा)

positive, *adj.* pakkA (पक्का),
sakArAtmak (सकारात्मक)

possess, *v.* rAkhnu (राख्नु),
hAt pArnu (हात पार्नु)

possession, *n.* bhog (भोग),
adhikAr (अधिकार),
swAmitwa (स्वामित्व)

possessions, *n.* dhan sampatti
(धन-सम्पत्ति), jethA (जेथा)

possibility, *n.* sambhAwanA
(सम्भावना),
sambhAwyatA (सम्भाव्यता)

possible, *adj.* sambhaw
(सम्भव), huna sakne (हुनसक्ने)

possibly, *adv.* huna sakchha
(हुन सक्छ),
sambhawtah (सम्भवतः)

post, *n.* (pole) khambA (खम्बा),
khAmA (खामा), (mail) hulAk
(हुलाक), DAňk (डाँक),
(office) pad (पद), jAgIr
(जागीर), ohadA (ओहदा),
(station) chaukI (चौकी)
v. chiTThI khasAlnu
(चिट्ठी खसाल्नु),
parchA TAňsnu (पर्चा टाँस्नु)

postage, *n.* hulAk mahsul
(हुलाकमहसुल)

postage stamp, *n.* hulAk
TikaT (हुलाकटिकट)

postbox, *n.* posT baks
(पोस्टबक्स), patra maňjUshA
(पत्र मञ्जूषा)

postcard, *n.* posT kArD
(पोस्टकार्ड)

poster, n. parchA (पर्चा),
posTar (पोस्टर), istihAr (इस्तिहार)

postman, n. hulAkI (हुलाकी)

postmaster, n. hulAk aDDA
ko hAkim (हुलाकअड्डाको
हाकिम)

post office, n. hulAk aDDA
(हुलाकअड्डा),
DAňk ghar (डाँक घर),
posT aphis (पोस्टअफिस)

postpone, v. para/pachhi
sArnu (पर/पछि सार्नु)

posture, n. hAu bhAu
(हाउभाउ), DhAňchA (ढाँचा),
mudrA (मुद्रा)

pot, n. bhAňDA (भाँडा),
bhAňDA kuňDA (भाँडाकुँडा),
(drug) gAňjA (गाँजा), (coffee
pot) kaphI dAn (कफीदान),
(inkpot) masI dAnI
(मसीदानी), (teapot) chiyA
dAn (चियादान),
(flowerpot) gamlA (गमला)

potable, adj. piuna hune
(पिउन हुने), peya (पेय)

potato, n. Alu (आलु)

pot-bellied, adj. bhunDe (भुँडे)

pot (belly), n. bhuňDI (भुँडी)

potboiler, n. chhiTo paisA
kamAuna lekhieko pustak
(छिटो पैसा कमाउन लेखिएको
पुस्तक)

pothole, n. gahiro pwAl

(गहिरो प्वाल)

potter, n. kumhAle (कुम्हाले)

pottery, n. mATA kA
bhAňDA kuňDA
(माटाका भाँडाकुँडा)

pouch, n. thailo (थैलो),
khaltI (खल्ती)

poultry, n. hAňs, kukhurA Adi
(हाँस, कुखुरा आदि)

pound, n. (weight, currency)
pAuND (पाउण्ड)
v. dhUlo pITho pArnu (धूलो
पीठो पार्नु), piňdhnu (पिँध्नु),
kuTnu (कुट्नु)

pour, v. khanyAunu (खन्याउनु),
khatyAunu (खत्याउनु)
n. (downpour) musal dhAre
warshA (मुसलधारे वर्षा)

poverty, n. garIbI (गरीबी),
daridratA (दरिद्रता)

poverty-striken, adj. garIb
(गरीब), daridra (दरिद्र)

powder, n. pAuDar (पाउडर),
dhUlo (धूलो), chUrN (चूर्ण),
(gun powder) bArUd (बारूद)
v. dhUlo pArnu (धूलो पार्नु)

power, n. bal (बल),
shakti (शक्ति), (authority)
akhtiyAr (अख्तियार),
adhikAr (अधिकार),
(electricity) bijulI (बिजुली)

powerful, adj. baliyo (बलियो)
shakti shAlI (शक्तिशाली)

powerless, *adj.* shakti hIn (शक्तिहीन), asamarth (असमर्थ)

pox, *n.* biphar (बिफर)

practical, *adj.* wyAwhArik (व्यावहारिक), kAm lAgne (काम लाग्ने)

practice, *n.* abhyAs (अभ्यास), bAnI (बानी), *(out of practice)* abhyAs chhuTeko (अभ्यास छुटेको)

practise, *v.* abhyAs garnu (अभ्यास गर्नु)

pragmatic, *adj.* wyAwhArik (व्यावहारिक)

praise, *n.* prashamsA (प्रशंसा), tAriph (तारिफ) *v.* prashamsA/tAriph garnu (प्रशंसा/तारिफ गर्नु)

praiseworthy, *adj.* tAriph yogya (तारिफयोग्य), prashamsnIya (प्रशंसनीय)

pray, *v.* prArthanA/bintI garnu (प्रार्थना/बिन्ती गर्नु)

prayer, *n.* prArthanA (प्रार्थना), stuti (स्तुति)

prayer wheel, *n. (Buddhism)* mAne (माने)

preach, *v.* dharm phailAunu (धर्म फैलाउनु), dharm prachAr garnu (धर्म प्रचार गर्नु)

preacher, *n.* dharm prachArak (धर्मप्रचारक), updesh dine (उपदेश दिने)

precarious, *adj.* anishchit (अनिश्चित), nAjuk (नाजुक)

precaution, *n.* sAwdhAnI (सावधानी), surakshA (सुरक्षा)

precious, *adj.* kImtI (कीमती), mUlya wAn (मूल्यवान्)

precipice, *n.* paharo (पहरो), bhIr (भीर)

precise, *adj.* ThIk (ठीक), yathArth (यथार्थ)

precisely, *adv.* ThIk sanga (ठीकसंग), bilkul (बिलकुल)

predecessor, *n.* pUrwaj (पूर्वज), purkhA (पुर्खा), pUrwAdhikArI (पूर्वाधिकारी)

predicament, *n.* kharAb awasthA (खराब अवस्था), phasAd (फसाद)

predict, *v.* bhawishya batAunu (भविष्य बताउनु, bhawishya wANI garnu (भविष्यवाणी गर्नु)

prediction, *n.* bhawishya wANi (भविष्यवाणी)

predominant, *adj.* adhik (अधिक), prabal (प्रबल)

prefer, *v.* baDhI ruchAunu (बढी रुचाउनु), baDhI man parAunu (बढी मनपराउनु)

preferable, *adj.* baDhI ruchikar (बढी रुचिकर), baDhI man parne (बढी मन पर्ने)

pregnancy, *n.* peT bokeko awasthA (पेट बोकेको अवस्था), garbhAwasthA (गर्भावस्था)

pregnant, *adj.* garbh batI (गर्भवती), peT bokekI (पेट बोकेकी)

prejudice, *n.* pUrwAgraha (पूर्वग्रह), durAgraha (दुराग्रह)

preliminary, *adj.* shuru ko (शुरुको), prArambhik (प्रारम्भिक)

premature, *adj.* aparipakwa (अपरिपक्व), akAl (अकाल)

premier, *adj.* abbal (अब्बल), pratham (प्रथम) *n. (news)* pradhAn mantrI (प्रधानमन्त्री)

premises, *n.* hAtA (हाता)

preparation, *n.* tayArI (तयारी), parikAr tarjumA (परिकार तर्जुमा)

prepare, *v.* tayAr garnu (तयार गर्नु), *(food)* khAnA banAunu (खाना बनाउनु)

prescribe, *v.* toknu (तोक्नु), nirdishT garnu (निर्दिष्ट गर्नु), *(med.)* okhatI lekhnu (ओखति लेख्नु)

prescription, *n. (med.)* pUrjI (पूर्जी)

presence, *n.* hAjirI (हाजिरी), upasthiti (उपस्थिति)

present, *adj.* hAjir (हाजिर),

upasthit (उपस्थित), *(gram. time)* wartmAn (वर्तमान), *(gift)* uphAr (उपहार), **(at present)** ahile (अहिले), **(for the present)** ahile ko lAgi (अहिलेको लागि) *v.* dinu (दिनु), pesh garnu (पेश गर्नु)

preserve, *v.* hiphAjat / samrakshaN garnu (हिफाजत/संरक्षण गर्नु) *n. (food)* jAm (जाम), mADA (माडा), *(game)* Araksha (आरक्ष)

preservation, *n.* samrakshaN (संरक्षण), hiphAjat (हिफाजत)

preside, *v.* sabhApatitwa garnu (सभापतित्व गर्नु)

president, *n. (state)* rAshtra pati (राष्ट्रपति), *(orgn.)* adhyaksha (अध्यक्ष), sabhA pati (सभापति)

press, *n. (printing)* chhApA khAnA (छापाखाना), *(media)* pres (प्रेस) *v.* thichnu (थिच्नु), khAňdnu (खांद्नु)

press agency, *n.* samAchAr samiti (समाचार समिति)

press agent, *n.* pres samwAd dAtA (प्रेस संवाददाता)

press conference, *n.* patrakAr sammelan (पत्रकार सम्मेलन)

pressure, *n.* dabAb (दबाब),
chAp (चाप)
v. dabAb dinu (दबाब दिनु)

pressure group, *n.* dabAb
samUh (दबाब समूह)

prestige, *n.* ijjat (इज्जत),
maryAdA (मर्यादा)

presume, *v.* bhani ThAnnu
(भनिठान्नु)

pretend, *v.* bahanA garnu
(बहाना गर्नु),
bujh pachAunu (बुझ पचाउनु)

pretext, *n.* nihuṅ (निहुँ),
bahanA (बहाना)

pretty, *adj.* rAmro (राम्रो)

prevent, *v.* roknu (रोक्नु),
chheknu (छेक्नु)

prevention, *n.* rok thAm
(रोक थाम), nirodh (निरोध)

previous, *adj.* aghi ko (अधिको),
biti sakeko (बितिसकेको),
bhUt pUrwa (भूतपूर्व)

previously, *adv.* uhile (उहिले)

prey, *n.* shikAr (शिकार),
AhAr (आहार)

price, *n.* mUlya (मूल्य),
mol (मोल)

priceless, *adj.* amUlya
(अमूल्य), amol (अमोल)

price list, *n.* mUlya sUchi
(मूल्य सूचि)

prick, *n.* kAṅDA (काँडा)
v. ghochnu (घोच्नु),

ropnu (रोप्नु)

pride, *n.* ghamaND (घमण्ड),
garwa (गर्व), tujuk (तुजुक)

priest, *n.* pujArI (पुजारी),
puret (पुरेत)

primal, *adj.* Adim (आदिम)

primary, *adj.* mukhya (मुख्य),
mUl (मूल),
prAthmik (प्राथमिक)

prime, *adj.* mukhya (मुख्य),
uttam (उत्तम)
n. (state) sarbottam sthiti
(सर्वोत्तम स्थिति)

prime minister, *n.* pradhAn
mantrI (प्रधानमन्त्री)

primitive, *adj.* prAchIn
(प्राचीन), asabhya (असभ्य)

prince, *n.* rAj kumAr
(राजकुमार), *(Crown Prince)*
yuwarAj (युवराज)

princess, *n.* rAj kumArI
(राजकुमारी),
(Crown Princess)
yuwarAgyĩI (युवराज्ञी)

principal, *adj.* mukya (मुख्य),
pradhAn (प्रधान)
n. (school) pradhAnA-
dhyApak (प्रधानाध्यापक)

principle, *n.* siddhAnt
(सिद्धान्त), niyam (नियम)

print, *n.* chhApA (छापा),
taswIr (तस्वीर)
v. chhApnu (छाप्नु)

printing press, *n.* chhApA khAnA (छापाखाना)

prior, *adj.* pahile ko (पहिलेको), aghi ko (अघिको)

prior to, *adv.* bhandA aghi (भन्दा अघि)

priority, *n.* prAthmiktA (प्राथमिकता)

prison, *n.* jhyAlkhAn (भ्यालखान), jel (जेल)

prisoner, *n.* kaidI (कैदी), bandI (बन्दी)

privacy, *n.* gupti (गुप्ति)

private, *adj.* nijI (निजी), gupt (गुप्त), gopya (गोप्य), *(in private)* ekAnt mA (एकान्तमा)

private enterprise, *n.* nijI udyam (निजी उद्यम), sarkArI niyantraN na raheko udyam (सरकारी नियन्त्रण नरहेको उद्यम)

private eye, *n.* nijI gupt char (निजी गुप्तचर), khuphiyA (सुफिया)

privately, *adv.* gupt rUp mA (गुप्त रूपमा)

private parts, *n.* gupt ang (गुप्त अङ्ग), guptAng harU (गुप्ताङ्गहरू)

privilege, *n.* suwidhA (सुविधा), sahuliyat (सहुलियत) *v.* suwidhA dinu (सुविधा दिनु)

prize, *n.* inAm (इनाम), puraskAr (पुरस्कार) *v.* Adar garnu (आदर गर्नु)

probable, *adj.* huna sakne (हुन सक्ने), sambhaw (सम्भव)

probably, *adv.* holA (होला), shAyad (शायद)

probe, *n.* DAkTar ko shalAkA (डाक्टरको शलाका), sutlo (सुत्लो), *(fig.)* jAnch paDtAl (जाँच पडताल) *v.* khoj/jAnch paDtal garnu (खोज/जाँच पडताल गर्नु)

problem, *n.* samasyA (समस्या)

procedure, *n.* kArya widhi (कार्यविधि)

proceed, *v.* aghi baDhnu (अघि बढ्नु)

proceeding, *n.* kAm (काम), kArbAI (कारबाई)

proceedings, *n.* adAlatI kArbAI (अदालती कारबाई)

proceeds, *n.* nAphA (नाफा), Aeko rakam (आएको रकम)

process, *n.* prakriyA (प्रक्रिया), widhi (विधि) *v.* kArbAI mA rAkhnu (कारबाईमा राख्नु)

procession, *n.* julus (जुलुस), *(marriage)* jantI (जन्ती), *(funeral)* malAmI (मलामी)

proclaim, *v.* ghoshaNA garnu (घोषणा गर्नु)

proclamation, *n.* ghoshaNA
(घोषणा)

procure, *v.* prApt/hAsil garnu
(प्राप्त/हासिल गर्नु)

produce, *v.* paidA/utpAdan
garnu (पैदा/उत्पादन गर्नु)
n. upaj (उपज),
ubjanI (उब्जनी)

producer, *n.* utpAdak
(उत्पादक),
(film) nirmAtA (निर्माता)

product, *n.* upaj (उपज),
(result) phal (फल), *(math.)*
guNan phal (गुणनफल)

production, *n.* utpAdan
(उत्पादन),
(film) nirmAN (निर्माण)

productive, *adj.* ubjAu
(उब्जाउ),
utpAdan shIl (उत्पादनशील)

profession, *n.* peshA (पेशा),
wyawasAya (व्यवसाय),
pesA (पेसा)

professional, *adj.* pesewar
(पेसेवर)

professor, *n.* prAdhyApak
(प्राध्यापक), pesA gat (पेसागत)

profit, *n.* nAphA (नाफा),
phAidA (फाइदा)
v. nAphA hunu (नाफा हुनु),
phAidA uThAunu
(फाइदा उठाउनु)

profitable, *adj.* nAphA dine
(नाफा दिने),
phAidA janak (फाइदाजनक)

profound, *adj.* gahiro (गहिरो),
gahan (गहन)

profuse, *adj.* prachur (प्रचुर)

program(me), *n.* kArya kram
(कार्यक्रम)

progress, *n.* pragati (प्रगति),
unnati (उन्नति)
v. pragati/unnati garnu
(प्रगति/उन्नति गर्नु)

progressive, *adj.* pragati shIl
(प्रगतिशील),
unnati shIl (उन्नतिशील)

prohibit, *v.* manAhI garnu
(मनाही गर्नु),
rok lagAunu (रोक लगाउनु)

prohibition, *n.* manAhI (मनाही),
prati bandh (प्रतिबन्ध)

project, *n.* AyojanA (आयोजना),
pariyojanA (परियोजना)
v. yojanA banAunu (योजना
बनाउनु), prakshep garnu
(प्रक्षेप गर्नु), bAhira niskanu
(बाहिर निस्कनु)

prominent, *adj.* wishishT
(विशिष्ट), pramukh (प्रमुख)

promise, *n.* pratigy̌A
(प्रतिज्ञा), wAchA (वाचा)
v. pratigy̌A/kabul garnu
(प्रतिज्ञा/कबुल गर्नु)

promote, *v.* baDhAunu
(बढाउनु)

promotion, n. baDhautI (बढौती), prawardhan (प्रवर्धन), baDhuwA (बढुवा)

prompt, adj. chhiTo (छिटो), phurtilo (फुर्तिलो)

promptly, adv. turunt (तुरुन्त)

prone, adj. ghopTo (घोप्टो), ubhinDo (उभिन्डो), (attitude) jhukAw bhaeko (झुकाव भएको)

pronoun, n. sarwa nAm (सर्वनाम)

pronounce, v. uchchAraN garnu (उच्चारण गर्नु)

pronunciation, n. uchchAraN (उच्चारण), hijje (हिज्जे)

proof, n. pramAN (प्रमाण), nissA (निस्सा), sabut (सबुत)

proofread, v. sachyAunu (सच्याउनु)

prop, v. Teko dinu (टेको दिनु) n. Teko (टेको)

propaganda, n. jhUto prachAr (झूटो प्रचार)

propel, v. dhakelnu (धकेल्नु), ghacheTnu (घचेट्नु)

propeller, n. hawAI jahAj ko paṅkhA (हवाईजहाजको पङ्खा)

proper, adj. uchit (उचित), ThIk (ठीक)

properly, adv. uchit tarikA le (उचित तरिकाले), ThIk saṅga (ठीकसँग)

property, n. dhan sampatti (धन-सम्पत्ति)

proposal, n. prastAw (प्रस्ताव)

propose, v. prastAw rAkhnu (प्रस्ताव राख्नु), yojanA garnu (योजना गर्नु)

proprietor, n. mAlik (मालिक), dhanI (धनी)

prose, n. gadya (गद्य)

prosecute, v. muddA chalAunu (मुद्दा चलाउनु)

prospect, n. AshA (आशा), apekshA (अपेक्षा)

prosper, v. saprinu (सप्रिनु), unnati garnu (उन्नति गर्नु)

prosperity, n. unnati (उन्नति), samriddhi (समृद्धि)

prosperous, adj. sampanna (सम्पन्न), hune khAne (हुनेखाने)

prostitute, n. weshyA (वेश्या), raNDI (रण्डी)

prostitution, n. weshyA writti (वेश्यावृत्ति), raNDI bAjI (रण्डीबाजी)

prostrate, adj. ghopTo parera lampasAr pareko (घोप्टो परेर लम्पसार परेको) v. lampasAr parnu (लम्पसार पर्नु)

protect, v. bachAunu (बचाउनु), jogAunu (जोगाउनु)

protection, n. rakshA (रक्षा), samrakshaN (संरक्षण)

protective, *adj.* rakshA garne (रक्षा गर्ने), rakshAtmak (रक्षात्मक)

protein, *n.* proTIn (प्रोटीन)

protest, *n.* wirodh (विरोध), ujur (उजुर)
v. wirodh/ujur garnu (विरोध/उजुर गर्नु)

proud, *adj.* ghamaNDI (घमण्डी), ahaṅkArI (अहङ्कारी)

prove, *v.* sAbit/pramANit garnu (साबित/प्रमाणित गर्नु)

proverb, *n.* ukhAn (उखान), kahAwat (कहावत)

provide, *v.* juTAunu (जुटाउनु), pradAn garnu (प्रदान गर्नु)

Providence, *n.* Ishwar (ईश्वर)

province, *n.* prAnt (प्रान्त), pradesh (प्रदेश)

provision, *n.* wyawasthA (व्यवस्था), prabandh (प्रबन्ध)
v. rasad pAnI ko wyawasthA garnu (रसद पानीको व्यवस्था गर्नु)

provisions, *n.* dAnA pAnI (दानापानी), khAdyAnna (खाद्यान्न), kirAnA mAl (किराना माल)

provocation, *n.* uttejanA (उत्तेजना), ris (रिस)

provoke, *v.* ris uThAunu (रिस उठाउनु), uttejit garnu (उत्तेजित गर्नु)

proximity, *n.* nikaTatA (निकटता), hArA hArI (हाराहारी)

proxy, *n.* (*agent*) prati nidhi (प्रतिनिधि), arkA ko lAgi kAm garne (अर्काको लागि काम गर्ने)

prudent, *adj.* wiwekI (विवेकी), chatur (चतुर)

prune, *v.* chhimalnu (छिमलनु), kAtnu (काट्नु)

psychology, *n.* manowigỹAn (मनोविज्ञान)

pub, *n.* bhaTTI (भट्टी)

puberty, *n.* yauwanArambh (यौवनारम्भ), wayah sandhi (वयः सन्धि)

public, *n.* janatA (जनता), raitI (रैती), (*in public*) khulast (खुलस्त), jan sAdhAraN (जनसाधारण) *adj.* sArwajanik (सार्वजनिक), Am (आम)

publication, *n.* prakAshan (प्रकाशन)

publicity, *n.* prachAr (प्रचार)

public relation, *n.* jan sampark (जन सम्पर्क)

public transport, *n.* yAtAyAt kA sAdhan rel, bus (यातायातका साधन रेल, बस)

publish, *v.* prakAshit garnu (प्रकाशित गर्नु), chhApnu (छाप्नु)

publisher, *n.* prakAshak
(प्रकाशक)

puff, *n.* sAs ko jhokkA
(सासको भोक्का),
(cigarette) sarko (सर्को)

puff up, *v.* phulAunu (फुलाउनु)

pull, *n.* khichAw (खिचाव),
tanAi (तनाइ)
v. tAnnu (तान्नु),
khichnu (खिच्नु)

pull back, *v.* bhAgnu (भाग्नु),
palAyan garnu (पलायन गर्नु)

pull down, *v.* bhatkAunu
(भत्काउनु)

pull in, *v.* najik jAnu
(नजिक जानु)

pull off, *v.* chuNDAlnu
(चुँडाल्नु)

pull out, *v.* haTnu (हट्नु)

pull up, *v.* ukhelnu (उखेल्नु)

pulse, *n. (body)* nADI (नाडी),
(lentil) dAl (दाल)

pulverize, *v.* dhUlo pArnu
(धूलो पार्नु), chUrN banAunu
(चूर्ण बनाउनु)

pump, *n.* pAnI tAnne/hAwA
dine yantra (पानी तान्ने/हावा
दिने यन्त्र), pamp (पम्प),
(syringe) pichkArI (पिचकारी)
v. pAnI tAnnu (पानी तान्नु),
hAwA bharnu (हावा भर्नु)

pumpkin, *n.* pharsI (फर्सी)

punch, *n.* pwAl pArne yantra
(प्वाल पार्ने यन्त्र),
(blow) mukkA (मुक्का), mukkI
(मुक्की), muDkI (मुड्की),
(drink) sarbat (सर्बत)
v. pwAl pArnu (प्वाल पार्नु),
(blow) mukkI hAnnu
(मुक्की हान्नु)

punctual, *adj.* samaya ko
pAlnA garne
(समयको पालना गर्ने)

puncture, *n.* pwAl (प्वाल),
chhidra (छिद्र)
v. pwAl pArnu (प्वाल पार्नु),
chheDnu (छेड्नु)

pungent, *adj.* piro (पिरो)

punish, *v.* daND/sajAya dinu
(दण्ड/सजाय दिनु)

punishment, *n.* sajAya
(सजाय), daND (दण्ड)

pup, *n.* kukur ko chhAuro
(कुकुरको छाउरो)

pupil, *n.* chelA (चेला),
shishya (शिष्य)

puppet, *n.* kaTh putalI
(कठपुतली)

puppy, *n.* kukur ko chhAuro
(कुकुरको छाउरो)

purchase, *n.* kharId (खरीद)
v. kinnu (किन्नु),
kharId garnu (खरीद गर्नु)

pure, *adj.* shuddha (शुद्ध),
pawitra (पवित्र),
chokho (चोखो)

purgative, *n.* julAb (जुलाब)

purge, *v.* haTAunu (हटाउनु),
saphA pArnu (सफा पार्नु)

purify, *v.* shuddha tulyAunu
(शुद्ध तुल्याउनु),
chokhyAunu (चोख्याउनु)

purple, *adj.* pyAjI (प्याजी)

purpose, *n.* uddeshya
(उद्देश्य), irAdA (इरादा)

purposeful, *adj.* AñTilo
(आँटिलो)

purposely, *adv.* jAnA jAnI
(जानाजानी)

purse, *n.* thailA (थैला),
byAg (ब्याग),
(hold the purse strings), *phr.*
kharch mA añkush rAkhnu
(खर्चमा अङ्कुश राख्नु)

pursue, *v.* khednu (खेद्नु),
pachhi lAgnu (पछि लाग्नु)

pursuit, *n.* khedo (खेदो),
pichhA (पिछा), khoj (खोज)

pus, *n.* pIp (पीप)

push, *n.* dhakkA (धक्का)
v. dhakelnu (धकेल्नु),
ghacheTnu (घचेट्नु)

pushcart, *n.* ThelA gADA
(ठेलागाडा)

push down, *v.* basAunu
(बसाउनु), thachyAunu (थच्याउनु)

push in, *v.* hulnu (हुल्नु)

push off, *v.* jAnu (जानु)

pushover, *n.* sajilai hune kAm
(सजिलै हुने काम)

push through, *v.* ghusArnu
(घुसार्नु), chhirAunu (छिराउनु)

put, *v.* rAkhnu (राख्नु)

put across, *v.* saphaltA kA
sAth kAm garnu (सफलताका
साथ काम गर्नु)

put away, *v. (goods)*
thankyAunu (थन्क्याउनु),
(person) thunnu (थुन्नु)

put down, *v.* dabAunu (दबाउनु)

put in, *v.* samaya bitAunu
(समय बिताउनु)

put off, *v. (dress, etc.)*
phukAlnu (फुकाल्नु),
(programme) sthagit garnu
(स्थगित गर्नु)

put on, *v.* lagAunu (लगाउनु)

put out, *v.* nibhAunu (निभाउनु)

put together, *v.* milAunu
(मिलाउनु)

put up, *v.* banAunu (बनाउनु),
uThAunu (उठाउनु),
basnu (बस्नु)

put up with, *v.* sahanu (सहनु)

puzzle, *n.* rahasya (रहस्य),
bhrAnti (भ्रान्ति)
v. jilla parnu (जिल्ल पर्नु),
almalinu (अलमलिनु)

pyre, *n.* chitA (चिता)

python, *n.* ajiñgar (अजिङ्गर)

Q

quack, *n.* *(duck)* hAńs ko bolI (हाँसको बोली), *(med.)* Thag waidya (ठग वैद्य), nIm hakim (नीम हकिम)

quadrangle, *n.* chaukos maidAn (चौकोस मैदान), chok (चोक)

quadrangular, *adj.* chAr chuchche (चारचुच्चे), chAr kune (चारकुने)

quadruped, *n.* chaupAyA jantu (चौपाया जन्तु), chAr khuTTe janAwar (चारखुट्टे जनावर)

quadruple, *adj.* chaugunA (चौगुना)

quagmire, *n.* dhAp (धाप), dal dal (दलदल)

quail, *n.* baTTAI (बट्टाई) *v.* haTnu (हट्नु), DarAunu (डराउनु)

quaint, *adj.* anauTho (अनौठो), purAno khAl ko (पुरानो खालको)

quake, *n.* kampan (कम्पन), bhU kamp (भूकम्प) *v.* kAmnu (काम्नु), hallinu (हल्लिनु)

qualification, *n.* yogyatA (योग्यता)

qualified, *adj.* yogya (योग्य)

qualify, *v.* yogya bannu / banAunu (योग्य बन्नु / बनाउनु)

quality, *n.* guN (गुण)

qualm, *n.* phikrI (फिक्री), pareshAnI (परेशानी)

quantity, *n.* mAtrA (मात्रा), rAshi (राशि)

quantum, *n.* diieko mAtrA (दिइएको मात्रा), pradatta mAtrA (प्रदत्त मात्रा)

quarantine, *n.* samsarga nishedh (संसर्ग निषेध), bandej (बन्देज)

quarrel, *n.* jhagaDA (झगडा), kalaha (कलह) *v.* jhagaDA garnu (झगडा गर्नु), bAjhnu (बाझ्नु)

quarrelsome, *adj.* jhagaDAlu (झगडालु), kachińgale (कचिङ्गले)

quarry, *n.* DhuńgA khAnI (ढुङ्गाखानी), sang marmar ko khAnI (संगमरमरको खानी)

quarter, *n.* *(math.)* chauthAi (चौथाइ), chaturthAmsh (चतुर्थांश), *(area)* mohallA (मोहल्ला), Tol (टोल)

quarterly, *adj.* traimAsik
(त्रैमासिक),
tIn mahine (तीन महिने)
n. tIn mahine patrikA
(तीन महिने पत्रिका)
adv. tIn mahinA mA ek
palTa (तीन महिनामा एक-
पल्ट)

quarters, *n.* basne ghar (बस्ने
घर), kwATar (क्वाटर)

quartet, *n.* chAr janA ko
samUha (चारजनाको समूह)

quartz, *n.* phaTik (फटिक)

quash, *v.* radda/badar garnu
(रद्द/बदर गर्नु)

quaver, *v.* kANpnu (काँप्नु),
tharkanu (थर्कनु)

queen, *n.* rAnI (रानी), mahA
rAnI (महारानी), *(cards)*
mIm (मीम), begam (बेगम)

queen mother, *n.* mumA
baDA mahA rAnI
(मुमा बडामहारानी)

queer, *adj.* anauTho (अनौठो),
achamm ko (अचम्मको)

quell, *v.* dabAunu (दबाउनु),
shAnt garnu (शान्त गर्नु)

quench, *v.* tirkhA mArnu
(तिर्खा मार्नु)

query, *n.* prashna (प्रश्न),
sawAl (सवाल)
v. prashna garnu (प्रश्न गर्नु),
sodhnu (सोध्नु)

quest, *n.* khoj (खोज),
anweshaN (अन्वेषण)
v. prashna garnu
(प्रश्न गर्नु), sodhnu (सोध्नु)

question, *n.* parashna (प्रश्न),
sawAl (सवाल)

(out of the question), *phr.*
chhal phal garna na parne
(छलफल गर्ने नपर्ने)

question mark, *n.* prashna
chinha (प्रश्नचिन्ह)

questionable, *adj.* shañ-
kAspad (शंकास्पद)

questionnaire, *n.* prashnAwalI
(प्रश्नावली)

queue, *n.* lAin (लाइन),
katAr (कतार), kyU (क्यू)
v. lAin/kyU ma basnu
(लाइन/क्यूमा बस्नु)

quick, *adj.* chhiTo (छिटो),
chAñDo (चाँडो)

quicken, *v.* chAñDo garnu /
garAunu (चाँडो गर्नु/गराउनु)

quickly, *adv.* jhaTTai (झट्टै),
chAñDai (चाँडै)

quicksilver, *n.* pAro (पारो)

quid pro quo, *n.* kshati pUrti
ko rUp mA diieko wastu
(क्षतिपूर्तिको रूपमा दिइएको
वस्तु)

quiet, *adj.* shAnt (शान्त),
sunsAn (सुनसान)
n. shAnti (शान्ति), maun (मौन)

quietly, *adv.* shAnti sanga (शान्तिसंग)

quill, *n.* pwAñkh (प्वाँख), pwAñkh ko DAñTh (प्वाँखको डाँठ)

quilt, *n.* sirak (सिरक), dolAiñ (दोलाइँ)

quinsy, *n.* ghAñTI ko sUj (घाँटीको सूज), ghAñTI sunine rog (घाँटी सुनिने रोग)

quintal, *n.* saya kilo (१०० किलो)

quintet, *n.* pAñch janA ko ToII (पाँच जनाको टोली)

quip, *n.* tAnA (ताना), ghoch pech (घोचपेच) *v.* tAnA mArnu (ताना मार्नु), ghoch pech garnu (घोचपेच गर्नु)

quit, *v.* chhoDnu (छोड्नु), tyAgnu (त्याग्नु)

quits, *n.* phachchhe (फच्छे)

quite, *adv.* bilkul (बिलकुल), ek dam (एकदम)

quiver, *n.* Thokro (ठोक्रो) *v.* kAmnu (काम्नु)

quixotic, *adj.* anauTho

(अनौठो), nirAIA (निराला)

quiz, *n.* sAmAnya gyAn ko prashna (सामान्य ज्ञानको प्रश्न)

quizzical, *adj.* beDhang ko (बेढङ्गको), ThaTyaulo (ठट्यौलो)

quorum, *n.* koram (कोरम), sankhyA (सङ्ख्या)

quota, *n.* tokieko mAtrA (तोकिएको मात्रा), koTA (कोटा)

quotable, *adj.* uddhrit garna lAyak ko (उद्धृत गर्न लायकको)

quotation, *n.* uddharaN wAkya (उद्धरण वाक्य), *(market)* lAgat bhAu (लागत भाउ)

quote, *v.* uddhrit garnu (उद्धृत गर्नु), kasai ko kurA dohryAunu (कसैको कुरा दोह्-याउनु), *(bus.)* dar batAunu (दर बताउनु)

quotient, *n.* bhAg phal (भागफल), *(I.Q.)* buddhi wA jehen janAune anupAt añk (बुद्धि वा जेहेन जनाउने अनुपात अंक)

R

rabbit, *n.* kharAyo (खरायो)

rabid, *adj.* risAhA (रिसाहा),
krodhI (क्रोधी),
(dog) baulAhA (बौलाहा)

rabies, *n.* kukur Adi lAI lAgne
rog (कुकुर आदिलाई लाग्ने
रोग), tyastA pashu le TokdA
manis baulAune, marne rog
(त्यस्ता पशुले टोक्दा मानिस
बौलाउने, मर्ने रोग),
jal trAs (जलत्रास)

race, *n. (sect)* jAti (जाति),
kul (कुल),
(athletic) dauD (दौड)

racism, *n.* jAti bhed (जातिभेद)

racist, *n.* jAti wAdI
(जातिवादी)

rack, *n. (shelf)* khulA darAj
(खुला दराज),
takhatA (तखता), *(cloud)*
uDne bAdal (उड्ने बादल)
v. maroDnu (मरोड्नु),
satAunu (सताउनु),
(rack one's brain) ThUlo
mAnsik prayatna garnu
(ठूलो मानसिक प्रयत्न गर्नु)

racketeer, *n.* beimAnI Dhang
bATa paisA kamAune

(बेइमानी ढङ्गबाट पैसा कमाउने),
ghusyAhA (घुस्याहा)

radar, *n.* reDAr (रेडार)

raddle, *n.* geru rang (गेरु रङ्ग)

radiant, *adj.* chamkilo
(चम्किलो), ujjwal (उज्ज्वल)

radiation, *n.* wikiraN
(विकिरण)

radical, *adj.* AmUl (आमूल)
n. ugra wAdI (उग्रवादी)

radio, *n.* reDiyo (रेडियो)

radioactive, *adj.* reDiyo
dharmI (रेडियोधर्मी)

radish, *n.* mUlA (मूला)

raffle, *n.* chiTThA (चिट्ठा)

raft, *n.* muDhA harU ko beDA
(मुढाहरूको बेडा),
ryapht (च्याफ्ट)

rafting, *n.* jal yAtrA (जलयात्रा)

rag, *n.* jhutro (भुत्रो),
TAlo (टालो)

rage, *n.* ris (रिस), jhok (भोक)

ragged, *adj.* thAnne (थाङ्ने),
jhutre (भुत्रे)

raid, *n.* dhAwA (धावा),
hamlA (हमला)
v. chhApA mArnu (छापा मार्नु),
hamlA garnu (हमला गर्नु)

rail, *n.* phalAme bAr (फलामे बार), rel ko lik (रेलको लिक)

railroad, *n.* rel mArg (रेलमार्ग), relwe (रेल्वे)

railway, *n.* rel mArg (रेलमार्ग), relwe (रेल्वे)

railway carriage, *n.* rel ko DibbA (रेलको डिब्बा)

railway engine, *n.* rel ko injin (रेलको इन्जिन)

railway train, *n.* rel gADI (रेलगाडी)

rain, *n.* pAnI (पानी), warshA (वर्षा), barkhA (बर्खा), *v.* pAnI parnu (पानी पर्नु), barsanu (बर्सनु)

rainbow, *n.* indreNI (इन्द्रेणी), indra dhanush (इन्द्रधनुष)

raincoat, *n.* barsAdI (बर्सादी)

rainfall, *n.* warshA (वर्षा), barkhA (बर्खा)

rainy, *adj.* barkhe (बर्खे)

rainy days, *n.* duhkh kA din (दुःखका दिन)

rainy season, *n.* warshA ritu/yam (वर्षा ऋतु/याम)

raise, *v.* uThAunu (उठाउनु), ubhyAunu (उभ्याउनु), hurkAunu (हुर्काउनु), pAlnu (पाल्नु), *(increase)* baDhAunu (बढाउनु) *n.* talab wriddhi (तलब वृद्धि)

raisin, *n.* kismis (किसमिस), dAkh (दाख)

rally, *n.* bhelA (भेला), ryAlI (र्‍याली) *v.* bhelA/jammA garnu (भेला/जम्मा गर्नु)

ram, *n.* bheDA (भेडा), thumo (थुमो)

ramp, *n.* jamIn kA duI tah laI joDne bATo (जमीनका दुई तहलाई जोड्ने बाटो)

rampage, *n.* himsAtmak wyawahAr (हिंसात्मक व्यवहार), upadro (उपद्रो) *v.* himsAtmak kAm garnu (हिंसात्मक काम गर्नु)

rampant, *adj.* aniyantrit (अनियन्त्रित)

ramshackle, *adj.* purAno (पुरानो), thotro (थोत्रो), bhatke bigreko (भत्के बिग्रेको)

random, *adj.* jathA bhAwI (जथाभावी), aniyamit (अनियमित), *(at random)* jathA bhAbI (जथाभाबी)

range, *n. (scope)* kshetra (क्षेत्र), *(Mt.)* shreNI (श्रेणी), *(distance)* phAslA (फासला), dUrI (दूरी)

rank, *n.* darjA (दर्जा), *(row)* lahar (लहर), pañkti (पंक्ति)

rank and file, *n.* sAdhAraN sipAhI (साधारण सिपाही), samsthA ko sAdhAraN sadasya (संस्थाको साधारण सदस्य)

ransack, *v. (search)* khUb
khojnu (खूब खोज्नु),
(loot) luTnu (लुट्नु)

ransom, *n.* phirautI rakam
(फिरौती रकम)
v. dhan dwArA mukti pAunu
(धनद्वारा मुक्ति पाउनु)

rap, *n.* halukA ghussA
(हलुका घुस्सा)
v. halukA ghussA hAnnu
(हलुका घुस्सा हान्नु)

rapacious, *adj.* lobhI (लोभी),
lAlchI (लालची)

rape, *n.* karaNI (करणी),
balAtkAr (बलात्कार)

rapid, *adj.* chhiTo (छिटो),
chAñDo (चाँडो)

rapids, *n.* tala jharne wegwAn
nadI (तल झर्ने वेगवान् नदी)

rapidly, *adv.* chhiTai (छिटै),
chAñDai (चाँडै)

rapport, *n.* sambandh
(सम्बन्ध), nAtA (नाता)

rapprochement, *n.* rAmro
sambandh punasthApnA
(राम्रो सम्बन्ध पुनर्स्थापना),
mel milAp (मेलमिलाप)

rapture, *n.* harsh (हर्ष),
Anand (आनन्द)

rare, *adj.* durlabh (दुर्लभ),
kam pAine (कम पाइने)

rascal, *n.* dushT (दुष्ट),
pAjI (पाजी)

rash, *n. (med.)* bimirA (बिमिरा)
adj. haDbaDe (हड्बडे),
shUro (शूरो)

raspberry, *n.* aiñselu (ऐंसेलु)

rat, *n.* mUso (मूसो),
(smell a rat) na rAmro kurA
ko shañkA hunu (नराम्रो
कुराको शङ्का हुनु)

rate, *n.* dar (दर), bhAu (भाउ)
v. dar kiTnu (दर किट्नु)

rather, *adv.* baru (बरु)

ratify, *v.* manjur garnu (मन्जुर
गर्नु), swIkriti dinu (स्वीकृति दिनु)

ration, *n.* rasad pAnI
(रसद पानी)
v. rasad Theknu (रसद ठेक्नु)

rational, *adj.* wiwekI (विवेकी),
tark shII (तर्कशील)

rationale, *n.* AdhAr bhUt
kAraN/tark (आधारभूत
कारण/तर्क)

rattle, *n.* tharkeko AwAj
(थर्केको आवाज)
v. AwAj Aune garI
hiñDnu/laDnu (आवाज
आउनेगरी हिंड्नु/लड्नु)

ravage, *v.* barbAd/nashT
garnu (बर्बाद/नष्ट गर्नु)
n. noksAn (नोक्सान),
hAni (हानि)

rave, *v.* pAgal kurA garnu
(पागल कुरा गर्नु),
garjera bolnu (गर्जेर बोल्नु)

rave-up, *n.* vrihat pArTI
(वृहत् पार्टी)

ravine, *n.* kholsA (खोल्सा),
kholchA (खोल्चा)

raw, *adj.* kAñcho (काँचो),
kachchA (कच्चा)

raw-boned, *adj.* jyAdai dublo
(ज्यादै दुब्लो)

raw deal, *n.* anuchit
wyawahAr (अनुचित व्यवहार)

raw material, *n.* kachchA mAl
(कच्चा माल)

ray, *n.* kiraN (किरण)

razor, *n.* chhurA (छुरा)

razor blade, *n.* pattA chhurA
(पत्ता छुरा)

razzle-dazzle, *n.* dauDA dauD
(दौडादौड), chaTAro (चटारो)

reach, *v.* pugnu (पुग्नु),
bheTTaunu (भेट्टाउनु),
puryAunu (पुर्‍याउनु)
n. pahuñch (पहुँच)

react, *v.* prati kriyA janAunu
(प्रतिक्रिया जनाउनु)

reaction, *n.* prati kriyA
(प्रतिक्रिया), asar (असर)

reactionary, *n.* prati kriyA
wAdI (प्रतिक्रियावादी)

read, *v.* paDhnu (पढ्नु),
paDhera sunAunu
(पढेर सुनाउनु)

readable, *adj.* paDhna
lAyak ko (पढ्न लायकको),

paTh nIya (पठनीय)

reader, *n.* pAThak (पाठक),
wAchak (वाचक), *(univ.)* sah
prAdhyApak (सहप्राध्यापक)

readily, *adv.* turunt (तुरुन्त)

readiness, *n.* tayArI (तयारी),
tatpartA (तत्परता),
ichchhA (इच्छा)

reading, *n.* paThan pAThan
(पठनपाठन), paDhAi (पढाइ)

ready, *adj.* tayAr (तयार)

ready-made, *n.* tayArI wastu
(तयारी वस्तु)

ready money, *n.* nagad (नगद)

real, *adj.* sAñcho (साँचो),
yathArth (यथार्थ)

real estate, *n.* ghar jaggA
(घरजग्गा)

realism, *n.* yathArth wAd
(यथार्थवाद)

reality, *n.* wAstawiktA
(वास्तविकता), yathArthatA
(यथार्थता), *(in reality)*
wAstaw mA (वास्तवमा)

realize, *v.* mahsus garnu
(महसुस गर्नु), bujhnu (बुझ्नु),
(bus.) wasul garnu (वसुल गर्नु)

really, *adv.* sAñchchai (साँच्चै),
pakkA (पक्का)

ream, *n.* kAgaj ko pAñch saya
tAu (कागजको ५०० ताउ)
v. pwAl ThUlo pArnu
(प्वाल ठूलो पार्नु)

reap, *v.* bAlI kATnu
(बाली काट्नु)

reappear, *v.* pheri dekhA
parnu (फेरि देखा पर्नु)

reappoint, *v.* pheri bahAl
garnu (फेरि बहाल गर्नु)

rear, *adj.* pachhADi ko
(पछाडिको)
n. pachhADi ko bhAg
(पछाडिको भाग)
v. pAlnu (पाल्नु),
hurkAunu (हुर्काउनु)

rearrange, *v.* pheri milAunu
(फेरि मिलाउनु)

reason, *n.* kAraN (कारण),
(faculty) buddhi (बुद्धि)
v. tark garnu (तर्क गर्नु)

reasonable, *adj.* manAsib
(मनासिब), uchit (उचित)

rebel, *n.* bAgI (बागी),
widrohI (विद्रोही)
v. widroh garnu (विद्रोह गर्नु)

rebellion, *n.* widroh (विद्रोह),
rAj droh (राजद्रोह)

rebellious, *adj.* widrohI
(विद्रोही), wirodhI (विरोधी),
bAgI (बागी)

rebirth, *n.* punar janma (पुनर्जन्म)

rebuild, *v.* pheri banAunu
(फेरि बनाउनु), punar nirmAN
garnu (पुनर्निर्माण गर्नु)

rebuke, *n.* hapkI (हप्की),
DAnT (डाँट), gAlI (गाली)

v. hapkAunu (हप्काउनु),
DAnTnu (डाँट्नु)

recall, *v. (pol., etc.)* phirtA
bolAunu (फिर्ता बोलाउनु),
(person, event) samjhanu
(सम्झनु)
n. khArejI (खारेजी),
pratyAhwAn (प्रत्याह्वान)

recapture, *v.* pheri pakranu
(फेरि पक्रनु)

receipt, *n.* bharpAI (भर्पाई)

receive, *v.* pAunu (पाउनु),
swAgat garnu (स्वागत गर्नु)

receiver, *n.* prApt garne
(प्राप्त गर्ने), *(phone, etc.)*
rishibhar (रिसिभर)

recent, *adj.* hAl sAl ko
(हालसालको), tAjA (ताजा)

reception, *n.* swAgat (स्वागत),
swAgat samAroh
(स्वागत समारोह)

receptionist, *n.* swAgat garne
(स्वागत गर्ने)

recess, *n. (leisure)* awkAsh
(अवकाश), *(niche)* khopA
(खोपा), *(secret place)* gupt
sthAn (गुप्तस्थान)

recipe, *n.* nuskhA (नुस्खा),
parikAr banAune sAmAn ra
tarikA (परिकार बनाउने सामान
र तरिका)

recipient, *n.* pAune wyakti
(पाउने व्यक्ति)

reciprocal, *adj.* ApasI (आपसी), badlA mA garine (बदलामा गरिने)

reciprocate, *v.* len den garnu (लेनदेन गर्नु)

recital, *n.* wAchan (वाचन), gAyan (गायन), so kArya kram (सो कार्यक्रम)

reckless, *adj.* lAparbAh (लापरबाह), ujjaND (उज्जण्ड)

reckon, *v.* ThAnnu (ठान्नु), sochnu (सोच्नु)

reckoning, *n.* gaNanA (गणना), mAn (मान)

recline, *v.* leTnu (लेट्नु), palTanu (पल्टनु)

recognition, *n.* mAnyatA (मान्यता), pahichAn (पहिचान)

recognize, *v.* chinnu (चिन्नु)

recoil, *v.* *(gun, etc.)* pachhil tira dhakkA hAnnu (पछिल्तिर धक्का हान्नु), pachhi haTnu (पछि हट्नु)

recollect, *v.* samjhanu (सम्झनु), yAd garnu (याद गर्नु)

recommend, *v.* siphArish garnu (सिफारिश गर्नु)

recommendation, *n.* siphArish (सिफारिश)

reconcile, *v.* mel milAp garnu (मेलमिलाप गर्नु)

reconciliation, *n.* mel milAp (मेलमिलाप)

reconfirm, *v.* dohoro pushTi garnu (दोहोरो पुष्टि गर्नु)

reconnaissance, *n.* sainik sarwekshaN (सैनिक सर्वेक्षण)

record, *n.* likhat (लिखत), rekarD (रेकर्ड), *(game, etc.)* kIrti mAn (कीर्तिमान), rekarD (रेकर्ड) *v.* dartA garnu (दर्ता गर्नु), lekhnu (लेख्नु)

(off the record), *phr.* anaupchArik rUp le (अनौपचारिक रूपले),

(on record) kAnUnI likhat (कानूनी लिखत)

recorder, *n.* rekarD garne yantra (रेकर्ड गर्ने यन्त्र)

recording, *n.* *(sound)* rekarD garne kAm (रेकर्ड गर्ने काम)

recount, *v.* warNan/bakhAn garnu (वर्णन/बखान गर्नु) *n.* punar gaNanA (पुनर्गणना)

recover, *v.* niko/ArAm hunu (निको/आराम हुनु), pAunu (पाउनु)

recovery, *n.* swAsthya lAbh (स्वास्थ्यलाभ)

recreate, *v.* tAjA pArnu (ताजा पार्नु), dil bahalAunu (दिल बहलाउनु)

recreation, *n.* manorañjan (मनोरञ्जन)

recruit, *n.* rañg ruT (रङ्गरुट), nayAñ sipAhI (नयाँ सिपाही) *v.* bhartI garnu (भर्ती गर्नु)

rectangle, *n.* Ayat (आयत),
chAr kune AkAr
(चारकुने आकार)

rectangular, *adj.* AyatAkAr
(आयताकार),
chAr pATe (चारपाटे)

rectify, *v.* sachyAunu (सच्याउनु),
shuddha garnu (शुद्ध गर्नु)

rector, *n.* (*univ.*) shikshA-
dhyaksha, (शिक्षाध्यक्ष,
rekTar (रेक्टर)

recumbent, *adj.* aDes lAgeko
(अडेस लागेको), leTeko (लेटेको)

recuperate, *v.* ArAm huṅdai
jAnu (आराम हुँदै जानु)

recuperation, *n.* swAsthya
lAbh (स्वास्थ्य लाभ)

recur, *v.* pheri samjhinu
(फेरि सम्झिनु),
pheri hunu (फेरि हुनु)

recurrence, *n.* punArwritti
(पुनरावृत्ति),
doharine kAm (दोहोरिने काम)

red, *adj.* rAto (रातो), *(in the
red)* riNI hunu (ऋणी हुनु)

Red Cross, *n.* reD kras
(रेडक्रस)

reddish, *adj.* ali ali rAto
(अलिअलि रातो)

redeem, *v.* mukta garnu (मुक्त गर्नु)

red-handed, *adv.* thalai mA
(थलैमा), aprAdh gardA
gardai (अपराध गर्दागर्दै)

red-hot, *adj.* tAtera rAto
bhaeko (तातेर रातो भएको)

red-letter day, *n.* khushI ko
smarNIya din
(खुशीको स्मरणीय दिन)

red light, *n.* khatarA ko battI
(खतराको बत्ती),
rokne saṅket (रोक्ने सङ्केत)

red-light area, *n.* weshyA
mohallA (वेश्या मोहल्ला)

redress, *v.* ThIk garnu (ठीक
गर्नु), sachyAunu (सच्याउनु),
n. sudhAr (सुधार),
kshati pUrti (क्षतिपूर्ति)

red tape, *n.* (*office*) ati aupchAriktA (अति औपचारिकता)

reduce, *v.* kam garnu (कम गर्नु),
ghaTAunu (घटाउनु)

reduction, *n.* kamI (कमी),
kaTTA (कट्टा)

reed, *n.* nigAlo (निगालो),
narkaT (नर्कट)

re-elect, *v.* pheri chhAnnu
/chunnu (फेरि छान्नु/चुन्नु)

refer, *v.* sandarbh dekhAunu
(सन्दर्भ देखाउनु),
hawAlA dinu (हवाला दिनु)

referee, *n.* rephrI (रेफ्री),
nirNAyak (निर्णायक)

reference, *n.* sandarbh
(सन्दर्भ), hawAlA (हवाला)

reference library, *n.* sandarbh
pustakAlaya (सन्दर्भ पुस्तकालय)

referendum, *n.* jan mat saṅgraha (जनमत संग्रह)

refill, *v.* pheri bharnu (फेरि भर्नु)

refine, *v.* shuddha garnu (शुद्ध गर्नु), khArnu (खार्नु)

refinery, *n.* tel saphA garne kAr khAnA (तेल सफा गर्ने कारखाना)

reflect, *v.* chhAyA pArnu (छाया पार्नु), prati wimbit garnu (प्रतिविम्बित गर्नु), wichAr garnu (विचार गर्नु)

reflection, *n.* chhAyA (छाया), prati wimba (प्रतिविम्ब), chintan (चिन्तन)

reform, *n.* sudhAr (सुधार) *v.* sudhAr garnu (सुधार गर्नु)

reformation, *n.* sudhAr (सुधार)

refrain, *v.* roknu (रोक्नु), parai rahanu (परै रहनु)

refresh, *v.* tAjA garAunu (ताजा गराउनु), nayAṅ josh prApt garnu (नयाँ जोश प्राप्त गर्नु)

refreshment, *n.* jal pAn (जलपान)

refrigerator, *n.* chiso pArne mesin (चिसो पार्ने मेसिन), rephrijeTar (रेफ्रिजेटर)

refuge, *n.* sharaN (शरण), Ashraya (आश्रय), *(take refuge)* sharaN linu (शरण लिनु)

refugee, *n.* sharNArthI (शरणार्थी)

refund, *v. (bus.)* paisA phirtA dinu (पैसा फिर्ता दिनु)

refuse, *v.* aswIkAr garnu (अस्वीकार गर्नु), na mAnnu (नमान्नु), *n.* phohar mailA (फोहरमैला), kasiṅgar (कसिङ्गर)

regal, *adj.* shAhI (शाही)

regard, *v.* Adar garnu (आदर गर्नु), wichAr garnu (विचार गर्नु), ThAnnu (ठान्नु), *(as regards/with regards to)* bAre mA (बारेमा)

regarding, *prep.* bAre ma (बारेमा)

regardless, *adj.* lAparbAh (लापर्बाह)

regency, *n.* rAj pratinidhi ko pad (राज प्रतिनिधिको पद)

regeneration, *n.* punar janma (पुनर्जन्म)

regent, *n.* nAyawI pad (नायवी पद)

regime, *n.* shAsan kAl (शासनकाल)

regimen, *n.* shAsan wyawasthA (शासन व्यवस्था)

regiment, *n.* palTan (पल्टन)

region, *n.* kshetra (क्षेत्र)

regional, *adj.* kshetrIya (क्षेत्रीय)

register, *v.* dartA garnu
(दर्ता गर्नु)
n. srestA (स्रेस्ता),
rajisTar (रजिस्टर)

registered, *adj.* dartA gareko
(दर्ता गरेको)

registrar, *n.* pañjikAdhikArI
(पञ्जिकाधिकारी)

registration, *n.* dartA (दर्ता)

regret, *n.* aphsos (अफसोस),
khed (खेद)
v. aphsos garnu (अफसोस
गर्नु), khed prakaT garnu
(खेद प्रकट गर्नु)

regrettable, *adj.* shochnIya
(शोचनीय)

regular, *adj.* niyamit (नियमित)

regularly, *adv.* niyamit rUp
mA (नियमित रूपमा)

regulate, *v.* niyamit /
niyantraN garnu (नियमित /
नियन्त्रण गर्नु)

regulation, *n.* niyam widhi
(नियम विधि)

rehabilitation, *n.* punarwAs
(पुनर्वास)

rehearsal, *n.* *(acting)*
pUrwAbhyAs (पूर्वाभ्यास)

reign, *n.* rAj (राज)
v. rAj garnu (राज गर्नु)

rein, *n.* lagAm (लगाम)
v. kAbU mA rAkhnu
(काबूमा राख्नु)

reincarnation, *n.* awtAr
(अवतार)

reinforce, *v.* arU baliyo
banAunu (अरू बलियो बनाउनु),
bal dinu (बल दिनु), prabal
banAunu (प्रबल बनाउनु)

reject, *v.* inkAr/aswIkAr garnu
(इन्कार/अस्वीकार गर्नु)
n. chhADieko wastu wA wyakti
(छाडिएको वस्तु वा व्यक्ति)

rejection, *n.* inkAr (इन्कार),
aswIkAr (अस्वीकार)

rejoice, *v.* khush hunu (खुश
हुनु), ramAunu (रमाउनु)

rejoicing, *n.* khushI (खुशी),
Anand (आनन्द)

relapse, *v.* ulTinu (उल्टिनु),
pharkinu (फर्किनु), bimArI
ulTinu (बिमारी उल्टिनु)
n. bimArI ko ulTAi
(बिमारीको उल्टाइ)

relate, *v.* bayAn/bakhAn garnu
(बयान/बखान गर्नु)

related, *adj.* sambandhit
(सम्बन्धित)

relation, *n.* nAtA (नाता),
sAino (साइनो)

relationship, *n.* sambandh
(सम्बन्ध)

relative, *n.* nAtA gotA
(नातागोता),
bhAi bandhu (भाइबन्धु)
adj. sApekshik (सापेक्षिक)

relax, *v.* ArAm garnu (आराम गर्नु), tanAu kam garnu (तनाउ कम गर्नु)

relaxation, *n.* holo (होलो), ArAm (आराम)

relay, *v.* sandesh puryAunu (सन्देश पुर्‍याउनु), prasAraN garnu (प्रसारण गर्नु)

relay race, *n.* rile dauD (रिले दौड)

release, *v.* chhoDnu (छोड्नु), rihA garnu (रिहा गर्नु), (*information*) prakAshit garnu (प्रकाशित गर्नु) *n.* chhuTkAra (छुट्कारा), rihAi (रिहाइ)

relent, *v.* naram hunu (नरम हुनु), paglanu (पग्लनु)

relentless, *adj.* nirdayI (निर्दयी), kaDA (कडा)

reliable, *adj.* bhar pardo (भरपर्दो), wishwasnIya (विश्वसनीय)

reliance, *n.* bharosA (भरोसा)

relic, *n.* awshesh (अवशेष), yAdgAr (यादगार)

relief, *n.* ArAm (आराम), (*aid*) madad (मदद)

relief fund, *n.* uddhAr kosh (उद्धार कोष)

relieve, *v.* chhoDi dinu (छोडिदिनु), uddhAr garnu (उद्धार गर्नु), (*job*) nikAlnu (निकाल्नु)

relieving, *adj.* pAlo dine (पालो दिने)

religion, *n.* dharm (धर्म)

religious, *adj.* dhArmik (धार्मिक), dharm garne (धर्म गर्ने)

reluctant, *adj.* ichchhA na garne (इच्छा नगर्ने), anichchhuk (अनिच्छुक)

rely, *v.* bhar garnu/parnu (भर गर्नु/पर्नु)

remain, *v.* rahanu (रहनु), basnu (बस्नु), (*food*) ubranu (उब्रनु)

remainder, *n.* bAñkI (बाँकी), shesh (शेष)

remaining, *adj.* bAñkI (बाँकी), bacheko (बचेको)

remains, *n.* lAsh (लाश), awshesh (अवशेष)

remark, *n.* bhanAi (भनाइ), udgAr (उद्गार), AlochanA (आलोचना) *v.* bhannu (भन्नु), AlochanA garnu (आलोचना गर्नु)

remarkable, *adj.* wishishT (विशिष्ट), herna lAyak ko (हेर्न लायकको)

remedy, *n.* ilAj (इलाज), upchAr (उपचार), upAya (उपाय) *v.* niko pArnu (निको पार्नु), ThIk garnu (ठीक गर्नु)

remember, *v.* samjhanu
(सम्झनु), yAd garnu (याद गर्नु)

remembrance, *n.* samjhanA
(सम्झना), yAd (याद)

remind, *v.* samjhanA
garAunnu(सम्झना गराउनु),
yAd dilAunu (याद दिलाउनु)

reminder, *n.* samjhauTo
(सम्झौटो), janAu (जनाउ)

remnant, *n.* bAňkI bhAg
(बाँकी भाग), shesh (शेष)

remorse, *n.* pachhuto (पछुतो),
pachhutAu (पछुताउ)

remorseless, *adj.* nirdayI
(निर्दयी), niThurI (निठुरी)

remote, *adj.* TADhA ko
(टाढाको), durgam (दुर्गम)

removable, *adj.* haTAuna
lAyak ko (हटाउन लायकको)

removal, *n.* khArejI (खारेजी)

remove, *v.* haTAunu
(हटाउनु), khosnu (खोस्नु)

remuneration, *n.* pArishramik
(पारिश्रमिक),
dakshiNA (दक्षिणा)

render, *v.* sewA/pesh garnu
(सेवा/पेश गर्नु), badlA mA
dinu (बदलामा दिनु)

rendezvous, *n.* bheT ghAt
(भेटघाट), bhelA hune ThAuň
(भेला हुने ठाउँ)
v. tokieko ThAuň mA
bheTnu (तोकिएको ठाउँमा

भेट्नु)

renegade, *n.* siddhAnt wA dal
chhoDne wyakti
(सिद्धान्त वा दल छोड्ने व्यक्ति)

renew, *v.* nayAň pArnu
(नयाँ पार्नु), nawIkaraN garnu
(नवीकरण गर्नु)

renewal, *n.* nayAň banAune
kAm (नयाँ बनाउने काम),
nawIkaraN (नवीकरण)

renounce, *v.* parityAg garnu
(परित्याग गर्नु),
sannyAs linu(सन्न्यास लिनु)

renovate, *v.* nayAň banAunu
(नयाँ बनाउनु), mar marmat
garnu (मर्मर्मत गर्नु)

renowned, *adj.* nAmI (नामी),
prasiddha (प्रसिद्ध),
wikhyAt (विख्यात)

rent, *n.* bahAl (बहाल), bhADA
(भाडा), kirAyA (किराया)
v. bhADA mA dinu
(भाडामा दिनु)

rental, *n.* bhADA bATa Aune
rakam (भाडाबाट आउने रकम)

repair, *v.* marammat garnu
(मर्म्मत गर्नु)
n. mar marmat (मर्मर्मत)

repay, *v.* chukAunu
(चुकाउनु), tirnu (तिर्नु)

repeal, *v.* badar/radda garnu
(बदर/रद्द गर्नु)
n. badar (बदर)

repeat, *v.* dohoryAunu
(दोहोऱ्याउनु)

repeatedly, *adv.* dohoryAeko
(दोहोऱ्याएको),
bArambAr (बारम्बार)

repel, *v.* pachhi haTAunu
(पछि हटाउनु)

repent, *v.* pachhutAunu
(पछुताउनु)

repentance, *n.* pachhuto
(पछुतो)

repetition, *n.* dohoryAune
kAm (दोहोऱ्याउने काम)

replace, *v.* badalnu (बदल्नु),
phernu (फेर्नु)

replacement, *n.* pratisthApan
(प्रतिस्थापन), badalI (बदली)

replica, *n.* nak kal (नक्कल),
prati kriti (प्रतिकृति)

reply, *v.* jawAph dinu
(जवाफ दिनु)
n. jawAph (जवाफ),
uttar (उत्तर)

report, *n.* riporT (रिपोर्ट), prati
wedan (प्रतिवेदन), samwAd
(संवाद), samAchAr (समाचार)
v. riporT garnu (रिपोर्ट गर्नु),
samAchar dinu (समाचार दिनु)

reportedly, *adv.* sune anusAr
(सुनेअनुसार)

reporter, *n.* samwAd dAta
(संवाददाता), samAchAr dAta
(समाचारदाता)

represent, *v.* saTTA mA
khaDA hunu (सट्टामा खडा
हुनु), prati nidhitwa garnu
(प्रतिनिधित्व गर्नु)

representation, *n.* prati
nidhitwa (प्रतिनिधित्व)

representative, *n.* prati nidhi
(प्रतिनिधि), wAris (वारिस)

repression, *n.* daman (दमन)

reprimand, *n.* nasihat (नसिहत),
Tokaso (टोकसो)
v. hapkAunu (हप्काउनु),
nasihat dinu (नसिहत दिनु)

reprint, *n.* nayAǹ prakAshan
(नयाँ प्रकाशन)
v. pheri chhApnu
(फेरि छाप्नु)

reproduce, *v.* pheri paidA
garnu (फेरि पैदा गर्नु),
(child) janmAunu (जन्माउनु)

reproduction, *n* punarutpAdan
(पुनरुत्पादन),
prajanan (प्रजनन),
(copy) nakkal (नक्कल),
prati rUp (प्रतिरूप)

reprove, *v.* hapkAunu
(हप्काउनु), hakArnu (हकार्नु)

reptile, *n.* ghasrane jantu (घस्रने
जन्तु), sarIsrip (सरीसृप)

republic, *n.* gaN tantra
(गणतन्त्र)

repulse, *v.* haTAunu (हटाउनु),
lakhaTnu (लखाट्नु)

repulsive, *adj.* ghIn lAgdo
(घिनलाग्दो)

reputation, *n.* ijjat (इज्जत),
mAn (मान), kIrti (कीर्ति)

reputed, *adj.* prasiddha
(प्रसिद्ध), mashhUr (मशहूर)

request, *n.* anurodh (अनुरोध),
bintI (बिन्ती)
v. anurodh/bintI garnu
(अनुरोध/बिन्ती गर्नु)

require, *v.* mAgnu (माग्नु),
Awashyak hunu
(आवश्यक हुनु)

required, *adj.* Awashyak
(आवश्यक), jarurI (जरुरी)

requirement, *n.* AwashyaktA
(आवश्यकता), mAg (माग),
chAhieko kurA
(चाहिएको कुरा)

requisite, *n.* chAhine sAmAn
(चाहिने सामान)
adj. chAhieko (चाहिएको)

rescue, *n.* uddhAr (उद्धार),
rakshA (रक्षा)
v. bachAunu (बचाउनु),
uddhAr garnu (उद्धार गर्नु)

research, *n.* anusandhAn
(अनुसन्धान), khoj (खोज)
v. anushandhAn garnu
(अनुसन्धान गर्नु)

researcher, *n.* anusandhAn
garne (अनुसन्धान गर्ने),
khoj kartA (खोजकर्ता)

resemblance, *n.* samarUptA
(समरूपता)

resemble, *v.* milnu (मिल्नु),
ek nAsh hunu (एकनाश हुनु)

resent, *v.* niko na mAnnu
(निको नमान्नु), risAunu (रिसाउनु)

resentment, *n.* ris (रिस),
krodh (क्रोध)

reservation, *n.* ArakshaN
(आरक्षण), shart (शर्त),
(area) Arakshit kshetra
(आरक्षित क्षेत्र)

reserve, *v.* surakshit garnu
(सुरक्षित गर्नु), jageDA
rAkhnu (जगेडा राख्नु),
rijarb garnu (रिजर्ब गर्नु)
n. surakshit sañchaya
(सुरक्षित सञ्चय), *(mil.)*
rijarbh senA (रिजर्भ सेना),
shart (शर्त), *(sports)* atirikt
khelADI (अतिरिक्त खेलाडी),
(faculty) Atma samyam
(आत्मसंयम), sañkoch(संकोच),
rUkhopan (रूखोपन),
(area) Araksha (आरक्ष)

reserved, *adj.* surakshit
(सुरक्षित), samyamI (संयमी),
sañkochI (सङ्कोची),
rUkho (रूखो)

reservoir, *n.* jalAshaya
(जलाशय)

reshuffle, *n.* her pher (हेरफेर)
v. her pher garnu (हेरफेर गर्नु)

reside, *v.* basnu (बस्नु)

residence, *n.* ghar (घर),
niwAs (निवास)

resident, *n.* niwAsI (निवासी),
bAsindA (बासिन्दा)

residential, *adj.* AwAsIya
(आवासीय)

resign, *v.* rAjI nAmA dinu
(राजीनामा दिनु),
jAgir choDnu (जागिर छोड्नु),
santushT hunu (सन्तुष्ट हुनु)

resignation, *n.* rAjI nAmA
(राजीनामा),
sahishNutA (सहिष्णुता)

resist, *v.* sAmnA/wirodh
garnu (सामना/विरोध गर्नु)

resistance, *n.* wirodh (विरोध),
bAdhA (बाधा)

resolution, *n.* sañkalp
(सङ्कल्प), prastAw (प्रस्ताव),
driDhtA (दृढता),
samAdhAn (समाधान)

resolve, *v.* nishchaya garnu
(निश्चय गर्नु), samAdhAn
garnu (समाधान गर्नु)

resort, *n.* Ashraya (आश्रय),
v. Ashraya linu (आश्रय लिनु)

resource, *n.* srot (स्रोत),
sAdhan (साधन)

resourceful, *adj.* chatur (चतुर),
chAñDo upAya sochne
(चाँडो उपाय सोच्ने)

respect, *n.* Adar (आदर),

sammAn (सम्मान), *(in respect
of)* bAre mA (बारेमा)
v. Adar/kadar garnu
(आदर/कदर गर्नु),
mAnnu (मान्नु)

respectable, *adj.* AdarNIya
(आदरणीय)

respectful, *adj.* sammAn janak
(सम्मानजनक)

respectfully, *adj.* sAdar (सादर)

respective, *adj.* A Aphnu
(आ-आफ्नु)

respectively, *adv.* kramai le
(क्रमैले)

respiration, *n.* shwAs
prashwAs (श्वासप्रश्वास), sAs
pherne kAm (सास फेर्ने काम)

respond, *v.* uttar dinu
(उत्तर दिनु)

response, *n.* jawAph (जवाफ),
uttar (उत्तर)

responsibility, *n.* uttar
dAyitwa (उत्तरदायित्व),
jimme dArI (जिम्मेदारी)

responsible, *adj.* uttar dAyI
(उत्तरदायी),
jimme dAr (जिम्मेदार)

rest, *n.* ArAm (आराम),
chain (चैन),
(part) bAñkI (बाँकी),
(at rest) sthir (स्थिर),
Dhukka (ढुक्क),
(for the rest) arU ko bAremA

(अरूको बारेमा), *(lay to rest)*
mareko lAI gADnu
(मरेकोलाई गाड्नु)
v. ArAm garnu (आराम गर्नु),
thakAi mArnu (थकाइ मार्नु)

restaurant, *n.* bhojnAlaya
(भोजनालय), resTurAñ (रेस्टुराँ)

restless, *adj.* chanchal (चन्चल),
ashAnt (अशान्त)

restlessness, *n.* chhaTpaTI
(छटपटी), bechainI (बेचैनी)

restoration, *n.* punarsthApnA
(पुनर्स्थापना)

restore, *v.* phirtA garnu
(फिर्ता गर्नु), pheri banAunu
(फेरि बनाउनु)

restrain, *v.* roknu (रोक्नु),
dabAunu (दबाउनु)

restraint, *n.* wirodh (विरोध),
rok thAm (रोकथाम)

restrict, *v.* roknu (रोक्नु),
sImit garnu (सीमित गर्नु)

restriction, *n.* rokkA (रोक्का),
prati bandh (प्रतिबन्ध)

result, *n.* pariNAm (परिणाम),
natijA (नतिजा),
v. natIjA niskanu (नतीजा
निस्कनु), *(as a result of)*
phal swarUp (फलस्वरूप)

resultant, *adj.* pariNAm dine
(परिणाम दिने)

resume, *v.* pheri suru garnu
(फेरि सुरु गर्नु)

resumé, *n.* sAr (सार),
bAyo DATA (बायोडाटा)

resumption, *n.* nayAñ suruAt
(नयाँ सुरुआत)

resuscitate, *v.* sas ra hos
pharkAunu (सास र होस
फर्काउनु)

retail, *n.* khudrA bikrI
(खुद्रा बिक्री)

retailer, *n.* khudrA pasale
(खुद्रा पसले)

retain, *v.* kAyam rAkhnu
(कायम राख्नु)

retaliate, *v.* badlA linu
(बदला लिनु)

retaliation, *n.* badlA (बदला)

retinue, *n.* anuchar (अनुचर),
lAwA laskar (लावालस्कर)

retire, *v.* awkAsh linu
(अवकाश लिनु),
(rest) sutna jAnu (सुत्न जानु)

retired, *adj.* awkAsh prApt
(अवकाशप्राप्त), awkAsh lieko
(अवकाश लिएको)

retirement, *n.* awkAsh
(अवकाश)

retreat, *n.* pacchi haTne kAm
(पछि हट्ने काम), palAyan
(पलायन), *(place)* lukne wA
sharaN line ThAuñ (लुक्ने वा
शरण लिने ठाउँ)
v. pachhi haTnu (पछि हट्नु),
bhAgnu (भाग्नु)

return, *n.* wApasI (वापसी),
phirtA (फिर्ती),
(bus.) phAidA (फाइदा),
(election) wijaya (विजय),
(in return for) saTTA mA
(सट्टामा)
v. pharkanu (फर्कनु)

return ticket, *n.* phirtI TikaT
(फिर्ती टिकट)

reunite, *v.* pheri saṅgaThit
hunu (फेरि सङ्गठित हुनु)

reunion, *n.* punar milan
(पुनर्मिलन)

reveal, *v.* kholnu (खोल्नु),
bhaNDA phor garnu
(भण्डाफोर गर्नु)

revel, *v.* ho hallA garI
ramAilo garnu (होहल्ला गरी
रमाइलो गर्नु)

revelation, *n.* kholAi (खोलाइ),
bhaNDA phor (भण्डाफोर)

revelry, *n.* ramAilo (रमाइलो),
moj majjA (मोजमज्जा)

revenge, *n.* badlA (बदला)
v. badlA linu (बदला लिनु)

revenue, *n.* rAjaswa (राजस्व)

reverberate, *v.* ghankanu
(घन्कनु), guñjnu (गुँज्नु)

reverberation, *n.* guñjan
(गुँजन), ghankAi (घन्काइ)

revere, *v.* mAn garnu
(मान गर्नु)

reverence, *n.* Adar (आदर),

sammAn (सम्मान)

reverie, *n.* chintan (चिन्तन),
dhyAn (ध्यान)

reverse, *n.* wiparIt (विपरीत),
ulTo (उल्टो)

review, *n.* samIkshA (समीक्षा),
simhAwalokan (सिंहावलोकन)
v. samIkshA garnu
(समीक्षा गर्नु)

revise, *v.* dohoryAunu
(दोहोर्‍याउनु),
sachyAunu (सच्याउनु)

revision, *n.* samshodhan
(संशोधन)

revive, *v.* punar jIwit garnu
(पुनर्जीवित गर्नु)

revoke, *v.* radda/khArej garnu
(रद्द/खारेज गर्नु)

revolt, *n.* widroh (विद्रोह)
v. widroh garnu
(विद्रोह गर्नु)

revolution, *n.* Andolan
(आन्दोलन), krAnti (क्रान्ति),
(earth) parikramA
(परिक्रमा), phanko (फन्को)

revolutionary, *n.* krAnti kArI
(क्रान्तिकारी)
adj. parikramA garne
(परिक्रमा गर्ने)

revolve, *v.* ghumnu (घुम्नु),
phanko mArnu (फन्को मार्नु)

revolver, *n.* pistaul (पिस्तौल),
pistol (पिस्तोल)

reward, *n.* inAm (इनाम),
baksis (बक्सिस), bakas (बकस)
v. inAm dinu (इनाम दिनु)

rewrite, *v.* pheri lekhnu
(फेरि लेख्नु)

rhesus monkey, *n.* sAno
puchchhar bhaeko bAñdar
(सानो पुच्छर भएको बाँदर)

rhetoric, *n.* AlañkArik
bhAshA (आलङ्कारिक भाषा)

rheumatic, *adj.* bAt rog
lAgeko (बातरोग लागेको)

rheumatism, *n.* bAt/bAth rog
(बात/बाथरोग)

rhinoceros, *n.* gaiñDA (गैंडा)

rhododendron, *n.* gurAñs
(गुराँस)

rhythm, *n.* tAl (ताल),
laya (लय)

rib, *n.* karañ (करड)

ribbon, *n.* riban (रिबन),
phittA (फित्ता)

rice, *n. (uncooked)* chAmal
(चामल), *(cooked)* bhAt (भात),
(beaten rice, rice flakes)
chiurA (चिउरा)

rich, *adj.* dhanI (धनी)

riches, *n.* dhan (धन),
daulat (दौलत)

rickshaw, *n.* riksA (रिक्सा)

rid, *v.* haTAunu (हटाउनु)

riddle, *n.* gAuñ khAne kathA
(गाउँखाने कथा)

ride, *v.* ghoDA chaDhnu
(घोडा चढ्नु), moTar
chaDhnu (मोटर चढ्नु)
n. ghoDA chaDhAi
(घोडा चढाइ), moTar
chaDhAi (मोटर चढाइ),
sawArI (सवारी)

rider, *n.* sawAr (सवार)

ridge, *n.* DAñDA (डाँडा),
lAmo Dhisko (लामो ढिस्को)

ridicule, *n.* hañsI (हँसी),
ThaTTA (ठट्टा)

ridiculous, *adj.* hañso (हाँसो),
hAsyAspad (हास्यास्पद),
wAhiyAt (वाहियात)

riff-raff, *n.* nimna warg laI
hochyAI korkAlI Adi
bhanine pArA (निम्न वर्गलाई
होच्याई कोर्काली आदि भनिने
पारा)

rifle, *n.* banduk (बन्दुक),
rAiphal (राइफल)

rift, *n.* darAr (दरार),
phATo (फाटो)

rigging, *n.* dhAñdhalI
(धाँधली), kapaT (कपट)

right, *adj. (direction)* dAyAñ
(दायाँ), dAhine (दाहिने),
(judgement) ThIk (ठीक),
uchit (उचित), *(law)* hak
(हक), adhikAr (अधिकार)

righteous, *adj.* nyAyI (न्यायी),
charitra wAn (चरित्रवान्)

rightful, *adj.* hak dAr
(हकदार), jAyaj (जायज)

right-hand man, *n.* mukhya
sahAyak (मुख्य सहायक)

right-minded, *adj.* ThIk
wichAr bhaeko (ठीक विचार
भएको)

rigid, *adj.* kaDA (कडा),
na galne (नगल्ने)

rigorous, *adj.* kaThor
(कठोर), kaDA (कडा)

rigo(u)r, *n.* kaThortA
(कठोरता), kaDai (कडाइ)

rim, *n.* biT (बिट),
kinArA (किनारा)

ring, *n.* mundrI (मुन्द्री),
munro (मुन्रो), auñThI (औंठी),
(circle) gherA (घेरा),
(echo) guñjan (गुञ्जन)
v. (bell) bajAunu (बजाउनु),
(echo) guñjnu(गुँज्नु)

ring finger, *n.* sAhilI auñlA
(साहिली औंला)

ringleader, *n.* netA (नेता),
nAike (नाइके)

ring road, *n.* chakra path
(चक्रपथ)

ringworm, *n.* dAd (दाद)

rinse, *v.* pakhAlnu (पखाल्नु),
chuThnu (चुठ्नु)

riot, *n.* hUl daṅgA (हूलदङ्गा)

rioter, *n.* hulyAha (हुल्याहा),
daṅgyAhA (दङ्ग्याहा)

rip, *v.* chyAtnu (च्यात्नु),
udhArnu (उधार्नु)

rip-off, *n.* chorI (चोरी),
nakkal (नक्कल), ThagI (ठगी)

ripe, *adj.* pAkeko (पाक्केको)

ripen, *v.* pAknu (पाक्नु)

ripple, *n.* sAno lahar
(सानो लहर)
v. lahar paidA garnu
(लहर पैदा गर्नु)

rise, *v.* uThnu (उठ्नु),
(sun) udAunu (उदाउनु)
n. udaya (उदय), utthAn
(उत्थान), *(give rise to)*
kAraN bannu (कारण बन्नु)

rising, *adj.* udIya mAn
(उदीयमान)

risk, *n.* jokhim (जोखिम)
v. jokhim uThAunu
(जोखिम उठाउनु)

risky, *adj.* jokhim pUrN
(जोखिमपूर्ण)

rite, *n.* dhArmik rIti
(धार्मिक रीति), kriyA (क्रिया)

ritual, *n.* saṃskAr widhi
widhAn (संस्कार विधिविधान)

rival, *n.* jorI pArI (जोरीपारी),
prati dwandwI (प्रतिद्वन्द्वी)

river, *n.* nadI (नदी),
kholA (खोला)

rivulet, *n.* kholA (खोला),
kholA nAlA (खोलानाला)

road, *n.* saDak (सडक),

bATo (बाटो), *(main road)*
mUl bAto (मूलबाटो),
(on the road) saphar gari
rahane (सफर गरिरहने)

road hog, *n.* man parI moTar
hAṅkne (मनपरी मोटर हाँक्ने)

road map, *n.* mArg chitra
(मार्गचित्र)

roam, *v.* ghum phir garnu
(घुमफिर गर्नु), Dulnu (डुल्नु)

roar, *n.* garjan (गर्जन)
v. garjanu (गर्जनु)

roast, *n.* sekuwA (सेकुवा)
v. seknu (सेक्नु)

rob, *v.* chornu (चोर्नु),
luTnu (लुट्नु)

robber, *n.* DAku (डाकु),
chor (चोर)

robbery, *n.* DakaitI (डकैती)

robe, *n.* poshAk (पोशाक),
gAun (गाउन)

robot, *n.* roboT (रोबोट),
yantra mAnaw (यन्त्रमानव)

rock, *n.* chaTTAn (चट्टान),
DhuṅgA (ढुङ्गा)
(on the rock), *phr.*
TAT bhaeko (टाट भएको)

rocket, *n.* rakeT (रकेट)

rod, *n.* chhaDI (छडी),
laTThI (लट्ठी)

rodent, *n.* mUso, chhuchundro
Adi (मूसो, छुचुन्द्रो आदि)

rogue, *n.* bad mAs (बदमास),

upadryAha (उपद्रयाहा)

role, *n.* bhUmikA (भूमिका)

roll, *n.* muThA (मुठा), *(cloth)*
thAn (थान), *(list)* sUchI
(सूची), kramAṅk (क्रमाङ्क)
v. bernu (बेर्नु), laDI buDI
garnu (लडीबुडी गर्नु)

roll away, *v.* palTiṅdai jAnu
(पल्टिँदै जानु)

roll-call, *n.* hAjir (हाजिर)

rolled gold, *n.* sun ko jalap
(सुनको जलप)

roller, *n.* belnA (बेलना), bATo
pelne injin (बाटो पेल्ने इन्जिन)

romance, *n.* premAlAp
(प्रेमालाप), romAns (रोमान्स)

romantic, *adj.* kAlpanik
(काल्पनिक), romAnI (रोमानी),
romAñch kArI (रोमाञ्चकारी)

roof, *n.* chhAnA (छाना),
chhAnu (छानु)

rook, *n.* kAg (काग)

room, *n.* koThA (कोठा),
(space) ThAuṅ (ठाउँ)

roomy, *adj.* pharAkilo
(फराकिलो)

rooster, *n.* *(cock)* bhAle (भाले)

root, *n.* jarA (जरा),
mUl (मूल), *(take root)* jaro
hAlnu (जरो हाल्नु)

root out, *n.* ukhelnu (उखेल्नु),
dhwaṃsa pArnu (ध्वंस पार्नु)

rope, *n.* DorI (डोरी)

rope in, v. bhAg lina kar garnu (भाग लिन कर गर्नु)

rosary, n. jap mAlA (जपमाला)

rose, n. gulAph (गुलाफ),
(bed of roses) sukh ko sajilo kAm (सुखको सजिलो काम),
(path strewn with roses) sukh ko jIwan (सुखको जीवन)

rosebud, n. *(fig.)* rAmrI strI (राम्री स्त्री)

rose water, n. gulAph jal (गुलाफजल)

rose without a thorn, adj. nish kaNTak Anand (निष्कण्टक आनन्द)

roster, n. nAmAwalI (नामावली)

rostrum, n. mañch (मञ्च)

rosy, adj. gulAphI (गुलाफी)

rot, v. kuhinu (कुहिनु), saDnu (सड्नु)

rotary, n. ghumne yantra (घुम्ने यन्त्र), klab (क्लब)

rotation, n. chakkar (चक्कर), ghumawaT (घुमावट)

rotten, adj. saDe galeko (सडे-गलेको), kuhieko (कुहिएको)

rough, adj. *(level)* khasro (खस्रो), *(estimate)* andAjI (अन्दाजी), *(behaviour)* michAhA (मिचाहा), Tarro (टर्रो), *(road)* apThero (अप्ठेरो)

rough-and-ready, adj. asabhya bhae pani kArgar (असभ्य भए पनि कारगर)

rough and tumble, n. hAt pAt (हातपात)
adj. aniyamit (अनियमित), ulTo sulTo (उल्टोसुल्टो)

rough house, n. jhagaDA (झगडा), gol mAl (गोलमाल), hAt pAt (हातपात)

roughly, adv. andAjI (अन्दाजी), lag bhag (लगभग)

roughneck, n. hulyAhA (हुल्याहा), gunDa (गुण्डा)

rough-tongued, adj. abhadra bolne (अभद्र बोल्ने)

round, adj. gol (गोल), golo (गोलो), bATulo (बाटुलो), Dallo (डल्लो), *(all-round)* sarwatomukhI (सर्वतोमुखी) n. *(gunfire)* golI (गोली) v. ghumnu (घुम्नु), phanko lagAunu (फन्को लगाउनु)

roundabout, adj. andAjI (अन्दाजी)

round-table conference, n. gol mej sammelan (गोलमेज सम्मेलन)

round up, v. samAtnu (समात्नु), jammA pArnu (जम्मा पार्नु)

round-up, n. sAr saṅkshep (सार-सङ्क्षेप), pakrAu (पक्राउ), mAnis Adi thupArne kAm (मानिस आदि थुपार्ने काम)

rouse, v. jagAunu (जगाउनु),

(stir) bhaDkAunu (भड्काउनु)

rout, *n.* daṅgA (दंगा),
ho hallA (होहल्ला)
v. bhagAunu (भगाउनु),
haTAunu (हटाउनु)

route, *n.* bATo (बाटो),
mArg (मार्ग)
v. kunai bATo bATa
paThAunu (कुनै बाटोबाट
पठाउनु)

routine, *n.* niyamit kArya
(नियमित कार्य)

rove, *v.* ghum phir garnu
(घुमफिर गर्नु)

rover, *n.* ghumakkaD (घुमक्कड)

row, *n.* lahar (लहर),
paṅkti (पंक्ति), *(noise)* hallA
khallA (हल्लाखल्ला)
v. (boat) duṅgA khyAunu
(डुङ्गा ख्याउनु)

rowdy, *adj.* guNDA (गुण्डा)

rowdyism, *n.* guNDA gardI
(गुण्डागर्दी)

royal, *adj.* shAhI (शाही),
rAj kIya (राजकीय)

royal road, *n.* sajilo upAya
(सजिलो उपाय)

royalty, *n.* rAj sattA (राजसत्ता),
rAj pariwAr (राज परिवार),
(book) royalTI (रोयल्टी),
lekhakaswa (लेखकस्व)

rub, *v.* dalnu (दल्नु), malnu
(मल्नु), *(oil)* ghasnu (घस्नु)

rubber, *n.* rabaD (रबड),
rabar (रबर)

rubbernecker, *n.* gAdI bATa
TolAera heri rahane
paryaTak (गाडीबाट टोलाएर
हेरिरहने पर्यटक)

rubber stamp, *n.* rabaD ko
chhAp (रबडको छाप)

rubber-stamp, *v.* nabichArI
swIkriti dinu (नबिचारी
सवीकृति दिनु)

rubbish, *n.* kasiṅgar (कसिङ्गर)

rub in, *v.* mAlis garnu
(मालिस गर्नु), dhasnu (धस्नु)

rub out, *v.* meTnu (मेट्नु)

ruby, *n.* mANik (माणिक),
lAl maNi (लालमणि)

rucksack, *n.* pITh mA bokne
jholA (पीठमा बोक्ने झोला)

rude, *adj.* asabhya (असभ्य),
pAkhe (पाखे), gaṅwAr
(गँवार), ThADo (ठाडो)

rudiment, *n.* shuru (शुरु),
prAthmik siddhAnt
(प्राथमिक सिद्धान्त)

ruffian, *n.* hulyAha (हुल्याहा),
bad mAsh (बदमाश)

rug, *n.* rADI (राडी), pAkhI
(पाखी), maNDI (मण्डी)

rugged, *adj.* rUkho (रूखो),
ubaD khAbaD (उबडखाबड)

ruin, *n.* winAsh (विनाश),
barbAdI (बर्बादी)

v. nAsh garnu (नाश गर्नु)

ruins, *n.* awshesh (अवशेष),
khanD har (खन्डहर)

rule, *n. (law)* niyam (नियम),
kAnUn (कानून), *(pol.)*
shAsan (शासन), *(as a rule)*
sAmAnya rUp le (सामान्य
रूपले), *(by rule)* chaleko
niyam anusAr (चलेको नियम-
अनुसार), *(hard and fast rule)*
kaThor niyam (कठोर नियम)
v. shAsan garnu (शासन गर्नु)

ruler, *n. (pol.)* shAsak (शासक),
(scale) rular (रुलर)

rule of thumb, *n.* anubhaw ra
wyawahAr ko AdhAr mA
chaleko niyam (अनुभव र
व्यवहारको आधारमा चलेको
नियम)

rule out, *v.* haTAunu (हटाउनु),
panchhAunu (पन्छाउनु)

rules and regulations, *n.*
niyam kAnUn (नियम कानून)

rule the roost, *v.* warchaswa
hunu (वर्चस्व हुनु)

rumo(u)r *n.* hallA (हल्ला)

rump, *n.* chAk (चाक),
philo (फिलो), nitamb (नितम्ब)

run, *v.* dagurnu (दगुर्नु),
dauDanu (दौडनु),
(mech.) chalAunu (चलाउनु),
(water) bagnu (बग्नु),
bahanu (बहनु),

(shop) chalAunu (चलाउनु)
n. dauDAi (दौडाइ), chAl
(चाल), *(cricket)* ran (रन),
(in the long run) Akhir mA
(आखिरमा), *(on the run)*
bhAgi raheko (भागिरहेको),
antya mA (अन्त्यमा),

run away, *v.* bhAgnu (भाग्नु)

run down, *v.* dam sakinu
(दम सकिनु),
kam jor hunu (कमजोर हुनु)

run-down, *adj.* upekshit
(उपेक्षित)

rundown, *n.* sañkhyA mA
kaTautI (संख्यामा कटौती)

run low, *v.* thorai bAñkI
rahanu (थोरै बाँकी रहनु)

rung, *n.* bhareñ ko khuD kilA
(भरेङको खुड्किला)

runner, *n.* dauDane mAnchhe
(दौडने मान्छे), dhAwak (धावक),
(state, etc.) dUt (दूत),
sandesh wAhak (सन्देशवाहक)

runner-up, *n.* up wijetA
(उपविजेता)

running water, *n.* kholA wA
dhArA ko pAnI (खोला वा
धाराको पानी)

run off, *v.* bhAgnu (भाग्नु)

run-of-the-mill, *adj.* sAdhAraN
(साधारण), sAmAnya (सामान्य)

run out, *v.* samApt hunu
(समाप्त हुनु)

run out on, v. chhADi dinu (छाडिदिनु)

run over, v. (water) pokhinu (पोखिनु), (vehicle) kulchinu (कुल्चिनु)

run short, v. kamI hunu (कमी हुनु)

run up, chANDai baDhnu (चाँडै बढ्नु)

run up against, v. kaThinAi jhelnu (कठिनाइ झेल्नु)

runway, n. ranwe (रनवे), dhAwan mArg (धावन मार्ग)

rupee, n. rupiyAN (रुपियाँ), rupaiyaN (रुपैयाँ)

rural, adj. gAuNle (गाउँले), grAmIN (ग्रामीण)

rush, n. chaTAro (चटारो),

ghuiNcho (घुइँचो), bhID (भीड)

v. dauDanu (दौडनु), hurrinu (हुर्रिनु)

rust, n. khiyA (खिया)

v. khiyA lAgnu (खिया लाग्नु)

rustic, adj. pAkhe (पाखे), kANThe (काँठे), dehAtI (देहाती)

rusticate, v. (exam., etc.) nikAlnu (निकाल्नु)

rustle, n. (leaf, cloth, etc.) saryAk suruk hune (स्याक्सुरुक हुने)

v. syAr syAr AwAj niklanu (स्यार्स्यार आवाज निक्लनु)

rusty, adj. khiyA lAgeko (खिया लागेको)

ruthless, adj. niThur (निठुर)

S

sabotage, n. toD phoD (तोडफोड), widhwaṃsa (विध्वंस) v. widhwaṃsa garnu (विध्वंस गर्नु), toD phoD garnu (तोडफोड गर्नु)

sack, n. borA (बोरा), thailA (थैला) v. borA mA kochnu (बोरामा कोच्नु), (job) barkhAst garnu (बर्खास्त गर्नु),

(crime) luTnu (लुट्नु)

sacred, adj. pawitra (पवित्र)

sacredness, n. pawitratA (पवित्रता)

sacrifice, n. (animal) balidAn (बलिदान), (person) tyAg (त्याग) v. bali dinu (बलि दिनु), tyAg garnu (त्याग गर्नु)

sad, *adj.* dik dAr (दिक्दार), duhkhI (दुःखी)

saddle, *n. (horse)* kAThI (काठी), *(hills)* bhañjyAñ (भञ्ज्याङ)

sadhu, *n.* sAdhu (साधु), jogI (जोगी)

sadness, *n.* shok (शोक), udAsI (उदासी)

safari, *n.* shikAr ko abhiyAn (शिकारको अभियान), *(Africa)* jaṅgal mA shikAr wa paryaTan (जङ्गलमा शिकार वा पर्यटन)

safe, *adj.* kushal (कुशल), surakshit (सुरक्षित), Dar na lAgne (डर नलाग्ने) *n.* seph (सेफ), tijoDI (तिजोडी)

safe conduct, *n.* abhaya patra (अभयपत्र)

safeguard, *n.* rakshA (रक्षा), surakshA (सुरक्षा) *v.* rakshA garnu (रक्षा गर्नु)

safely, *adv.* subistA saṅga (सुबिस्तासँग), surakshA sAth (सुरक्षासाथ)

safety, *n.* surakshA (सुरक्षा), kushaltA (कुशलता)

safety pin, *n.* sepTi pin (सेप्टिपिन), Alpin (आल्पिन)

safety razor, *n.* surakshit chhurA (सुरक्षित छुरा)

saffron, *n.* keshar (केशर)

sag, *v.* jhulnu (झुल्नु), jhuNDinu (झुण्डिनु)

saga, *n.* AkhyAn (आख्यान)

sage, *n.* rishi (ऋषि), muni (मुनि)

Sagittarius, *n.* dhanu rAshi (धनुराशि)

sago, *n.* sAbu dAnA (साबुदाना)

sail, *n.* jahAj ko pAl (जहाजको पाल) *v.* jahAj hiññDnu (जहाज हिँड्नु), jahAj mA saphar garnu (जहाजमा सफर गर्नु)

sailor, *n.* jahAjI (जहाजी), nAwik (नाविक)

saint, *n.* sant (सन्त), mahAtmA (महात्मा)

sake, *n.* kAraN (कारण), nimitta (निमित्त), *(for the sake of)* ko lAgi (को लागि)

salad, *n.* salAd (सलाद)

salad days, *n.* kishorAwasthA (किशोरावस्था)

salamander, *n.* mAusulI (माउसुली)

salary, *n.* talab (तलब), tankhA (तनखा)

sale, *n.* bikrI (बिक्री), *(for/on sale)* bikrI kA lAgi (बिक्रीका लागि)

saleable, *adj.* bechna lAyak (बेच्नलायक)

salesman, *n.* wikretA (विक्रेता)

salient, *adj.* pramukh (प्रमुख), mUl (मूल)

saline, *adj.* nunilo (नुनिलो)

saliva, *n.* thuk (थुक), rAl (राल)

saloon, *n.* ThUlo koThA (ठूलो कोठा), baiThak (बैठक)

salt, *n.* nun (नुन),

(take with a pinch of salt) shaṅkA garnu (शंका गर्नु), na patyAunu (नपत्याउनु)

salted, *adj.* nunilo (नुनिलो)

saltless, *adj.* alino (अलिनो)

salty, *adj.* nunilo (नुनिलो)

salute, *n.* salAmI (सलामी), salAm (सलाम)

v. salAm garnu (सलाम गर्नु)

salvation, *n.* mukti (मुक्ति), nirwAN (निर्वाण)

same, *adj.* uhI (उही), tyahI (त्यही), ekai nAs ko (एकैनासको), *(just the same)* tathApi (तथापि)

sample, *n.* namUnA (नमूना)

v. namUnA linu/dinu (नमूना लिनु/दिनु)

sanatorium, *n.* Arogya shAlA (आरोग्यशाला)

sanction, *n.* mañjurI (मञ्जुरी), swIkriti (स्वीकृति)

v. mañjurI dinu (मञ्जुरी दिनु)

sanctity, *n.* pawitratA (पवित्रता)

sanctuary, *n.* Ashraya (आश्रय), Araksha (आरक्ष)

sand, *n.* bAluwA (बालुवा)

sandal, *n.* chaTTI (चट्टी), chappal (चप्पल)

sandalwood, *n.* shrI khaND (श्रीखण्ड), chandan (चन्दन)

sandpaper, *n.* khAksI (खाक्सी)

sands, *n.* balauTe samudrI taT (बलौटे समुद्रीतट)

sandwich, *n.* syAND wIch (स्याण्डवीच)

sandy, *adj.* balauTe (बलौटे)

sane, *adj.* swasth (स्वस्थ), sadde (सट्टे)

sanitary, *adj.* swAsthyakar (स्वास्थ्यकर), sar saphAi yukta (सरसफाइयुक्त)

sanitation, *n.* sar saphAi (सरसफाइ)

sap, *n. (watery)* ras (रस), *(sticky)* chop (चोप)

v. ras sukAunu (रस सुकाउनु)

sapling, *n.* sAnu bot (सानुबोट), biruwA (बिरुवा)

sapphire, *n.* nIl maNi (नीलमणि), nIr (नीर)

sarcasm, *n.* ghoch pech (घोचपेच), wyaṅgya (व्यङ्ग्य)

sarcastic, *adj.* wyaṅgya pUrN (व्यङ्ग्यपूर्ण), Akshep yukta (आक्षेपयुक्त)

sari, *n.* sADI (साडी), dhotI (धोती)

Satan, *n.* shaitAn (शैतान)

satellite, *n.* up graha (उपग्रह), *(follower)* anuchar (अनुचर)

satin, *n.* sATan (साटन)

satire, *n.* wyaṅgyAtmak lekh/kawitA (व्यङ्ग्यात्मक लेख/कविता)

satirical, *adj.* wyaṅgya/uphAs pUrN (व्यङ्ग्य/उपहासपूर्ण)

satisfaction, *n.* santosh (सन्तोष), santushTi (सन्तुष्टि)

satisfactory, *adj.* santosh janak (सन्तोषजनक)

satisfied, *adj.* santushT (सन्तुष्ट)

satisfy, *v.* santushT pArnu (सन्तुष्ट पार्नु), chitta bujhAunu (चित्त बुझाउनु)

Saturday, *n.* shani wAr (शनिवार)

Saturn, *n.* shani graha (शनिग्रह), shanishchar (शनिश्चर)

sauce, *n.* rasdAr wyañjan (रसदार व्यञ्जन), sas (सस)

saucepan, *n.* tApke (ताप्के)

saucer, *n.* rikAbI (रिकाबी)

sausage, *n.* sasej (ससेज), pakAeko bose Andro (पकाएको बोसे आन्द्रो)

savage, *adj.* jaṅgalI (जङ्गली)

savagery, *n.* jaṅgalI pan (जङ्गलीपन), barbartA (बर्बरता)

save, *v.* bachAunu (बचाउनु), jogAunu (जोगाउनु), *(money)* sAnchnu (साँच्नु) *prep.* bAhek (बाहेक)

save one's face, *v.* ijjat bachAunu (इज्जत बचाउनु)

savings, *n.* bachat (बचत)

savio(u)r, *n.* mukti dAtA (मुक्तिदाता)

saw, *n.* karauṅtI (करौँती) *v.* kATh chirnu (काठ चिर्नु)

sawdust, *n.* kATh ko dhulo (काठको धुलो)

sawmill, *n.* kATh chhirne kAr khAnA (काठ चिर्ने कारखाना)

sawyer, *n.* kATH chirne mAnchhe (काठ चिर्ने मान्छे)

say, *v.* bhannu (भन्नु) *n.* phaisalA mA hissA (फैसलामा हिस्सा), hak (हक)

saying, *n.* AhAn (आहान), ukhAn (उखान)

scab, *n.* ghAu ko pAprA (घाउको पाप्रा)

scabbard, *n.* myAn (म्यान), dAp (दाप)

scabies, *n.* luto (लुतो)

scaffold, *n.* machAn (मचान)

scaffolding, *n.* khaT (खट), machAn (मचान)

scald, *v.* tAto pAnI wA bAph le polnu (तातो पानी वा बाफ्ले पोल्नु)

scale, n. (fish) katlA (कत्ला),
(weight) tarAju ko palarA
(तराजुको पलरा),
(measure) rular (रुलर)
v. (Mt.) chaDhnu (चढ्नु),
(measure) nApnu (नाप्नु)

scaly, adj. katlA bhaeko
(कत्ला भएको)

scan, v. dhyAn saṅga hernu
(ध्यानसँग हेर्नु)

scandal, n. bad nAm (बदनाम),
kAND (काण्ड)

scant, adj. thorai (थोरै)

scanty, adj. thorai (थोरै),
kam (कम)

scapegoat, n. arkA ko dosh
bokne(अर्काको दोष बोक्ने),
bali ko boko(बलिको बोको)

scar, n. khat (खत), dAg (दाग)
v. khat lAgnu (खत लाग्नु)

scarce, adj. apug (अपुग),
thorai (थोरै), durlabh (दुर्लभ)

scarcely, adv. muskil le
(मुस्किलले)

scarcity, n. kamI (कमी),
abhAw (अभाव)

scare, v. tarsanu (तर्सनु),
tarsAunu (तर्साउनु)
n. trAs (त्रास)

scarecrow, n. bukhyAchA
(बुख्याचा), juluṅgo (जुलुङ्गो)

scarf, n. gal bandI (गलबन्दी),
skArph (स्कार्फ)

scarlet, adj. gADhA rAto raṅg
(गाढा रातो रङ्ग)

scatter, v. chharnu (छर्नु),
chharinu (छरिनु),
(crowd) titar bitar garnu/hunu
(तितरबितर गर्नु/हुनु)

scavenger, n. (animal) sinu
khAne pashu/charA
(सिनु खाने पशु/चरा), (person)
kUchI kAr (कूचीकार),
meh tar (मेहत्तर), poDe (पोडे)

scene, n. drishya (दृश्य),
(behind the scene) adrishya
(अदृश्य),
pardA pachhADi (पर्दपछाडि)

scenery, n. prAkritik drishya
(प्राकृतिक दृश्य)

scenic, adj. ramNIya
(रमणीय)

scent, n. (odour) bAsnA
(बास्ना), gandh (गन्ध),
(essence) attar (अत्तर)
v. gandh dwArA khojI garnu
(गन्धद्वारा खोजी गर्नु)

schedule, n. samaya tAlikA
(समयतालिका), kArya kram
(कार्यक्रम), (list) sUchI (सूची)
v. sUchI banAunu (सूची
बनाउनु), kArya kram mA
samAwesh garnu (कार्यक्रममा
समावेश गर्नु)

scheduled, adj. tokieko
(तोकिएको), niyamit (नियमित)

scheme, *n.* yojanA (योजना), jukti (जुक्ति)
  v. tarkib sochnu (तरकिब सोच्नु), yojanA banAunu (योजना बनाउनु)

scholar, *n.* widwAn (विद्वान्), paNDit (पण्डित)

scholarship, *n.* chhAtra writti (छात्रवृत्ति)

school, *n.* pATh shAlA (पाठशाला), skUl (स्कूल), widyAlaya (विद्यालय), *(boarding school)* borDing skUl (बोर्डिङ स्कूल), AwAsIya widyAlaya (आवासीय विद्यालय), *(primary school)* prAthmik widyAlaya (प्राथमिक विद्यालय), *(secondary school)* mAdhyamik widyAlaya (माध्यमिक विद्यालय)

science, *n.* wigỹAn (विज्ञान), shAstra (शास्त्र)

scientific, *adj.* waigỹAnik (वैज्ञानिक)

scientist, *n.* waigỹAnik (वैज्ञानिक)

scissors, *n.* kaiñchI (कैंची)

scold, *v.* hapkAunu (हप्काउनु), jhapArnu (झपार्नु)

scoop, *n.* paniuṅ (पनिउँ), DADU (डाडु)
  v. ujhelnu (उझेल्नु),

khokro pArnu (खोक्रो पार्नु), *(journalism)* samAchAr baTuldA arU lAI uchhinnu (समाचार बटुल्दा अरूलाई उछिन्नु)

scooter, *n.* skUTar (स्कूटर)

scope, *n.* kArya kshetra (कार्यक्षेत्र), maukA (मौका)

scorch, *v.* jhurrinu (झुर्रिनु), khaharinu (खहरिनु)

score, *n. (number)* bIs Than (बीस थान), *(exam., etc.)* aṅk (अंक), *(mark)* chinha (चिन्ह)
  v. chino lAunu (चिनो लाउनु), aṅk kornu (अङ्क कोर्नु)

scorer, *n.* aṅk korne (अङ्क कोर्ने), hisAb rAkhne (हिसाब राख्ने)

scorn, *v.* hepnu (हेप्नु), helA garnu (हेला गर्नु)
  n. ghriNA (घृणा), helA (हेला)

Scorpio, *n.* wrishchik rAshi (वृश्चिक राशि)

scorpion, *n.* bichchhI (बिच्छी)

scot-free, *adj.* binA sajAya umkeko (बिनासजाय उम्केको)

scoundrel, *n.* bad mAs (बदमास)

scourge, *n. (whip)* korrA (कोर्रा), *(affliction)* mahA mArI (महामारी)
  v. korrA hAnnu (कोर्रा हान्नु), pIDA dinu (पीडा दिनु)

scout, *n.* bAl char (बालचर), skAuT (स्काउट)

scramble, *v.* muskil le uklanu (मुस्किले उक्लनु)
n. ghisrAi (घिस्राइ)

scrape, *v.* khurkanu (खुर्कनु), tAchhnu (ताछ्नु)
n. khurkane kAm (खुर्कने काम)

scraps, *n.* *(food)* juTho purA (जुठो पुरा), *(bits)* kAgaj kA TukrA (कागजका टुक्रा), TAlA TulI (टालाटुली)

scratch, *n.* *(med.)* ghau (घाउ), *(athletics)* prasthAn rekhA (प्रस्थान रेखा), *(from scratch)* shuru dekhi (शुरुदेखि)
v. kornu (कोर्नु), koparnu (कोपर्नु)

scream, *n.* chichyAhaT (चिच्याहट)
v. chichyAunu (चिच्याउनु)

screen, *n.* pardA (पर्दा)
v. lukAunu (लुकाउनु)

screw, *n.* pech (पेच)
v. pech kasnu (पेच कस्नु), *(twist)* nimoThnu (निमोठ्नु)

screwdriver, *n.* pech kas (पेचकस), mArtol (मार्तोल)

script, *n.* lipi (लिपि), hast lipi (हस्तलिपि)

scripture, *n.* dharm granth (धर्मग्रन्थ)

scrub, *v.* dalera saphA garnu (दलेर सफा गर्नु)

scrutinize, *v.* dhyAn saṅga jAnchnu (ध्यानसँग जाँच्नु)

scrutiny, *n.* sUksham parIkshaN (सूक्ष्म परीक्षण), *(exam.)* sam parIkshaN (सम्परीक्षण)

scuffle, *n.* jhagaDA (झगडा), bhiDant (भिडन्त)
v. jhagaDA garnu (झगडा गर्नु)

sculptor, *n.* mUrti kAr (मूर्तिकार)

sculpture, *n.* mUrti kalA (मूर्तिकला)

scurf, *n.* chAyA (चाया)

scythe, *n.* haṅsiyA (हँसिया)

sea, *n.* samudra (समुद्र), sAgar (सागर)

sea beach, *n.* samudrI taT (समुद्रीतट)

seafarer, *n.* samudrI yAtrI (समुद्री यात्री)

seafood, *n.* samudrI khAnA (समुद्री खाना)

seal, *n.* *(stamp)* chhAp (छाप), nishAnA (निशाना), *(animal)* sIl (सील)
v. sil mArnu (सिल मार्नु), chhAp lAunu (छाप लाउनु), *(close)* band garnu (बन्द गर्नु), TAlnu (टाल्नु)

sea level, *n.* samudrI sataha (समुद्री सतह)

sealing wax, *n.* lAhA (लाहा)

seal of love, *n.* chumban
(चुम्बन)

seal off, *v.* bATo band garnu
(बाटो बन्द गर्नु)

seam, *n.* kapaDA ko jornI
(कपडाको जोर्नी), siunI(सिउनी)

seamster, *n.* darjI (दर्जी),
damAI (दमाई)

seamstress, *n.* darjinI
(दर्जिनी), daminI (दमिनी)

seaport, *n.* bandar gAh
(बन्दरगाह),
samudrI ghAT (समुद्री घाट)

search, *n.* khoj talAsh
(खोजतलाश),
khAn talAshI (खानतलाशी)
v. khojnu (खोज्नु)

search party, *n.* khojI dal
(खोजी दल)

search warrant, *n.* khAn
talAsh garne adAlatI Adesh
(खान तलाश गर्ने अदालती
आदेश)

seashore, *n.* samudrI kinAr
(समुद्री किनार)

seasickness, *n.* samudrI
bimArI (समुद्री बिमारी),
wAk wAk (वाकवाक)

season, *n.* ritu (ऋतु),
mausam (मौसम)
v. pAko banAunu
(पाको बनाउनु)

seasonal, *adj.* mausamI
(मौसमी),
samayochit (समयोचित)

seasoned, *adj.* pAko (पाको),
chhippieko (छिप्पिएको)

seat, *n.* basne ThAuñ (बस्ने
ठाउँ), *(chair)* mech (मेच),
kursI (कुर्सी)
v. basAlnu (बसाल्नु)

seaweed, *n.* samudrI jhAr
(समुद्री झार)

seclusion, *n.* ekAnt bAs
(एकान्तबास)

second, *n.* dosro mAnchhe
(दोस्रो मान्छे),
(time) sekeND (सेकेण्ड)
adj. dosro (दोस्रो)
v. samarthan garnu
(समर्थन गर्नु)

second best, *adj.* dosro
sarwottam (दोस्रो सर्वोत्तम)

second fiddle, *n.* dosro sthAn
(दोस्रो स्थान)

second-hand, *adj.* purAno
(पुरानो), jaDaurI (जडौरी)

second thought, *n.* nayAñ
wichAr (नयाँ विचार)

secrecy, *n.* gopnIyatA
(गोपनीयता)

secret, *n.* gupti kurA(गुप्ति कुरा)
adj. gopya (गोप्य), gupt (गुप्त)

secretariat, sachiwAlaya
(सचिवालय)

secretary, *n.* sachiw (सचिव), secreTarI (सेक्रेटरी)

Secretary General, *n.* mahA sachiw (महासचिव)

secretly, *adv.* gupt Dhang le (गुप्त ढङ्गले)

secret police, *n.* gupt pulis (गुप्त पुलिस)

secret service, *n.* gupti sewA (गुप्ति सेवा), jAsUsI kAm (जासूसी काम)

sect, *n.* sampradAya (सम्प्रदाय), matAwlambI (मतावलम्बी)

section. *n.* (branch) shAkhA (शाखा), khaND (खण्ड), (law, etc.) dhArA (धारा), daphA(दफा)

sector, *n.* kshetra (क्षेत्र), (*private sector*) nijI kshetra (निजी क्षेत्र), (*public sector*) sArwjanik kshetra (सार्वजनिक क्षेत्र)

secular, *adj.* dharm nirapeksha (धर्मनिरपेक्ष)

secure, *v.* surakshit garAunu (सुरक्षित गराउनु) *adj.* surakshit (सुरक्षित), nishank (निशङ्क)

security, *n.* surakshA (सुरक्षा), (*guarantee*) jamAnI (जमानी)

sediment, *n.* thegro (थेग्रो), kasar (कसर)

sedition, *n.* rAj droh (राजद्रोह)

seduce, *v.* bahakAunu (बहकाउनु), charitra nashT garnu (चरित्र नष्ट गर्नु)

seduction, *n.* satItwa nAsh (सतीत्व नाश), bahakAu (बहकाउ)

see, *v.* hernu (हेर्नु), dekhnu (देख्नु), (*visit*) bheTnu (भेट्नु), (*understand*) bujhnu (बुझ्नु), (*find out*) pattA lAunu (पत्ता लाउनु)

seed, *n.* bIu (बीउ), bijan (बिजन) *v.* bIu chharnu (बीउ छर्नु)

seedling, *n.* bernA (बेर्ना), biruwA (बिरुवा)

seek, *v.* khojnu (खोज्नु)

seem, *v.* dekhinu (देखिनु), lAgnu (लाग्नु)

seemingly, *adv.* dekhdA (देख्दा), herdA (हेर्दा)

seemly, *adj.* sushIl (सुशील), shishT (शिष्ट)

see off, *v.* puryAuna jAnu (पुर्‍याउन जानु)

see red, *v.* jyAdai risAunu (ज्यादै रिसाउनु)

seesaw, *n.* Dhiki chyAun khel (ढिकिच्याउँ खेल)

see-through, *adj.* pAr darshak (पारदर्शक)

see to, *v.* dhyAn rAkhnu (ध्यान राख्नु), marammat garnu (मर्म्मत गर्नु)

segment, n. khaND (खण्ड)

seize, v. samAtnu (समात्नु),
pakranu (पक्रनु)

seizure, n. pakaD (पकड),
giraphtArI (गिरफ्तारी)

seldom, adv. kahile kAhiǹ
mAtrai (कहिलेकाहीं मात्रै),
wirlai (विरलै)

select, v. chhAnnu (छान्नु),
chunnu (चुन्नु), rojnu (रोज्नु)

selection, n. chhanoT
(छनोट), chunAu (चुनाउ)

self, n. Aphu (आफु),
Aphai (आफै)

self-abuse, n. hast maithun
(हस्तमैथुन)

self-confident, adj. Atma
wishwAsI (आत्मविश्वासी)

self-conscious, adj. (shy)
sañkochI (सङ्कोची), (phil.)
Atma chetan (आत्मचेतन)

self-control, n. Atma
niyantraN (आत्मनियन्त्रण)

self-determination, n. Atma
nirNaya (आत्मनिर्णय)

self-evident, adj. swayaṃ
siddha (स्वयंसिद्ध)

self-help, n. swAwlamban
(स्वावलम्बन)

self-indulgent, adj. wilAsI
(विलासी), shokhI (शोखी)

self-interest, n. swArth (स्वार्थ)

selfish, adj. swArthI (स्वार्थी),

matlabI (मतलबी)

selfishness, n. swArth (स्वार्थ)

selfless, adj. nisswArth
(निस्स्वार्थ)

self-made, adj. Aphai baneko
(आफै बनेको)

self-possessed, adj. dhairya
wAn (धैर्यवान)

self-reliant, adj. Atma nirbhar
(आत्मनिर्भर),
swAwlambI (स्वावलम्बी)

self-respect, n. Atma sammAn
(आत्मसम्मान)

self-sacrifice, n. Atma balidan
(आत्म बलिदान)

self-sufficient, adj. Atma
nirbhar (आत्मनिर्भर)

sell, v. bechnu (बेच्नु)

seller, n. wikretA (विक्रेता),
bech bikhan garne
(बेचबिखन गर्ने)

sell off, v. kam dAm mA
bAñkI mAl bechnu
(कम दाममा बाँकी माल बेच्नु)

sell out, v. (thing) bechi dinu
(बेचिदिनु), (person)
dhokhA dinu (धोका दिनु)

semen, n. wIrya (वीर्य),
shukra (शुक्र)

semester, n. satra (सत्र),
semesTar (सेमेस्टर)

semicircle, n. AdhA writta
(आधा वृत्त)

seminar, *n.* goshThI (गोष्ठी), seminAr (सेमिनार)

senate, *n.* sineT (सिनेट), rAjya sabhA (राज्यसभा)

senator, *n.* sineTar (सिनेटर)

send, *v.* paThAunu (पठाउनु)

send for, *v.* (person) bolAuna paThAunu (बोलाउन पठाउनु), (thing) magAunu (मगाउनु)

send off, *v.* bidA garnu (बिदा गर्नु)

senior, *adj.* jeTho (जेठो), Thulo (ठूलो), warishTh (वरिष्ठ)

sensation, *n.* sansanI (सनसनी), halchal (हलचल)

sensational, *adj.* sansanI pUrN (सनसनीपूर्ण)

sense, *n.* gỹAn (ज्ञान), akkal (अक्कल), buddhi (बुद्धि), **(come to one's senses)** hosh mA Aunu (होशमा आउनु), **(lose one's senses)** hosh gumAunu (होश गुमाउनु) *v.* thAhA pAunu (थाहा पाउनु), bujhnu (बुझ्नु)

senseless, *adj.* mUrkh (मूर्ख), (med.) behosh (बेहोश)

sensible, *adj.* samajh dAr (समझदार), manAsib (मनासिब)

sensitive, *adj.* saṃwedan shIl (संवेदनशील), bhAwuk (भावुक)

sentence, *n.* wAkya (वाक्य), (law) daND (दण्ड), sajAya (सजाय)

sentiment, *n.* bhAwanA (भावना), bhAw (भाव)

sentimental, *adj.* bhAwuk (भावुक)

sentinel, *n.* chapaTe (चपटे), pAle (पाले)

sentry, *n.* chapaTe (चपटे), pAle (पाले)

separate, *adj.* alag (अलग), chhuTTai (छुट्टै), beglai (बेग्लै) *v.* alag garnu (अलग गर्नु), chhuTyAunu (छुट्याउनु)

separately, *adv.* beglA beglai (बेग्लाबेग्लै)

separation, *n.* bichhoD (बिछोड), bichchhed (विच्छेद)

sequence, *n.* kram (क्रम), silsilA (सिलसिला)

serene, *adj.* shAnt (शान्त), gambhIr (गम्भीर)

serial, *n./adj.* dhArA wAhik (धारावाहिक)

series, *n.* shreNI (श्रेणी), kram (क्रम)

serious, *adj.* gambhIr (गम्भीर), mahattwa pUrN (महत्त्वपूर्ण), sAñchchi ko (साँच्चिको), (med.) sikista (सिकिस्त)

serpent, *n.* sarpa (सर्प)

servant, *n.* nokar (नोकर)

serve, *v.* sewA/nokarI garnu (सेवा/नोकरी गर्नु), *(food)* paskanu (पस्कनु), *(game)* sarbh garnu (सर्भ गर्नु)

service, *n.* sewA (सेवा), nokarI (नोकरी), jAgir (जागिर) *v.* her chAh/mar marmat garnu (हेरचाह/मर्मर्मत गर्नु)

servicing, *n.* mar marmat (मरमर्मत), her chAh (हेरचाह)

sesame, *n.* til (तिल)

session, *n.* satra (सत्र), baiThak (बैठक)

set, *n.* seT (सेट), samUha (समूह), *(habit)* bAnI (बानी) *v.* ThIk garnu (ठीक गर्नु), *(mus.)* dhun milAunu (धुन मिलाउनु), *(gems)* jaDnu (जड्नु), basAlnu (बसाल्नु), nishchit garnu (निश्चित गर्नु), *(sun, moon)* astAunu (अस्ताउनु) *adj.* astAeko (अस्ताएको), ast (अस्त)

set about, *v.* shuru garnu (शुरु गर्नु)

set an example, *v.* udAharaN dekhAunu (उदाहरण देखाउनु)

setback, *n.* nirAshA (निराशा), dhakkA (धक्का)

set eyes on, *v.* dekhnu (देख्नु), AňkhA gADnu (आँखा गाड्नु)

set forth, *v.* prasthAn garnu (प्रस्थान गर्नु), rawAnA hunu (रवाना हुनु)

set off, *v.* prasthAn garnu (प्रस्थान गर्नु), prawritta garnu (प्रवृत गर्नु)

set out, *v.* prasthAn garnu (प्रस्थान गर्नु), *(show)* pradarshit garnu (प्रदर्शित गर्नु)

settle, *v. (live)* basobAs garnu (बसोबास गर्नु), *(decide)* chhinA phAnA garnu (छिनाफाना गर्नु), *(debts)* chuktA garnu (चुक्ता गर्नु)

settlement, *n.* bastI (बस्ती), AbAdI (आबादी), chhinA phAnA (छिनाफाना), *(debts)* chuktA (चुक्ता), *(dispute)* Tuňgo (टुङ्गो), pharsyoT (फर्स्योट)

settler, *n.* nayAň bastI mA basne (नयाँ बस्तीमा बस्ने)

set-up, *n.* wyawasthA (व्यवस्था), DhAňchA (ढाँचा)

set upon, *v.* AkramaN garnu (आक्रमण गर्नु), AkramaN garna lagAunu (आक्रमण गर्न लगाउनु)

seven, *n.* sAt (सात)

seventeen, *n.* satra (सत्र)

seventeenth, *n./adj.* satrauň (सत्रौं)

seventh, *n./adj.* sAtauň (सातौं)

seventy, n. sattarI (सत्तरी)

sever, v. alag/wichchhed garnu (अलग/विच्छेद गर्नु)

several, adj. dherai (धेरै), kati paya (कतिपय)

severe, adj. kaDA (कडा), kaThor (कठोर)

sew, v. siunu (सिउनु), silAunu (सिलाउनु)

sewing machine, n. siune kal (सिउने कल)

sewer, n. Dhal (ढल), nAl (नाल)

sex, n. liṅg (लिङ्ग)

sex appeal, n. yaunAkarshaN (यौनाकर्षण)

sexy, adj. kAmuk (कामुक), kAmottejak (कामोत्तेजक)

shackle, n. hat kaDI (हतकडी), bandhan (बन्धन)
v. hat kaDI lAunu (हतकडी लाउनु)

shade, n. chhAyA (छाया), chhahArI (छहारी), (paint) raṅg (रङ्ग)
v. chhAya pArnu (छाया पार्नु)

shadow, n. chhAya (छाया), pratiwimb (प्रतिविम्ब)
v. (things) chhAyA pArnu (छाया पार्नु),
(person) pichhA/chiyo garnu (पिछा/चियो गर्नु)

shady, adj. chhAyA dAr (छायादार)

shaft, n. DaNDA (डण्डा), DAṅTh (डाँठ)

shake, v. hallAunu (हल्लाउनु), hallanu (हल्लनु)

shake down, v. jhArnu (झार्नु), khasAlnu (खसाल्नु)

shake hands, v. hAt milAunu (हात मिलाउनु)

shake off, v. piND chhuTAunu (पिण्ड छुटाउनु)

shake-out, n. hal chal (हलचल)

shake-up, n. halchal (हलचल)

shaky, adj. chañchal (चञ्चल), dhar marAune (धरमराउने)

shall, mod. lA (ला), lI (ली), (pl) lAn (लान्), lin (लिन्)

shallow, adj. kam gahiro (कम गहिरो)

sham, adj. nakkalI (नक्कली), jhuTTo (झुट्टो)
v. nakal/swAṅ pArnu (नकल/स्वाङ पार्नु)

shame, n. lAj (लाज), lajjA (लज्जा), sharm (शर्म)

shamefaced, adj. lajjAlu (लज्जालु)

shameless, adj. nirlajja (निर्लज्ज), nakachcharo (नकच्चरो)

shampoo, n. syAmpU (स्याम्पू), jhol sAbun (झोल साबुन)

shape, *n.* AkAr (आकार),
chhAŇT kAŇT (छाँटकाँट),
rUp (रूप)
v. AkAr dinu (आकार दिनु),
DhAlnu (ढाल्नु)

shapely, *adj.* rUp watI
(रूपवती), suDaul (सुडौल)

share, *n.* amsh (अंश),
hissA (हिस्सा), sheyar (शेयर),
(lion's share) ThUlo bhAg
(ठूलो भाग)
v. bhAg lagAunu (भाग लगाउनु),
sAjhA garnu (साभा गर्नु)

shareholder, *n.* sAjhe dAr
(साभेदार),
sheyar wAlA (शेयरवाला)

sharp, *adj. (point)* tIkho
(तीखो), **(blade)** dhArilo
(धारिलो), *(person)* tej (तेज),
(time) Thik (ठिक)

sharpen, *v.* tikhArnu (तिखार्नु),
dhAr lAunu (धार लाउनु)

sharply, *adv.* tej le (तेजले)

shatter, *v.* phuTAunu
(फुटाउनु), phornu (फोर्नु)

shave, *n.* khaurAi (खौराइ),
muNDan (मुण्डन)
v. khauranu (खौरनु),
muNDan garnu (मुण्डन गर्नु)

shawl, *n.* pachhyaurA
(पछ्यौरा), oDhne (ओढ्ने),
dosallA (दोसल्ला)

she, *pron.* U (ऊ), unI (उनी),

tinI (तिनी), un le (उनले)

sheath, *n.* khol (खोल), dAp (दाप)

shed, *n.* kaTero (कटेरो),
chhApro (छाप्रो), **(cowshed)**
gAI goTh (गाईगोठ)
v. jhArnu (भार्नु),
khasAlnu (खसाल्नु)

sheep, *n.* bheDA (भेडा)

sheepish, *adj.* lajjAlu (लज्जालु),
sharmAune (शर्माउने)

sheet, *n. (bed)* tannA (तन्ना),
(paper) pAnA (पाना),
(steel) pATA (पाता)

shelf, *n.* takhtA (तखता),
darAj (दराज),
(wall) khopA (खोपा)

shelter, *n.* sharaN (शरण),
Ashraya (आश्रय)
v. sharaN dinu (शरण दिनु)

shepherd, *n.* bheDA goThAlo
(भेडागोठालो)

shield, *n.* DhAl (ढाल)
v. rakshA garnu (रक्षा गर्नु),
bachAunu (बचाउनु)

shift, *n.* sATo (साटो), pAlo (पालो)
v. sarnu (सर्नु), sArnu (सार्नु)

shin, *n.* nali hAD (नलिहाड)

shine, *n.* chamak (चमक),
prakAsh (प्रकाश)
v. chamkanu (चम्कनु),
Talkanu (टल्कनु)

shining, *adj.* chamkilo
(चम्किलो), ujyAlo (उज्यालो)

ship, *n.* jahAj (जहाज), pAnI jahAj (पानीजहाज)
v. jahAj mA paThAunu (जहाजमा पठाउनु)

shipment, *n.* jahAj mA chalAn garieko mAl (जहाजमा चलान गरिएको माल)

shirt, *n.* kamij (कमिज), kurtA (कुर्ता), labedA (लबेदा)

shiver, *n.* kampan (कम्पन),
v. kAmnu (काम्नु), thatharAunu (थरथराउनु)

shock, *n.* dhakkA (धक्का), AghAt (आघात),
(electric shock) kareNT lAgnu (करेन्ट लाग्नु)
v. dhakkA lAgnu (धक्का लाग्नु)

shocking, *adj.* choT puryAune (चोट पुर्‍याउने)

shoe, *n.* juttA (जुत्ता)

shoehorn, *n.* baglis (बगलिस)

shoelace, *n.* juttA ko phittA (जुत्ताको फित्ता)

shoemaker, *n.* sArkI (सार्की)

shoestring, *n.* juttA ko phittA (जुत्ताको फित्ता)

shoot, *n.* TusA (टुसा), munA (मुना), aṅkur (अँकुर)
v. golI/wAN hAnnu (गोली/वाण हान्नु)

shooting, *n.* banduk wA pistol hAnne kAm (बन्दुक वा पिस्तोल हान्ने काम)

shooting star, *n.* sAno ulkA (सानो उल्का)

shop, *n.* pasal (पसल), dokAn (दोकान)
v. kin mel garnu (किनमेल गर्नु), mAl kinnu (माल किन्नु)

shopkeeper, *n.* pasale (पसले), sAhujI (साहुजी)

shopping, *n.* kin mel (किनमेल)

shore, *n.* bagar (बगर), kinArA (किनारा)

short, *adj.* chhoTo (छोटो), puDko (पुड्को), hocho (होचो), *(supply)* kam (कम)

shortage, *n.* kamI (कमी), abhAw (अभाव)

shortcoming, *n.* kam jorI (कमजोरी), dosh (दोष)

shortcut, *n.* chhoto bATo (छोटो बाटो)

shorten, *v.* chhoTo pArnu (छोटो पार्नु), chhoTyAunu (छोट्याउनु)

shortfall, *n.* ghATA (घाटा), kamI (कमी)

shorthand, *n.* chhiTo lekhne widhi (छिटो लेख्ने विधि), sharT hyAND (शर्टह्‍याण्ड)

short-lived, *adj.* chhoTo jIwan bhaeko (छोटो जीवन भएको), alp jIwI (अल्पजीवी)

shortly, *adv.* chAñDai (चाँडै), chhiTai nai (छिटै नै)

short of, *prep.* siwAya (सिवाय)

shorts, *n.* kaTTu (कट्टु)

short-sighted, *adj.* nikaT
  darshI (निकटदर्शी),
  adUr darshI (अदूरदर्शी)

short-tempered, *adj.* chAñDai
  risAune (चाँडै रिसाउने)

short-term, *adj.* alp kAlik
  (अल्पकालिक)

short-witted, *adj.* mUrkh
  (मूर्ख), alp buddhi (अल्पबुद्धि)

shot, *n.* golI (गोली), top golA
  (तोपगोला), chharrA (छर्रा),
  (sports) hirkAi (हिर्काइ),
  shaT (शट)

shotgun, *n.* banduk (बन्दुक)

should, *v./mod.* parchha (पर्छ)

shoulder, *n.* kum (कुम),
  kAñdh (काँध)
  v. bhAr uThAunu
  (भार उठाउनु), boknu (बोक्नु)

shout, *v.* karAunu (कराउनु),
  kurlinu (कुर्लिनु)
  n. DAñko (डाँको)

shove, *v.* ghacheTnu (घचेट्नु),
  dhakkA dinu (धक्का दिनु)

shovel, *n.* sAbhel (साभेल),
  khanitro (खनित्रो)

show, *n.* ramitA (रमिता),
  tamAshA (तमाशा),
  pradarshanI (प्रदर्शनी)
  v. dekhAunu (देखाउनु),
  pradarshan garnu (प्रदर्शन गर्नु)

show off, *v.* rabAph
  dekhAunu (रबाफ देखाउनु)

shower, *n.* jharI (झरी),
  warshA (वर्षा),
  (bath) snAn (स्नान)
  v. panI parnu (पानी पर्नु),
  barsanu (बर्सनु),
  nuhAunu (नुहाउनु)

showy, *adj.* dekhAwaTI
  (देखावटी)

shred, *n.* tyAndro (त्यान्द्रो),
  dhujA (धुजा)
  v. dhujA pArnu (धुजा पार्नु)

shrew, *n. (woman)* karkash
  nArI (कर्कश नारी), *(animal)*
  chhuchundro (छुचुन्द्रो)

shrewd, *adj.* chalAkh
  (चलाख), dhUrt (धूर्त)

shriek, *n.* chichyAhaT
  (चिच्याहट)
  v. chichyAunu (चिच्याउनु)

shrill, *adj.* karkash (कर्कश),
  tIkho (तीखो)
  v. tIkho awAj le bolnu
  (तीखो आवाजले बोल्नु)

shrine, *n.* tIrth (तीर्थ),
  dhAm (धाम), mandir (मन्दिर)

shrink, *v.* khumchinu
  (खुम्चिनु), ghaTnu (घट्नु)

shroud, *n.* kAtro (कात्रो),
  AwraN (आवरण)
  v. kAtro bernu (कात्रो बेर्नु),
  DhAknu (ढाक्नु)

shrug, *v.* kAňdh khum-
chyAunu (काँध खुम्च्याउनु)

shudder, *v.* Dar le kAmnu
(डरले काम्नु)
n. Dar (डर), trAs (त्रास)

shuffle, *v.* khuTTA ghisArera
hiňDnu (खुट्टा घिसारेर हिँड्नु),
(cards) phiňTnu (फिँट्नु)

shun, *v.* TADha rahanu
(टाढा रहनु), tyAgnu (त्याग्नु)

shut, *v.* band garnu
(बन्द गर्नु), thunnu (थुन्नु)

shut down, *v. (door, work,*
computer) band garnu
(बन्द गर्नु)

shut off, *v.* prawAh band
garidinu (प्रवाह बन्द गरिदिनु)

shut up, *v.* thunnu (थुन्नु),
(imp., coll.) chup lAg (चुप लाग)

shutter, *n.* saTar (सटर),
(window) jhil mil (झिलमिल)

shy, *adj.* lajjAlu (लज्जालु),
kAtar (कातर)

sick, *adj.* birAmI (बिरामी),
rogI (रोगी)

sickle *n.* haňsiyA (हँसिया)

sickness, *n.* bimArI (बिमारी),
rog (रोग)

side, *n.* kinarA (किनारा),
chheu (छेउ)
v. paksha linu (पक्ष लिनु)

side by side, *adv.* saňg saňgai
(सँगसँगै)

sideshow, *n.* mUl bhandA
pharak tamAsha wA khel
(मूलभन्दा फरक तमाशा वा खेल)

sidewalk, *n.* peTI (पेटी)

sideways, *adv.* bagal tira
(बगलतिर)

siege, *n.* gherA (घेरा)
v. ghernu (घेर्नु),
gherA hAlnu (घेरा हाल्नु)

sieve, *n.* chalnI (चल्नी)
v. (sift) chAlnu (चाल्नु),
chhAnnu (छान्नु)

sigh, *n.* Ah (आह),
uchchh wAs (उच्छ्वास)
v. lAmo sAs phernu
(लामो सास फेर्नु)

sight, *n.* herAi (हेराइ), drishTi
(दृष्टि), drishya (दृश्य),
(at first sight) pahilo herAi
mA (पहिलो हेराइमा),
(on sight) dekhnA sAth
(देख्नासाथ), *(out of sight)* na
dekhine (नदेखिने)
v. dekhnu (देख्नु), hernu (हेर्नु)

sightless, *adj.* andho (अन्धो)

sightseer, *n.* paryaTak (पर्यटक)

sign, *n.* isArA (इसारा), saňket
(सङ्केत), chinha (चिन्ह),
sakun (सकुन),
(symbol) pratIk (प्रतीक),
hastAkshar (हस्ताक्षर)
v. sahI/hastAkshar garnu
(सही/हस्ताक्षर गर्नु)

signal, *n.* saṅket (सङ्केत)
   v. saṅket garnu (सङ्केत गर्नु)

signature, *n.* sahI (सही),
   hastAkshar (हस्ताक्षर)

signature tune, *n.* reDio Adi
   shuru hunu aghi bajAine
   dhun (रेडियो आदि शुरु हुनु
   अघि बजाइने धुन)

signboard, *n.* sUchanA pATI
   (सूचनापाटी),
   sAin borD (साइनबोर्ड)

significance, *n.* mahattwa
   (महत्त्व)

signficant, *adj.* mahattwa
   pUrN (महत्त्वपूर्ण)

signify, *v.* janAunu
   (जनाउनु),
   sUchit garnu (सूचित गर्नु)

silence, *n.* chup chAp
   (चुपचाप), maun (मौन)

silent, *adj.* chup lAgeko
   (चुप लागेको), maun (मौन),
   khAmosh (खामोश)

silently, *adv.* chup lAgera
   (चुप लागेर),
   chup chAp (चुपचाप)

silk, *n.* resham (रेशम)

silkworm, *n.* resham kIrA
   (रेशमकीरा)

silky, *adj.* naram (नरम),
   resham jasto (रेशमजस्तो)

silly, *adj.* sillI (सिल्ली),
   laThuwA (लठुवा)

silver, *n.* chAṅdI (चाँदी)
   adj. chAṅdI ko (चाँदीको)

silvery, *adj.* chAṅdI jasto seto
   (चाँदीजस्तो सेतो)

similar, *adj.* ustai (उस्तै),
   samAn (समान)

similarly, *adv.* tyasai garI
   (त्यसैगरी)

simmer, *v.* wistArai umlanu
   (विस्तारै उम्लनु),
   (fig.) bhitra bhitrai gumsanu
   (भित्रभित्रै गुम्सनु)

simmer down, *v.* kam uttejit
   hunu (कम उत्तेजित हुनु)

simple, *adj.* sajilo (सजिलो),
   sojho (सोझो)

simpleton, *n.* mUrkh (मूर्ख),
   bekuph (बेकुफ)

simply, *adv.* khAli (खाली),
   kewal (केवल)

simultaneously, *adv.* ekai
   choTi (एकैचोटि)

sin, *n.* pAp (पाप)
   v. pAp garnu (पाप गर्नु)

since, *adv.* tyas belA dekhi
   (त्यस बेलादेखि)
   prep. bATa (बाट),
   pachhi (पछि)
   conj. kina bhane (किनभने)

sincere, *adj.* sAṅcho (साँचो),
   imAn dAr (इमान्दार)

sincerely, *adv.* shuddha
   man le (शुद्ध मनले)

sine die, *adv.* anishchit kAl
samma (अनिश्चित कालसम्म)

sine qua non, *n.* aniwArya
shart (अनिवार्य शर्त)

sinew, *n.* nasA (नसा)

sinewy, *adj.* gaThilo (गठिलो)

sinful, *adj.* pApI (पापी)

sing, *v.* gAunu (गाउनु)

singe, *v.* polnu (पोल्नु),
khaharyAunu (खह्‌र्याउनु)

singer, *n.* gawaiyA (गवैया),
gAyak (गायक),
(fem.) gAyikA (गायिका)

single, *adj.* eklo (एक्लो),
kumAr (कुमार)
n. (number) ek (एक),
(sports) ekal khel (एकल खेल)

single-handed, *adj./adv.* eklai
le (एक्लै ले), eklai (एक्लै)

single-minded, *adj.* ek nishTh
(एकनिष्ठ)

singleton, *adj.* euTai
(एउटै), eklo (एक्लो)

sinister, *adj.* anishT
(अनिष्ट), dushT (दुष्ट)

sink, Dubnu (डुब्नु),
DubAunu (डुबाउनु), bhAsinu
(भासिनु), khasnu (खस्नु),
(sun) Dubnu (डुब्नु),
Dhlnu (ढल्नु)

sinner, *n.* pApI (पापी)

sinus infection, *n.* pinAs
(पिनास)

sir, *n.* sAheb (साहेब), sar (सर),
mahA shaya (महाशय),

sister, *n. (elder)* didI (दिदी),
(younger) bahinI (बहिनी)

sister-in-law, *n. (elder
brother's wife)* bhAujU
(भाउजू), *(younger brother's
wife)* buhArI (बुहारी),
*(huband's elder brother's
wife)* jeThAnI (जेठानी),
*(husband's younger brother's
wife)* deurAnI (देउरानी),
(wife's elder sister) jeThI
sAsU (जेठीसासू), *(wife's
younger sister)* sAlI (साली)

sit, *v.* basnu (बस्नु), *(sit cross-
legged)* palenTI mArera
basnu (पलेंटी मारेर बस्नु)
(sit on one's heels)
Tukrukka basnu (टुक्रुक्क
बस्नु)

site, *n.* kAm hune ThAuň
(काम हुने ठाउँ),
nirmAN sthal (निर्माणस्थल)

sit tight, *v.* aDAn linu (अडान
लिनु), na galnu (नगल्नु)

situation, *n.* sthiti (स्थिति),
paristhiti (परिस्थिति),
(job) nokarI (नोकरी),
jAgir (जागिर)

six, *n.* chha (छ)

sixteen, *n.* sorha (सोह्र)

sixth, *n./adj.* chhaiTauň (छैटौँ)

sixty, *n.* sAThI (साठी)

size, *n.* nAp (नाप), AkAr
(आकार), *(stature)* DAl (डाल)

skeleton, *n.* kaṅkAl (कङ्काल),
asthi panjar (अस्थिपन्जर)

skeleton key, *n.* dherai tAlchA
mA milne sAÑcho (धेरै
तालचामा मिल्ने साँचो)

sketch, *n.* hAt le banAeko
chitra (हातले बनाएको चित्र),
(map) naksA (नक्सा),
nAp naksA (नापनक्सा)
v. chitra banAunu
(चित्र बनाउनु)

skill, *n.* sIp (सीप),
kaushal (कौशल)

skilled, *adj.* sipAlu (सिपालु),
kushal (कुशल)

skim, *v. (milk)* tar jhiknu
(तर झिक्नु), *(pass over)*
mAthi bATa niskanu/bahanu
(माथिबाट निस्कनु/बहनु),
(book, etc.) sarsartI paDhnu
(सरसर्ती पढ्नु)

skim(med) milk, *n.* tar jhikeko
dUdh (तर झिकेको दूध)

skin, *n.* chhAlA (छाला),
(hide) chhAlA (छाला),
(fruit) bokrA (बोक्रा)
v. chhAlA kADhnu
(छाला काढ्नु)

skip, *v.* burukka uphranu
(बुरुक्क उफ्रनु)

skirmish, *n.* bhiDant
(भिडन्त), laDAiṅ (लडाई)
v. bhiDant garnu (भिडन्त गर्नु)

skirt, *n.* skarT (स्कर्ट), jAmA (जामा)
v. chheu chheu jAnu
(छेउ छेउ जानु)

skull, *n.* khopaDI (खोपडी),
khappar (खप्पर)

sky, *n.* AkAsh (आकाश)
v. akAsinu (अकासिनु)

sky-blue, *adj.* AkAshe nIlo
(आकाशे नीलो)

skyjack, *v.* wimAn ap haraN
garnu (विमान अपहरण गर्नु)

skyline, *n.* kshitij (क्षितिज)

skyscraper, *n.* gagan chumbI
bhawan (गगनचुम्बी भवन)

slab, *n.* shilA (शिला), paTTI (पट्टी)

slack, *adj.* phitalo (फितलो),
khukulo (खुकुलो),
mand (मन्द), sust (सुस्त)
n. DhilAi (ढिलाइ), mandI (मन्दी)

slacks, *n.* khukulo
patlun/pAijAmA (खुकुलो
पतलुन/पाइजामा)

slam, *v.* bajArnu (बजार्नु),
(door) DhyAmma lAunu
(ध्याम्म लाउनु)

slander, *n.* Arop (आरोप),
bad nAm (बदनाम)
v. jhUTA Arop lAunu
(भूटा आरोप लाउनु),
bad nAm garnu (बदनाम गर्नु)

slang, *n.* ap bhAshA
(अपभाषा), nimn star ko
bhAshA (निम्नस्तरको भाषा)

slant, *adj.* terso (तेर्सो),
chhaDke (छड्के)
v. tersinu (तेर्सिनु)

slap, *n.* thappaD (थप्पड),
jhApaD (झापड),
chapeTA (चपेटा)
v. thappaD hAnnu
(थप्पड हान्नु),
chaDkAunu (चड्काउनु)

slash, *v.* chirnu (चिर्नु),
kATnu (काट्नु), *(lash)* korrA
hAnnu (कोर्रा हान्नु)
n. kATeko ghAu (काटेको घाउ)

slate, *n.* siloT (सिलोट),
pATI (पाटी),
(tile) sleT pAta (स्लेट पाता)
v. sleT le DhAknu (स्लेटले
ढाक्नु), *(fig.)* gAlI garnu
(गाली गर्नु), AlochanA garnu
(आलोचना गर्नु)

slaughter, *v.* kATnu (काट्नु),
chhapkAunu (छप्काउनु)
n. hatyA (हत्या)

slave, *n.* dAs (दास),
kamArA (कमारा)

slavery, *n.* dAstA (दासता),
gulAmI (गुलामी)

slay, *v.* mArnu (मार्नु),
hatyA garnu (हत्या गर्नु)

sledgehammer, *n.* ThUlo ghan

(ठूलो घन)

sleek, *adj. (hair, skin)* chiplo
(चिप्लो), naram (नरम), *(body)*
moTA tAjA (मोटाताजा)

sleep, *v.* sutnu (सुत्नु),
nidAunu (निदाउनु)
n. nidrA (निद्रा),
(sound sleep) mast nidrA
(मस्त निद्रा)

sleeping bag, *n.* slipiñ byAg
(स्लिपिङ ब्याग)

sleeping partner, *n.* kArobAr
mA samlagna na hune sAjhe
dAr (कारोबारमा संलग्न नहुने
साभेदार)

sleeping pill, *n.* nidrA lAgne
chakkI (निद्रा लाग्ने चक्की)

sleepy, *adj.* nidrA lAgeko
(निद्रा लागेको), nidAuro (निदाउरो)

sleeve, *n.* bAhulA (बाहुला)

sleeveless, *adj.* bAhulA na
bhaeko (बाहुला नभएको)

slender, *adj. (thing)* jhino
(झिनो), *(person)* dublo
pAtalo (दुब्लोपातलो),
(weight) halkA (हल्का)

slice, *n.* chAnA (चाना),
kesrA (केश्रा)
v. chAnA pArnu (चाना पार्नु)

slide, *v.* chiplanu (चिप्लनु),
chipleTI khelnu (चिप्लेटी खेल्नु)
n. chipleTI (चिप्लेटी),
(transparency) slAiD (स्लाइड)

slight, *adj.* jhino (झिनो),
halkA (हल्का), thorai (थोरै)
v. hepnu (हेप्नु),
hochyAunu (होच्याउनु)

slightly, *adv.* ali kati
(अलिकति),
halkA saṅga (हल्कासँग)

slim, *adj.* chharito (छरितो),
dublo (दुब्लो),
(scant) kam (कम)
v. moTAi ghaTAunu
(मोटाइ घटाउनु)

sling, *n. (med.)* bhAñchieko
hAt aDyAune kapaDA
(भाँचिएको हात अड्याउने
कपडा)
v. phyAñknu (फ्याँक्नु),
hAnnu (हान्नु)

slingshot, *n.* guleII (गुलेली),
ghuñyetro (घुँयेत्रो)

slip, *n. (error)* bhUl (भूल),
(cloth) khukulo lugA
(खुकुलो लुगा), *(paper)* parchA
(पर्चो), TukrA (टुक्रा)

slip, *v.* chiplanu (चिप्लनु),
suTukka jAnu (सुटुक्क जानु),
bhUl garnu (भूल गर्नु),
chuknu (चुक्नु)

slip-knot, *n.* surkenI gAñTho
(सुर्केनी गाँठो)

slippers, *n.* chaTTI (चट्टी),
chappal (चप्पल)

slippery, *adj.* chiplo (चिप्लो)

slipshod, *adj.* phohorI
(फोहोरी), asAwdhAn
(असावधान), lAparbAh
(लापरबाह), galat (गलत),
beDhaṅg (बेढङ्ग)

slit, *n.* chirA (चिरा),
lAmo pwAl (लामो प्वाल)
v. chirnu (चिर्नु),
kATnu (काट्नु)

slogan, *n.* nArA (नारा)

slope, *n. (up)* ukAlo (उकालो),
(down) orAlo (ओरालो),
(hillside) bhirAlo (भिरालो)

sloppy, *adj.* beDhaṅg (बेढङ्ग),
be rIt ko (बेरीतको)

slot, *n.* chirA (चिरा), pwAl (प्वाल)

slow, *adj.* DhIlo (ढीलो),
sust (सुस्त), jumso (जुम्सो)

slowly, *adv.* DhIlo garI
(ढीलोगरी), sustarI (सुस्तरी),
bistArai (बिस्तारै)

slug, *n.* chiple kIro (चिप्लेकीरो)

slum, *n.* gandA bastI
(गन्दा बस्ती)

slumber, *n.* nidrA (निद्रा)

sly, *adj.* dhUrt (धूर्त),
chalAkh (चलाख)

small, *adj.* sAno (सानो)

small arms, *n.* sAnA hatiyAr
(साना हतियार)

small change, *n.* khudrA (खुद्रा),
rechkI (रेच्की),
chAn chun (चानचुन)

small hours, *n.* AdhA rAt
pachhi ko samaya
(आधारातपछिको समय)

smallpox, *n.* biphar (बिफर),
shItalA (शीतला)

small talk, *n.* sAnA tinA kurA
(सानातिना कुरा), gaph (गफ)

smart, *adj.* tej (तेज),
chatur (चतुर), bATho (बाठो),
saphA sugghar (सफा-सुग्घर),
chhAñT pareko (छाँट परेको)
v. pIDA hunu (पीडा हुनु),
dukhnu (दुख्नु)

smartly, *adv.* phurtI sañga
(फुर्तीसँग)

smash, *v.* phoDnu (फोड्नु),
chaknAchUr garnu
(चकनाचूर गर्नु)
n. mukkA prahAr (मुक्का
प्रहार), ghussA (घुस्सा)

smear, *v.* ghasnu (घस्नु),
potnu (पोत्नु)
n. dhabbA (धब्बा), dAg (दाग)

smell, *n.* sugandh (सुगन्ध),
suwAs (सुवास),
v. suñghnu (सुँघ्नु)

smile, *n.* muskAn (मुस्कान),
muskurAhaT (मुस्कुराहट)
v. muskurAunu (मुस्कुराउनु),
hAñsnu (हाँस्नु)

smiling, *adj.* hañsilo (हाँसिलो),
prasanna (प्रसन्न)

smoke, *n.* dhuwAñ (धुवाँ),

churoT (चुरोट)
v. dhuwAñunu (धुवाँउनु),
(tobacco) churoT khAnu
(चुरोट खानु), dhumra pAn
garnu (धुम्रपान गर्नु)

smokeless, *adj.* dhuwAñ na
bhaeko (धुवाँ नभएको),
dhuwAñ rahit (धुवाँरहित)

smoker, *n.* churoT/tamAkhu
khAne (चुरोट/तमाखु खाने)

smoking, *n.* dhumra pAn
(धुम्रपान)

smoky, *adj.* dhwAñse (ध्वाँसे)

smooth, *adj.* samma (सम्म),
chiplo (चिप्लो), chillo (चिल्लो)
v. samma/chiplo pArnu
(सम्म/चिप्लो पार्नु)

smoothly, *adv.* rAmro sañga
(राम्रोसँग), nirwighna (निर्विघ्न)

smooth-tongued, *adj.* mItho
bolne (मीठो बोल्ने),
mridu bhAshI (मृदुभाषी),
chiplo dhasne (चिप्लो धस्ने)

smother, *v.* sAs roki dinu
(सास रोकिदिनु),
nisAssine pArnu
(निसास्सिने पार्नु)

smuggle, *v.* taskarI garnu
(तस्करी गर्नु)

smuggler, *n.* taskar wyApArI
(तस्कर व्यापारी)

snack, *n.* khAjA (खाजा),
chamenA (चमेना)

snack bar, *n.* chamenA ghar (चमेनाघर)

snag, *n.* samasyA (समस्या), bAdhA (बाधा)

snail, *n.* chiple/shaṅkhe kIro (चिप्ले/शङ्खे कीरो)

snake, *n.* sarpa (सर्प), sAṅp (साँप)
v. nAg belI garI hiṅDnu/chalnu (नागबेली गरी हिँड्नु/चल्नु)

snakebite, *n.* sarpa ko TokAi (सर्पको टोकाइ)

snake charmer, *n.* sapero (सपेरो)

snake-gourd, *n.* chichiNDo (चिचिण्डो)

snake in the grass, *n.* lukeko shatru (लुकेको शत्रु)

snakes and ladders, *n. (ludo)* baikuNTh khel (बैकुण्ठ खेल)

snap, *v.* nyAkka Toknu (न्याक्क टोक्नु), jhamTanu (फम्टनु), chuṇDAlnu (चुँडाल्नु), *(crackle)* auṅlA/pistol paDkAunu (औंला/पिस्तोल पड्काउनु)
n. taswIr (तस्वीर)

snapshot, *n.* taswIr (तस्वीर), phoTo (फोटो)

snare, *n.* pAso (पासो)
v. pAso thApnu (पासो थाप्नु), jAl mA pArnu (जालमा पार्नु)

snarl, *v.* ñyAr ñyur garnu (ङ्यार्ङ्गुर गर्नु), gurrinu (गुर्रिनु)

snatch, *v.* khosnu (खोस्नु), jhamTanu (फम्टनु)
n. hArA luchh (हारालुछ), luchhA chuṇDI (लुछाचुँडी)

sneak, *v.* suTukka/lukera jAnu (सुटुक्क/लुकेर जानु)
n. Dar chheruwA (डरछेरुवा)

sneak thief, *n.* chor (चोर), jhyAl DhokA bATa hAt chhirAera chorne (भ्याल ढोकाबाट हात छिराएर चोर्ने)

sneer, *v.* gillA garnu (गिल्ला गर्नु), hAṅso uDAunu (हाँसो उडाउनु)

sneeze, *n.* Achchhiuṅ (आच्छिउँ), chhiṅk (छिङ्क)
v. chhyuṅ/Achchhiuṅ garnu (छ्युँ/आच्छिउँ गर्नु)

sniff, *v.* surknu (सुर्क्नु), siṅ̄An tannu (सिङ्गान तान्नु), suṅghnu (सुँघ्नु)
n. suṅghAi (सुँघाइ)

snob, *n.* ghamaNDI mAnchhe (घमण्डी मान्छे)

snore, *v.* ghurnu (घुर्नु)
n. ghurAi (घुराइ)

snout, *n.* thutuno (थुतुनो)

snow, *n.* hiuṅ (हिउँ)
v. hiuṅ parnu (हिउँ पर्नु)

snowball, *n.* hiuṅ ko Dallo (हिउँको डल्लो)

snow-capped, *adj.* hiuñ le DhAkeko (हिउँले ढाकेको)

snowfall, *n.* him pAt (हिमपात)

snow leopard, *n.* hiuñ chituwA (हिउँ चितुवा)

snowline *n.* him rekhA (हिमरेखा)

snowstorm, *n.* barphilo tUphAn (बर्फिलो तूफान)

snowman, *n.* him mAnaw (हिममानव), yatI (यती)

snow-white, *adj.* shuddha seto (शुद्ध सेतो)

snuff, *n.* nas (नस)
v. nas hAlnu (नस हाल्नु), *(candle lamp)* lotA kATnu (लोता काट्नु), nibhAunu (निभाउनु)

so, *adv./conj.* tyas kAraN (त्यसकारण), yasto (यस्तो), tyasai le (त्यसैले), tasarth (तसर्थ)

so-and-so, *pron.* phalAnu (फलानु), chilAnu (चिलानु) DhiskAnu (ढिस्कानु)

soap, *n.* sAbun (साबुन)
v. sAbun lAunu (साबुन लाउनु)

soar, *v.* akAsinu (अकासिनु)

sob, *n.* ruwAi (रुवाइ), rodan (रोदन)
v. suñkka suñkka runu (सुँक्क सुँक्क रुनु)

sober, *adj.* shAnt (शान्त),

samyamI (संयमी)

so-called, *adj.* tathA kathit (तथाकथित), bhanAuñdo (भनाउँदो)

soccer, *n.* phuT bal (फुटबल), bhakunDo (भकुन्डो)

social, *adj.* sAmAjik (सामाजिक), *(person)* milan sAr (मिलनसार)

socialism, *n.* samAj wAd (समाजवाद)

social science, *n.* sAmAjik wigỹAn (सामाजिक विज्ञान)

social security, *n.* sAmAjik surakshA (सामाजिक सुरक्षा)

social services, *n.* sAmAjik sewA (सामाजिक सेवा)

social worker, *n.* samAj sewI (समाजसेवी)

society, *n.* samAj (समाज), *(orgn.)* sañgh (सङ्घ), *(person)* sañgat (सङ्गत), *(highbrow)* mAthillo warg (माथिल्लो वर्ग)

sock, *n.* mojA (मोजा)

soda, *n.* soDA (सोडा)

soda water, *n.* soDA pAnI (सोडा पानी)

sofa, *n.* sophA (सोफा)

soft, *adj.* kamalo (कमलो), komal (कोमल), naram (नरम)

soft drink, *n.* halukA peya (हलुका पेय)

soft-hearted, adj. kamalo
(कमलो), dayAlu (दयालु)

soft(ly)-spoken, adj. mijAsilo
(मिजासिलो),
naram bolne (नरम बोल्ने)

software, n. kampyuTar kArya
kram (कम्प्युटर कार्यक्रम)

soil, n. mATo (माटो)
v. phohor pArnu (फोहोर
पार्नु), mailyAunu (मैल्याउनु)

sojourn, n. bAs (बास)
v. bAs basnu (बास बस्नु)

solace, n. sAntwana (सान्त्वना)

solar, adj. sUrya ko (सूर्यको),
sUrya sambandhI
(सूर्यसम्बन्धी)

solar eclipse, n. sUrya grahaN
(सूर्यग्रहण)

solar system, n. saur maNDal
(सौरमण्डल)

soldier, n. sipAhI (सिपाही)

sole, n. (foot) paitAlA (पैताला),
(shoe) taluwA (तलुवा)
adj. ek mAtra (एक मात्र),
eklo (एक्लो)

solely, adv. khAli (खालि),
mAtrai (मात्रै)

solemn, adj. gambhIr (गम्भीर),
pawitra (पवित्र),
aupchArik (औपचारिक)

solicit, v. bintI bhAu garnu
(बिन्तीभाउ गर्नु),
anurodh garnu (अनुरोध गर्नु)

solid, adj. Thos (ठोस),
khaNDilo (खंदिलो)

solitary, adj. eklo (एक्लो),
nirjan (निर्जन),
ekAnt (एकान्त)

so long, inter. (inf.) bidA
(बिदा), namaste (नमस्ते)

so long as, adv. tyaso bhae
mA (त्यसो भएमा), yas shart
mA ki (यस शर्तमा कि)

solution, n. (liquid) ghol (घोल),
(difficulty) samAdhAn
(समाधान)

solve, v. hal/samAdhAn garnu
(हल/समाधान गर्नु)

some, adj. kehI (केही),
kohI (कोही)
adv. lag bhag (लगभग),
karIb (करीब)
pron. kehI (केही),
kohI kohI (कोही कोही)

somebody, pron. kohI (कोही),
kunai wyakti (कुनै व्यक्ति)

somehow, adv. yena kena
(येन केन),
kunai kisim le (कुनै किसिमले)

someone, pron. kohI (कोही),
kohI khAs wyakti
(कोही खास व्यक्ति)

something, pron. kehI wastu
(केही वस्तु)

sometimes, adv. kahile kAhIň
(कहिलेकाहीं)

somewhere, *adv.* kahIň (कहीं), katai (कतै)

son, *n.* chhorA (छोरा), putra (पुत्र)

song, *n.* gIt (गीत), gAnA (गाना)

so on, *pron.* ityAdi (इत्यादि)

soon, *adv.* chAňDai (चाँडै), jhaTTa (झट्ट), turunt (तुरुन्त), *(as soon as)* jasai (जसै), hunA sAth (हुनासाथ), *(as soon as possible)* sake samma chAňDo (सकेसम्म चाँडो)

sooner or later, *adv.* Dhilo wA chAňDo (ढिलो वा चाँडो), kunai na kunai belA (कुनै न कुनै बेला)

soot, *n.* dhwAňso (ध्वाँसो), moso (मोसो)

soothe, *v.* shAnt/shaman garnu (शान्त/शमन गर्नु)

soothsayer, *n.* jyotishI (ज्योतिषी), bhawishya waktA (भविष्यवक्ता)

sorcerer, *n.* bokso (बोक्सो), jAdu gar (जादुगर)

sore, *n.* ghAu (घाउ), khaTirA (खटिरा) *adj.* dukhne (दुख्ने), dukhad (दुखद)

sorrow, *n.* duhkha (दुःख), surtA (सुर्ता), pIr (पीर)

sorrowful, *adj.* dukhI (दुखी), udAs (उदास)

sorry, *adj.* dukhI (दुखी), khinna (खिन्न), udAs (उदास), *(I am sorry)* aphsos! (अफसोस!), mAph garnus! (माफ गर्नुस्!)

sort, *n.* kisim (किसिम), tharI (थरी) *v.* chhAňTnu (छाँट्नु), chhoTyAunu (छोट्याउनु)

sort out, *v.* chhuTyAunu (छुट्याउनु)

so-so, *adj/adv.* Thikkai (ठिक्कै), besai (बेसै)

soul, *n.* AtmA (आत्मा)

sound, *n.* AwAj (आवाज), dhwani (ध्वनि) *adj.* swasth (स्वस्थ), tandurust (तन्दुरुस्त) *v.* AwAj nikAlnu (आवाज निकाल्नु), *(view)* wyakt garnu (व्यक्त गर्नु), *(test)* jAňchnu (जाँच्नु)

sound asleep, *adv.* mast nidAeko (मस्त निदाएको)

sound off, *v. (coll.)* joD le kurA garnu (जोडले कुरा गर्नु)

soundproof(ed), *adj.* AwAj na chhirne (आवाज नछिर्ने)

sound sleep, *n.* mast nidrA (मस्तनिद्रा)

soup, *n.* suruwA (सुरुवा), ras (रस), jhol (झोल)

sour, *adj.* amilo (अमिलो)

source, *n.* srot (स्रोत), mUl (मूल)

south, *n.* dakkhin (दक्खिन), dakshiN (दक्षिण)

southern, *adj.* dakshiNI (दक्षिणी), dakshiN ko (दक्षिणको)

southward, *adj.* dakshiNI (दक्षिणी) *adv.* dakshiN paTTi (दक्षिणपट्टि)

souvenir, *n.* chinu (चिनु), samjhauTo (सम्झौटो)

sovereign, *n.* rAjA (राजा), shAsak (शासक) *adj.* prabhu sattA sampanna (प्रभुसत्ता सम्पन्न)

sovereignty, *n.* prabhu sattA (प्रभुसत्ता), sArwbhaum sattA (सार्वभौमसत्ता)

sow, *v. (seed)* chharnu (छर्नु) *n.* suṅgurnI (सुँगुर्नी)

soya bean/soybean, *n.* bhaT mAs (भटमास)

space, *n.* ThAuṅ (ठाउँ), sthAn (स्थान), *(universe)* antariksha (अन्तरिक्ष) *v.* khAlI ThAuṅ chhoDnu (खाली ठाउँ छोड्नु)

space age, *n.* antariksha yug (अन्तरिक्ष युग)

spacecraft, *n.* antariksha yAn (अन्तरिक्षयान)

spaceman, *n.* antariksha yAtrI (अन्तरिक्षयात्री)

spaceship, *n.* antariksha yAn (अन्तरिक्षयान)

space station, *n.* antariksha sTesan (अन्तरिक्ष स्टेसन)

spacesuit, *n.* antariksha poshAk (अन्तरिक्ष पोशाक)

spacious, *adj.* pharAkilo (फराकिलो)

spade, *n.* kodAlo (कोदालो), kodAlI (कोदाली) *v.* mATo khannu (माटो खन्नु)

spades, *n. (cards)* surath (सुरथ), hukum (हुकुम)

spadework, *n. (fig.)* kaThin, shuru ko kAm (कठिन, शुरुको काम)

span, *n. (measure)* bittA (बित्ता), *(extent)* wistAr (विस्तार), *(time)* awadhi (अवधि) *v.* wAr pAr garnu (वारपार गर्नु)

spare, *n.* jageDA (जगेडा) *adj.* phAltu (फाल्तु) *v.* phAro garnu (फारो गर्नु), bachAunu (बचाउनु)

spare parts, *n.* jageDA purjA harU (जगेडा पुर्जाहरू)

spare time, *n.* phursad ko samaya (फुर्सदको समय)

spark, *n.* jhilko (झिल्को), jhilkA (झिल्का) *v.* jhilkA nikAlnu (झिल्का निकाल्नु)

sparkle, *v.* chamkanu (चम्कनु),
  jhilkinu (झिल्किनु)

sparrow, *n.* bhaṅgerA (भँगेरा)

sparse, *adj.* pAtlieko
  (पातलिएको)

spate, *n.* bADhI (बाढी), bhel (भेल)

spatter, *v.* chharkinu (छर्किनु),
  chhyApnu (छ्याप्नु)

speak, *v.* bolnu (बोल्नु),
  kurA garnu (कुरा गर्नु),
  (lecture) bhAshaN garnu
  (भाषण गर्नु)

speaker, *n.* waktA (वक्ता),
  bolne mAnis (बोल्ने मानिस),
  (Lower House) sabhA mukh
  (सभामुख)

spear, *n.* bhAlA (भाला),
  barchhA (बर्छा)
  v. ghopnu (घोप्नु),
  chheDnu (छेड्नु)

special, *adj.* wishesh (विशेष),
  khAs (खास)

specialist, *n.* wisheshagȳa
  (विशेषज्ञ),
  jAniph kAr (जानिफकार)

specially, *adv.* wishesh garI
  (विशेषगरी),
  khAs garI (खासगरी)

species, *n.* kisim (किसिम),
  jAt (जात), warg (वर्ग)

specific, *adj.* tokieko
  (तोकिएको),
  nirdishT (निर्दिष्ट)

specified, *adj.* tokieko
  (तोकिएको)

specify, *v.* toknu (तोक्नु)

specimen, *n.* namUnA (नमूना)

speck, *n.* sAno kaN (सानो
  कण), thoplo (थोप्लो)

spectacle, *n.* tamAshA
  (तमाशा), ramitA (रमिता)

spectacles, *n.* chasmA (चस्मा)

spectacular, *adj.* herna lAyak
  ko (हेर्न लायकको),
  shAndAr (शान्दार)

spectator, *n.* tamAshe (तमाशे),
  darshak (दर्शक)

speculate, *v.* anumAn/tarkanA
  garnu (अनुमान/तर्कना गर्नु)

speculation, *n.* anumAn
  (अनुमान), tarkanA (तर्कना)

speech, *n.* bolI (बोली), kurA
  (कुरा), bhAshaN (भाषण)

speechless, *adj.* lATo (लाटो),
  maun (मौन)

speed, *n.* gati (गति),
  weg (वेग), chAl (चाल),
  raphtAr (रफ्तार)

speedboat, *n.* beg saṅga
  chalne moTar DuṅgA
  (वेगसँग चल्ने मोटर डुङ्गा)

speed limit, *n.* gati sImA
  (गति सीमा)

speedy, *adj.* tejilo (तेजिलो)

spell, *v.* hijje garnu (हिज्जे गर्नु)

spelling, *n.* hijje (हिज्जे)

spend, n. *(money)* kharch garnu (खर्च गर्नु), *(time)* bitAunu (बिताउनु)

spendthrift, n./adj. phajul kharchI (फजुलखर्ची)

sphere, n. *(things)* Dallo (डल्लो), *(geo.)* prithwI (पृथ्वी), *(area)* kshetra (क्षेत्र)

sphere of influence, n. prabhAw kshetra (प्रभाव क्षेत्र)

spherical, adj. golo (गोलो), Dallo (डल्लो)

spice(s), n. maslA (मसला)

spicy, adj. masAle dAr (मसालेदार)

spider, n. mAkuro (माकुरो), mAkurA (माकुरा)

spider's web, n. mAkurA ko jAlo (माकुराको जालो)

spike, n. suro (सुरो), dhAtu ko kAňTA (धातुको काँटा) v. kAňTA le ghopnu (काँटाले घोप्नु)

spill, v. pokhnu (पोख्नु), pokhinu (पोखिनु), chhachalkinu (छछल्किनु)

spill the beans, v. kurA kholnu (कुरा खोल्नु), pardA phAs garnu (पर्दाफास गर्नु)

spin v. phan phanI ghumnu (फनफनी घुम्नु), ghumAunu (घुमाउनु), *(thread)* kAtnu (कात्नु),

n. ghumAi (घुमाइ), chakkar (चक्कर)

spinach, n. pAluňgo (पालुङ्गो)

spine, n. DaňDAlno (डँडाल्नो)

spinning top, n. laTTu (लट्टु), bhuruňg (भुरुङ्ग)

spinning wheel, n. charkhA (चर्खा)

spirit, n. *(soul)* AtmA (आत्मा), *(ghost)* pret (प्रेत), *(attitude)* swabhAw (स्वभाव), *(morale)* hausalA (हौसला), *(alcohol)* raksI (रक्सी)

spiritual, adj. AdhyAtmik (आध्यात्मिक), daiwI (दैवी) n. dhArmik gIt (धार्मिक गीत)

spit, n. thuk (थुक) v. thuknu (थुक्नु)

spiteful, adj. ikhAlu (इखालु), ibI rAkhne (इबी राख्ने)

spittle, n. thuk (थुक), khakAr (खकार)

splash, n. jhwAmlyAňg (झ्वाम्ल्याङ्ग), chhyAp chhyAp (छ्यापछ्याप) v. pAnI chhyApnu (पानी छ्याप्नु), chharkanu (छर्कनु)

spleen, n. phiyo (फियो)

splendid, adj. shAn dAr (शान्दार), bhawya (भव्य)

splendo(u)r, n. chahak (चहक), bhaDak (भडक), shAn (शान)

splint, *n.* choiTo (चोइटो)

splinter, *n.* choiTA (चोइटा),
TukrA (टुक्रा)

split, *n.* bAñDieko mat
(बाँडिएको मत)
 adj. wibhAjit (विभाजित)
 v. chirnu (चिर्नु),
phuTnu (फुट्नु)

split personality, *n.* wibhAjit
wyaktitwa (विभाजित व्यक्तित्व)

split second, *n.* jyAdai
chhoTo samaya
(ज्यादै छोटो समय)

split up, *v.* wichchhed hunu
(विच्छेद हुनु)

spoil, *v.* bigArnu (बिगार्नु),
bhAñDnu (भाँड्नु)
 n. lUT (लूट)

spoilsport, *n.* khel bigArne
mAnchhe (खेल बिगार्ने मान्छे)

spokesperson, *n.* prawaktA
(प्रवक्ता)

sponge, *n.* spoñj (स्पोञ्ज)
 v. sosnu (सोस्नु)

spongy, *adj.* sosilo (सोसिलो)

sponsor, *n.* prAyojak (प्रायोजक)
 v. prAyojit garnu
(प्रायोजित गर्नु)

spontaneous, *adj.* Aphai
bhaeko (आफै भएको),
Aphu khushI (आफुखुशी)

spool, *n.* dhAgo wA philim
berne ril (धागो वा फिलिम बेर्ने

रिल), laTTai (लट्टाइ)

spoon, *n.* chamchA (चम्चा)

sport(s), *n.* khel kUd (खेलकूद)

sportsperson, *n.* khelADI
(खेलाडी)

spot, *n.* *(stain)* dAg (दाग),
TATo (टाटो), *(dot)* thoplo
(थोप्लो), *(place)* ThAuñ (ठाउँ),
(in a spot) kaThinAi mA
(कठिनाइमा),
sañkaT mA (सङ्कटमा),
(on the spot) tatkAl (तत्काल),
jahAñ ko tahIñ (जहाँको तहीँ)
 v. dAg lagAunu (दाग लगाउनु),
(see) dekhnu (देख्नु),
(locate) pattA lagAunu (पत्ता
लगाउनु)

spotless, *adj.* bedAg (बेदाग),
nirmal (निर्मल)

spotted, *adj.* chhirbire (छिर्बिरे),
TATe pATe (टाटेपाटे)

spouse, *n.* jahAn (जहान),
joI poi (जोईपोइ)

spout, *n.* dhAro (धारो),
TuTI (टुटी)
 v. dhAro lAgnu (धारो लाग्नु)

sprain, *n.* markAi (मर्काइ)
 v. markanu (मर्कनु)

sprained, *adj.* markeko (मर्केको)

spray, *n.* sirko (सिर्को),
pichkArI (पिचकारी)
 v. chharkanu (छर्कनु),
sirko chhoDnu (सिर्को छोड्नु)

spread, v. phailanu (फैलनु),
phijAunu (फिजाउनु),
(legs) pasArnu (पसार्नु),
phaTTyAunu (फट्याउनु),
(body) tankyAunu
(तन्क्याउनु)
n. wistAr (विस्तार),
pasAro (पसारो)

spring, n. *(season)* basant
(बसन्त), *(metal)* kamAnI
(कमानी), *(water)* mUl (मूल),
panero (पनेरो)
v. uphranu (उफ्रनु),
phAl hAlnu (फाल हाल्नु)

spring on, v. jhamTanu
(भम्टनु)

sprinkle, v. chharkanu (छर्कनु),
chhamkanu (छम्कनु)

sprout, n. TusA (टुसा),
aṅkur (अंकुर), munA (मुना)
v. TusAunu (टुसाउनु),
palAunu (पलाउनु)

spur, n. *(horseman)*
kurkuchchA (कुर्कुच्चा),
(cock's leg) ThelA (ठेला),
(ridge) thumko (थुम्को),
(on the spur of the moment)
utni kherai (उत्निखेरै),
tatkAl (तत्काल)
v. *(man)* prerit garnu (प्रेरित
गर्नु), *(horse)* kurkuchcha le
hAnnu (कुर्कुच्चाले हान्नु),
(walk) tej chalnu (तेज चल्नु)

sputum, n. kaph (कफ),
khakAr (खकार)

spy, n. jAsUs (जासूस)
v. jAsUsI garnu (जासूसी गर्नु),
dekhnu (देख्नु)

squad, n. TolI (टोली), dal (दल)

squalid, adj. phohor (फोहोर),
daridra (दरिद्र)
n. daridrI (दरिद्री),
malintA (मलिनता)

squander, v. phajul kharch
garnu (फजुल खर्च गर्नु),
uDAunu (उडाउनु)

square, n. chAr pATe
(चारपाटे), warg (वर्ग),
chaukos (चौकोस),
(area) chok (चोक)
adj. wargAkAr (वर्गाकार),
(sl.) paramparA wAdI
(परम्परावादी)
v. chaukos pArnu
(चौकोस पार्नु), *(math.)* warg
banAunu (वर्ग बनाउनु),
(bus.) chuktA garnu
(चुक्ता गर्नु)

square deal, n. nish kapaT
saude bAjI (निष्कपट
सौदेबाजी), rAmro wyawahAr
(राम्रो व्यवहार)

square meal, n. peT bhar
bhojan (पेटभर भोजन)

square root, n. warg mUl
(वर्गमूल)

squash, *n. (game)* skwAs khel
(स्क्वास खेल), *(gourd)* pharsI
(फर्सी), laukA (लौका)
v. kichnu (किच्नु)

squat, *v.* Tukrukka basnu
(टुक्रुक्क बस्नु), basnu (बस्नु)

squatter, *n.* sukum bAsI
(सुकुम्बासी)

squeak, *v.* chIň chIň garnu
(चीं चीं गर्नु)
n. chIň chIň AwAj
(चीं चीं आवाज)

squeeze, *v.* nicharnu (निचर्नु),
nimoThnu (निमोठ्नु),
kochchinu (कोच्चिनु)
n. nimoThAi (निमोठाइ),
(crowd) bhID (भीड)

squint, *adj.* DeDho (ढेढो)
v. DeDho AňkhA le hernu
(ढेढो आँखाले हेर्नु)
n. terso herAi (तेर्सो हेराइ),
chhaDke najar (छड्के नजर)

squirrel, *n.* lokharke (लोखर्के)

stab, *n.* chhurA prahAr
(छुरा प्रहार)
v. chhurA dhasnu (छुरा घस्नु)

stab in the back, *n.* piň hyun
mA prahAr (पिठ्यूँमा प्रहार),
dhokhA (घोका)

stable, *adj.* sthir (स्थिर),
achal (अचल)
n. (horse) tabelA (तबेला)

stadium, *n.* rang shAlA

(रङ्गशाला)

staff, *n.* karm chArI
(कर्मचारी), sTAph (स्टाफ),
(stick) laTThI (लट्ठी),
lauro (लौरो)
v. karm chArI rAkhnu
(कर्मचारी राख्नु)

stag, *n.* bhAle jarAyo
(भाले जरायो), hariN (हरिण)

stag party, *n.* logne mAnchhe
harU ko pArTI
(लोग्नेमान्छेहरूको पार्टी)

stage, *n.* rang mañch
(रङ्गमञ्च), sTej (स्टेज),
(development) awasthA
(अवस्था),
(progress) charaN (चरण)
v. nATak dekhAunu
(नाटक देखाउनु)

stagger, *v.* larkharAunu
(लर्खराउनु),
larbarAunu (लर्बराउनु)
n. larkhar (लर्खर),
Dhal mal (ढलमल)

stain, *n.* dAg (दाग),
TATo (टाटो), dhabbA (धब्बा)
v. dAg lAunu (दाग लाउनु),
dhabbA lAunu (धब्बा लाउनु)

stainless, *adj.* be dAg (बेदाग),
nirmal (निर्मल)

stainless steel, *n.* khiyA na
lAgne ispAt (खिया नलाग्ने
इस्पात)

stairs, *n.* bharen̐ (भरेङ),
siñDhI (सिँढी)

staircase, *n.* bharen̐ (भरेङ),
bharyAn̐ (भर्‍याङ)

stake, *(post)* ghocho (घोचो),
sUlI (सूली), *(game)* bAjI
(बाजी), dAu (दाउ),
(at stake) dAu mA (दाउमा)

stale, *adj. (food)* bAsI (बासी),
thotro (थोत्रो),
purAno (पुरानो)

stalemate, *n. (chess)* chAl
band (चालबन्द),
(fig.) gati rodh (गतिरोध)

stalk, *n. (plant)* DAn̐Th (डाँठ),
(gait) hiñDAi (हिँडाइ),
chAl (चाल)
v. (stride) tankera hin̐dnu
(तन्केर हिँड्नु), *(hunting)*
lukera hin̐Dnu (लुकेर हिँड्नु)

stall, *n. (animal)* tabelA/goTh
ko kabal (तबेला/गोठको
कबल), *(bus.)* sTal (स्टल),
pasal (पसल),
(seat) sIT (सीट),
Asan (आसन)
v. kabal mA rAkhnu
(कबलमा राख्नु), *(work)* Dhilo
garnu (ढिलो गर्नु)

stallion, *n.* An̐Du ghoDA
(आँडु घोडा)

stamina, *n.* aDne shakti
(अड्ने शक्ति), dam (दम)

stammer, *v.* bhak bhakAunu
(भकभकाउनु)

stammerer, *n.* bhak bhake
(भकभके)

stamp, *n. (seal)* chhAp (छाप),
(postage) TikaT (टिकट)
v. (imprint) chhAp lAunu
(छाप लाउनु), Tak mArnu
(ठक मार्नु), *(influence)*
prabhAw pArnu (प्रभाव पार्नु),
(foot) khuTTA bajArnu (खुट्टा
बजार्नु), *(affix)* TikaT TAn̐snu
(टिकट टाँस्नु)

stand, *v.* ubhinu (उभिनु),
khaDA hunu (खडा हुनु),
(pain, etc.) sahanu (सहनु)
n. (stopping) gati rodh
(गतिरोध), *(firm position)*
nishchitatA (निश्चितता),
sthiti (स्थिति), aDAn (अडान),
(bus.) sTal (स्टल), pasal (पसल)

standard, *n. (flag)* jhaNDA
(झण्डा), *(degree)* star (स्तर),
(quality) koTI (कोटी),
(school) shreNI (श्रेणी)

standard-bearer, *n.* dhwajA
wAhak (ध्वजावाहक)

standard of living, *n.* jIwan
star (जीवन स्तर)

stand by, *v. (support)* samarthan
garnu (समर्थन गर्नु), *(readiness)*
tayAr rahanu (तयार रहनु)

standby, *n.* sahArA (सहारा),

milne sAthI (मिल्ने साथी)
n./adj. (person, thing)
Awashyak pardA tayAr
rAkhine
(आवश्यक पर्दा तयार राखिने)

stand for, *v. (person)* prati
nidhitwa garnu
(प्रतिनिधित्व गर्नु), *(word)*
janAunu (जनाउनु), *(election)*
laDnu khaDA hunu (लड़नु
खड़ा हुनु), *(bear)* sahanu (सहनु)

standing, *adj.* khaDA (खड़ा),
(orgn.) sthAyI (स्थायी),
achal (अचल)
n. (repute) nAm
(नाम), pratishThA (प्रतिष्ठा)

standing order, *n.* sthAyI
Adesh (स्थायी आदेश)

standing committee, *n.* sthAyI
samiti (स्थायी समिति)

stand off, *v.* haTnu (हट्नु),
alag hunu (अलग हुनु),
(employees) haTAunu
(हटाउनु), chhAnTnu (छाँट्नु)

standpoint, *n.* drishTi koN
(दृष्टिकोण)

standstill, *n. (stoppage)*
mukAm (मुकाम), aDai (अडाइ),
awrodh (अवरोध)

staple, *adj. (food)* mukhya
(मुख्य)
n. steplar ko pin (स्टेप्लरको पिन)

star, *n.* tArA (तारा),

(film) sitArA (सितारा),
mahAn kalA kAr
(महान कलाकार)

stargazer, *n. (coll.)* jyotishI
(ज्योतिषी)

starch, *n.* mAD (माड),
kalap (कलप)
v. mAD lAunu (माड लाउनु),
kalap hAlnu (कलप हाल्नु)

stare at one another, *v.* herA
her garnu (हेराहेर गर्नु)

stark, *adj.* daro (दरो),
kaDA (कड़ा), *(stark naked)*
pUrai nAngo (पूरै नाङ्गो)

start, *n.* shuru (शुरु),
Arambh (आरम्भ),
(journey) prasthAn (प्रस्थान)
v. rawAnA hunu (रवाना हुनु),
prasthAn garnu (प्रस्थान गर्नु),
shuru garnu (शुरु गर्नु),
chalAunu (चलाउनु)

startle, *v.* jhaskinu (झस्किनु),
jhaskAunu (झस्काउनु)

starvation, *n.* bhok (भोक),
bhok marI (भोकमरी),
anikAl (अनिकाल)

starve, *v.* bhokai hunu/marnu
(भोकै हुनु/मर्नु)

state, *n.* hAlat (हालत), sthiti
(स्थिति), *(pol.)* rAjya (राज्य),
sarkAr (सरकार), *(lie in state)*
(body) darshanArth rAkhinu
(दर्शनार्थ राखिनु)

v. batAunu (बताउनु),
bhannu (भन्नु)
adj. rAjya (राज्य),
rAjkIya (राजकीय),
sarkArI (सरकारी)

statement, *n.* waktawya
(वक्तव्य), bayAn (बयान)

state of affairs, *n.* paristhiti
(परिस्थिति)

state of mind, *n.* manasthiti
(मनस्थिति)

statesman, *n.* rAj netA
(राजनेता)

station, *n.* sthAn (स्थान),
mukAm (मुकाम)
v. rAkhnu (राख्नु),
ThAuṅ toknu (ठाउँ तोक्नु)

stationary, *adj.* achal (अचल),
sthir (स्थिर)

stationery, *n.* masland
(मसलन्द)

statistics, *n.* tathyAṅk
(तथ्याङ्क)

statue, *n.* sAlik (सालिक),
pratimA (प्रतिमा),
mUrti (मूर्ति)

status, *n.* aukAt (औकात),
gachchhe (गच्छे)

status quo, *n.* yathA sthiti
(यथास्थिति)

status symbol, *n.* jethA
(जेथा), waibhaw (वैभव)

staunch, *adj.* baphA dAr

(बफादार), pakkA (पक्का),
wishwAsilo (विश्वासिलो)

stay, *v.* rahanu (रहनु),
basnu (बस्नु)
n. bAs (बास), mukAm (मुकाम)

staying power, *n.* aDne shakti
(अड्ने शक्ति)

stay put, *v.* jahAṅ ko tyhIṅ
rahanu (जहाँको त्यहीं रहनु)

steady, *adj.* sthir (स्थिर),
darilo (दरिलो)

steal, *v.* chornu (चोर्नु),
chorI garnu (चोरी गर्नु)

steam, *n.* bAph (बाफ),
bAshpa (बाष्प),
(let off steam) man ko
baha/gumseko bhAw pokhnu
(मनको बह/गुम्सेको भाव पोख्नु)
adj. bAph ko (बाफको),
bAshpIya (बाष्पीय)
v. bAph uThAunu (बाफ
उठाउनु), usinnu (उसिन्नु)

steel, *n.* ispAt (इस्पात)

steep, *adj.* ThADo (ठाडो),
bhirAlo (भिरालो)

steer, *v.* hAṅknu (हाँक्नु),
parichAlan garnu
(परिचालन गर्नु)

steer clear of, *v.* alag/bachera
rahanu (अलग/बचेर रहनु)

steering committee, *n.*
nirdeshak/sañchAlak samiti
(निर्देशक/संचालक समिति)

steering wheel, *n. (vehicles)* sTeriñ (स्टेरिङ)

stem, *n.* DAñTh (डाँठ)

stench, *v.* ganAunu (गनाउनु)

stenographer, *n.* sañket lekhak (संकेत लेखक)

step, *n. (ladder)* khuDkilA (खुड्किला), *(pace)* kadam (कदम), pAilA (पाइला), *(mind one's step)* sAwdhAn hunu (सावधान हुनु) *v.* pAilA chAlnu (पाइला चाल्नु), Teknu (टेक्नु)

stepbrother, *n.* sautinI bhAi/dAju (सौतिनी भाइ/दाजु)

stepdaughter, *n.* jhaTkelI chhorI (भट्केली छोरी)

step down, *v.* rAjI nAmA dinu (राजीनामा दिनु)

stepfather, *n.* jhaDkelo bAbu (भड्केलो बाबु)

step in, *v.* bhitra pasnu (भित्र पस्नु)

stepladder, *n.* Aphai aDne bhareñ (आफै अड्ने भरेङ)

stepmother, *n.* sautinI AmA (सौतिनी आमा)

stepsister, *n.* sautinI bahinI/didI (सौतिनी बहिनी/दिदी)

stepson, *n.* jhaTkelo chhorA (भट्केलो छोरा)

step up, *v.* baDhAun (बढाउन),

thapnu (थप्नु)

stereotyped, *adj.* ekai nAse (एकैनासे), na badline (नबदलिने)

sterile, *adj.* bAñjho (बाँझो), banjar (बन्जर), *(med.)* jIwANu hIn (जीवाणुहीन)

stew, *n.* baphAeko parikAr (बफाएको परिकार) *v.* baphAunu (बफाउनु), usinnu (उसिन्नु)

steward, *n.* prabandhak (प्रबन्धक), parichArak (परिचारक)

stick, *n.* laTThI (लट्ठी), chhaDI (छडी) *v.* TAñsnu (टाँस्नु), TAñsinu (टाँसिनु), aljhinu (अल्झिनु)

stick around, *v. (sl.)* najikai rahanu (नजिकै रहनु)

stick-in-the-mud, *n.* purAno DharrA ko mAnis (पुरानो ढर्राको मानिस)

stick out, *v.* bAhira nikleko hunu (बाहिर निक्लेको हुनु)

stiff, *adj.* daro (दरो), kaDA (कडा), kaThin (कठिन)

still, *adv.* ajhai (अझै) *adj.* shAnt (शान्त), na chalne (नचल्ने), nishchal (निश्चल) *v.* shAnt garnu (शान्त गर्नु)

stillborn, *adj.* janmadA

mareko (जन्मदा मरेको)

still life, *n.* nirjIw wastu ko chitra (निर्जीव वस्तुको चित्र)

stimulate, *v.* uttejit garnu (उत्तेजित गर्नु), jagAunu (जगाउनु)

stimulation, *n.* uttejan (उत्तेजन), uddIpan (उद्दीपन)

sting, *n.* chilne khil (चिल्ने खिल) *v.* chilnu (चिल्नु), Dasnu (डस्नु), Toknu (टोक्नु)

stingy, *adj.* kanjus (कन्जुस), makkhI chus (मक्खीचुस)

stink, *v.* ganAunu (गनाउनु)

stipend, *n.* bhattA (भत्ता), writti (वृत्ति)

stipulation, *n.* shart (शर्त), bhAkhA patra (भाखापत्र)

stir, *v.* chalAunu (चलाउनु), hallinu (हल्लिनु) *n.* tahalkA (तहलका), hal chal (हलचल)

stitch, *n.* TAñkA (टाँका) *v.* siunu (सिउनु), TAñkA dinu (टाँका दिनु)

stock, *n.* (*bus.*) mAl (माल), sAmAn (सामान), korA mAl (कोरा माल), mUl pUñjI (मूल पूँजी), (*tree*) dhaD (धड), (*family*) wamsh (वंश), kul (कुल) *v.* mAl rAkhnu (माल राख्नु), jammA garnu (जम्मा गर्नु)

stocking, *n.* lAmo mojA (लामो मोजा), jurAb (जुराब)

stockpile, *n.* mAl ko sañgAlo (मालको सँगालो) *v.* mAl thuprAunu (माल थुप्राउनु)

stocky, *adj.* gaThilo (गठिलो), khañdilo (खँदिलो)

stomach, *n.* peT (पेट), bhuñDI (भुँडी) *adj.* peT ko (पेटको) *v.* (*oft. neg.*) khAna saknu (खान सक्नु), (*endure*) sahanu (सहनु), khapnu (खप्नु)

stone, *n.* DhuñgA (ढुङ्गा), patthar (पत्थर), (*fruit*) koyA (कोया) *adj.* Dhuñge (ढुङ्गे), patthar ko (पत्थरको) *v.* DhuñgA le hAnnu (ढुङ्गाले हान्नु)

Stone Age, *n.* Dhuñge/patthar yug (ढुङ्गे/पत्थरयुग)

stone's throw, *n.* chhoTo dUrI (छोटो दूरी)

stool, *n.* tripAi (त्रिपाइ), pirkA (पिर्का), (*faeces*) disA (दिसा)

stool pigeon, *n.* phasAune mAnis/wastu (फसाउने मानिस/वस्तु)

stoop, *v.* nihuranu (निहुरनु), jhuknu (झुक्नु)

stop, *v.* roknu (रोक्नु),

rokinu (रोकिनु), aDnu (अड्नु),
(close) band garnu (बन्द गर्नु)
n. birAm (विराम), rokkA
(रोक्का), bisaunI (बिसौनी),
(gram.) pUrN wirAm (पूर्णविराम)
stop dead, *v.* Takka aDnu
(टक्क अड्नु)
stoppage, *n.* rok (रोक),
awrodh (अवरोध)
stop press, *n.* chhAptA
chhAptai ko samAchAr
(छाप्ता छाप्तैको समाचार)
stop short, *v.* achAnak aDnu
(अचानक अड्नु)
storage, *n. (goods)* sañgraha
(संग्रह), *(place)* bhaNDAr
(भण्डार), godAm (गोदाम)
store, *n.* bhaNDAr (भण्डार),
godAm (गोदाम)
v. godAm mA rAkhnu
(गोदाममा राख्नु),
jammA garnu (जम्मा गर्नु)
storehouse, *n.* bhaNDAr
(भण्डार), godAm (गोदाम)
storekeeper, *n.* bhaNDAre
(भण्डारे), pasale (पसले)
storeroom, *n.* bhaNDAr
(भण्डार)
storey, *n.* talA (तला)
stork, *n.* sAras (सारस)
storm, *n.* AñdhI (आँधी),
AñdhI berhI (आँधीबेह्री)
v. (wind) tej bahanu

(तेज बहनु), (army) dhAwA
bolnu (धावा बोल्नु)
stormy, *adj.* AñdhI chaleko
(आँधी चलेको)
story, *n.* kathA (कथा), kahAnI
(कहानी), wiwaraN (विवरण),
bayAn (बयान),
(news) samAchAr (समाचार)
stout, *adj.* baliyo (बलियो),
haTTA kaTTA (हट्टाकट्टा)
stove, *n.* chulho (चुल्हो),
sTobh (स्टोभ)
straight, *adj.* sIdhA (सीधा),
sojho (सोझो),
(go straight) sajAya pAe
pachhi imAn dArI kA sАth
basnu (सजाय पाएपछि
इमान्दारीका साथ बस्नु)
straight away, *adv.* turunt
(तुरुन्त)
straighten, *v.* sIdhA pArnu
(सीधा पार्नु)
straight face, *adj.* gambhIr
mudrA (गम्भीर मुद्रा)
straightforward, *adj.* kharo
(खरो), spashT (स्पष्ट)
strain, *n.* tanAu (तनाउ),
markAi (मर्काइ),
(lit.) shailI (शैली)
v. tankyAunu (तन्क्याउनु),
adhik bhAr pArnu (अधिक भार
पार्नु), markAunu (मर्काउनु)
strange, *adj.* anauTho

(अनौठो), naulo (नौलो)

stranger, n. naulo/parAi mAnchhe (नौलो/पराइ मान्छे)

strangle, v. ghAnTI thunnu/nimoThnu (घाँटी थुन्नु/निमोठ्नु)

strap, n. phittA (फिता), lotA (लोता)

strategy, n. raN nIti (रणनीति)

straw, n. parAl (पराल), triN (तृण)

strawberry, n. stra berI (स्ट्रबेरी), bhuiñ ainselu (भुइँ ऐंसेलु)

stray, v. bATo birAunu (बाटो बिराउनु)

stream, n. kholA (खोला), nAlA (नाला), kholsA (खोल्सा), (flow) prawAh (प्रवाह)
v. bagnu (बग्नु)

streamline, v. sajilo ra saphal banAunu (सजिलो र सफल बनाउनु)

street, n. saDak (सडक), bATo (बाटो), path (पथ), (man in the street) sAdhAraN mAnis (साधारण मानिस), (on the streets) weshyA peshA (वेश्या पेशा)

streetwalker, n. weshyA (वेश्या), raNDI (रण्डी)

strength, n. bal (बल), tAgat (तागत)

strengthen, v. baliyo banAunu (बलियो बनाउनु)

stress, n. chAp (चाप),

joD (जोड), dabAu (दबाउ), tanAu (तनाउ)
v. joD/bal dinu (जोड/बल दिनु)

stretch, n. tankAi (तन्काइ), pasAr (पसार), (area) dUrI (दूरी), (at a stretch) nirantar (निरन्तर)
v. tankAunu (तन्काउनु), (body) Ang tAnnu (आंग तान्नु), pasArnu (पसार्नु)

stretcher, n. sTrechar (स्ट्रेचर)

stretch out, v. pasArnu (पसार्नु)

strict, adj. kaDA (कडा), sakht (सख्त)

stride, n. kadam (कदम), pAilA (पाइला), v. lamkanu (लम्कनु)

strife, n. jhagaDA (भगडा), wiwAd (विवाद)

strike, v. hAnnu (हान्नु), hirkAunu (हिर्काउनु), hamlA garnu (हमला गर्नु), Thakkar khAnu (ठक्कर खानु) n. haDtAl (हडताल), mAr (मार), prahAr (प्रहार), AkramaN (आक्रमण), hamlA (हमला)

strike home, v. marm prahAr garnu (मर्म प्रहार गर्नु)

strike off, v. kATnu (काट्नु), meTnu (मेट्नु)

string, n. DorI (डोरी), dhAgo

(धागो), *(mus.)* tAr (तार), *(series)* tAntI (तांती), katAr (कतार)
v. DorI hAlnu (डोरी हाल्नु), kasnu (कस्नु)

strip, *v.* lugA phukAlnu (लुगा फुकाल्नु), nangyAunu (नङ्ग्याउनु), *(skin, bark)* kADhnu (काढ्नु)

striptease, *n.* lugA phukAldai garne uttejak nAch (लुगा फुकाल्दै गर्ने उत्तेजक नाच)

stripe, *n.* dharko (धर्को), *(whip)* korrA ko mAr (कोर्राको मार)

striped, *adj.* dharke (धर्के)

strive, *v.* kosis garnu (कोसिस गर्नु), mari meTnu (मरिमेट्नु), sangharsh garnu (संघर्ष गर्नु)

stroke, *n.* prahAr (प्रहार), dhakkA (धक्का)
v. musArnu (मुसार्नु), sum sumyAunu (सुमसुम्याउनु)

stroll, *v.* Dulnu (डुल्नु), sair garnu (सैर गर्नु)
n. Dul phir (डुलफिर)

strong, *adj.* baliyo (बलियो), shakti shalI (शक्तिशाली)

strong-arm, *adj.* bal prayog garine (बल प्रयोग गरिने)

stronghold, *n.* gaDh (गढ), killA (किल्ला)

strong-minded, *adj.* driDh nischayI (दृढनिश्चयी)

strong point, *n.* wishishTtA (विशिष्टता), wishesh yogyatA

(विशेष योग्यता)

structure, *n.* samrachnA (संरचना), banoT (बनोट)

struggle, *n.* sangharsh (संघर्ष), bhiDant (भिडन्त)
v. sangharsh garnu (संघर्ष गर्नु), bhiDnu (भिड्नु)

stubborn, *adj.* haThI (हठी), jiddI wAl (जिद्दीवाल), jarkaTo (जर्कटो)

student, *n.* widyArthI (विद्यार्थी), chhAtra (छात्र)

studio, *n.* sTuDio (स्टुडियो)

study, *n.* paDhAi (पढाइ), adhyayan (अध्ययन)
v. paDhnu (पढ्नु), adhyayan garnu (अध्ययन गर्नु)

stuff, *n.* chIj (चीज), mAl (माल), kapaDA (कपडा)
v. kochnu (कोच्नु), jAknu (जाक्नु)

stumble, *v.* Thes lAgnu (ठेस लाग्नु), laDnu (लड्नु)

stump, *n. (tree)* ThuTA (ठुटा), *(cigarette)* ThuTo (ठुटो), *(cricket)* sTamp (स्टम्प)
v. (walk) khuTTA bajArera hindnu (खुट्टा बजारेर हिंड्नु), *(speak)* bhAshaN dindai hindnu (भाषण दिंदै हिंड्नु)

stunned, *adj.* dukhI (दुखी), *(feelings)* stambhit (स्तम्भित)

stunt, *n.* kamAl (कमाल),

kalA bAjI (कलाबाजी)

stupid, *adj.* mUrkh (मूर्ख),
bekuph (बेकुफ)

stupor, *n.* tandrA (तन्द्रा),
moh (मोह)

style, *n.* shailI (शैली),
DhAṅchA (ढाँचा)
v. saṅgỹA dinu (संज्ञा दिनु)

stylish, *adj.* DhAṅchA wAl
(ढाँचावाल), jhilke (भ्रिल्के)

subconscious, *adj.* aw chetan
(अवचेतन)

subject, *n.* wishaya (विषय),
(state) nAgrik (नागरिक),
(pl.) prajA (प्रजा)
v. adhIn garnu (अधीन गर्नु),
dabAunu (दबाउनु)

subjection, *n.* adhIntA
(अधीनता), kabjA (कब्जा)

submerge, *v.* pAnI le
DhAknu/DubAunu (पानीले
ढाक्नु/डुबाउनु)

submission, *n.* adhIntA
(अधीनता), *(plea)* bintI
(बिन्ती), anurodh (अनुरोध)

submit, *v.* bintI/anurodh garnu
(बिन्ती/अनुरोध गर्नु),
(yield) mAnnu (मान्नु),
jhuknu (भुक्नु)

subordinate, *adj.* mAt hat
(मातहत), adhIn (अधीन)
n. tallo karm chArI
(तल्लो कर्मचारी)

subscribe, *v.* samarthan garnu
(समर्थन गर्नु), *(paper, cable)*
grAhak bannu (ग्राहक बन्नु),
(sign) sahI garnu (सही गर्नु)

subscriber, *n.* grAhak (ग्राहक),
chandA dAtA (चन्दादाता)

subscription, *n.* chandA (चन्दा)

subside, *v.* ghaTnu (घट्नु),
shAnt hunu (शान्त हुनु)

substance, *n.* *(matter)* chIj
(चीज), padArth (पदार्थ),
(gist) sAr (सार)

substantiate, *v.* pramANit /
sAbit garnu (प्रमाणित /
साबित गर्नु)

substitute, *n.* sATo (साटो),
badlA (बदला)
v. sATnu (साट्नु),
badli dinu (बदलिदिनु)

subtle, *adj.* kushAgra (कुशाग्र),
(matter) gUDh (गूढ),
jaTil (जटिल),
(person) chatur (चतुर)

subtract, *v.* ghaTAunu (घटाउनु)

subtraction, *n.* ghaTAu (घटाउ)

suburb, *n.* kAṅTh (कांठ),
shahar ko bAhirI bhAg
(शहरको बाहिरी भाग)

succeed, *v.* saphal hunu (सफल
हुनु), *(post)* kasai ko ThAuṅ
mA kAm garnu (कसैको
ठाउँमा काम गर्नु)

success, *n.* saphaltA (सफलता)

successful, *adj.* saphal (सफल)

successor, *n.* uttarAdhikArI (उत्तराधिकारी)

such, *adj.* yasto (यस्तो), yatro (यत्रो), *(as such)* tyas haisiyat le (त्यस हैसियतले)

such-and-such, *pron.* phalAno (फलानो), tyasto (त्यस्तो)

such as, *adv.* udAharaN kA lAgi (उदाहरणका लागि), jasto ki (जस्तो कि)

suck, *v.* chusnu (चुस्नु), *(breast)* dUdh chusnu (दूध चुस्नु) *n.* chusne kAm (चुस्ने काम)

suckle, *v.* dUdh khwAunu (दूध ख्वाउनु)

sudden, *adj.* achAnak (अचानक), Akasmik (आकस्मिक)

suddenly *adj.* akasmAt (अकस्मात्), ekA ek (एकाएक)

suffer, *v.* sahanu (सहनु), bhognu (भोग्नु), *(pain)* duhkha bhognu (दुःख भोग्नु)

suffering, *n.* kashT (कष्ट), pIDA (पीडा)

sufficient, *adj.* kAphI (काफी), paryApt (पर्याप्त)

suffocate, *v.* nisAssinu (निसास्सिनु), galA dabAunu (गला दबाउनु)

sugar, *n.* chinI (चिनी)

sugar beet, *n.* chukandar (चुकन्दर)

sugar cane, *n.* ukhu (उखु)

suggest, *v.* sujhAu dinu (सुझाउ दिनु)

suggestion, *n.* sujhAu (सुझाउ)

suicide, *n.* Atma hatyA (आत्महत्या), ap hatte (अपहत्ते)

suit, *n.* sUT (सूट), *(law)* muddA (मुद्दा), nAlis (नालिस), *(marriage)* wiwAh prastAw (विवाह प्रस्ताव) *v.* suhAunu (सुहाउनु), rAmro dekhinu (राम्रो देखिनु)

suitable, *adj.* suhAuṅdo (सुहाउँदो), lAyak (लायक)

suitcase, *n.* lugA rAkhne bAkas (लुगा राख्ने बाकस), suT kes (सुटकेस)

suitor, *n.* jhagaDiyA (झगडिया), *(man)* premI (प्रेमी)

sulk, *v.* Thussinu (ठुस्सिनु)

sullen, *adj.* Thussa pareko (ठुस्स परेको)

sulphur/sulfur, *n.* gandhak (गन्धक)

sultry, *adj.* garmI (गर्मी), *(person)* kAmuk (कामुक)

sum, *n.* jammA (जम्मा), *(money)* rakam (रकम), *(gist)* sAr (सार), *(math.)* hisAb (हिसाब)

sum up, *v.* joDnu (जोड्नु),

jammA garnu (जम्मा गर्नु),
sAr nikAlnu (सार निकाल्नु)

summary, *n.* sArAmsh (सारांश)

summer, *n. (season)* garmI
(गर्मी), barkhA (बर्खा)

summit, *n.* chulI (चुली),
Tuppo (टुप्पो)
adj. shIrshasth (शीर्षस्थ)

summon, *v.* DAkI bolAI
paThAunu (डाकी बोलाई
पठाउनु), DAknu (डाक्नु)

summons, *n.* bolAhaT
(बोलाहट)

sumptuous, *adj.* bhawya (भव्य),
rabAphilo (रबाफिलो)

sun, *n.* sUrya (सूर्य), ghAm (घाम)

sunbath, *n.* sUrya snAn
(सूर्य स्नान)

sunburnt, *adj.* ghAm le
DaDheko (घामले डढेको)

Sunday, *n.* Ait bAr (आइतबार),
rawi wAr (रविवार)

sundown, *n.* sUryAst (सूर्यास्त)

sunflower, *n.* sUrya mukhI
phUl (सूर्यमुखी फूल)

sunglasses, *n.* ghAm chasmA
(घाम चस्मा)

sunny, *adj.* ghamAilo (घमाइलो),
ghAm lAgeko (घाम लागेको)

sunrise, *n.* sUryodaya (सूर्योदय)

sunset, *n.* sUryAst (सूर्यास्त)

sunshine, *n.* ghAm (घाम)

sunstroke, *n.* lU (लू)

suntanned, *adj.* ghAm le
DaDhera khairo bhaeko
(घामले डढेर खैरो भएको)

superb, *adj.* shAn dAr
(शान्दार), uttam (उत्तम)

superhuman, *adj.* daiwI (दैवी)

supermarket, *n.* wishAl bajAr
(बिशालबजार)

supernatural, *adj.* alaukik
(अलौकिक), amAnush (अमानुष)

superintendent, *n.* sañchAlak
(सञ्चालक),
supariwekshak (सुपरिवेक्षक)

superior, *adj.* shreshTh (श्रेष्ठ),
utkrishT (उत्कृष्ट)
n. (position) mAthillo hAkim
(माथिल्लो हाकिम)

superstition, *n.* andh wishwAs
(अन्धविश्वास)

superstitious, *adj.* andh
wishwAsI (अन्धविश्वासी)

supervise, *v.* rekh dekh garnu
(रेखदेख गर्नु)

supervisor, *n.* supariwekshak
(सुपरिवेक्षक),
supar bhAijar (सुपरभाइजर)

supper, *n.* belukA dhilo
khAine khAnA (बेलुका ढिलो
खाइने खाना)

supplies, *n.* sar sAmAn
(सरसामान),
khAdya sAmagrI (खाद्यसामग्री)

supply, *n.* ApUrti (आपूर्ति),

sambharaN (सम्भरण)
v. puryAunu (पुर्‍याउनु),
juTAunu (जुटाउनु),
ApUrti garnu (आपूर्ति गर्नु)

support, n. AD (आड),
sahArA (सहारा), sahAyatA
(सहायता), samarthan (समर्थन)
v. AD dinu (आड दिनु),
sahAyatA garnu
(सहायता गर्नु), (person)
samarthan garnu (समर्थन गर्नु)

supporter, n. samarthak
(समर्थक)

suppose, v. anumAn garnu
(अनुमान गर्नु),
bhanThAnnu (भन्ठान्नु)

suppress, v. daman garnu
(दमन गर्नु), dabAunu (दबाउनु)

supreme, adj. sarwochcha
(सर्वोच्च)

sure, adj. pakkA (पक्का),
jarur (जरुर), *(make sure)*
pakkA garnu (पक्का गर्नु)

sure-fire, adj. pakkA (पक्का),
asaphal na hune (असफल
नहुने), achUk (अचूक)

sure-footed, adj. khuTTA na
kamAune (खुट्टा नकमाउने)

surface, n. satah (सतह),
bAhirI hissA (बाहिरी हिस्सा)
v. mAthi utranu (माथि उत्रनु)

surgeon, n. chir phAr garne
DAkTar (चिरफार गर्ने

DAkTar), sarjan (सर्जन)

surgery, n. chir phAr
(चिरफार),
shalya kriyA (शल्यक्रिया)

surname, n. thar (थर),
up nAm (उपनाम)

surpass, v. uchhinnu (उछिन्नु),
jitnu (जित्नु)

surplus, n. baDhI (बढी),
jageDA (जगेडा)

surprise, n. Ashcharya
(आश्चर्य), tAjup (ताजुप)
v. chakit/jilla pArnu
(चकित/जिल्ल पार्नु)

surprised, adj. chakit (चकित),
tAjup (ताजुप)

surprising, adj. achamma
lAgdo (अचम्म लाग्दो)

surrender, v. hAr mAnnu (हार
मान्नु), Atma samarpaN garnu
(आत्मसमर्पण गर्नु)
n. Atma samarapaN
(आत्मसमर्पण), hAr (हार)

surround, v. ghernu (घेर्नु)

surrounding, n. sero phero
(सेरोफेरो)

survey, v. chArai tira hernu
(चारैतिर हेर्नु), sarwekshaN
garnu (सर्वेक्षण गर्नु)
n. sarwekshaN (सर्वेक्षण),
(land) nApI (नापी)

survive, v. bAñchnu (बाँच्नु)

suspect, v. shañkA garnu

(शंका गर्नु)
n. shañkA lAgeko mAnis
(शंका लागेको मानिस)

suspend, v. jhunDyAunu
(भुन्ड्याउनु), (job) nilamban
garnu (निलम्बन गर्नु)

suspense, n. anyol (अन्योल),
duwidhA (दुविधा)

suspension, n. jholuñge
(भोलुङ्गे), TañgAi (टँगाइ)

suspension bridge, n.
jholuñge pul (भोलुङ्गे पुल)

suspicion, n. shañkA (शंका),
sandeh (सन्देह)

suspicious, adj. shañkA lAgne
(शंका लाग्ने), shañkit (शंकित)

sustain, v. thegnu (थेग्नु),
dhAnnu (धान्नु)

swagger, v. akaDera hiñDnu
(अकडेर हिंड्नु), gamkanu (गम्कनु)

swallow, n. gauñthalI (गौंथली)
v. nilnu (निल्नु)

swamp, n. dhAp (धाप),
dal dal (दलदल)
v. gADinu (गाडिनु), dhassinu
(धस्सिनु), (flood) pAnI le
DhAki dinu (पानीले ढाकिदिनु),
(person) hairAn garnu (हैरान गर्नु)

swan, n. rAj hAñs (राजहाँस)

swarm, n. bathAn (बथान),
thupro (थुप्रो)
v. bathAn banAera hiñDnu
(बथान बनाएर हिंड्नु),

jhummlnu (भुम्मिनु)

sway, v. hallanu (हल्लनु),
jhulnu (भुल्नु)
n. kampan (कम्पन)

swear, v. kiriyA khAnu
(किरिया खानु),
sapath linu (सपथ लिनु)

sweat, n. pasinA (पसिना)
v. pasinA jhiknu
(पसिना भिक्नु)

sweater, n. sweTar (स्वेटर)

sweep, v. kucho lAunu (कुचो
लाउनु), baDhArnu (बढार्नु)

sweep the board, v. pUrA
bAjI mArnu (पूरा बाजी मार्नु)

sweeper, n. kucho lAune
mAnchhe (कुचो लाउने मान्छे),
kUchI kAr (कूचीकार)

sweet, adj. guliyo (गुलियो),
mITho (मीठो), (voice)
madhur (मधुर), surilo (सुरिलो)
n. miThAI (मिठाई)

sweetheart, n. premI (प्रेमी),
premikA (प्रेमिका)

sweetmeat, n. miThAI (मिठाई)

sweetpea, n. kerAu ko phUl
(केराउको फूल)

sweet potato, n. sakhar
khaND (सखरखण्ड)

swell, v. suninu (सुनिनु),
phulnu (फुल्नु)
adj. bes (बेस), uttam (उत्तम)

swift, adj. chhiTo (छिटो),

chAṅDo (चाँडो)

swim, *v.* pauDI khelnu
(पौडी खेल्नु)
n. pauDI (पौडी), tairaN (तैरण)

swimmer, *n.* pauDI bAj
(पौडीबाज)

swimming, *n.* pauDI (पौडी)

swimming costume, *n.* pauDI
kheldA lAune poshAk
(पौडी खेल्दा लाउने पोशाक)

swimming pool, *n.* pauDI
pokharI (पौडी पोखरी)

swimming suit, *n.* pauDI
khelne poshAk
(पौडी खेल्ने पोशाक)

swine, *n.* suṅgur (सुँगुर)

swing, *v.* piṅ (पिङ),
jhulanA (झुलना),
jholuṅgo (झोलुङ्गो)
v. piṅ khelnu/jhulnu
(पिङ खेल्नु/झुल्नु),
machchAunu (मच्चाउनु)

switch, *n.* *(electric)* swIch
(स्वीच), *(change)* pher badal
(फेरबदल),
(stick) chhaDI (छडी)
v. badalnu (बदल्नु)

switch off, *v.* *(bulb, etc.)*
nibhAunu (निभाउनु),
mArnu (मर्नु)

sword, *n.* tar bAr (तरबार),
khaDga (खड्ग)

syllabus, *n.* pAThya kram
(पाठ्यक्रम),
(list) tAlikA (तालिका)

symbol, *n.* chinha (चिन्ह),
pratIk (प्रतीक)

sympathy, *n.* sahAnu bhUti
(सहानुभूति)

symptom, *n.* chinha (चिन्ह),
lakshaN (लक्षण)

synonym, *n.* uhI arth
bujhAune shabd (उही अर्थ
बुझाउने शब्द),
paryAya (पर्याय)

synopsis, *n.* sArAṃsh
(सारांश), majbUn (मजबून)

synthetic, *n.* kritrim (कृत्रिम),
nakkalI (नक्कली)

syphilis, *n.* bhiriṅgI rog
(भिरिङ्गी रोग)

syringe, *n.* pachkA (पच्का),
sirinj (सिरिन्ज),
pichkArI (पिचकारी)

syrup, *n.* chAsnI (चासनी),
sarbat (सर्बत)

system, *n.* rIti (रीति),
wyawasthA (व्यवस्था)

systematic, *adj.* rIti/niyam
pUrwak (रीति/नियमपूर्वक)

table   259   take out

T

table, *n.* Tebul (टेबुल)
v. tAlikA baddh garnu
(तालिकाबद्ध गर्नु),
sUchi mA rAkhnu
(सूचिमा राख्नु)

tablecloth, *n.* Tebul posh
(टेबुलपोश)

tablet, *n. (writing)* pATI
(पाटी), *(slab)* phalak (फलक),
(med.) chakkI (चक्की)

taboo, *n.* bArnA (बारना),
warjit kAm (वर्जित काम)

tact, *n.* sIp (सीप), dakshatA
(दक्षता), buddhi (बुद्धि)

tactful, *adj.* nipuN (निपुण),
sipAlu (सिपालु)

tactics, *n.* dAu pech (दाउपेच),
yukti (युक्ति),
(war) raN nIti (रणनीति)

tag, *n.* lebul (लेबुल),
(shoe) phittA ko chheu ko
dhAtu ko bhAg (फित्ताको
छेउको धातुको भाग)
v. lebul lagAunu (लेबुल
लगाउनु), joDnu (जोड्नु)

tail, *n.* puchchhar (पुच्छर),
puchhAr (पुछार)
v. puchchhar hAlnu

(पुच्छर हाल्नु),
pIchhA garnu (पीछा गर्नु)

tail away/off, *v.* pachhi parnu
(पछि पर्नु), chhuTTinu (छुट्टिनु)

tailor, *n.* darjI (दर्जी),
sujI kAr (सुजीकार)

tailor-made, *adj.* nAp milAera
tayAr garieko (नाप मिलाएर
तयार गरिएको),
khup mileko (खुप मिलेको)

tailpiece, *n.* antim bhAg
(अन्तिम भाग)

take, *v.* pakranu (पक्रनु),
lai jAnu (लैजानु), linu (लिनु),
puryAunu (पुर्‍याउनु),
(time, etc.) lAgnu (लाग्नु),
(receive) thAppnu (थाप्नु)

take away, *v.* lAnu (लानु),
lai jAnu (लैजानु)

take hold, *v.* samAtnu (समाल्नु)

take-home pay, *n.* kar Adi
kaTAI diyeko talab (कर
आदि कटाई दिएको तलब)

take off, *v.* phukAlnu
(फुकाल्नु),
(plane) uDnu (उड्नु)

take out, *v.* jhiknu (भिक्नु),
nikAlnu (निकाल्नु)

take over, *v.* samhAlnu (सम्हाल्नु), bujhnu (बुझ्नु), *(control)* niyantraN garnu (नियन्त्रण गर्नु)

take place, *v.* ghaTit hunu (घटित हुनु)

take to, *v. (work)* shuru garnu (शुरु गर्नु), *(drug)* lat lAgnu (लत लाग्नु)

take to pieces *v.* bhatkAunu (भत्काउनु)

tale, *n.* kathA (कथा)

talent, *n.* sIp (सीप), yogyatA (योग्यता), pratibhA (प्रतिभा)

talented, *adj.* daksha (दक्ष), pratibhA shAlI (प्रतिभाशाली)

talk, *n.* kurA (कुरा), kurA kAnI (कुराकानी), wArtA (वार्ता), prawachan (प्रवचन) *v.* kurA garnu (कुरा गर्नु), kurA kAnI garnu (कुराकानी गर्नु), bolnu (बोल्नु)

talkative, *adj.* bature (बतुरे), gaphI (गफी), kurauTe (कुरौटे)

talk over, *v.* chhal phal garnu (छलफल गर्नु)

talk tall, *v.* guDDI hAṅknu (गुड्डी हाँक्नु)

tall, *adj.* aglo (अग्लो), algo (अल्गो)

tall order, *n.* anuchit mAg (अनुचित माग)

tally, *n. (debt)* len den (लेनदेन), *(number)* goTA (गोटा) *v.* mel khAnu (मेल खानु), milnu (मिल्नु)

tamarind, *n.* imalI (इमली), amlI (अम्ली), amilI (अमिली)

tame, *adj.* pAltu (पाल्तु), rattieko (रत्तिएको), gharelu (घरेलु), shAnt (शान्त) *v.* pAltu garAunu (पाल्तु गराउनु), ratyAunu (रत्याउनु)

tamper, *v.* bigArnu (बिगार्नु)

tan, *n.* ghAm le poleko khairo raṅg (घामले पोलेको खैरो रंग) *adj.* khairo (खैरो) *v.* ghAm le DaDhnu (घामले डढ्नु), *(leather)* tayArI chhAlA banAunu (तयारी छाला बनाउनु)

tangerine, *n.* suntalA (सुन्तला)

tank, *n.* talAu (तलाउ), pokharI (पोखरी), *(reservoir)* jalAshaya (जलाशय), *(mil.)* TyAṅk (ट्याङ्क)

tap, *n.* dhArA (धारा), kal dhArA (कलधारा), *(pat)* thapkI (थप्की) *v.* TuTI lagAunu (टुटी लगाउनु), *(let out)* nikAlnu (निकाल्नु), *(pierce)* chheDnu (छेड्नु)

tape, *n.* phittA (फित्ता), Tep (टेप) *v.* phittA le bAṅdhnu (फित्ताले बाँध्नु)

tapeworm, *n.* phitte jukA
(फितेजुका)

tar, *n.* alkatrA (अलकत्रा)

target, *n.* nishAnA (निशाना),
tAro (तारो)

tariff, *n.* bhansAr mahsul
(भन्सार महसुल)

tarnish, *n.* dhabbA (धब्बा),
TATo (टाटो)
v. Talak dhamilyAunu
(टलक धमिल्याउनु),
dhabbA lAunu (धब्बा लाउनु)

taro, *n.* piñDAlu (पिंडालु)

task, *n.* kAm (कम),
(lesson) pATh (पाठ)
v. kAm dinu/ladAunu
(काम दिनु/लदाउनु)

taste, *n.* swAd (स्वाद),
ruchi (रुचि)
v. swAd linu (स्वाद लिनु),
chAkhnu (चाख्नु)

tasteful, *adj.* swAdilo (स्वादिलो),
ruchi kar (रुचिकर)

tasty, *adj.* swAdilo (स्वादिलो),
mITho (मीठो)

tattoo, *n. (skin)* godna (गोदना),
(mil.) rAt ko bigul
(रातको बिगुल)
v. khopAunu (खोपाउनु),
khop hAlnu (खोप हाल्नु)

taunt, *v.* tanA mArnu (ताना
मार्नु), gijyAunu (गिज्याउनु)

tavern, *n* bhaTTI (भट्टी)

tax, *n.* kar (कर),
mahsul (महसुल)
v. kar lagAunu (कर लगाउनु),
(burden) bhAr hAlnu
(भार हाल्नु)

taxi, *n.* TyAksI (ट्याक्सी)

T.B., *n.* TibI (टि.बी.),
kshya rog (क्षयरोग)

tea, *n.* chiyA (चिया)

tea break, *n.* chiyA khAne
chhuTTI (चिया खाने छुट्टी)

teach, *v.* paDhAunu (पढाउनु),
sikAunu (सिकाउनु)

teacher, *n.* shikshak (शिक्षक),
guru (गुरु)

tea estate, *n.* chiyA bagAn
(चियाबगान)

teak, *n.* sAgwAn kATh
(सागवान काठ)

team, *n.* TolI (टोली),
dal (दल), samUha (समूह)
v. milera kAm garnu
(मिलेर काम गर्नु)

teamwork, *n.* milera garine
kAm (मिलेर गरिने काम)

teapot, *n.* chiyA dAn
(चियादान)

tear, *n. (eye)* Añsu (आँसु),
(opening) chirA (चिरा)
v. chyAtnu (च्यात्नु),
phADnu (फाड्नु)

tear to pieces, *v.* luchhnu
(लुछ्नु)

tear up, v. chyAt chut pArnu
(च्यातचुत पार्नु)

tease, v. gijyAunu (गिज्याउनु),
jiskyAunu (जिस्क्याउनु)

teaspoon, n. sAno chamchA
(सानो चम्चा)

teat, n. thun (थुन), dUdh ko
muNTo (दूधको मुण्टो)

technical, adj. prAwidhik
(प्राविधिक)

technician, n. prAwidhigya
(प्राविधिज्ञ),
jAniph kAr (जानिफकार)

technique, n. prawidhi
(प्रविधि), widhi (विधि)

technology,n. prawidhi
(प्रविधि)

tedious, adj. uchchAT lAgne
(उच्चाट लाग्ने),
thakAune (थकाउने)

teens, n. kishorAwasthA
(किशोराअवस्था)

teeth, n. dAnt harU (दाँतहरू)

telegram, n. tAr (तार),
Teli grAm (टेलिग्राम)

telephone, n. Teli phon
(टेलिफोन)

telescope, n. dUrbIn (दूरबीन)

television, n. Teli bhijan
(टेलिभिजन)

tell, v. bhannu (भन्नु),
batAunu (बताउनु), (relate)
bayAn garnu (बयान गर्नु)

teller, n. gaNak (गणक),
(bank) noT ganne jAnchne
(नोट गन्ने जाँच्ने)

tell-tale, n. kathA bhanne
wyakti (कथा भन्ने व्यक्ति)

telltale, n. chhuske bachchA
(छुस्के बच्चा), kurauTe
bachchA (कुरौटे बच्चा)

temper, n. mijAs (मिजास),
bAnI (बानी)
v. ghaTAunu (घटाउनु),
roknu (रोक्नु), (steel) pAnI
chaDhAunu (पानी चढाउनु),
(in a temper) risAeko
(रिसाएको), (loose one's
temper) risAunu (रिसाउनु)

tempered, adj (bad/hot-
tempered) risAhA (रिसाहा)

temperament,n. swabhAw
(स्वभाव), mijAs (मिजास)

temperamental adj. chir chire
(चिरचिरे)

temperature, n.tAp kram
(तापक्रम)

tempest, n. AndI (आँधी),
tUphAn (तूफान)

temple, n. mandir (मन्दिर),
dewal (देवल), kan chaT
(कन्चट), kan pAo (कन्पारो)

tempo, n. (mus.) tA (ताल),
(activity) raphtAr (रफ्तार)

temporary, adj. asthAyI
(अस्थायी)

tempt, *v.* phasAunu (फसाउनु),
lobhyAunu (लोभ्याउनु)

temptation, *n.* lAlach (लालच),
pralobhan (प्रलोभन)

tempting, *adj.* lobh lAgdo
(लोभलाग्दो),
Akarshak (आकर्षक)

ten, *n.* das (दस)

tenacious, *adj.* driDh (दृढ),
aTal (अटल), chAmro (चाम्रो)

tenant, *n. (house)* bahAl
wAlA (बहालवाला), *(land)*
mohI (मोही), asAmI (असामी)

tend, *v.* her wichAr garnu
(हेरविचार गर्नु),
(cattle) pAlnu (पाल्नु),
(attitude) Dhalkanu (ढल्कनु),
prawritta hunu (प्रवृत्त हुनु)

tendency, *n.* jhukAu
(झुकाउ), prawritti (प्रवृत्ति)

tender, *adj.* kalilo (कलिलो),
kamalo (कमलो)
n. bol patra (बोलपत्र),
TeNDar (टेण्डर)
v. dinu (दिनु),
prastut garnu (प्रस्तुत गर्नु)

tennis, *n.* Tenis khel
(टेनिस खेल)

tense, *adj. (body)* tankieko
(तन्किएको),
(person) Attieko (आत्तिएको),
tanAu pUrN (तनाउपूर्ण)
n. (gram.) kAl (काल)

tent, *n.* pAl (पाल), tambU (तम्बू),
(pitch a tent) pAl TAñnu
(पाल टाङ्नु)

tenure, *n. (land)* hak (हक),
swAmitwa (स्वामित्व),
(office) kArya kAl (कार्यकाल)

term, *n. (period)* awadhi
(अवधि), myAd (म्याद),
(word) shabd (शब्द)
v. bhannu (भन्नु),
sañgYA dinu (संज्ञा दिनु)

terms, *n.* shart (शर्त),
(come to terms) milnu (मिल्नु),
dabnu (दब्नु),
(in terms of) sambandh mA
(सम्बन्धमा)

terms of reference, *n.*
wichArArth wishaya
(विचारार्थ विषय)

terminate, *v.* samApt garnu
(समाप्त गर्नु), siddhinu (सिद्धिनु)
adj. sImit (सीमित)

termination, *n.* samApti
(समाप्ति), samApan (समापन),
antya (अन्त्य)

termite, *n.* dhamiro (धमिरो)

terrace, *n. (land, field)* garA
(गरा), *(altitude)* aglo ThAuñ
(अग्लो ठाउँ),
(house) kausI (कौसी)

terrible, *adj.* Dar lAgdo
(डरलाग्दो),
bhayañkar (भयङ्कर)

terrific, *adj.* Dar lAgdo (डरलाग्दो), ghor (घोर)

terrify, *v.* atyAunu (अत्याउनु), tarsAunu (तर्साउनु)

terror, *n.* Dar (डर), trAs (त्रास), Ataṅk (आतङ्क)

territorial, *adj.* kshetrIya (क्षेत्रीय)

territory, *n.* kshetra (क्षेत्र), ilAkA (इलाका)

test, *n.* (trial) jA̐ch (जाँच), parakh (परख), (exam.) jA̐ch (जाँच), parIkshA (परीक्षा) *v.* jA̐chnu (जाँच्नु), ajmAunu (अजमाउनु)

testicle, *n.* gulA (गुला), aND kosh (अण्डकोष)

testify, *v.* sAkshI baknu (साक्षी बक्नु), pramANit garnu (प्रमाणित गर्नु)

testimonial, *n.* pramAN patra (प्रमाणपत्र), siphArish patra (सिफारिशपत्र)

testimony, *n.* gawAhI (गवाही), sAkshI (साक्षी)

tetanus, *n.* (med.) dhanush TaṅkAr (धनुष्टङ्कार)

text, *n.* mUl pATh (मूल पाठ)

textbook, *n.* pAThya pustak (पाठ्यपुस्तक)

textile, *n.* kapaDA (कपडा), wastra (वस्त्र)

than, *prep.* bhandA (भन्दा)

thank, *v.* dhanya wAd dinu (धन्यवाद दिनु)

thank you, *inter.* dhanya wAd (धन्यवाद)

thankful, *adj.* AbhArI (आभारी), kritagȳa (कृतज्ञ)

thanks, *inter.* dhanya wAd (धन्यवाद)

that, *pron.* tyo (त्यो), tyahI (त्यही) *adj.* tyo (त्यो), yo (यो) *conj.* ki (कि)

that is, *conj.* arthAt (अर्थात्)

thatch, *n.* phus ko chhAnA (फुसको छाना) *v.* phus ko chhAnA lAunu (फुसको छाना लाउनु)

thaw, *v.* paglanu (पग्लनु)

the, *def. art.* tyo (त्यो)

theatre/theater, *n.* nAch ghar (नाचघर), raṅg mañch (रङ्गमञ्च), (hall) koThA (कोठा), kaksha (कक्ष)

theft, *n.* chorI (चोरी)

their, *pron.* tinI/unI harU ko (तिनी/उनीहरूको)

them, *pron.* tinI/unI harU lAI (तिनी/उनीहरूलाई)

theme, *n.* wishaya (विषय)

then, *adj.* tyas belA ko (त्यसबेलाको) *adv.* tyas belA (त्यसबेला), taba (तब), tyas pachhi (त्यसपछि), ani (अनि) *conj.* tasarth (तसर्थ)

thence, *adv.* tyahAň bATa (त्यहाँबाट), tyas pachhi (त्यसपछि)

thenceforth, *adv.* tyas uprAnta (त्यसउप्रान्त)

theory, *n.* siddhAnt (सिद्धान्त), mat (मत)

there, *adv.* tyahAň (त्यहाँ), uhAň (उहाँ)

thereafter, *adv.* tyas pachhi (त्यसपछि)

thereby, *adv.* tyas us le (त्यस उसले), tyasarI (त्यसरी), phal swarUp (फलस्वरूप)

therefore, *adv.* tyas kAraN (त्यसकारण), tasarth (तसर्थ)

therein, *adv.* tyahAň (त्यहाँ), tyas mA (त्यसमा)

thereupon, *adv.* tyas pachhi (त्यसपछि)

thermometer, *n.* tAp nApne (ताप नाप्ने), tAp mApak yantra (तापमापक यन्त्र)

thermos, *n.* tharmas (थर्मस)

these, *pron.* yI (यी), yinI harU (यिनीहरू)

they, *pron.* tinI harU (तिनीहरू), yinI harU (यिनीहरू)

thick, *adj.* moTo (मोटो), bAklo (बाक्लो)

thicket, *n.* jhAň (झाड), jhADI (झाडी)

thickness, *n.* moTAi (मोटाइ),

gADhA pan (गाढापन)

thief, *n.* chor (चोर)

thigh, *n.* tighrA (तिघ्रा)

thin, *adj.* pAtalo (पातलो), masino (मसिनो), *(person)* dublo (दुब्लो), *(thing)* jhinU (झिनु)

thing, *n.* chIj (चीज), wastu (वस्तु), kurA (कुरा), *(affair)* kurA (कुरा), wishaya (विषय)

think, *v.* wichAr garnu (विचार गर्नु), sochnu (सोच्नु), *(imagine)* ThAnnu (ठान्नु)

thinker, *n.* wichArak (विचारक)

third, *adj.* tesro (तेस्रो), tritIya (तृतीय)

third-rate, *adj.* ghaTiyA (घटिया)

thirst, *n.* pyAs (प्यास), tirkhA (तिर्खा)

thirsty, *adj.* tirkhAeko (तिर्खाएको), pyAso (प्यासो)

thirteen, *n.* terha (तेह्र)

thirty, *n.* tIs (तीस)

this, *pron.* yo (यो)

this day, *n.* Aja (आज)

this morning, *n./adv.* Aja bihAna (आज बिहान)

thither, *adv.* utA (उता), tyatA (त्यता)

thorn, *n.* kAňDA (काँडा)

thorny, *adj.* kAňDe (काँडे), *(fig.)* pechilo (पेचिलो)

thorough, *adj.* pakkA (पक्का),
pUrA (पूरा), *(person)* ati
sAwdhAn (अति सावधान)

thoroughfare, *n.* mUl bATo
(मूल बाटो)

thoroughly, *adv.* pUrA
tawar le (पूरा तवरले),
ek dam (एकदम)

those, *pron.* unI harU(उनीहरू),
yinI harU (यिनीहरू)

though, *conj.* tA pani (तापनि),
yadyapi (यद्यपि),
(as though) mAno (मानो)

thought, *n.* wichAr (विचार),
chintan (चिन्तन)
v. *(pt. of think)* sochyo
(सोच्यो)

thoughtful, *adj.* wichAr shIl
(विचारशील)

thoughtless, *adj.* wAstA na
garne (वास्ता नगर्ने),
wichAr hIn (विचारहीन)

thousand, *n.* hajAr (हजार)

thousands, *n.* hajArauñ (हजारौँ)

thread *n.* dhAgo (धागो)
v. dhAgo hAlnu (धागो हाल्नु),
(beads) unnu (उन्नु)

threadbare, *adj.* jhyAñg
pwAle (भ्याङ्प्वाले)

threat, *n.* dhamkI (धम्की),
trAs (त्रास)

threaten, *v.* dhamkyAunu
(धम्क्याउनु),

dhamkI dinu (धम्की दिनु)

three, *n.* tIn (तीन)

threshold, *n.* sañghAr (संघार)

thrifty, *adj.* kam kharch garne
(कम खर्च गर्ने),
kam kharchilo (कम खर्चिलो)

thrill, *n.* san sanI (सनसनी),
romAñch (रोमाञ्च)
v. romAñchit garnu
(रोमाञ्चित गर्नु)

thrilling, *adj.* romAñch kArI
(रोमाञ्चकारी)

thrive, *v.* sapranu (सप्रनु),
phasTAunu (फस्टाउनु)

throat, *n.* ghAñTI (घाँटी),
galA (गला)

throb, *v.* balkanu (बल्कनु),
dhaDkanu (धड्कनु)
n. dhaDkan (धड्कन),
kampan (कम्पन)

throne, *n.* rAj gaddI (राजगद्दी),
simhAsan (सिंहासन)
v. gaddI mA basnu/basAunu
(गद्दीमा बस्नु/बसाउनु)

through, *prep.* mArphat
(मार्फत), *(via)* bhaera (भएर),
dwArA (द्वारा),
(Am.) samma (सम्म)

through and through, *adv.*
pUrN rUp le (पूर्णरूपले)

throughout, *adv./prep.* pUrN
tayA (पूर्णतया), sampUrN
(सम्पूर्ण), wAr pAr (वारपार)

throw, v. phyAṅknu (फ्याँक्नु), milkAunu (मिल्काउनु), *(wrestling)* pachhArnu (पछार्नु) n. pheṅkAi (फेँकाइ), prakshep (प्रक्षेप)

throw a party, v. pArTI dinu (पार्टी दिनु)

throwaway, n. kAm sake phAline wastu (काम सके फालिने वस्तु)

throw away, v. milkAunu (मिल्काउनु)

throw cold water on, v. nirutsAhit pArnu (निरुत्साहित पार्नु)

throw dust into the eyes, v. AṅkhA mA chhAro hAlnu (आँखामा छारो हाल्नु)

throw one's lot with, v. sAth dinu (साथ दिनु)

throw open, v. khulA garAunu (खुला गराउनु)

throw out, v. nikAlnu (निकाल्नु)

thumb, n. bUDhI auṅlo (बूढी औंलो) v. chalAunu (चलाउनु), palTAunu (पल्टाउनु)

thumbnail sketch, n. laghu chitra (लघुचित्र)

thumbprint, n. lyApche (ल्याप्चे), auṅThA chhAp (औंठाछाप)

thunder, n. garjan (गर्जन) v. garjanu (गर्जनु), chaDkanu (चड्कनु)

thunderbolt, n. chaTyAṅ (चट्याङ), bajra (बज्र)

thunderous, adj. garjane (गर्जने)

Thursday, n. bihI bAr (बिहीबार), brihaspati wAr (बृहस्पतिवार)

thus, adv. yasarI (यसरी), yas prakAr (यसप्रकार)

tiara, n. trimukuT (त्रिमुकुट)

tick, n. *(insect)* kirnA (किर्ना), *(clock)* Tik-Tik AwAj (टिक टिक आवाज) v. chino lAunu (चिनो लाउनु)

ticket, n. TikaT (टिकट), parchA (पर्चा)

tickle, v. kAukutI lAunu (काउकुती लाउनु) n. kAukutI (काउकुती), kutkutI (कुत्कुती)

ticklish, adj. chAṅDo kutkutI lAgne (चाँडो कुत्कुती लाग्ने)

tide, n. *(sea)* jwAr bhATA (ज्वारभाटा) v. *(season)* samaya (समय), kAl (काल), *(river)* bagnu (बग्नु), *(surge)* urlanu (उर्लनु)

tidy, adj. saphA (सफा), sugghar (सुग्घर)

tie, v. bAňdhnu (बाँध्नु), kasnu (कस्नु), gAňTho pArnu (गाँठो पार्नु), joDnu (जोड्नु), *(sport)* barAbar hunu (बराबर हुनु) *n.* nek TAi (नेकटाइ), bandhan (बन्धन), *(sport)* barAbarI (बराबरी)

tiebreak(er), *n.* wijayI ko nidho garne arko khel/ prashna (विजयीको निधो गर्ने अर्को खेल/प्रश्न)

tier, *n.* talA (तला), taha (तह)

tiffin, *n.* khAjA (खाजा), chamenA (चमेना)

tiger, *n.* bAgh (बाघ)

tight, *adj.* kasieko (कसिएको), Tamma (टम्म), tankeko (तन्केको), khaňdieko (खाँदिएको), na chuhine (नचुहिने)

tight-fisted, *adj.* kanjUs (कन्जुस)

tight-lipped, *adj.* kehI na bolne (केही नबोल्ने)

tightrope, *n.* kalA bAjI dekhAune kasieko DorI (कलाबाजी देखाउने कसिएको डोरी)

tile, *n.* jhiňgaTI (झिँगटी), khapaDA (खपडा), TAyal (टायल), tele IňT (तेले ईंट) *v.* jhiňgaTI wA TAyal chhApnu (झिँगटी वा टायल छाप्नु)

till, *prep.* samma (सम्म) *adv.* jaba samma (जबसम्म) *v.* (field) jotnu (जोल्नु)

tillage, *n.* khan jot (खनजोत)

tiller, *n.* jotAhA (जोताहा), kisAn (किसान)

tilt, *n.* jhukAu (भुकाउ) *v.* jhuknu (भुक्नु), Dhalkinu (ढल्किनु)

timber, *n.* kATh (काठ), kATh pAt (काठपात), TimbA (टिम्बा)

time, *n.* samaya (समय), kAl (काल), belA (बेला), yug (युग), *(occasion)* choTi (चोटि), paTak (पटक), mausam (मौसम), jIwan kAl (जीवनकाल), *(all the time)* hameshA (हमेशा), sadhaiň (सधैं), *(at no time)* kadApi hoina (कदापि होइन), *(at the same time)* ek sAth (एकसाथ), *(behind time)* aber Aune (अबेर आउने), *(for a time)* kehI samaya samma (केही समयसम्म), *(for the time being)* asthAyI rUp le (अस्थायी रूपले), *(free time)* phursat (फुर्सत), *(from time to time)* kahile kAhiň (कहिलेकाहीं), *(in no time)* turunt (तुरुन्त), *(in time)* belai mA (बेलैमा), *(once upon a time)* ekA desh mA (एकादेशमा), *(on time)* ThIk samaya mA (ठीक समयमा), *(out of time)* bemaukA ko (बेमौकाको), *(take your time)* hatAr na gara (हतार नगर) *v.* samaya toknu (समय तोक्नु), samaya nirdhArit garnu (समय निर्धारित गर्नु) *adj.* sAmayik (सामयिक), myAdI (म्यादी)

time and again, *adv.* bArambAr (बारम्बार)

time and tide, *n.* kholA ra belA (खोला र बेला)

time-hono(u)red, *adj.* chir sammAnit (चिरसम्मानित)

time immemorial, *n.* ati prAchIn kAl (अति प्राचीन काल)

time lag, *n.* samaya ko antar (समयको अन्तर), antarAl (अन्तराल)

time limit, *n.* nishchit awadhi (निश्चित अवधि), antim samaya (अन्तिम समय)

timely, *adj.* sAmayik (सामयिक)

time off, *n.* wishrAm garne nishchit samaya (विश्राम गर्ने निश्चत समय)

timepiece, *n.* ghaDI (घडी)

times, *n.* yug (युग),

jamAnA (जमाना), kAl (काल), *(math.)* gunA (गुना), gune (गुने), *(at all times)* sadhaiñ (सधैं), hameshA (हमेशा), *(at times)* kahile kAhIñ (कहिलेकाहीं) *(behind the times)* purAno wichAr ko (पुरानो विचारको)

timetable, *n.* samaya tAlikA (समयतालिका)

timid, *adj.* kAthar (कातर), Dar pok (डरपोक)

tin, *n.* Tin (टिन)

tint, *n.* rañg (रङ्ग) *v.* rañg lagAunu (रङ्ग लगाउनु)

tiny, *adj.* dherai sAno (धेरै सानो)

tip, *n. (top)* tuppo (टुप्पो), *(waiter, etc.)* baksis (बक्सिस), *(hint)* sañket (सङ्केत)

tiptoe, *v.* khuTTA ko auñlA mA Tekera hiñDnu (खुट्टाको औंलामा टेकेर हिंड्नु)

tip-top, *adj.* atyuttam (अत्युत्तम)

tire, *v.* thAknu (थाक्नु), thakAi lAgnu (थकाइ लाग्नु)

tired, *adj.* thAkeko (थाकेको), thakit (थकित)

tireless, *adj.* athak (अथक), na thAkne (नथाक्ने)

tiring, *adj.* thakAune (थकाउने)

title, *n.* darjA (दर्जा), mAn (मान), padwI (पदवी), *(book, etc.)* shIrshak (शीर्षक)

title page, n. mukh prishTh (मुखपृष्ठ)

title role, n. pramukh bhUmikA (प्रमुख भूमिका)

to, prep. lAI (लाई), (motion) mA (मा)

to and fro, adv. yatA uti (यताउति)

toad, n. khasre bhyAguto (खस्रे भ्यागुतो)

toast, n. (bread) sekAeko pAuroTI (सेकाएको पाउरोटी), (wish) shubh kAmnA (शुभकामना) v. seknu (सेक्नु), (for.) su swAsthya ko kAmnA gardai madya pAn garnu (सुस्वास्थ्यको कामना गर्दै मद्यपान गर्नु)

tobacco, n. (plant) surtI (सुर्ती), tamAkhu (तमाखु)

today, n./adv. Aja (आज)

toe, n. khuTTA ko auṅlA (खुट्टाको औंला), (on the toes) pañjA mA (पञ्जामा) v. auṅlA le hAnnu (औंलाले हान्नु),

toehold, n. sAno AdhAr (सानो आधार)

toenail, n. khuTTA ko naṅ (खुट्टाको नङ)

toe the line/mark, v. Adesh ko pAlan garnu (आदेश पालन गर्नु)

toffee, n. miThAI (मिठाई), TaphI (टफी)

together, adv. saṅgai (सँगै), sAth sAth (साथसाथ)

toil, n. kAm (काम), shram (श्रम) v. khaTnu (खट्नु), parishram garnu (परिश्रम गर्नु)

toilet, n. shriṅgAr (शृंगार), poshAk (पोशाक), (lavatory) shauchAlaya (शौचालय), charpI (चर्पी)

token, n. chinha (चिन्ह), saṅket (सङ्केत), chino (चिनो)

token strike, n. sAṅketik haDtAl (साङ्केतिक हडताल)

tolerable, adj. sahya (सह्य), sahanIya (सहनीय), kAm chalAu (कामचलाउ)

tolerance, n. sahan shIltA (सहनशीलता)

tolerate, v. sahanu (सहनु)

tomato, n. gol bheṅDA (गोलभेंडा), TamATar (टमाटर)

tomb, n. chihAn (चिहान), samAdhi (समाधि)

tome, n. grantha (ग्रन्थ)

tomorrow, n./adv. bholi (भोलि), (day after tomorrow) parsi (पर्सि)

ton(ne), n. Tan (टन)

tone, *n.* AwAj (आवाज),
dhwanI (ध्वनि),
(mus.) sur (सुर), tAn (तान),
(mood) bhAw (भाव)
v. sur milAunu (सुर
मिलाउनु), *(colour)* raṅg
milAunu (रङ्ग मिलाउनु)

tone down, *v.* namra hunu
(नम्र हुनु)

tone up, *v.* tIwra pArnu
(तीव्र पार्नु)

tongs, *n.* chimTA (चिम्टा),
sanAso (सनासो)

tongue, *n.* jibro (जिब्रो), *(lg.)*
bhAshA (भाषा), bolI (बोली)

tongue-tied, *adj.* awAk
(अवाक्), chUp (चुप),
saṅkochI (सङ्कोची)

tonic, *n. (med.)* rasAdi (रसादि),
tAgat ko aushadhi
(तागतको औषधि)

tonight, *n./adv.* Aja rAtI
(आज राती)

too, *adv.* ati (अति), jyAdA
(ज्यादा), *(also)* pani (पनि)

tool, *n.* aujAr (औजार),
jyAwal (ज्यावल),
(means) sAdhan (साधन)

tooth, *n.* dAṅt (दाँत),
dant (दन्त), *(tools)* dAṅtI
(दाँती), *(tusk, fang)* dArho
(दाह्रो), **(fight tooth and nail)**
pUrA shakti kA sAth

(पूरा शक्तिका साथ), **(in the
teeth of)** wiruddha (विरुद्ध)

toothache, *n.* dAṅt dukhAi
(दाँत दुखाइ), dant pIDA (दन्तपीडा)

toothpaste, *n.* manjan (मन्जन),
missI (मिस्सी)

toothpick, dAṅt koTyAune
sinko (दाँत कोट्याउने सिन्को)

top, *n.* laTTu (लट्टु), bhuruṅg
(भुरुङ्ग), *(hill, etc.)* Tuppo
(टुप्पो), shikhar (शिखर),
TAkurA (टाकुरा), chulI (चुली),
(page) shir (शिर),
(reach top) TuppA mA pugnu
(टुप्पामा पुग्नु), *(exam, etc.)*
pahilA hunu (पहिला हुनु)
v. DhAknu (ढाक्नु),
shir hAlnu (शिर हाल्नु)
adj. mAthillo (माथिल्लो),
uparI (उपरी)

topaz, *n.* pushpa rAj (पुष्पराज)

(top) brass, *n.* mAthillA darjA
kA aphisar harU (माथिल्ला
दर्जाका अफिसरहरू)

topcoat, *n. (paint)* bAhirI taha
(बाहिरी तह),
(dress) obhar koT (ओभरकोट)

top dog, *n.* pratispardhA mA
abbal wyakti Adi (प्रतिस्पर्धामा
अब्बल ब्यक्ति आदि),
(sl.) mAlik (मालिक)

topic, *n.* wishaya (विषय),
prasaṅg (प्रसङ्ग)

top-notch, *adj. (coll.)* pahilo darjA ko (पहिलो दर्जाको)

top secret, *adj.* ati gopya (अति गोप्य)

topsoil, *n.* mATo ko mAthillo patra (माटोको माथिल्लो पत्र)

topsy-turvy, *adj.* ulTo pAlTo (उल्टोपाल्टो), lathA liṅg (लथालिङ्ग)

torch, *n.* mashAl (मशाल), Tarch lAiT (टर्चलाइट)

torment, *v.* duhkh/yAtnA dinu (दुःख/यातना दिनु) *n.* yAtnA (यातना), pIDA (पीडा)

torrent, *n.* muslo (मुस्लो), dhArA (धारा), bhal (भल)

torrential, *adj.* musal dhAre (मुसलधारे)

tortoise, *n.* kachhuwA (कछुवा), ThoTarI (ठोटरी)

torture, *n.* yAtnA (यातना), sAstI (सास्ती) *v.* yAtnA dinu (यातना दिनु)

toss, *v.* mAs tira phyAṅknu (मास्तिर फ्याँक्नु) *n.* sikkA ko huttyAi (सिक्काको हुत्त्याइ)

toss up, *v.* sikkA huttyAunu (सिक्का हुत्त्याउनु)

total, *n.* jammA hisAb (जम्मा हिसाब) *adj.* jammA (जम्मा) *v.* jammA garnu (जम्मा गर्नु)

totally, *adv.* jammai (जम्मै), pUrai (पूरै)

touch, *n.* sparsh (स्पर्श), chhuwAi (छुवाइ), *(trace)* sAno mAtrA (सानो मात्रा), *(fig.)* shailI (शैली), samparka (सम्पर्क), ***(be in touch)*** sampark mA rahanu (सम्पर्कमा रहनु) *v.* chhunu (छुनु), *(subject)* charchA garnu (चर्चा गर्नु), *(feelings)* prabhAwit garnu (प्रभावित गर्नु), asar pArnu (असर पार्नु)

touch-and-go, *adj.* jokhim pUrN (जोखिमपूर्ण), anishchit (अनिश्चित)

touch down, *v. (plane)* utranu (उत्रनु)

touching, *adj.* man chhune (मन छुने), mAyA lAgdo (मायालाग्दो)

touchstone, *n.* kasI (कसी), jAňch (जाँच)

touchy, *adj.* chir chire (चिर-चिरे), ati bhAwuk (अति भावुक), sukumAr (सुकुमार)

tough, *adj.* kaDA (कडा), chAmro (चाम्रो), sakht (सख्त)

tour, *n.* yAtrA (यात्रा), saphar (सफर), bhramaN (भ्रमण) *v.* yAtrA/saphar garnu (यात्रा/सफर गर्नु)

tourism, *n.* paryaTan (पर्यटन)

tourist, *n.* paryaTak (पर्यटक), yAtrI (यात्री), TurisT (टुरिस्ट)

tournament, *n.* khel prati-yogitA (खेल प्रतियोगिता)

tow, *v.* tAnnu (तान्नु), ghisArnu (घिसार्नु)

towards, *prep.* tira (तिर)

towel, *n.* tauliyA (तौलिया), rumAl (रुमाल) *v.* jiu puchhnu (जिउ पुछ्नु)

tower, *n.* aglo burjA (अग्लो बुर्जा), minAr (मिनार), dhar harA (धरहरा) *v.* aglinu (अग्लिनु)

town, *n.* nagar (नगर), *(go to town)* ramAilo garnu (रमाइलो गर्नु), *(talk of town)* nagar bhari ko charchA (नगरभरिको चर्चा)

town hall, *n.* sabhA griha (सभागृह)

town planning, *n.* nagar yojanA (नगर योजना)

toxic, *adj.* bikhAlu (बिखालु)

toxin, *n.* wish (विष)

toy, *n.* khelaunA (खेलौना) *v.* khelnu (खेल्नु), dil bahalAunu (दिल बहलाउनु)

trace, *n.* khoj (खोज),*(person)* pAilA (पाइला), *(sign)* chinha (चिन्ह), nishAn (निशान), *(amount)* sAno mAtrA (सानो

मात्रा), *(not a trace)* atto na patto (अत्तो न पत्तो) *v.* nakkal utArnu (नक्कल उतार्नु), *(things)* pattA lagAunu (पत्ता लगाउनु)

trachoma, *n.* phulo (फुलो)

track, *n.* pAilo (पाइलो), *(path, way)* bATo (बाटो), goreTo (गोरेटो), *(lose track of)* dhyAn bATa jAnu (ध्यानबाट जानु), sampark chhuTnu (सम्पर्क छुट्नु), *(off the beaten track)* asAmAnya (असामान्य), *(off the track)* wishaya bATa bAhira (विषयबाट बाहिर) *v.* pahilyAunu (पहिल्याउनु), surAk lAunu (सुराक लाउनु), khoj khabar rAkhnu (खोज खबर राख्नु)

track down, *v.* surAk lAunu (सुराक लाउनु)

tractor, *n.* TryAkTar (ट्र्याक्टर)

trade, *n.* bepAr (बेपार), wyApAr (व्यापार) *v.* wyApAr garnu (व्यापार गर्नु), sATnu (साट्नु)

trader, *n.* wyApArI (व्यापारी)

trademark, *n.* wyApArik chinha (व्यापारिक चिन्ह), mArkA (मार्का)

trade off, *v.* samjhautA sarI sAT pher garnu (सम्भौतासरी साटफेर गर्नु)

trade on, *v.* phAidA uThAunu
(फाइदा उठाउनु)

trade union, *n.* majdur sangh
(मजदुर संघ)

tradition, *n.* paramparA
(परम्परा), rIti thiti (रीतिथिति)

traditional, *adj.* paramparA gat
(परम्परागत)

traffic, *n.* yAtA yAt (यातायात),
TrAphik (ट्राफिक)
v. (drug, etc.) awaidh
wyApAr garnu (अवैध व्यापार गर्नु)

trafficker, *n.* awaidh wyApArI
(अवैध व्यापारी)

tragedy, *n.* duhkhad ghaTnA
(दुःखद घटना),
wiyogAnt (वियोगान्त)

tragic, *adj.* duhkhad (दुःखद)

trail, *n.* khoj (खोज),
goreTo (गोरेटो)
v. khojI garnu (खोजी गर्नु),
ghisArnu (घिसार्नु)

train, *n.* rel (रेल), *(line)* pankti
(पंक्ति), tАМtI (ताँती),
(train of thought) wichAr
dhArA (विचारधारा)
v. sikAunu (सिकाउनु),
tAllm dinu (तालीम दिनु)

trained, *adj.* tAllm pAeko
(तालीम पाएको),
prashikshit (प्रशिक्षित)

trainee, *n.* tAlime (तालिमे),
prashikshArthI (प्रशिक्षार्थी)

training, *n.* tallm (तालीम),
prashikshaN (प्रशिक्षण)

trait, *n.* swabhAw (स्वभाव),
guN (गुण)

traitor, *n.* desh drohI (देशद्रोही),
wishwAs ghAtI (विश्वासघाती)

tramp, *n.* ghumante (घुमन्ते),
AwArA (आवारा)
v. khuTTA bajArera hinDnu
(खुट्टा बजारेर हिंड्नु)

trample, *v.* kulchinu (कुल्चिनु)

trance, *n.* tandrA (तन्द्रा),
moh (मोह)
v. moh pArnu (मोह पार्नु)

tranquillity, *n.* shAnti (शान्ति)

transfer, *v.* saruwA garnu
(सरुवा गर्नु), sArnu (सार्नु)
n. saruwA (सरुवा)

transform, *v.* rUp badalnu
(रूप बदल्नु)

transit, *n.* pAr wahan (पारवहन)

translate, *v.* ulthA/anuwAd
garnu (उल्था/अनुवाद गर्नु)

translation, *n.* ulthA (उल्था),
anuwAd (अनुवाद)

translator, *n.* anuwAdak
(अनुवादक)

transparent, *adj.* pAr darshI
(पारदर्शी), nirmal (निर्मल)

transplant, *v.* arko ThAuň mA
ropnu (अर्को ठाउँमा रोप्नु),
(med.) AropaN garnu
(आरोपण गर्नु)

transport, n. yAtA yAt
(यातायात), DhuwAnI (ढुवानी)
v. DhuwAnI garnu
(ढुवानी गर्नु)

trap, n. dharAp (धराप),
pAso (पासो)
v. pAso mA pArnu
(पासोमा पार्नु),
phasAunu (फसाउनु)

trash, n. kasiṅgar (कसिंगर),
thotrA raddI mAl
(थोत्रा रद्दी माल)
v. pAt jhiknu (पात भिक्नु)

travel, v. yAtrA/saphar garnu
(यात्रा/सफर गर्नु),
n. yAtrA(यात्रा), saphar (सफर)

travel agent, n. TrAbhal
ejeNT (ट्राभल एजेण्ट)

travel(l)er, n. yAtrI (यात्री),
baTuwA (बटुवा)

tray, n. kistI (किस्ती),
thAlI (थाली)

treacherous, adj. kapaTI
(कपटी), chhalI (छली)

treachery, n. dhokhA (धोखा)
chhal (छल), kapaT (कपट)

tread, v. hiñDnu (हिँड्नु),
kulchanu (कुल्चनु)

treason, n. rAj droh (राजद्रोह),
desh droh (देशद्रोह)

treasure, n. dhan (धन), daulat
(दौलत), khajAnA (खजाना)
v. sAñchnu (साँच्नु),

samjhi rAkhnu (सम्झिराख्नु)

treasurer, n. khajAñchI
(खजाञ्ची),
koshAdhyaksha (कोषाध्यक्ष)

treasury, n. DhukuTI (ढुकुटी),
rAj kosh (राजकोष)

treat, v. upchAr/aushadhi
garnu (उपचार/औषधि गर्नु),
wyawahAr garnu (व्यवहार
गर्नु), samjhanu (सम्झनु),
(feast) khwAunu (ख्वाउनु)
n. Anand (आनन्द),
manorañjan (मनोरञ्जन),
sair (सैर), bhoj (भोज)

treatment, n. (med.) upchAr
(उपचार), ilAj (इलाज),
wyawahAr (व्यवहार)

treaty, n. sandhi (सन्धि),
samjhautA (सम्झौता)

treble, adj. tIn gunA (तीनगुना),
tehro (तेहरो), tebbar (तेब्बर)
v. tebryAunu (तेब्र्याउनु)

tree, n. rUkh (रूख),
wriksha (वृक्ष)

trek, v. paidal yAtrA garnu
(पैदल यात्रा गर्नु)

trekker, n. pad yAtrI (पदयात्री)

trekking, n. pad yAtrA
(पदयात्रा), trekiṅg (ट्रेकिङ्ग)

tremble, v. kAmnu (काम्नु),
thar tharAunu (थरथराउनु)
n. kamp (कम्प),
kampan (कम्पन)

tremendous, *adj.* ghor (घोर),
(*colloq.*) nikai (निकै)

tremor, *n.* kamp (कम्प),
kampan (कम्पन)

trench, *n.* suruñ (सुरुङ),
khADal (खाडल)
v. khADal khannu
(खाडल खन्नु)

trend, *n.* prawritti (प्रवृत्ति),
jhukAu (भुकाउ)

trend of thought, *n.* wichAr
dhArA (विचारधारा)

trepidation, *n.* Dar (डर),
AshañkA (आशंका)

trespass, *v.* binA adhikAr
prawesh garnu (बिनाअधिकार
प्रवेश गर्नु), khicholA garnu
(खिचोला गर्नु)
n. aprAdh (अपराध),
ati kramaN (अतिक्रमण)

trial, *n.* jAñch (आँच), prayog
(प्रयोग), (*law*) muddA (मुद्दा),
purpaksha (पुर्पक्ष)

triangle, *n.* tri bhuj (त्रिभुज),
tIn kune (तीनकुने)

tribal, *adj.* jAtIya (जातीय),
jAti wishesh ko
(जातिविशेषको)

tribe, *n.* jan jAti (जनजाति),
jAti (जाति)

tributary, *n.* sahAyak nadI
(सहायक नदी)

tribute, *n.* (*bilateral*) kar

(कर), shulk (शुल्क),
(*praise*) prashamsA (प्रशंसा),
shraddhAñjalI (श्रद्धाञ्जली)

trick, *n.* dAu (दाउ), chhal
(छल), chalAkhI (चलाखी)
v. chhalnu (छल्नु),
chalAkhI garnu (चलाखी गर्नु)

trickery, *n.* chhal (छल),
kapaT (कपट)

trickster, *n.* chhalI (छली),
chAl bAj (चालबाज)

trickle, *n.* thopA (थोपा),
sAno dhAro (सानो धारो)
v. Tapkanu (टप्कनु)

tricycle, *n.* tIn pAñgre sAikal
(तीनपाङ्ग्रे साइकल),
riksA (रिक्सा)

trident, *n.* trishUl (त्रिशूल)

trigger, *n.* banduk ko jibrI
(बन्दुकको जिब्री)

trigger-happy, *n.* sahaj golI
chalAuna man garne
(सहज गोली चलाउन मन गर्ने)

trill, *n.* kampit swar (कम्पित स्वर)

trim, *adj.* TAm Tume (टामटुमे),
chhAñT pareko (छाँट परेको)
v. sugghar saphA garnu
(सुग्घर सफा गर्नु),
(*plants*) kAT chhAñT garnu
(काटछाँट गर्नु)

trim one's sails, *v.* badliñdo
sthiti mA Dhalnu (बदलिंदो
स्थितिमा ढल्नु)

trinity, *n.* tri mUrti (त्रिमूर्ति)

trinket, *n.* gahanA guriyA (गहनागुरिया), sasto sAno mAl (सस्तो सानो माल)

trio, *n.* TIn janA ko samUha (तीनजनाको समूह)

trip, *n.* sair (सैर), yAtrA (यात्रा), saphar (सफर), *(stumble)* laD khaDAhaT (लडखडाहट)
v. laD khaDAunu (लडखडाउनु), laDnu (लड्नु), *(walk)* halukA saṅga hiṅDnu (हलुकासँग हिंड्नु)

triple, *adj.* tebbar (तेब्बर), tehro (तेह्रो)

tripod, *n.* tri khuTI (त्रिखुटी), odhAn (ओधान)

trite, *adj.* sahaliyA(सहलिया), sAmAnya (सामान्य)

triumph, *n.* jaya (जय), wijaya (विजय), jIt (जीत) *v.* jitnu (जित्नु), wijaya prApt garnu (विजय प्राप्त गर्नु)

triumphant, *adj.* wijayI (विजयी), praphulla (प्रफुल्ल)

trolly, *n.* TralI (ट्रली), *(vechicle)* TralI bas (ट्रली बस)

troop, *n.* dal (दल), TolI (टोली), *(artist)* maNDalI (मण्डली)

troops, *n.* senA (सेना), phauj (फौज)

trophy, *n.* smArak (स्मारक), *(prize)* uphAr (उपहार), puraskAr (पुरस्कार), chino (चिनो), nishAnI (निशानी)

tropical, *adj.* garmI sambandhI (गर्मीसम्बन्धी)

trouble, *n.* muskil (मुस्किल), duhkh (दुःख), pareshAnI (परेशानी), asuwidhA (असुविधा), ashAnti (अशान्ति), gaD baDI (गडबडी) *v.* duhkh dinu (दुःख दिनु)

troublemaker, *n.* bAuṅTho (बाउँठो), upadrawI (उपद्रवी), ashAnti phailAune (अशान्ति फैलाउने)

troubleshooter, *n.* ashAnti wA gaD baDI haTAune (अशान्ति वा गडबडी हटाउने)

troublesome, *adj.* jhanjhaTilo (भन्भटिलो)

trousers, *n.* pyANT (प्याण्ट), pAijAmA (पाइजामा)

truce, *n.* yuddha wirAm (युद्धविराम), wirAm (विराम)

truck, *n.* Trak (ट्रक) *v.* Trak mA lai jAnu (ट्रकमा लैजानु)

true, *adj.* sAṅcho (साँचो), satya (सत्य), sahI (सही), ThIk (ठीक), *(person, etc.)* sakkalI (सक्कली), asalI (असली)

truly, *adv.* wAstaw mA
(वास्तवमा),
sAňchchai nai (साँच्चै नै),
(letter) bhawdIya (भवदीय)

trump, *n.* *(cards)* turup (तुरुप)

trump up, *v.* banAunu (बनाउनु),
ulto lAunu (उल्टो लाउनु)

trumpet, *n.* bigul (बिगुल),
nar simhA (नरसिंहा)
v. turahI/bigul bajAunu
(तुरही/बिगुल बजाउनु)

trunk, *n.* *(torso)* mUl jIu (मूल
जीउ), giňD (गिँड), *(box)*
bAkas (बाकस), sanduk
(सन्दुक), *(tree)* thAmo (थामो),
(elephant) sUňD (सूँड)

trunk call, *n.* TADhA bATa
garine Teli phon
(टाढाबाट गरिने टेलिफोन)

trust, *n.* wishwAs (विश्वास),
patyAr (पत्यार), *(orgn.)* saňgh
(संघ), guThI (गुठी)
v. wishwAs/patyAr garnu
(विश्वास/पत्यार गर्नु)

trustworthy, *adj.* bhar pardo
(भरपर्दो), wishwAs garna
hune (विश्वास गर्न हुने)

truth, *n.* satya (सत्य), satyatA
(सत्यता), sachchAi (सच्चाइ)

truthful, *adj.* sAňcho (साँचो),
satya wAdI (सत्यवादी)

try, *v.* koshish garnu
(कोशिश गर्नु), *(things)* prayog

garnu (प्रयोग गर्नु), *(test)*
jAňch garnu (जाँच गर्नु),
(dress) lAi hernu (लाइहेर्नु),
muddA hernu (मुद्दा हेर्नु)
n. koshish (कोशिश),
prayatna (प्रयत्न)

trying, *adj.* gArho (गाह्रो),
kashT prad (कष्टप्रद)

try out, *v.* parIkshA linu
(परीक्षा लिनु)

try on, *v.* lagAera hernu
(लगाएर हेर्नु)

tub, *n.* Tab (टब), bATA (बाटा)

tube, *n.* nalI (नली), sote (सोते)

tuberculosis, *n.* kshaya rog
(क्षयरोग), sukenAs (सुकेनास)

Tuesday, *n.* maňgal bAr
(मंगलबार)

tuft, *n.* guchchhA (गुच्छा),
gujulTo (गुजुल्टो)
v. guchchhA pArnu (गुच्छा पार्नु)

tug, *v.* joD le tAnnu (जोडले तान्नु)

tug of war, *n.* DorI tAnne khel
(डोरी तान्ने खेल)

tuition, *n.* paDhai shulk (पढाइ
शुल्क), Tyusan (ट्युसन),
shikshaN (शिक्षण)

tumble, *v.* laDnu (लड्नु), khur
murinu (खुर्मुरिनु), palTan
bAjI khAnu(पल्टनबाजी खानु)
n. *(fall)* patan (पतन),
(somersaults) palTan bAjI
(पल्टनबाजी)

tummy, *n.* peT (पेट),
bhuǹDI (भुँडी)

tumo(u)r, *n.* gAñTho (गाँठो),
gAno(गानो), Tyumar(ट्युमर)

tumult, *n.* khailA bailA
(खैलाबैला), hallA (हल्ला)

tune, *n.* *(melody)* laya (लय),
tAn (तान), *(change one's*
tune) rañg badalnu (रङ्ग बदल्नु),
(out of tune) be surA (बेसुरा)
v. sur milAunu (सुर मिलाउनु)

tunic, *n.* lugA (लुगा),
kurtA (कुर्ता)

tunnel, *n.* suruǹ (सुरुङ)
v. suruǹ khannu (सुरुङ खन्नु)

turban, *n.* pheTA (फेटा)

turbid, *adj.* dhamilo (धमिलो)

turbulent, *adj.* ugra (उग्र)

turf, *n.* ghAǹse chaur
(घाँसे चौर)

turmeric, *n.* *(root)* haledo
(हलेदो), besAr (बेसार)

turmoil, *n.* utpAt (उत्पात),
ho hallA (होहल्ला)

turn, *n.* ghumAu (घुमाउ),
(revolution) chakkar
(चक्कर), moD (मोड),
pariwartan (परिवर्तन),
palaT (पलट), pAli (पालि),
(by turns) pAlai pAlo sañga
(पालैपालो सँग), *(in turn)*
krama ile (क्रमैले), *(out of*
turn) binA silsilA ko (बिना

silsilAko), *(take turn)* pAlai
pAlo sañga garnu
(पालैपालोसँग गर्नु)
v. (wheel) ghumnu (घुम्नु),
ghumAunu (घुमाउनु),
(head) chakkar khAnu
(चक्कर खानु), *(lathe)* kharAj
garnu (खराज गर्नु),
(direction) moDinu (मोडिनु),
moDnu (मोड्नु),
(return) pharkanu (फर्कनु),
(pages) palTAunu (पल्टाउनु),
(change) badalnu (बदल्नु),
(become) hunu (हुनु),
bannu (बन्नु)

turn against, *v.* wiruddha
hunu (विरुद्ध हुनु)

turncoat, *n.* dal chhoDAhA
(दल छोडाहा),
dal badal garne (दलबदल गर्ने)

turn down, *v.* aswIkAr /
nAmanjur garnu (अस्वीकार /
नामन्जुर गर्नु)

turning, *n.* moD (मोड),
ghumtI (घुम्ती)

turning point, *n.* moD (मोड),
pariwartan windu
(परिवर्तन विन्दु)

turnip, *n.* salgam (सलगम)

turnkey, *n.* jelar (जेलर)
adj. (comp.) tatkAl prayog
garna milne (तत्काल प्रयोग
गर्न मिल्ने)

turn off, v. band garnu (बन्द गर्नु), roknu (रोक्नु)

turn of the century, n. yug sandhi (युगसन्धि)

turn on, v. kholnu (खोल्नु), nirbhar hunu (निर्भर हुनु)

turn out, v. nikAlnu (निकाल्नु), (person) upasthit hunu (उपस्थित हुनु)

turn over, v. ulTAunu (उल्टाउनु), kolTe phernu (कोल्टे फेर्नु), sumpinu (सुम्पिनु)

turnover, n. upasthiti (उपस्थिति), (bus.) Aya (आय)

turnpike, n. shulk dwAr (शुल्कद्वार)

turn to, v. lAgnu (लाग्नु), ruchi linu (रुचि लिनु)

turn turtle, v. ghopTinu (घोप्टिनु)

turn up, v. ekatra hunu (एकत्र हुनु), Ai pugnu (आइपुग्नु)

turquoise, n. phiroj dhungA (फिरोज ढुङ्गा)

turtle, n. kachhuwA (कछुवा)

tusk, n. hAttI ko dArho (हात्तीको दाह्रो)

tussle, n. ghamsA ghamsI (घम्साघम्सी), jhagaDA (झगडा)

tutor, n. guru (गुरु), shikshak (शिक्षक)

twelve, n. bArha (बाह्र)

twentieth, adj. bIsauň (बीसौं)

twenty, n. bIs (बीस)

twice, adv. duI palTa (दुईपल्ट)

twig, n. jhiňjhA (झिंझा), DAňTh (डाँठ)

twilight, n. go dhUli (गोधूलि)

twin, n. jumlyAhA (जुम्ल्याहा)

twinkle, v. chamkanu (चम्कनु), jhalkanu (झल्कनु) n. jhil mil (झिलमिल)

twist, v. baTArnu (बटार्नु), bATnu (बाट्नु), ghumAunu (घुमाउनु), moDnu (मोड्नु) n. bATeko DorI (बाटेको डोरी), (tobacco) surtI (सुर्ती), (rotary action) toD maroD (तोड मरोड), (dance) TwisT nAch (ट्विस्ट नाच)

two, n. duI (दुई), (put two and two together) sojho arth nikAlnu (सोझो अर्थ निकाल्नु)

two-dimensional, adj. duI AyAm ko (दुई आयामको)

two-edged, adj. duI dhAre (दुईधारे)

two-faced, adj. kapaTI (कपटी), pAkhaNDI (पाखण्डी)

two-way, adj. dohoro (दोहोरो)

type, n. kisim (किसिम), prakAr (प्रकार), namUnA (नमूना), (printing) TAip (टाइप)

typewriter, n. TAip rAiTar (टाइपराइटर)

typhoid, *n.* atisAr jaro
(अतिसार जरो),
TAiphAiD (टाइफाइड)

typist, *n.* TAipisT (टाइपिस्ट)

typical, *adj.* khAs (खास),
prati rUpI (प्रतिरूपी)

tyrannical, *adj.* nirañkush
(निरङ्कुश),
atyAchArI (अत्याचारी)

tyranny, *n.* atyAchAr
(अत्याचार), *(pol.)* nirañkush
shAsan (निरङ्कुश शासन)

tyrant, *n.* krUr/nirañkush
shAsak (क्रूर/निरङ्कुश शासक)

U

udder, *n.* kal chauñDo
(कल्चौंडो)

ugly, *adj.* na rAmro (नराम्रो),
kurUp (कुरूप)

ulcer, *n.* khaTiro (खटिरो),
ghAu (घाउ)

ultimate, *adj.* AkhirI
(आखिरी), antim (अन्तिम)

ultimately, *adv.* ant mA
(अन्तमा),
Akhir mA (आखिरमा)

ultimatum, *n.* AkhirI shart
(आखिरी शर्त)

umbilical cord, *n.* sAl (साल),
nAl (नाल)

umbrella, *n.* chhAtA (छाता)

umpire, *n.* nirNAyak
(निर्णायक), madhyasth
(मध्यस्थ), rephrI (रेफ्री)
v. madhyasth hunu
(मध्यस्थ हुनु)

unable, *adj.* na sakne (नसक्ने),
asamarth (असमर्थ)

unacquainted, *adj.* chinA
parchI na bhaeko
(चिनापर्ची नभएको),
aparichit (अपरिचित)

unaffected, *adj.* sIdhA sAdhA
(सीधासाधा),
nish kapaT (निष्कपट)

unanimous, *adj.* ek mat
(एकमत)

unarmed, *adj.* nihatthA
(निहत्था), nirastra (निरस्त्र)

unattached, *adj.* khukulo
(खुकुलो), phukkA (फुक्का)

unaware, *adj.* thAhA na
pAeko (थाहा नपाएको),
anjAn (अनजान)

uncalled for, *adj.* na chAhiñdo
(नचाहिंदो),
anAwashyak (अनावश्यक)

uncanny, *adj.* rahasya maya (रहस्यमय), daiwI (दैवी)

uncertain, *adj.* anishchit (अनिश्चित), anyol ko (अन्योलको)

uncle, *n.* *(paternal, older)* Thulo bA (ठूलो बा), *(paternal, younger)* kAkA (काका), sAno bA (सानो बा), *(maternal)* mAmA (मामा), phupAjU (फुपाजू)

uncomfortable, *adj.* asajilo (असजिलो)

unconscious, *adj.* achet (अचेत), be hosh (बेहोश)

uncooked, *adj.* kAñcho (काँचो)

uncultured, *adj.* somat na bhaeko (सोमत नभएको), asabhya (असभ्य)

undecided, *adj.* anirNit (अनिर्णित), anishchit (अनिश्चित)

under, *prep.* tala (तल), muni (मुनि), antargat (अन्तर्गत)

under age, *adj.* nA bAlak (नाबालक), awayask (अवयस्क)

underdog, *n.* haruwA (हरुवा), upekshit (उपेक्षित)

underground, *adj.* bhUmi gat (भूमिगत), gupt (गुप्त), lukeko (लुकेको)

undermine, *v.* khoiro khannu (खोइरो खन्नु), gupt rUp le nashT garnu (गुप्त रूपले नष्ट गर्नु)

underneath, *adv.* mun tira (मुन्तिर), tala tira (तलतिर)

underrate, *v.* kam mahattwa dinu (कम महत्त्व दिनु)

undersized, *adj.* sAnu kad ko (सानु कदको)

understand, *v.* bujhnu (बुझ्नु), samjhanu (सम्झनु)

understanding, *n.* samajh dArI (समझदारी), mel (मेल) *adj.* samajh dAr (समझदार)

undertake, *v.* kabul garnu (कबुल गर्नु), kAm thAlnu (काम थाल्नु), jimmA linu (जिम्मा लिनु)

undertaking, *n.* kAm (काम), kArobAr (कारोबार)

underwear, *n.* bhitrI lugA (भित्री लुगा), kachhAD (कछाड)

underworld, *n.* *(hades)* pAtAl (पाताल), *(crime)* aprAdh jagat (अपराधजगत्)

undesirable, *adj.* awAñchha-nIya (अवाञ्छनीय)

undo, *v.* phukAunu (फुकाउनु), kholnu (खोल्नु)

undoubtedly, *adv.* nissandeh (निस्सन्देह)

undressed, *adj.* lugA na lAeko (लुगा नलाएको), nAñgo (नाङ्गो), *(wounds)* binA malam paTTI ko (बिनामलम पट्टीको)

undue, *adj.* anuchit (अनुचित),
jyAdA (ज्यादा), ati (अति)

uneasy, *adj.* asajilo (असजिलो)

uneconomical, *adj.* kharchilo
(खर्चिलो), mahaṅgo (महङ्गो)

unemployed, *adj.* bekAr
(बेकार), DhAkre (ढाक्रे)

unemployment, *n.* bekArI
(बेकारी), berojgArI (बेरोजगारी)

unequal, *adj.* asamAn (असमान)

uneven, *adj. (figure)* bijor
(बिजोर), asam (असम)

unfair, *adj.* anuchit (अनुचित),
paksh pAtI (पक्षपाती),
anyAya pUrN (अन्यायपूर्ण)

unfasten, *v.* kholnu (खोल्नु),
phukAunu (फुकाउनु)

unfavo(u)rable, *adj.* prati kUl
(प्रतिकूल)

unfit, *adj.* ayogya (अयोग्य)

unfold, *v.* kholnu (खोल्नु),
phailAunu (फैलाउनु)

unfortunate, *adj.* abhAgI
(अभागी), bicharA (बिचरा)

unfortunately, *adv.* durbhAgya
wash (दुर्भाग्यवश)

unicameral, *adj. (parliament)*
ek sadanIya (एक सदनीय)

uniform, *n.* bardI (बर्दी),
jaṅgI poshAk (जङ्गी पोशाक)
adj. ek nAs (एकनास),
ek samAn (एक समान)
v. ek rUp garAunu

(ek rUp garAunu)

uniformity, *n.* ek rUptA
(एकरूपता)

unify, *v.* ek garAunu (एक
गराउनु), milAunu (मिलाउनु)

unimportant, *adj.* mahattwa
hIn (महत्त्वहीन)

union, *n.* ekatA (एकता),
mel (मेल), *(orgn.)* saṅgh (संघ),
sabhA (सभा)

unique, *adj.* bejoD (बेजोड),
apUrwa (अपूर्व)

unit, *n. (math.)* ekAi (एकाइ),
(mil.) palTan (पल्टन),
TukaDI (टुकडी)

unite, *v.* joDnu (जोड्नु),
milnu (मिल्नु), *(marriage)*
bihA garnu (बिहा गर्नु)

united, *adj.* saṃyukta (संयुक्त)

United Nations Organization,
n. saṃyukta rAshtra saṅgh
(संयुक्त राष्ट्र संघ)

unity, *n.* ekatA (एकता)

universal, *adj.* wishwa wyApI
(विश्वव्यापी),
sarwa wyApak (सर्वव्यापक)

universe, *n.* brahmAND (ब्रह्माण्ड)

university, *n.* wishwa
widyAlaya (विश्वविद्यालय)

unjust, *adj.* anyAyI (अन्यायी),
anyAya pUrN (अन्यायपूर्ण)

unknown, *adj.* agYAt (अज्ञात),
aparichit (अपरिचित)

unleash, *v.* kholnu (खोल्नु), unmukt garnu (उन्मुक्त गर्नु)

unless, *conj.* jaba samma ... huṅdaina (जबसम्म ... हुँदैन)

unlike, *adj.* asamAn (असमान), bhinna (भिन्न)

unlimited, *adj.* asImit (असीमित)

unload, *v.* mAl utArnu (माल उतार्नु), jhArnu (झार्नु)

unlucky, *adj.* abhAgI (अभागी)

unmarried, *adj.* wiwAh na bhaeko (विवाह नभएको), awiwAhit (अविवाहित)

unnatural, *adj.* aprAkritik (अप्राकृतिक), aswAbhAwik (अस्वाभाविक)

unnecessary, *adj.* na chAhiṅdo (नचाहिँदो), anAwashyak (अनावश्यक)

unobstructed, *adj.* na chhekieko (नछेकिएको), khulA (खुला)

unpack, *v.* kholnu (खोल्नु), phukAunu (फुकाउनु)

unpaid, *adj.* na tirieko (नतिरिएको), bAṅkI (बाँकी)

unpleasant, *adj.* na ramAilo (नरमाइलो)

unprecedented, *adj.* pahile na bhaeko (पहिले नभएको), apUrwa (अपूर्व)

unprepared, *adj.* tayAr na bhaeko (तयार नभएको)

unpublished, *adj.* aprakAshit (अप्रकाशित)

unqualified, *adj.* ayogya (अयोग्य)

unreasonable, *adj.* be manAsib (बेमनासिब)

unrest, *n.* ashAnti (अशान्ति), gaD baD (गडबड)

unripe, *adj.* kAncho (काँचो)

unruly, *adj.* aTerI (अटेरी), arAjak (अराजक)

unsatisfactory, *adj.* asantosh janak (असन्तोषजनक)

unseen, *adj.* na dekhieko (नदेखिएको), adrishya (अदृश्य)

unsophisticated, *adj.* sojho (सोझो), saral swabhAw ko (सरल स्वभावको), bholA (भोला)

unspeakable, *adj.* awarNanIya (अवर्णनीय), akathnIya (अकथनीय)

unsuccessful, *adj.* asaphal (असफल), wiphal (विफल)

unsuitable, *adj.* aphAp (अफाप), anmel (अनमेल)

unsuspecting, *adj.* shaṅkA na garine (शंका नगरिने)

untie, *v.* phukAunu (फुकाउनु), kholnu (खोल्नु)

until, *conj.* jaba samma ... huṅdaina (जबसम्म ... हुँदैन)

untimely, *adj.* asAmayik (असामयिक), kubelA ko (कुबेलाको)

untouchable, *n.* achhUt (अछूत)

untoward, *adj.* apriya (अप्रिय), ashubh (अशुभ)

unusual, *adj.* asAdhAraN (असाधारण), anauTho (अनौठो)

unveil, *v.* anAwaraN garnu (अनावरण गर्नु)

unwell, *adj.* bisañcho (बिसञ्चो), aswasth (अस्वस्थ)

unwilling, *adj.* birAjI (बिराजी), anichchhuk (अनिच्छुक)

unworthy, *adj.* ayogya (अयोग्य), anuchit (अनुचित)

up, *prep.* mAthi (माथि)
adv. mAs tira (मास्तिर)
adj. khaDA (खडा), mAs tira ko (मास्तिरको)

up against, *adv.* nikaT (निकट), sampark mA (सम्पर्कमा)

up against it, *adv. (colloq.)* ThUlo kaThinAi mA (ठूलो कठिनाइमा)

up and coming, *adj.* honhAr (होनहार), pragati gardai (प्रगति गर्दै)

upbringing, *n.* lAlan pAlan (लालनपालन), sikshA dIkshA (शिक्षादीक्षा)

upheaval, *n.* uthal puthal (उथलपुथल), hUl dangA (हूलदङ्गा)

uphill, *adj.* ukAlo (उकालो)

uphold, *v.* samarthan garnu (समर्थन गर्नु), thAmnu (थाम्नु),

anumodan garnu (अनुमोदन गर्नु)

uplift, *n.* unnati (उन्नति), utthAn (उत्थान)
v. mAthi uThAunu (माथि उठाउनु), *(fig.)* unnat tulyAunu (उन्नत तुल्याउनु)

upon, *prep.* mA (मा), mAthi (माथि)

upper, *adj.* mAthillo (माथिल्लो)

upperhand, *n.* mAthillo hAt (माथिल्लो हात)

uppermost, *adj.* sab bhandA mAthillo (सबभन्दा माथिल्लो), sarwochcha (सर्वोच्च)

upright, *adj. (thing)* khaDA (खडा), *(person)* sojho (सोझो), sachchA (सच्चा), imAn dAr (इमान्दार)

uprising, *n.* Andolan (आन्दोलन), widroh (विद्रोह)

uproar, *n.* ho hallA (होहल्ला), kolAhal (कोलाहल), kachingal (कचिङ्गल)

uproot, *v.* ukhelnu (उखेल्नु)

ups and downs, *n.* tala mAthi (तल माथि), sudin durdin (सुदिन दुर्दिन)

upset, *v.* ulTinu (उल्टिनु), ghopTinu (घोप्टिनु), ashAnt gari dinu (अशान्त गरिदिनु)
n. gaD baD (गडबड), pareshAnI (परेशानी),

upside down, *adj./adv.*
ubhiNDo (उभिण्डो),
ulTo pAlTo (उल्टोपाल्टो)

upstairs, *n.* mAthillo talA
(माथिल्लो तला)
adj. mAthi (माथि)

upstart, *adj.* lAuke (लाउके),
baDhtA (बढ्ता)

upstream, *adv.* prawAh
wiparIt (प्रवाहविपरीत)

upto, *prep.* samma (सम्म)

upwards, *adv.* mAthi tira
(माथितिर), mAs tira (मास्तिर)

urban, *adj.* shaharI (शहरी),
nagarIya (नगरीय)

urge, *v.* jor/tAkitA garnu
(जोर/ताकिता गर्नु)
n. jor (जोर), Aweg (आवेग)

urgency, *n.* mahattwa (महत्त्व),
AwashyaktA (आवश्यकता)

urgent, *adj.* jarurI (जरुरी),
awilamb (अविलम्ब)

urinal, *n.* shauchAlaya
(शौचालय)

urinate, *v.* pishAb garnu
(पिसाब गर्नु), mutnu (मुत्नु)

urine, *n.* pisAb (पिसाब),
mUt (मूत)

us, *pron.* hAmI lAI (हामीलाई),
hamI harU lAI (हामीहरूलाई)

use, *v.* prayog/bhog garnu
(प्रयोग/भोग गर्नु)
n. prayog (प्रयोग), upyog

(उपयोग), *(make use of)*
prayog garnu (प्रयोग गर्नु)

useful, *adj.* upyogI (उपयोगी)

useless, *adj.* nikammA
(निकम्मा), phAltu (फाल्तु)

used, *adj.* purAno (पुरानो),
abhyast (अभ्यस्त)

use up, *v.* siddhyAunu
(सिद्ध्याउनु)

usher, *n.* basne ThAuṅ
dekhAune (बस्ने ठाउँ देखाउनु)
v. Agantuk ko sammAn
garnu (आगन्तुकको सम्मान गर्नु)

usual, *adj.* sAdhAraN (साधारण),
sAmAnya (सामान्य)

usually, *adv.* aksar (अक्सर),
sadhaiṅ jaso (सधैंजसो),
prAyah (प्रायः)

utensils, *n.* bhaṅDA kuṅDA
(भाँडाकुँडा)

uterus, *n.* pAThe ghar (पाठेघर)

utilization, *n.* upyog (उपयोग),
wyawahAr (व्यवहार)

utilize, *v.* upyog garnu
(उपयोग गर्नु)

utmost, *adj.* param (परम),
sarwopari (सर्वोपरि)

utter, *v.* bhannu (भन्नु),
bolnu (बोल्नु)
adj. pUrA (पूरा), param (परम)

uvula, *n.* kilkile (किलकिले),
liglige (लिगलिगे)

vacant, *adj.* khAlI (खाली),
ritto (रित्तो)

vacation, *n.* lamo chhuTTI
(लामो छुट्टी), bidA (बिदा)

vaccinate, *v.* khopAunu
(खोपाउनु), khop dinu (खोप दिनु)

vaccination, *n.* khop (खोप),
TIkA (टीका)

vaccine, *n.* khop (खोप)

vacuum, *n.* shUnya (शून्य),
ritto (रित्तो)

vagabond, *n.* phirantA
(फिरन्ता), AwArA (आवारा)

vagina, *n.* bhag (भग),
yoni mArg (योनिमार्ग)

vague, *adj.* aspashT (अस्पष्ट)

vain, *adj.* wyarth (व्यर्थ),
nirarthak (निरर्थक)

vainglorious, *adj.* ghamaNDI
(घमण्डी), garwilo (गर्विलो)

valet, *n.* baiThake (बैठके)

valid, *adj.* manAsib (मनासिब),
jAyaj (जायज), waidh (वैध)

validity, *n.* waidhtA (वैधता),
mAnyatA (मान्यता)

valley, *n.* khAlTo (खाल्टो),
upatyakA (उपत्यका)

valo(u)r, *n.* sAhas (साहस),
parAkram (पराक्रम)

valuable, *adj.* mUlya wAn
(मूल्यवान्)

valuation, *n.* mUlya
nirdhAraN (मूल्यनिर्धारण)

value, *n.* mUlya (मूल्य),
mol (मोल), mahattwa (महत्त्व)
v. mol/kadar garnu
(मोल/कदर गर्नु)

valueless, *adj.* nikammA
(निकम्मा),
bekAr ko (बेकारको)

van, *n.* band gADI (बन्द गाडी),
bhyAn (भ्यान)

vanish, *v.* alpinu (अल्पिनु),
harAunu (हराउनु),
gAyab hunu (गायब हुनु)

vanity, *n.* ghamaND (घमण्ड),
abhimAn (अभिमान)

vanity bag, *n.* siṅgAr ko
baTTA (सिंगारको बट्टा)

vanquish, *v.* jitnu (जित्नु),
harAunu (हराउनु)

vapo(u)r, *n.* bAph (बाफ)
v. bAphinu (बाफिनु)

variation, *n.* pariwartan
(परिवर्तन),
wibhinnatA (विभिन्नता)

varied, *n.* wiwidh (विविध)

variety entertainment, *n.* wiwidh manorañjan (विविध मनोरञ्जन)

various, *adj.* wibhinna (विभिन्न), nAnA tharI ko (नानाथरीको)

vary, *v.* badlinu (बदलिनु), pharak pArnu (फरक पार्नु)

vase, *n.* phUl dAn (फूलदान), ghaDA (घडा)

vasectomy, *n.* nas chchhedan (नसच्छेदन)

vast, *adj.* wishAl (विशाल), wipul (विपुल)

vault, *n.* gumbaj dAr chhAnA (गुम्बजदार छाना), *(strong room)* DhukuTI (ढुकुटी) *v.* gumbaj hAlnu (गुम्बज हाल्नु), *(jump)* hAt le Tekera uphranu (हातले टेकेर उफ्रनु)

vegetable, *n.* tarkArI (तरकारी), sAg pAt (सागपात)

vegetarian, *n.* shAkA hArI (शाकाहारी)

vegetation, *n.* wanaspati (वनस्पति), rUkh pAt (रूखपात)

vehement, *adj.* prachaND (प्रचण्ड), prabal (प्रबल)

vehicle, *n.* sawArI (सवारी), yAn (यान), gADI (गाडी)

veil, *n.* ghumTo (घुम्टो),

pardA (पर्दा), *(draw a veil over)* kurA na jhiknu (कुरा नझिक्नु), dhyAn na khichnu (ध्यान नखिच्नु) *v.* ghumTo hAlnu (घुम्टो हाल्नु), chhopnu (छोप्नु)

vein, *n.* nasA (नसा), naso (नसो), shirA (शिरा)

velocity, *n.* gati (गति), weg (वेग)

velvet, *n.* makh mal (मखमल) *adj.* makh malI (मखमली), makh mal jasto naram (मखमलजस्तो नरम)

velvet glove, *n.* bAhira naram bhitra kaThor swabhAw (बाहिर नरम भित्र कठोर स्वभाव)

vendor, *n.* wikretA (विक्रेता), pherI wAlA (फेरीवाला)

venerable, *adj.* Adar NIya (आदरणीय), pUjya (पूज्य)

vengeance, *n.* badlA (बदला), *(with a vengeance)* ajha charko saṅga (अझ चर्कोसँग)

venom, *n.* wish (विष), bikh (बिख)

venomous, *adj.* wishAlu (विषालु), bikhAlu (बिखालु)

vent, *n.* *(outlet)* nikAs (निकास) *(flue)* dhUwAñ kash (धूवाँकश) *v.* pwAl pArnu (प्वाल पार्नु), bATo dinu (बाटो दिनु)

ventilation, *n.* wAyu sañchAlan (वायु सञ्चालन)

venture, *n.* sAhas ko kAm (साहसको काम),
(bus.) wyApArik kAm (व्यापारिक काम)
v. AñT garnu (आँट गर्नु)

Venus, *n.* shukra graha (शुक्रग्रह)

verb, *n.* kriyA pad (क्रियापद)

verbal, *adj.* maukhik (मौखिक),
shAbdik (शाब्दिक)

verdict, *n.* phaislA (फैसला),
nirNaya (निर्णय)

verification, *n.* pramANI karaN (प्रमाणीकरण)

verify, *v.* rujU/pramANit garnu (रुजु/प्रमाणित गर्नु)

vermilion, *n.* abir (अबिर),
sindUr (सिन्दूर)

vernacular, *n.* swadeshI bhAshA (स्वदेशी भाषा),
bol chAlI bhAshA (बोलचाली भाषा), dev nAgarI (देवनागरी)

vernal, *adj.* wasant ko (वसन्तको)

verse, *n.* kawitA (कविता),
shlok (श्लोक)

version, *n.* bayAn (बयान),
bhAshAntar (भाषान्तर)

versus, *prep.* wiruddha (विरुद्ध), khilAph (खिलाफ)

vertical, *adj.* ThADo (ठाडो),
khaDA (खडा)

very, *adv.* dherai (धेरै),

khUb (खूब)

vessel, *n.* bhAñDo (भाँडो),
(ship) jahAj (जहाज)

vest, *n.* ganjI (गन्जी),
isT koT (इस्टकोट)

veteran, *n.* anubhawI wyakti (अनुभवी व्यक्ति)
adj. anubhawI (अनुभवी),
ghAgDAn (घागडान)

veto, *n.* nishedh (निषेध),
bhiTo (भिटो)
v. nishedh garnu (निषेध गर्नु),
roknu (रोक्नु)

via, *prep.* bhaera (भएर),
huṅdai (हुँदै)

viable, *adj.* bAñchna sakne (बाँच्न सक्ने),
dhAnna sakne (धान्न सक्ने)

vibrate, *v.* tharkanu (थर्कनु),
(sound) guñjnu (गुँज्नु),
kAmnu (काम्नु)

vibration, *n.* kampan (कम्पन),
jhan jhanAhaT (फनफनाहट)

vice, *n.* pAp (पाप),
durwyasan (दुर्व्यसन)

vice chancellor, *n.* up kul pati (उपकुलपति)

vice president, *n.* up rAshtra pati (उपराष्ट्रपति)

vice versa, *adv.* ulTo (उल्टो),
wiprIt (विपरीत)

vicinity, *n.* As pAs (आसपास),
chhar chhimek (छरछिमेक)

vicious, *adj.* dushT (दुष्ट), anaitik (अनैतिक)

vicissitude, *n.* ulaT pher (उलटफेर), anukram (अनुक्रम)

victim, *n. (prey)* shikAr (शिकार), *(sacrifice)* bali (बलि), *(med.)* ghAite (घाइते), mritak (मृतक)

victimize, *v.* shikAr banAunu (शिकार बनाउनु), satAunu (सताउनु)

victor, *n.* wijetA (विजेता), jitne mAnchhe (जित्ने मान्छे)

victorious, *adj.* wijayI (विजयी), jituwA (जितुवा)

victory, *n.* jIt (जीत), wijaya (विजय)

video, *n.* bhiDiyo (भिडियो)

view, *n.* drishya (दृश्य), wichAr (विचार), nirIkshaN (निरीक्षण), uddeshya (उद्देश्य), *(in view of)* kAraN Ie (कारणले), dhyAn mA rAkhera (ध्यानमा राखेर), *(on view)* pradarshit (प्रदर्शित), *(point of view)* drishTi koN (दृष्टिकोण), *(with a view to)* ko uddeshya le(को उद्देश्यले) *v.* hernu (हेर्नु), nirIkshaN garnu (निरीक्षण गर्नु), wichAr garnu (विचार गर्नु),

viewpoint, *n.* drishTi koN (दृष्टिकोण)

vigilant, *adj.* chanAkho (चनाखो), jAgruk (जागरुक)

vigorous, *adj.* joD dAr (जोडदार), prabal (प्रबल)

vigorously, *adv.* joD sanga (जोडसँग), ek dam (एकदम)

vigo(u)r, *n.* shakti (शक्ति), joD (जोड)

vile, *adj.* nIch (नीच), adham (अधम)

villa, *n.* dehAtI niwAs (देहाती निवास), grAm niwAs (ग्राम निवास)

village, *n.* gAuñ (गाउँ), dehAt (देहात)

villager, *n.* gauñle (गाउँले), dehAtI (देहाती)

villain, *n.* dushT (दुष्ट), khal nAyak (खलनायक)

vine, *n.* laharA (लहरा)

vinegar, *n.* sirkA (सिरका), chuk (चुक), amilo (अमिलो)

violate, *v.* ullanghan garnu (उल्लंघन गर्नु)

violation, *n.* ullanghan (उल्लंघन), bhang (भङ्ग)

violence, *n.* himsA (हिंसा), jor julum (जोरजुलुम)

violent, *adj.* himsAtmak (हिंसात्मक)

violet, *adj.* baijanI (बैजनी)

violin, *n.* belA (बेला)

violinist, *n.* belA wAdak
(बेलावादक)

virgin, *n.* kanyA keTI
(कन्याकेटी)

Virgo, *n.* kanyA rAshi
(कन्या राशि)

virtual, *adj.* jhaNDai jhaNDai
(झण्डैझण्डै)

virtue, *n.* sad guN (सद्गुण),
puNya (पुण्य),
(by virtue of) ... ko kAraN
Ie (... को कारणले)

virtuous, *adj.* guNI (गुणी),
sadA chArI (सदाचारी)

virus, *n.* rogANu (रोगाणु),
bhAiras (भाइरस)

visa, *n.* bhisA (भिसा),
praweshAgyA (प्रवेशाज्ञा)

visible, *adj.* dekhine (देखिने),
dekhna sakine (देख्न सकिने)

vision, *n.* drishTi (दृष्टि),
drishya (दृश्य)

visit, *n.* Agaman (आगमन),
bheT (भेट)
v. bheTna jAnu/Aunu
(भेट्न जानु/आउनु)

visitor, *n.* Agantuk (आगन्तुक)

visitor's book, *n.* Agantuk
pustikA (आगन्तुक पुस्तिका)

vista, *n.* drishya (दृश्य)

visual, *n.* drishTi sambandhI
(दृष्टिसम्बन्धी)

vital, *adj.* Awashyak (आवश्यक),

(life) prAN dAtA (प्राणदाता)

vitality, *n.* jIwan shakti
(जीवनशक्ति), oj (ओज)

vitamin, *n.* bhiTAmin
(भिटामिन)

vivacious, *adj.* sajIw (सजीव),
phurtilo (फुर्तिलो)

vivid, *adj.* ujyAlo (उज्यालो),
spashT (स्पष्ट)

vocabulary, *n.* shabdAwalI
(शब्दावली)

vocal, *adj.* wAchik (वाचिक),
maukhik (मौखिक)

vocalist, *n.* gAyak (गायक)

vocation, *n.* peshA (पेशा),
wyawasAya (व्यवसाय)

vogue, *n.* chaltI (चल्ती),
prachalan (प्रचलन),
(in vogue) chaltI mA
(चल्तीमा)

voice, *n.* swar (स्वर),
AwAj (आवाज)
v. bhannu (भन्नु),
wyakt garnu (व्यक्त गर्नु)

voiceless, *adj.* lATo (लाटो),
mUk (मूक)

volatile, *adj.* chAñDai uDne
(चाँडै उड्ने),
bAph banne (बाफ बन्ने)

volcano, *n.* jwAlA mukhI
(ज्वालामुखी)

volleyball, *n.* bhali bal
(भलिबल)

volume, *n.* pustak (पुस्तक),
(*amount*) parimAN (परिमाण),
mAtrA (मात्रा),
(*sound*) bholyum (भोल्युम),
(*size*) Ayatan (आयतन)

voluminous, *adj.* moTo
(मोटो), ThUlo (ठूलो)

voluntary, *adj.* Aphu khushI
(आफ़ुखुशी), aichchhik (ऐच्छिक)

volunteer, *n.* swayaṃ sewak
(स्वयंसेवक)

voluptuous, *adj.* kAmuk
(कामुक),
wishaya bhogI (विषयभोगी)

vomit, *n.* wAntA (वान्ता),
ulTI (उल्टी)
v. wAntA garnu (वान्ता गर्नु),
okalnu (ओकल्नु),

chhAdnu (छाद्नु)

voracious, *adj.* peTu (पेटु),
khanchuwA (खन्चुवा), (*fig.*)
khAna Adi nikai chAhane
(खान आदि निकै चाहने)

vote, *n.* mat (मत), bhoT (भोट)
v. bhoT dinu (भोट दिनु),
mat dAn garnu (मतदान गर्नु)

vote down, *v.* bahu mat le
aswIkAr garnu
(बहुमतले अस्वीकार गर्नु)

voter, *n.* mat dAtA (मतदाता)

vote of no confidence, *n.*
awishwAs kp prastAw
(अविश्वासको प्रस्ताव)

vote of thanks, *n.* dhanya
wAd gȳApan (धन्यवाद-ज्ञापन)

vulgar, *adj.* ashlII (अश्लील)

wade, *v.* nadI helera tarnu
(नदी हेलेर तर्नु)

wag, *v.* hallAunu (हल्लाउनु)

wage, *n.* talab (तलब), majdUrI
(मजदूरी), jyAlA (ज्याला)

wager, *n.* bAjI (बाजी),
shart (शर्त)
v. bAjI lagAunu (बाजी लगाउनु)

wag(g)on, *n.* chAr pAⁿgre
gADI (चारपाङ्ग्रे गाडी),

(*railway*) mAl DibbA
(माल डिब्बा), (*car*) wyAgan
(व्यागन), (**on the wagon**)
raksI chhADeko
(रक्सी छाडेको)

waist, *n.* kammar (कम्मर)

waistcoat, *n.* isT koT
(इस्टकोट)

wait, *v.* parkhanu (पर्खनु),
bATo hernu (बाटो हेर्नु)

waiter, *n.* beyarA (बेयरा),
(tray) kistI (किस्ती)

waiting list, *n.* pratIkshA
sUchi (प्रतीक्षा सूचि)

waiting room, *n.* pratI-
kshAlaya (प्रतीक्षालय)

waitress, *n.* beyarA keTI
(बेयरा केटी)

wake, *v.* byUňjhanu (ब्यूँझनु),
jAgnu (जाग्नु)
n. jAgrAm (जाग्राम), jAgA
(जागा), *(in the wake of)* ... ko
pachhi (... को पछि), ... ko
phal swarUp (को फलस्वरूप)

wake up, *v.* byUňjhAunu
(ब्यूँझाउनु),
jagAunu (जगाउनु)

walk, *v.* hiňDnu (हिँड्नु),
Dulnu (डुल्नु)
n. hiňDAi (हिँडाइ),
DulAi (डुलाइ)

walker, *n.* hiňDne (हिँड्ने),
Dulne (डुल्ने)

walk off with, *v.* chorera
laijAnu (चोरेर लैजानु)

walk of life, *n.* wyawasAya
(व्यवसाय), kAm (काम)

walkout, *n.* haDtAl (हडताल),
sabhA tyAg (सभात्याग)

walkover, *n.* sajilo jIt
(सजिलो जीत)

walk the street, *v.* weshyA
hunu (वेश्या हुनु)

walk the streets, *adv.* gallI
gallI ghumnu (गल्ली गल्ली
घुम्नु)

wall, *n.* gAro (गारो), bhittA
(भित्ता), parkhAl (पर्खाल),
(go to the wall) hArnu (हार्नु)
v. bhittA banAunu
(भित्ता बनाउनु)

wallet, *n.* byAg (ब्याग),
thailI (थैली)

walnut, *n.* okhar (ओखर)

wander, *v.* ghumnu (घुम्नु),
bhauňtArinu (भौंतारिनु)

wanderer, *n.* DuluwA
(डुलुवा), phirantA (फिरन्ता)

wanderlust, *n.* Dulne/ghumne
rahar (डुल्ने/घुम्ने रहर)

wane, *v.* ghaTnu (घट्नु),
kshaya hunu (क्षय हुनु)
n. rhAs (ह्रास),
(on the wane) ghaTne
paksha mA (घट्ने पक्षमा)

want, *v.* chAhanu (चाहनु),
ichchhA garnu (इच्छा गर्नु)
n. khAňcho (खाँचो),
abhAw (अभाव)

wanted, *adj.* Awashyak
(आवश्यक), khojeko (खोजेको)

wantonly, *adv.* be matlab
saňga (बेमतलबसँग)

war, *n.* laDAiň (लडाईं)
yuddha (युद्ध), *(at war)*
laDAiň mA samlagna

(लडाइँमा संलग्न)

v. laDAiñ garnu (लडाई गर्नु)

war cry, *n.* laDAiñ ko nArA (लडाईको नारा)

ward, *n. (minor)* Ashrit (आश्रित), *(town)* waDA (वडा), *(hospital)* wArD (वार्ड), wibhAg (विभाग)

v. rakshA garnu (रक्षा गर्नु)

ward off, *v.* roknu (रोक्नु), bachAunu (बचाउनु)

wardrobe, *n.* darAj (दराज)

warehouse, *n.* godAm (गोदाम)

warfare, *n.* laDAiñ (लडाई), yuddha (युद्ध), sañgrAm (संग्राम)

warlike, *adj.* laDAku (लडाकू)

warm, *adj.* nyAno (न्यानो), tAto (तातो), hArdik (हार्दिक), joshilo (जोशिलो)

v. tatAunu (तताउनु), garmAunu (गर्माउनु)

warm-hearted, *adj.* snehI (स्नेही), dayAlu (दयालु)

warmth, *n.* nyAno pan (न्यानोपन)

warm up, *v.* tatAunu (तताउनु)

warn, *v.* sAwdhAn garnu (सावधान गर्नु), chetAunu (चेताउनु)

warning, *n.* chetAwanI (चेतावनी), janAu (जनाउ)

warrant, *n.* pakrAu purjI (पक्राउ पुर्जी),

wAraNT (वारण्ट)

v. pramANit garnu (प्रमाणित गर्नु)

warrior, *n.* yoddhA (योद्धा), laDAkA (लडाका)

wart, *n.* musA (मुसा)

was, *v./aux.* thiyo (थियो)

wash, *v.* dhunu (धुनु), pakhAlnu (पखाल्नु)

washable, *adj.* dhuna hune (धुन हुने)

washbasin, *n.* hAt mukh dhune besin (हातमुख धुने बेसिन), koparA (कोपरा)

washed out, *adj.* thAkeko (थाकेको), nirAsh (निराश)

wash up, *v.* mAjhnu (माभ्नु)

washer, *n.* wAsar (वासर)

washerman, *n.* dhobI (धोबी)

wasp, *n.* bArulo (बारुलो)

wastage, *n.* khera (खेर), kshati (क्षति)

waste, *n.* khera (खेर), *(food)* juTho (जुठो), *(land)* ujAD (उजाड), *(litter)* kasiñgar (कसिंगर)

v. khera phAlnu (खेर फाल्नु), *(time)* samaya barbAd garnu (बर्बाद गर्नु), **(lay waste)** dhwamsa pArnu (ध्वंस पार्नु)

wasted, *adj.* khera gaeko (खेर गएको)

wasteland, *n.* banjAr jaggA

(बन्जार जग्गा)

waste paper, *n.* raddI kAgaj
(रद्दी कागज)

waste(-paper) basket, *n.* raddI
ko TokarI (रद्दीको टोकरी)

watch, *n.* ghaDI (घडी),
nADI ghaDI (नाडी घडी),
(vigil) nigrAnI निगरानी),
(keep watch) paharA dinu
(पहरा दिनु), *(on the watch)*
kunai ghaTanA lAI parkhera
basnu (कुनै घटनालाई पर्खेर बस्नु)
v. dhyAn pUrwak hernu
(ध्यानपूर्वक हेर्नु), nigrAnI
garnu (निगरानी गर्नु)

watchful, *adj.* sAwdhAn
(सावधान), satark (सतर्क)

watchmaker, *n.* ghaDI sAj
(घडीसाज)

watchman, *n.* pAle (पाले),
chaukI dAr (चौकीदार)

watch out, *v.* satark rahanu
(सतर्क रहनु)

watchword, *n.* sanket shabd
(संकेत शब्द), nArA (नारा)

water, *n.* pAnI (पानी), jal (जल),
(make water) mutnu (मुत्नु),
pisAb garnu (पिसाब गर्नु),
(of the first water) uchcha
koTi ko (उच्च कोटिको)
v. pAnI hAlnu(पानी हाल्नु)

water down, *v.* kam garI dinu
(कम गरी दिनु)

waterfall, *n.* jharnA (झरना),
chhAngo (छाँगो)

water lily, *n.* seto kamal
(सेतो कमल)

watermelon, *n.* tar bujA
(तरबुजा)

watermill, *n.* pAnI ghaTTa
(पानीघट्ट)

waterpipe, *n.* panI ko pAip
(पानीको पाइप)

waterproof, *adj.* pAnI le na
bigArne (पानीले नबिगार्ने),
panI na pasne (पानी नपस्ने)

watershed, *n.* jalAdhAr
(जलाधार),
nadI ghATI (नदीघाटी)

waterspout, *n.* jal stambha
(जलस्तम्भ), sirkA (सिर्का)

watery, *adj.* panyAlo (पन्यालो),
pAnI bharieko (पानी भरिएको)

wave, *n.* lahar (लहर),
chhAl (छाल), tarang (तरंग)
v. hallAunu (हल्लाउनु)

wavy, *adj.* lahar dAr (लहरदार),
nAg belI (नागबेली)

wax, *n.* main (मैन),
(sealing wax) lAhA (लाहा)

way, *n.* *(road)* bATo (बाटो),
(method) rIti (रीति), jukti
(जुक्ति), *(direction)* dishA
(दिशा), *(custom)* rIti(रीति),
riwAj (रिवाज), *(by the way)*
sunnos ta (सुन्नोस् त),

(by way of) bhaera (भएर), huṅdai (हुँदै), **(get out of the way)** haTnu (हट्नु), **(give way)** hAr mAnnu (हार मान्नु), **(make way)** bATo chhoDnu (बाटो छोड्नु), haTAunu (हटाउनु)

way back, n. (colloq.) dherai aghi (धेरैअघि)

wayfarer, n. baTuwA (बटुवा), rAhI (राही)

waylay, v. Dhuknu (ढुक्नु)

way of life, n. jIwan charyA (जीवनचर्या)

way out, adv. dherai bAhira (धेरै बाहिर)

way-out, adj. asAdhAraN (असाधारण)

wayside, n. bATo chheu (बाटोछेउ)

wayward, adj. jiddI (जिद्दी), haThI (हठी)

we, pron. hAmI (हामी), hAmI harU (हामीहरू)

weak, adj. kam jor (कमजोर), durbal (दुर्बल), (light) dhamilo (धमिलो)

weaken, v. kam jor tulyAunu (कमजोर तुल्याउनु)

weak-minded, adj. sust (सुस्त)

weakness, n. kam jorI (कमजोरी)

weal, n. kalyAN (कल्याण), hit (हित)

weal and woe, n. sukh duhkh (सुखदुःख)

wealth, n. dhan (धन)

wealthy, adj. dhanI (धनी)

weapon, n. hatiyAr (हतियार)

wear, v. lAunu (लाउनु)

wear and tear, n. TuT phuT (टुटफुट), khiyAi (खियाइ)

wear away, v. khiinu (खिइनु)

weariness, n. thakAi (थकाइ)

wear out, v. phATnu (फाट्नु)

weary, adj. thAkeko (थाकेको), thakit (थकित)

weasel, n. kAThe nyAurI mUso (काठे न्याउरीमूसो)

weather, n. mausam (मौसम), **(keep a weather eye open)** chanAkho hunu (चनाखो हुनु)

weather-beaten, adj. ghAm pAnI khAeko (घाम पानी खाएको)

weather forecast, n. mausam bhawishya wANI (मौसम भविष्यवाणी)

weave, v. bunnu (बुन्नु)

weaving, n. bunAi (बुनाइ)

web, n. jAlI (जाली), jAlo (जालो)

wed, v. bihe garnu (बिहे गर्नु)

wedding, n. bihe (बिहे), wiwAh (विवाह)

wedding ring, n. bihe ko auṅThI (बिहेको औंठी)

wedlock, n. wiwAh bandhan

(विवाहबन्धन)

wedge, *n.* chukul (चुकुल),
kII (कील)

Wednesday, *n.* budh bAr (बुधबार)

weed, *n.* jhAr (झार),
jhAr pAt (झारपात)
v. goDnu (गोड्नु)

week, *n.* sAtA (साता),
haptA (हप्ता)

weekend, *n.* haptA ko AkhirI
din (हप्ताको आखिरी दिन),
saptAhAnt (सप्ताहान्त)

weekly, *n. (magazine)*
sAptAhik patrikA
(साप्ताहिक पत्रिका)
adj. sAptAhik (साप्ताहिक),
harek sAtA (हरेक साता)

weep, *v.* runu (रुनु)

weigh, *v.* taulanu (तौलनु),
jokhnu (जोख्नु)

weight, *n.* taul (तौल),
Dhak (ढक), bhAr (भार)

weightless, *adj.* bhAr hIn
(भारहीन)

weighty, *adj.* garhuṅgo (गह्रुङ्गो),
bhArI (भारी)

weird, *adj.* bhayAnak
(भयानक), anauTho (अनौठो),
sankI (सनकी)

welcome, *n.* swAgat (स्वागत)
v. swAgat garnu (स्वागत गर्नु)

welcome arch, *n.* swAgat
dwAr (स्वागत द्वार)

welfare, *n.* kalyAN (कल्याण),
bhalAi (भलाइ)

welfare state, *n.* kalyAN kArI
rAjya (कल्याणकारी राज्य)

well, *adj. (health)* niko (निको),
jAtI (जाती)
n. (pit) kuwA (कुवा), inAr (इनार),
(as well) pani (पनि),
(as well as) atirikta (अतिरिक्त)
adv. rAmrarI (राम्ररी),
besharI (बेसरी)

well advised, *adj.* buddhi
mAn (बुद्धिमान्)

well and good, *adv.* bes (बेस),
yastai sahI (यस्तै सही)

well balanced, *adj.* santulit
(सन्तुलित)

well-being, *n.* kalyAN (कल्याण)

well bred, *adj.* sushIl (सुशील)

well done, *adj.* rAmrarI
garieko (राम्ररी गरिएको)
inter. syAbAsh (स्याबाश)

well informed, *adj.* jAniph kAr
(जानिफकार)

well intentioned, *adj.* rAmro
niyat ko (राम्रो नियतको)

well judged, *adj.* rAmrarI
garieko (राम्ररी गरिएको)

well known, *adj.* prasiddha
(प्रसिद्ध)

well off, *adj.* dhanI (धनी),
unnati shIl (उन्नतिशील)

well read, *adj.* supaThit

(सुपठित)

well-to-do, *adj.* khush hAl
(खुसहाल)

well tried, *adj.* rAmrarI koshish
gareko (राम्ररी कोशिश गरेको)

well-wisher, *n.* hitaishI (हितैषी)

wench, *n.* ThiTI (ठिटी),
tarunI (तरुनी)

were, *v./aux.* thie (थिए)

west, *n.* pashchim (पश्चिम),
(go west) *(sl.)* mArinu
(मारिनु)

western, *adj.* pashchimI
(पश्चिमी)

westernise, *v.* pashchimI
raṅga mA raṅginu (पश्चिमी
रंगमा रंगिनु)

westernmost, *adj.* sudUr
pashchim (सुदूरपश्चिम)

westward, *adv.* pashchim tira
(पश्चिमतिर)

wet, *adj.* bhijeko (भिजेको),
rujheko (रुझेको)

wet blanket, *n.* raṅga mA
bhaṅg garne (रंगमा भंग गर्ने)

wet nurse, *n.* dhAI (धाई)

whale, *n.* hwel mAchhA
(ह्वेल माछा)

what, *int. pron.* ke? (के?),
(know what's what) samajh
dAr hunu (समझदार हुनु)

whatever, *pron.* je sukai
(जेसुकै)

what for, *int. pron.* ke ko lAgi?
(केको लागि?)

what have you, *pron.* tyastai
arU kurA (त्यस्तै अरू कुरा)

whatsoever, *pron.* je sukai
(जेसुकै)

wheat, *n.* gahuṅ (गहुँ)

wheat stalk, *n.* chhwAlI
(छ्वाली)

wheel, *n.* pAṅgrA (पांग्रा),
chakkA (चक्का)

wheelchair, *n.* pAṅgre mech
(पांग्रे मेच)

when, *int. pron.* kahile?
(कहिले?)
adv. jaba (जब), jahile (जहिले)

where, *int. pron.* kahAṅ? (कहाँ?)
adv. jahAṅ (जहाँ)

whereabouts, *adv.* ThegAnA
(ठेगाना)

wherever, *adv.* jahAṅ sukai
(जहाँसुकै)

wherewithal, *n.* *(colloq.)*
paisA Adi (पैसा आदि)

whetstone, *n.* sAn lAune
patthar (सान लाउने पत्थर)

whether, *conj.* ki (कि)

which, *int. pron.* kun (कुन),
kun chAhiṅ (कुनचाहिँ)
rel. pron. jun (जुन)

while, *con.* jaba ki (जब कि),
yadyapi (यद्यपि),
(for a while) ek chhin ko

lAgi (एकछिनको लागि),
(in a while) chAñDai nai
(चाँडै नै), *(once in a while)*
kahile kAhiñ (कहिलेकाहीं),
(worthwhile) upyukta
(उपयुक्त), uchit (उचित)

whim, *n.* lahaD (लहड),
sanak (सनक)

whimsical, *adj.* lahaDI (लहडी),
sankI (सनकी)

whip, *n.* korrA (कोर्रा)
v. korrA hAnnu (कोर्रा हान्नु)

whipping boy, *n.* bali ko boko
(बलिको बोको)

whirl, *v.* phankA khwAunu
(फन्का ख्वाउनु),
ghumAunu (घुमाउनु)

whirlpool, *n.* pAnI ko bhumarI
(पानीको भुमरी)

whirlwind, *n.* bhumarI (भुमरी),
chakra wAt (चक्रवात)

whisker, *n.* juñgA (जुंगा),
jhus (भुस)

whisper, *v.* kAne khusI garnu
(कानेखुसी गर्नु),
sAutI garnu (साउती गर्नु)
n. sAutI (साउती),
kAne khusI (कानेखुसी)

whistle, *n.* siTThI (सिट्ठी),
suselI (सुसेली)
v. suselnu (सुसेल्नु), siTThI
bajAunu (सिट्ठी बजाउनु)

white, *adj.* seto (सेतो),

goro (गोरो)

white-collar, *adj.* Tebul mech
mA basI kAm garne
(टेबुल मेचमा बसी काम गर्ने)

white elephant, *n.* kashT maya
bhAr (कष्टमय भार),
kharchilo (खर्चिलो)

white flag, *n.* milA patra/Atma
samarpaN ko seto jhaNDA
(मिलापत्र/आत्मसमर्पणको सेतो
भण्डा)

white hope, *n.* AshA ko jyoti
(आशाको ज्योति)

white lie, *n.* nirdosh jhUT
(निर्दोष भूट)

White Paper, *n.* shwet patra
(श्वेतपत्र), sarkArI wiwaraN
(सरकारी विवरण)

whitewash, *n.* chun ko potAi
(चुनको पोताइ)

whitlow, *n.* nañ chhurI (नडछुरी)

who, *int. pron.* ko? (को?)
rel. pron. jo (जो)

whole, *adj./adv.* sampUrN
(सम्पूर्ण), sArA (सारा),
(on the whole) sabai milAera
(सबै मिलाएर)

wholehearted, *adj.* sachchA
(सच्चा), hArdik (हार्दिक)

wholesale, *n.* thok (थोक)
adj. thok ko (थोकको)

wholesome, *adj. (food)*
paushTik (पौष्टिक), *(healthy)*

swAsth kar (स्वास्थकर)

whom, *int. pron.* kas lAI? (कसलाई?), jas lAI (जसलाई)

whooping cough, *n.* lahare khokI (लहरे खोकी)

whore, *n.* weshyA (वेश्या), raNDI (रण्डी)

whose, *int. pron.* kasko?(कस्को?), *rel. pron.* jasko (जस्को)

why, *int. pron.* kina? (किन?) *rel. pron.* kina (किन)

wick, *n.* battI (बत्ती), sutalI (सुतली), saleto (सलेतो)

wicked, *adj.* bad mAs (बदमास), dushT (दुष्ट)

wicker, *n.* baTAre ko bet (बटारेको बेत)

wide, *adj.* chauDA (चौडा), pharAkilo (फराकिलो), *(far and wide)* jatA tatai (जताततै)

wide awake, *adj.* pUrA byuÑjheko (पूरा ब्यूँझेको), chanAkho (चनाखो)

wide-eyed, *adj.* chhakka pareko (छक्क परेको)

widespread, *adj.* wyApak (व्यापक)

widow, *n.* widhwA (विधवा)

widower, *n.* rAñDo (राँडो), widhur (विधुर)

width, *n.* chauDAi (चौडाइ)

wield, *v.* machchAunu

(मच्चाउनु), ujyAunu (उज्याउनु)

wife, *n.* swAsnI (स्वास्नी), strI (स्त्री), patnI (पत्नी)

wig, *n.* nakkalI kapAl (नक्कली कपाल)

wild, *adj.* jañgalI (जङ्गली), wanya (वन्य)

wildcat, *n.* ban birAlo (बनबिरालो) *adj.* asatte (असत्ते), *(person)* dussAhasI (दुस्साहसी), garam mijAs ko (गरम मिजासको)

wildfire, *n.* DaDhelo (डढेलो), dAwA nal (दावानल), wishphoTak tattwa (विष्फोटक तत्त्व)

wild goose chase, *n.* wyarth ko prayAs (व्यर्थको प्रयास)

wildlife, *n.* wanya jantu (वन्यजन्तु)

wilful, *adj.* jiddI (जिद्दी), aTerI (अटेरी)

will, *n.* ichchhA (इच्छा), sañkalpa (संकल्प) *mod.* lA (ला) *v.* chAhanu (चाहनु), ichchhA garnu (इच्छा गर्नु)

willing, *adj.* rAjI (राजी), ichchhuk (इच्छुक)

will power, *n.* ichchhA shakti (इच्छाशक्ति)

wilt, *v.* oilAunu (ओइलाउनु)

suknu (सुक्नु)

win, n. jIt (जीत)

v. jitnu (जित्नु)

wind, n. hAwA (हावा),
wAyu (वायु), batAs (बतास),
(get wind of) pattA lAgnu
(पत्ता लाग्नु), suiṅko pAunu
(सुईंको पाउनु), **(in the wind)**
(fig.) hune wAlA (हुनेवाला)
v. (pipe) phukera bajAunu
(फुकेर बजाउनु),
dam phulnu (दम फुल्नु),
baTArnu (बटार्नु),
(clock) dam dinu (दम दिनु)

windbag, n. bolakkaD
(बोलक्कड), ghanthane (गन्थ्ने)

windfall, n. (fig.) jhare ko phal
(झरेको फल), na chitAeko
lAbh (नचिताएको लाभ)

windmill, n. hAwA ghaTT
(हावाघट्ट)

window, n. jhyAl (भ्याल)

window-shopping, n. pasal ko
mAl herera mAtra chitta
bujhAune (पसलको माल हेरेर
मात्र चित्त बुझाउने)

windswept, adj. dherai hAwA
ko mAr pareko (धेरै हावाको
मार परेको)

wind up, v. samApt garnu
(समाप्त गर्नु),
siddhyAunu (सिद्ध्याउनु)

wine, n. raksI (रक्सी), mad (मद)

wing, n. pakheTA (पखेटा),
(on the wing) uDi raheko
(उडिरहेको)

wink at, v. AṅkhA jhimkyAunu
(आँखा भिम्क्याउनु)

winner, n. jituwA (जितुवा),
wijetA (विजेता)

winnow, v. niphannu (निफन्नु)

winnowing tray, n. nAṅlo
(नाङ्लो)

winsome, adj. rAmro (राम्रो),
Akarshak (आकर्षक)

winter, n. hiuṅd (हिउँद),
jADo mausam (जाडो मौसम)
v. jADo bitAunu
(जाडो बिताउनु)
adj. hiuṅde (हिउँदे)

winter sports, n. hiuṅde khel
kud (हिउँदे खेलकुद)

wipe, v. puchhnu (पुछ्नु)

wiper, n. puchhne wastu
(पुछ्ने वस्तु)

wipe out, v. meTnu (मेट्नु),
dhwamsa pArnu (ध्वंस पार्नु)

wire, n. tAr (तार)
v. tAr le baṅdhnu (तारले बाँध्नु),
tAr hAlnu (तार हाल्नु),
(telegram) tAr paThAunu
(तार पठाउनु)

wireless, n. be tAr (बेतार),
reDiyo (रेडियो)
adj. be tAr ko (बेतारको)
v. be tAr sandesh paThAunu

(बेतार सन्देश पठाउनु)

wirepulling, *n.* lukera garine kAm (लुकेर गरिने काम)

wiretapping, *n.* arkA ko Teli phon sunne kAm (अर्काको टेलिफोन सुन्ने काम)

wiring, *n.* bijulI ko tAr jaDAn (बिजुलीको तार जडान)

wisdom, *n.* gỹAn (ज्ञान), buddhi (बुद्धि)

wisdom tooth, *v.* buddhi baṅgaro (बुद्धि बङ्गारो)

wise, *adj.* buddhi mAn (बुद्धिमान्)

wisecrack, *n.* chuDkilA (चुड्किला), chheD pech (छेडपेच)

wisely, *adv.* buddhi mAnI sAth (बुद्धिमानीसाथ)

wish, *v.* ichchhA/kAmnA garnu (इच्छा/कामना गर्नु) *n.* ichchhA (इच्छा), kAmnA (कामना)

wishful, *adj.* ichchhuk (इच्छुक)

wishful thinking, *n.* chAhanA anusAr ko wichAr (चाहना अनुसारको विचार)

wisp, *n.* tyAndro (त्यान्द्रो), resA (रेसा)

wit, *n.* gỹAn (ज्ञान), buddhi (बुद्धि), *(at one's wit's end)* kimkartawya wimUDh (किंकर्तव्यविमूढ, *(out of one's wits)* pAgal

(पागल), sankeko (सन्केको)

witch, *n.* boksI (बोक्सी), daṅkinI (डइकिनी)

witchcraft, *n.* boksI widyA (बोक्सी विद्या), TunA (टुना)

witch doctor, *n.* dhAmI (धामी), jhAṅkrI (र्झाक्री)

witch-hunt, *n.* boksI ko khoj (बोक्सीको खोज), *(fig.)* shaṅkA yukt wyakti ko khoj (शङ्कायुक्त व्यक्तिको खोज)

with, *prep.* saṅga (सँग), sita (सित), le (ले)

withdraw, *v.* pachhi haTnu (पछि हट्नु), *(money)* jhiknu (झिक्नु)

withdrawal, *n.* wApasI (वापसी)

wither, *v.* oilAunu (ओइलाउनु)

within, *prep.* bhitra (भित्र)

without, *prep.* binA (बिना), na bhaikana (नभइकन)

withstand, *v.* wirodh garnu (विरोध गर्नु), roknu (रोक्नु)

witless, *adj.* bekuph (बेकुफ), mUrkh (मूर्ख)

witness, *n.* sAkshI (साक्षी), gabAh (गवाह), *(bear withness)* sAkshI baknu (साक्षी बक्नु) *v. (see)* dekhnu (देख्नु), hernu (हेर्नु)

wizard, *n. (sorcerer)* bokso (बोक्सो), *(conjurer)* chaTakI (चटकी), *(expert)* prawIN (प्रवीण),

wisheshagỹa (विशेषज्ञ)

wobble, v. hallanu (हल्लनु),
Dhun munAunu (धुनमुनाउनु)

woe, n. duhkha (दुःख),
sankaT (सङ्कट)

wolf, n. bwAñso (ब्वाँसो),
huñDAr (हुँडार), *(cry wolf)*
jhUTA Atank machAunu
(झूटा आतङ्क मचाउनु)

woman, n. Ai mAI (आइमाई),
mahilA (महिला), strI (स्त्री),
swAsnI mAnchhe
(स्वास्नीमान्छे)

womanizer, n. chhokaDI bAj
(छोकडीबाज), phuñDo (फुँडो)

womb, n. kokh (कोख), garbh
(गर्भ), pAThe ghar (पाठेघर)

women, n. AimAI harU
(आइमाईहरू),
mahilA harU (महिलाहरू)

wonder, n. Ashcharya (आश्चर्य),
udek (उदेक), chhakka (छक्क),
(no wonder) sahaj nai (सहज
नै), swAbhAwik (स्वाभाविक)
v. udek mAnnu (उदेक मान्नु),
utsuk hunu (उत्सुक हुनु)

wonderful, adj. achamma ko
(अचम्मको), gajab ko (गजबको),
Ashcharya janak
(आश्चर्यजनक)

woo, v. prem garnu (प्रेम गर्नु),
phakAunu (फकाउनु)

wood, n. kATh (काठ),

dAurA (दाउरा),
(forest) jangal (जङ्गल),
(out of the wood) khatarA
bATa bAhira (खतराबाट
बाहिर)

woodcutter, n. dAure (दाउरे)

wooded, adj. rUkh harU
bhaeko (रूखहरू भएको)

wooden, adj. kATh ko (काठको)

woodpecker, n. kATh koTero
(काठकोटेरो),
lAhAñche (लाहाँचे)

wool, n. Un (ऊन)

woollen, adj. UnI (ऊनी),
Un ko (ऊनको)

word, n. shabd (शब्द),
kurA (कुरा)
v. wAkya banAunu
(वाक्य बनाउनु)

word for word, adv.
aksharashaḥ (अक्षरशः)

word of honour, n. wachan
(वचन)

word of mouth, n. maukhik
(मौखिक)

work, n. kAm (काम),
kArya (कार्य)
v. kAm garnu (काम गर्नु)

workable, adj. kAm chalAu
(कामचलाउ)

worker, n. kAm dAr (कामदार),
majdUr (मजदूर)

workforce, n. prApt majdUr

saṅkhyA (प्राप्त मजदूर संख्या)

working knowledge, *n.* kAm chalAu gȳAn (कामचलाउ ज्ञान)

workload, *n.* kAm ko bhAr (कामको भार)

workmanship, *n.* shilp (शिल्प), kAli gaDhI (कालिगढी)

work out, *v.* hisAb garnu (हिसाब गर्नु),
(solve) hal garnu (हल गर्नु)

workshop, *n.* kArya shAlA (कार्यशाला)

world, *n.* samsAr (संसार), wishwa (विश्व),
(out of this world) *(colloq.)* bhawya (भव्य)

world-famous, *adj.* wishwa prasiddha (विश्वप्रसिद्ध)

worldly, *adj.* sAmsArik (सांसारिक)

worm, *n.* kIrA (कीरा),
(earthworm) gaDeuṅlo (गडेउँलो),
(hookworm) churnA (चुर्ना),
(roundworm) juko (जुको), jukA (जुका), *(tapeworm)* nAmle juko (नाम्ले जुको)

worn out, *adj.* jhutro (भुत्रो), thotro (थोत्रो),
(person) thAkeko (थाकेको)

worried, *adj.* chintit (चिन्तित)

worry, *n.* chintA (चिन्ता), pIr (पीर)
v. chintA garnu (चिन्ता गर्नु),

surtA linu (सुर्ता लिनु)

worse, *adj.* arU baDhI kharAb (अरू बढी खराब)

worsen, *v.* kharAb hunu (खराब हुनु), kharAb tulyAunu (खराब तुल्याउनु)

worship, *n.* pUjA (पूजा)
v. pUjA garnu (पूजा गर्नु)

worshipper, *n.* pUjak (पूजक), bhakta (भक्त)

worst, *adj.* sab bhandA kharAb (सबभन्दा खराब)

worth, *adj.* lAyak (लायक), yogya (योग्य),
(cost) mol parne (मोल पर्ने)
n. mUlya (मूल्य), mahattwa (महत्त्व)

worthiness, *n.* yogyatA (योग्यता), guN (गुण)

worthless, *adj.* nikammA (निकम्मा),
bekAr ko (बेकारको)

worthwhile, *adj.* uchit (उचित), kAm lAgne (काम लाग्ने)

worthy, *adj.* Adar NIya (आदरणीय), yogya (योग्य)

would, *mod.* bhayo (भयो), garyo (गर्यो)

would-be, *adj.* bhAwI (भावी), hune wAlA (हुनेवाला)

wound, *n.* ghAu (घाउ)

wounded, *adj.* ghAite (घाइते)

wow, *inter.* bAbh re bAph

(बाफरे बाफ)

wrap, *v.* bernu (बेर्नु),
lapeTnu (लपेट्नु)

wrap up, *v.* chhopnu (छोप्नु),
lapeTnu (लपेट्नु),
(story, news) samApt garnu
(समाप्त गर्नु)

wrath, *n.* ris (रिस), krodh (क्रोध)

wreath, *n.* mAlA (माला),
hAr (हार)

wreck, *v.* nAsh garnu
(नाश गर्नु), bigArnu (बिगार्नु)
n. nAsh (नाश),
dhwaṃsa (ध्वंस)

wreckage, *n.* bhagnAwshesh
(भग्नावशेष),
TukrA TukrI (टुक्राटुक्री)

wrench, *n.* renchu (रेन्चु)
v. baTArnu (बटार्नु),
nimoThnu (निमोठ्नु)

wrest, *v. (twist)* baTArnu
(बटार्नु), *(extort)* aiñchera
linu/khosnu (ऐंचेर लिनु/खोस्नु)

wrestle, *v.* kustI khelnu
(कुस्ती खेल्नु)

wrestler, *n.* kustI bAj
(कुस्तीबाज),
pahal mAn (पहलमान)

wrestling, *n.* kustI (कुस्ती)

wretched, *adj.* duhkhI (दुःखी),
bicharo (बिचरो)

wriggle, *v.* chal malAunu
(चलमलाउनु),

chhaT paTAunu (छटपटाउनु)
n. maDAr (मडार),
chhaT paT (छटपट)

wring, *v.* nichornu (निचोर्नु),
nimoThnu (निमोठ्नु)

wrinkle, *n.* chAurI (चाउरी)
v. chAurinu (चाउरिनु)

wrist, *n.* nADI (नाडी),
nArI (नारी)

wristwatch, *n.* nADI/nArI
ghaDI (नाडी/नारी घडी)

writ, *n.* riT (रिट),
paramAdesh (परमादेश)

write, *v.* lekhnu (लेख्नु),
rachnu (रच्नु)

write off, *v. (debt)* mAph
garnu (माफ गर्नु),
(money, etc.) nashT
samjhanu (नष्ट सम्झनु)

write up, *v.* warNan /
prashaṃsA garnu
(वर्णन/प्रशंसा गर्नु)

write-up, *n.* warNan lekh
(वर्णन लेख)

writer, *n.* lekhak (लेखक)

writing, *n.* lekhAi (लेखाइ),
lekh (लेख)

written, *adj.* lekheko (लेखेको),
likhit (लिखित)

writhe, *v.* duhkha le chhaT
paTAunu (दुःखले छटपटाउनु),
maDArinu (मडारिनु)
n. maDAr (मडार),

chhaT paT (छटपट)

wrong, *adj.* galat (गलत),
ashuddha (अशुद्ध),
(go wrong) galtI garnu
(गल्ती गर्नु)
v. birAunu (बिराउनु),

anyAya garnu (अन्याय गर्नु)

wrong doing, *n.* durAchAr
(दुराचार), adharm (अधर्म)

wrong-headed, *adj.* haThI
(हठी), durAgrahI (दुराग्रही)

xenophobia, *n.* wideshI prati
aruchi (विदेशीप्रति अरुचि)

xmas, *n.* krismas (क्रिस्मस),
baDA din (बडादिन)

xerox, *n.* phoTo kapI (फोटोकपी)
v. phoTo kapI garnu
(फोटोकपी गर्नु)

x-ray, *n.* eksre (एक्सरे)

yacht, *n.* pAl wAlA DuṅgA
(पालवाला डुङ्गा), naukA (नौका)

yahoo, *n.* nar pashu (नरपशु)

yak, *n.* chauṅrI gAI (चौंरी गाई)

yam, *n.* tarul (तरुल)

yard, *n.* gaj (गज),
(building) Aṅgan (आँगन),
chok (चोक)

yarn, *n.* sut (सुट), dhAgo (धागो)

yawn, *v.* hAI garnu (हाई गर्नु)
n. hAI (हाई)

year, *n.* warsh (वर्ष), sAl (साल),
(last year) pohor (पोहोर),

(next year) Aghauṅ (आघौं)

year in and year out, *adv.*
nirantar (निरन्तर)

yearly, *adj.* wArshik (वार्षिक)
adv. sAlindA (सालिन्दा)

yearn, *v.* rahar garnu (रहर
गर्नु), chAhanu (चाहनु)

yearning, *n.* dhoko (धोको),
chAhanA (चाहना)

yeast, *n.* khamir (खमिर),
marchA (मर्चा)

yell, *v.* karAunu (कराउनु),
chichyAunu (चिच्याउनु)

n. chichyAhaT (चिच्याहट), chitkAr (चित्कार)

yellow, *adj.* pahenlo (पहेंलो)

yellow fever, *n.* pIt jwar (पीतज्वर), kamal pitta ko jaro (कमलपित्तको जरो)

yellow press, *n.* pIt patra kArita (पीत पत्रकारिता)

yeoman, *n.* bhUmi dhar (भूमिधर)

yeoman service, *n.* khAncho pardA garine sewA (खाँचो पर्दा गरिने सेवा)

yes, *n.* ho (हो), hunchha (हुन्छ), an (अँ)

yesman, *n.* jI hajuriya (जीहजुरिया)

yesterday, *n./adv.* hijo (हिजो),
(the day before yesterday) asti (अस्ति)

yet, *adv.* ajhai (अझै)
conj. taipani (तैपनि)

yield, *n.* paidAwAr (पैदावार), utpAdan (उत्पादन)
v. paidA garnu (पैदा गर्नु), *(person)* hAr mAnnu (हार मान्नु)

yog(ho)urt, *n.* dahI (दही)

yoke, *n.* juwA (जुवा), dhur (धुर)
v. juwA hAlnu (जुवा हाल्नु)

yolk, *n.* aNDA ko pahenlo

bhAg (अण्डाको पहेंलो भाग)

yore, *n.* prAchIn samaya (प्राचीन समय)

you, *pron.* timI (तिमी), *(for.)* tapAIn (तपाईं), timI le (तिमीले), *(for.)* tapAIn le (तपाईंले)

young, *adj.* taruN (तरुण), jawAn (जवान), *(under age)* sAno (सानो), kalilo (कलिलो), *(male)* taruno (तरुनो), yuwak (युवक), *(fem.)* tarunI (तरुनी), yuwatI (युवती)

younger, *adj.* kAnchho (कान्छो), sAno (सानो)

youngest, *adj.* sab bhandA kAnchho (सबभन्दा कान्छो)

youngsters, *n.* bAl bAlikA (बालबालिका)

your, *pron.* timro (तिम्रो), timI harU ko (तिमीहरूको), *(for.)* tapAIn ko (तपाईंको)

yourself, *pron.* timI Aphai (तिमी आफै), *(for.)* tapAIn Aphai (तपाई आफै)

youth, *n.* yauwan (यौवन), jawAnI (जवानी)
adj. yuwA (युवा)

youthful, *adj.* taruN (तरुण)

Z

zany, *n.* maskharA (मसखरा), widUshak (विदूषक), bewkuph (बेवकुफ), gwAn̐ro (ग्वान्रो)

zeal, *n.* josh (जोश), utsAh (उत्साह)

zealot, *n.* kaTTar panthI (कट्टरपन्थी)

zealous, *adj.* utsAhI (उत्साही), joshilo (जोशिलो)

zebra, *n.* jebrA ghoDA (जेब्रा घोडा)

zero, *n.* shUnya (शून्य)

zest, *n.* utsAh (उत्साह), josh (जोश), majA (मजा)

zigzag, *adj.* bAn̐go Tin̐go (बाझ्टिङ्गो), nAg belI pareko (नागबेली परेको)

zinc, *n.* jastA (जस्ता)

zipper, *n.* jiper (जिपर),

phAsnar (फास्नर)

zodiac, *n.* rAshi chakra (राशिचक्र)

zone, *n.* añchal (अञ्चल), kaTibandh (कटिबन्ध)

zone of peace, *n.* shAnti kshetra (शान्तिक्षेत्र)

zoo, *n.* chiDiyA khAnA (चिडियाखाना)

zoologist, *n.* prANI shAstrI (प्राणीशास्त्री)

zoology, *n.* pashu wigỹAn (पशुविज्ञान)

zoological garden, *n.* chiDiyA khAnA (चिडियाखाना)

zoom, *v.* garjan̐dai ThADo uDnu (गर्जदै ठाडो उड्नु) *n.* tej ThADo uDAn (तेज ठाडो उडान)

For Further References

Adhikary, Kamal R. *A Concise English Nepali Dictionary with Transliteration and Devanagari*. Kathmandu: Author, 2001.

Adhikary, Sita Ram. *Modern Essential Dictionary*. Kathmandu: Utsab Books Prakashan, 2007.

Bhattarai, P. Harshanath (ed.) Rashtriya Nepali Shabdakosh. Kathmandu: Educational Publishing House, 2063 B.S.

Clark, T.W. *Introduction to Nepali*. Kathmandu: Ratna Pustak Bhandar, 1989.

Dixit, Narendra Mani Acharya. *Angreji Nepali Sajha Sankshipta Shabda Kosh*. Kathmandu: Sajha Prakashan, 2057 B.S.

Gautam, Choodamani. *Gautam's Up-To-Date Nepali English Dictionary*. Biratnagar: Gautam Prakashan, 2059 B.S.

Hornby, A.S. *Oxford Advanced Learner's Dictionary of Current English*. Oxford University Press, 6th ed., 2000.

Hutt, Michael and Abhi Subedi. *Teach Yourself Nepali*. London: Hodder & Stoughton, 2003.

Karki, Tika B. and Chij K. Shrestha. *Basic Course in Spoken Nepali*. Kathmandu: Authors, 1999.

Matthews, David. *A Course in Nepali*. London: School of Oriental and African Studies, University of London, 1984.

Pradhan, Babulall. *Ratna English Nepali Dictionary*. Kathmandu: Ratna Pustak Bhandar, 2003.

_____ . *Ratna Nepali Shabda Kosh*. Kathmandu: Ratna Pustak Bhandar, 2059 B.S.

____ . *Ratna's Nepali English Nepali Dictionary.* Kathmandu: Ratna Pustak Bhandar, 1997.

Pradhan, Raj Narayan. *Adhunik Angreji Nepali Shabda Kosh.* Kathmandu: Educational Enterprise, 2051 B.S.

Regmi, M.P. *Regmi's Anglo Nepali Dictionary.* Varanasi: Babu Madhav Prasad Sharma, 2001.

Schmidt, R.L. et al., eds. *A Practical Dictionary of Modern Nepali.* New Delhi: Ratna Sagar, 1993.

Sharma, Bal Chandra. *Nepali Shabda Kosh.* Kathmandu: Srishti Prakashan, 2057 B.S.

Sharma, Tara Nath. *Beginning Nepali for Foreign Learner.* Kathmandu: Sajha Prakashan, 1993.

Sharmma 'Nepal', B.K. *Nepali Shabda Sagar.* Kathmandu: Bhabha Pustak Bhandar, 2057 B.S.

Singh, Chandra Lal. *The Concise Dictionary of the Nepali Language.* Kathmandu: Educational Enterprise, 2000.

____ . *Nepali to English Dictionary.* Kathmandu: Educational Enterprise, 2002.

Tripathy, Basudev et al., eds. *Nepali Brihat Shabda Kosh.* Kathamndu: Royal Nepal Academy, 2060 B.S.

Turner, Ralph Lilley. *A Comparative and Etymological Dictionary of the Nepali Language.* New Delhi: Allied Publishers Limited, 1980.

Wagley, S.P. *Ratna English Nepali Pocket Dictionary.* Kathmandu: Ratna Pustak Bhandar, 2002.

Wagley, S.P. and B.K. Rauniyar. *Ratna Basic Nepali Dictionary.*